Law of the Sea: Caracas and Beyond

Law of the Sea: Caracas and Beyond

PROCEEDINGS

Law of the Sea Institute
Ninth Annual Conference
January 6–9, 1975

University of Rhode Island
Kingston, Rhode Island

Edited by Francis T. Christy, Jr.; Thomas
A. Clingan, Jr.; John King Gamble, Jr.;
H. Gary Knight; and Edward Miles

Ballinger Publishing Company ● Cambridge, Mass.
A Subsidiary of J.B. Lippincott Company

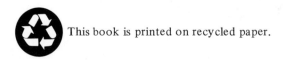 This book is printed on recycled paper.

Funds for the Ninth Annual Conference of the Law of the Sea Institute, held in Miami, Florida, in January 1975 were provided by the Ford Foundation (Grant No. 700-0438); the International Research and Exchanges Board; the National Sea Grant Program, NOAA, U.S. Department of Commerce (Grant No. 04-3-158-3); the Office of Naval Research, United States Department of the Navy (Task Order No. 0215-000-3); the United States Coast Guard (Contract No. DOT-CG-24240-A); and the University of Rhode Island.

Recently the Institute has decided to invite support from commercial concerns having an interest in the oceans. Thus far contributions have been received from the Chevron Corporation, the Exxon Corporation, the Royal Dutch Shell Group and the Tenneco Foundation in the name of Deepsea Ventures, Incorporated. The Institute gratefully acknowledges the support provided by these institutions.

International Standard Book Number: 0-88410-029-4

Library of Congress Catalog Card Number: 75-12540

Printed in the United States of America

Library of Congress Cataloging in Publication Data
1. Maritime law—Congresses. I. Christy, Francis T. II. Title.
JX4408.L37   1975   341.44'8   75-12540
ISBN 0-88410-029-4

Contents

List of Tables

List of Figures

Foreword

This conference, the ninth sponsored by the Law of the Sea Institute, was held January 6-9, 1975 in Miami, Florida. Principal planning for the program was done by William T. Burke; Francis T. Christy, Jr.; Thomas A. Clingan, Jr.; H. Gary Knight; and Edward Miles.

The planning and administration of a large conference like this one is complex. The Law of the Sea Institute wishes to express its appreciation to Tony Pajares and Arlene Jacobsohn of the University of Miami's Conference Center and to Clare Gamble for so ably handling all procedural matters. In addition, we wish to thank Warren S. Wooster, Dean of the Rosenstiel School of Marine and Atmospheric Science, for making his facilities available to us.

The conference would have been impossible were it not for the financial support provided by many sources among them the Ford Foundation, the U.S. Coast Guard, the Office of Naval Research, the National Sea Grant Program, the International Research and Exchanges Board, and, of course, the University of Rhode Island. The Institute is deeply appreciative of the support provided by these organizations.

John King Gamble, Jr.
Kingston, Rhode Island
March 16, 1975

Opening Remarks

William T. Burke
School of Law
University of Washington

Mr. Burke: I think we have waited long enough. There were a number of people out in the hall. My name is William Burke, listed here as chairman for the program. I want to welcome you to the Ninth Annual Meeting of the Law of the Sea Institute. We wish especially to extend our greetings and hospitality to those of you from outside the United States who have come here to join the discussions, and we hope your stay is as pleasant as the weather and productive and useful.

We have a message from the Secretary-General of the United Nations. I will read it.

> Your annual Conference has been one of the pioneering efforts in the attempt to review and modernize the Law of the Sea. Bringing together as it does representatives of Governments, jurists, figures in the academic world and other specialists in the many complex subjects it covers, your Conference can be of great assistance in helping those concerned to take stock of developments and to find solutions to their common problems. I wish you all success.

The planning and program development for this meeting has been carried out mainly by five people. They are Thomas A. Clingan, Edward L. Miles, Francis T. Christy, H. Gary Knight, and John K. Gamble. The first four of these are the chairpeople for the daily sessions responsible for the program content. John Gamble has backed them up with respect to the entire program. Regarding the program itself, I think it is pretty obvious we have attempted to place emphasis both on substantive problems under discussion in the law of the sea and on the process employed in attempting to reach decisions. While I think proportionately a little greater time is devoted to substantive problems on the agenda of this meeting we do not wish to underemphasize the importance of the process and will devote some time to that at this meeting and considerably more time to it at a future meeting.

The chairperson for this morning's session is Thomas Clingan, and I will turn the program over to him. Tom.

Law of the Sea:
Caracas and
Beyond

Part I

Report on the Course of Negotiations at Caracas

Chairman
Thomas A. Clingan, Jr.
Deputy Assistant Secretary of State for
Ocean Affairs

Mr. Clingan: Thank you very much, Bill. It is a great pleasure to be here and
to have the opportunity to chair this opening panel. We have had a couple of
changes on the program, so I would like to introduce the gentlemen who are
sitting with me. To my right is Mr. J.S. Warioba, Director for Legal Research
in International Organizations, from Tanzania. To my immediate left, Mr. John
Norton Moore, Chairman of the United States Interagency Task Force on Law
of the Sea. To his left, Mr. Paul Lapointe, of the Department of External Affairs,
Ottawa, Canada. We are quite fortunate to have these three gentlemen with us
this morning. They were not only participants at Caracas, but major players, I
believe, in the game, and therefore extremely well qualified to present to you
this morning a picture from different perspectives of what occurred at Caracas
last summer.

    The significance of this opening panel which I am honored to chair
is established not only by the distinction and experience of these panelists, but
also by the comprehensive structure of the program for this Law of the Sea Institute annual meeting as it is viewed in its unity.

    Subsequent papers and panels will deal with the dynamics of con-
ference diplomacy, ocean resource issues at the Caracas conference, dynamics
and ocean technology, and the obstacles to negotiations and their removal.
Clearly, these sessions have not been designed simply with a view toward an
analysis of past events solely for historical benefits, but rather they should be
considered as a part of the continuum in which we find ourselves restless participants. It is important, therefore, that we begin our meetings with an examination of what it was that occurred at Caracas.

    This, too, as we all recognize, is as much a matter of perception as it
is fact. In this sense we are particularly fortunate to have not one, but rather several points of view from those who were actively engaged in the negotiations.
My role in this portion of the program is one of moderator, and I shall not offer

1

comments of substance at this time. I do this by design for a number of reasons, not the least of which is that, since the conclusion of the Caracas meeting, I have changed my role vis à vis negotiations from that of a member of the advisory committee to participant. Thus, I am in that awkward stage of transition in which I lack the perspective of having fully participated and can no longer exercise the academic luxury of selecting between optimism and cynicism. Therefore I will leave this to others and attempt to content myself with briefly setting the stage this morning and raising a few preliminary inquiries.

Undoubtedly the ultimate question to be attacked during the next few days, regardless of the phraseology we might choose, will be was Caracas a success, with the necessary caveats to cover that extremely broad and sweeping inquiry. In my view such a question is not only dangerous, misleading, and self-serving, but it is intellectually irrelevant unless it is accompanied by a framework of objectives within which the term "success" is to be measured.

It is hoped that one or more such frameworks will evolve during the meetings of the next few days. Perhaps the range of objectives by which success or failure is measured will turn out to be more meaningful and more helpful than the objective conclusions we might reach themselves might be. Success was defined by one authority as a favorable or prosperous course or termination of anything attempted, a result corresponding to the aim or design entertained, prosperous or advantageous issue. Such a definition itself cries out for the kind of framework I am suggesting.

Within the context of the Law of the Sea Conference, success could be determined by as many sets of values as there were participants, or perhaps even more. If the single criterion is whether a document was signed containing agreed-upon sets of articles, one conclusion would have to be reached. If the question is whether a total, disastrous collapse of the negotiations was avoided, a second is foregone. Success or failure can further be defined in terms of progress, in terms of understanding the dynamics of large-scale international decision-making, the advancement of third-party nationalism, the attainment of perceived national goals, or even the degree to which one or another participant achieved recognition or personal satisfaction from the proceedings. Any of these and many more of course could be acceptable criteria of success, depending upon one's goals and perspectives.

Thus in the next few days I believe it would be a disservice to ourselves as a group to seek to isolate a single measure of success. Rather, we should focus on the dynamics of the process itself for what benefit that might provide for the future. Indeed, the ultimate criteria for success, those which history will utilize in evaluating our present efforts, may still elude our own understanding. If that is the case, then our energies must be renewed and our works reexamined toward that end.

It has been said that success is measured relative to the times. If that is true, then perhaps that order of success we seek is best described in terms of process or better yet, institutions, so structured as to defy the vagaries and the stresses of time. It has also been suggested that to achieve real success one must put aside mere national interests and find those flashes of insight that transcend the commonplace and inspire statesmanship. I do not believe it. This simply cannot be done in the real world of average humans. What can be accomplished, however, is a longer range view of national interests, examined within an appropriate institutional framework, designed to keep those interests in proper perspective at all times and for all times.

Time, in my view, not the product of the negotiations of men, is the great accommodator. The rationalizing of polar views can sometimes be accomplished by time, when the most skillful have failed. Thus we must be careful in our future work to structure institutions and establish sound processes, place these as our major objectives, and worry less about one's perception of success which may be frozen in time, particularly that time in which we live.

The driving force to succeed is narrow in simplistic terms, and in its simplistic terms is human. It is derived, I believe, from fear and uncertainty, and it seeks to defeat human frailties by the establishment of a particular order to maintain and sustain itself, unsullied by human hands. But if that is the meaning of success then success is the defiler of intelligent behavior. P.W. Bridgeman said, "I believe that the average man can be made to see that the imposition of restraints on the freedom to be intelligent betrays fear of the unknown and of himself, and that he be made to feel that this fear is an ignoble thing." My gamble is that the human race, once it has caught the vision, will not yield to fear of the consequences of its own intelligence.

Like Bridgeman, we must all develop the capability of believing in the right of the man to catch the vision and concentrate on an order capable of freeing him from the fear of the consequences of his intelligence and the rational and sound management of the oceans for future decades.

Now I would like to proceed with our panel this morning. It gives me great pleasure to begin to introduce to you Mr. John Norton Moore. John.

Commentary

John Norton Moore
Chairman
U.S. Interagency Task Force on Law of the Sea

Mr. Moore: Mr. Chairman, in trying to serve as a standin for Andres Aguilar I feel a little bit like the obscure official in the Cultural Affairs Bureau of the Department of State who found himself a year ago facing an audience of a thousand at the World Affairs Council in San Francisco as a standin for Henry Kissinger, with a title addressing the Middle East conflict. It is indeed a great pleasure to meet with this distinguished audience of experts on ocean affairs, to share with you a few thoughts on one of the most challenging international negotiations of our time, the effort to reach a comprehensive ocean agreement.

We are accustomed to rapid change. But in recent decades the change in ocean politics and ocean uses has been so fundamental as to constitute a basic change in the character of change itself. That change has taken many forms. In some cases it has been an intensification of traditional uses of the oceans. Fishing is a good example of that. A few years ago we felt that the oceans were going to be a nearly inexhaustible supply of proteins for man's use. With new knowledge we now know that we are moving into an era of scarcity. In a matter of a decade or so we will be at global maximum sustainable yield, at least for those ocean fisheries populations that we like to find and normally find on our dinner plate. At that point we can look around for the newer sources of protein, such as the pelagic squid and the great supplies of krill, but the change has taken place and it is going to be a change that we must live with.

In other cases the change has been the development of new ocean technology. For example, the development of the technology to mine manganese nodules from the deep-ocean floor, those interesting nodules, looking like a lump of coal, formed over at least a million years, and containing commercially attractive quantities of copper, nickel, manganese, and cobalt. In still other cases the change has resulted from an increasing interaction with land-based uses: for example, the increasing threat of pollution of the ocean environment, an area almost three-quarters of the surface of the earth and a vital part of the global ecosystem.

4

Although part of that pollution of the marine environment is certainly due to an intensification of traditional uses of the seas and part to the development of new ocean technologies—such as the supertanker, which poses special problems—the greater part of it is due to increasing land-based pollution. We estimate that more than half of all pollution of the world's oceans today is from land-based sources, in a very realistic sense an increasing threat to the ocean from an intensified interaction with land-based uses. Not surprisingly these changes have been accompanied by strains in the fabric of the international legal order for the oceans.

We could wait for the slow growth of customary international law to fill in those gaps and tears in the legal fabric, but there are strong reasons why that would not be a satisfactory solution or as satisfactory a solution as a comprehensive oceans treaty. First, the customary law process will for a long period be accompanied by substantial political tensions among nations and even by chances for increasing conflict and open military action. Thus, in the absence of agreement, the oceans will increasingly become a source of tension and conflict rather than providing the opportunity for cooperation which is their real heritage.

Second, the customary law process will for a long period not provide the essential stability of expectations which is required for the full development of the resource and other potentials of the oceans. Thus, in the absence of an agreement, the full potential of the oceans for protein, minerals, energy, transportation, and other benefits for man will go unrealized. Third, we have learned that a pattern of unilateral action favors simplistic and chauvinistic solutions rather than cooperative actions in the common interest as required by global problems and an interdependent world. For example, the 200-mile territorial sea can no longer solve the problem of conservation of highly migratory species or solve problems of global cooperation needed to protect the marine environment or a variety of other problems that today must be solved by cooperation on a global basis.

Against this background the United Nations General Assembly last year formally convened the Third United Nations Conference on the Law of the Sea. That conference began its substantive work last summer in a ten-week session in Caracas, Venezuela, and will resume in Geneva for an eight-week session from March 17 through May 10. This Third United Nations Conference on the Law of the Sea is the largest and most complex plenipotentiary conference in history, with 137 nations plus a number of observers participating at the Caracas session and more expected in Geneva, and with an agenda including 92 major and minor subheadings on the formal agenda of the conference.

In essence, as the experts in this room know full well, the conference is writing a global charter for an area approximately three-quarters of the surface of the earth. As is evident the task of reaching agreement is staggering. In fact, one wag at the Caracas session of the conference compared that task with having affairs with nine women simultaneously in an effort to produce a child in one month. Nevertheless, reach agreement we must, if the priceless opportunity for cooperation we now have is not to be forever lost.

Let me briefly review the principal issues dealt with by the Caracas session of the conference, and on each issue indicate where we stand after Caracas. First, the question of the breadth of the territorial sea and the protection of unimpeded transit through and over straits used for international navigation. The United States and many other maritime states recognize a maximum breadth of the territorial sea of only three nautical miles. There are a number of countries, very few, largely in Latin America, that recognize a maximum breadth of the territorial sea of up to 200 miles.

In between, the largest category of states, over fifty, includes the countries that recognize a maximum breadth of the territorial sea of up to 12 nautical miles. Most of the states that now have a three-nautical-mile territorial sea have indicated that in the context of an overall satisfactory treaty they are prepared to accept a twelve-nautical-mile territorial sea. Similarly, at least some, if not most, of the nine states with a 200-mile territorial sea have implied that, subject to satisfactory resolution of the economic zone, they might be willing to accept a territorial sea of not more than 12 nautical miles. In short, with respect to breadth of the territorial sea, I think that we can say after Caracas there is no possibility of agreement on any breadth of the territorial sea either less than or greater than twelve nautical miles.

The greatest problem, as you know, in connection with the question of territorial sea and the straits is the question of guarantees of unimpeded transit through, over, and under straits used for international navigation. The principal problem is that, when one shifts from a three-nautical-mile territorial sea to a twelve-nautical-mile territorial sea, there are over 100 straits used for international navigation which will be overlapped by territorial sea that formerly had a high-seas corridor through the strait.

The question is really one that is vital for the movement of commerce and for the maintenance of global stability. It is not surprising that the states that recognize the three-nautical-mile territorial sea, as well as some of those who recognize the twelve-nautical-mile territorial sea, but who maintain a theory of historic rights of transit through straits, have indicated in the strongest of terms that they must have guarantees of unimpeded transit of straits in order to conclude a successful treaty on the law of the sea.

On our part, we seek only the right to continue what we have been doing, and that is going from one side of a strait used for international navigation to the other side of the strait in the normal mode of transit. And that is overflight, if it is an aircraft; surface transit, if it is a surface vessel; submerged transit, if it is a submarine which normally transits in the submerged mode. We do not feel that this is the kind of practice which threatens or harms the interest of any other state, nor that we are asking a great deal simply to maintain the international community freedom of transit through these straits. This is certainly an issue, however, that must be resolved satisfactorily by the conference.

I am happy to say that though the trend is not yet fixed, and this is certainly still an issue that is very much in the negotiation, there was at least at Caracas a definite trend toward support for unimpeded transit of straits. For the first time in the history of these negotiations there were more speakers in favor of unimpeded transit than there were in favor of innocent passage. However, there were a few ominous signs on the horizon as some of the strait states sought to introduce a differentiation between military and commercial vessels.

Should that differentiation catch on, I personally think that it could seriously endanger the success of the Law of the Sea Conference. I was happy to see that we did not see any widespread signs of that catching on.

Shifting to the second set of issues—those concerning the resources under national jurisdiction, both the living resources and the mineral resources— first, with respect to fishing, as you know the traditional law has been to recognize only a twelve-mile fisheries contiguous zone. The difficulty is that the fish have not recognized the 12-mile contiguous zone and have a disarming habit of swimming back and forth across the lines that man tries to draw in the ocean. And the result is of course the classic common pool problem that Francis Christy and many others have educated us on through the years, and that is that if you do not have ownership or a common agreement which is coextensive with the range of a resource—in this case the range of the particular species of fish—you have the classic case, similar to the old Texas oil fields, of competing producers putting down wells and pumping at the most rapid rate they can on the common pool of the resource.

In fact when you game it out you will discover that there is a built-in disincentive to conserve and the only rational behavior, in the absence of an agreement or common management jurisdiction, is to pump as rapidly as you can vis à vis the other players. That has been exactly what has been happening to fisheries stocks worldwide. The solution to that has seemed to us to be an approach that basically gave jurisdiction over coastal species to the coastal state, and basically the 200-mile economic zone with preferential rights in the coastal state would for the most part place management jurisdiction over coastal species in coastal states.

On the other hand, with respect to anadromous species, such as salmon and highly migratory species, a different solution than the 200-mile economic zone or at least a provision consistent with that zone must be found. That would mean that salmon should be placed under the jurisdiction of the host state throughout their range on the high seas, and certainly beyond the territorial sea of the host state.

Similarly, with respect to the highly migratory species which do not have any special relation to any particular state, and whose range is over vast areas of the ocean, the only solution to the common-pool problem is a regional or international organization that can set the allowable catch and provide necessary regulation throughout the range of the species.

Turning to the question of the mineral resources of the continental

shelf in the margins, as you know, the issue is of particular importance because
we estimate that approximately 40 percent of the total world hydrocarbon reserves are located under salt water in the continental margins of the world. The
existing international law provided by the 1958 Continental Shelf Convention is
that the coastal state has the exclusive right to explore and exploit these mineral
resources out to 200 meters, plus to where the depth of the superjacent waters
admit of exploitation, the latter portion of the test of course being the classic
way in which many issues are resolved in international relations. That is, when
you cannot reach agreement, you resort to a deliberately ambiguous test, in this
case a test which changes through time as oceans technology develops to exploit
mineral resources of the margin.

The difficulty of course is that the kind of uncertainty we could live
with in 1958, when we did not have the technology to exploit in those depths, is
no longer the kind of uncertainty that is going to enable the most rational development of those resources on a worldwide basis, particularly when we remember
that the agency on the other side of the line is going to be the international
community through an international seabed resource authority.

Now the general trend at Caracas on these issues is fairly clear. That
is, there is a broad trend, in fact almost unanimous, toward acceptance of the
idea of a 200-mile economic zone, again in many cases very clearly conditioned
on a very satisfactory overall law of the sea settlement. The 200-mile economic
zone would at least include preferential rights over coastal species of fish and, in
addition to that, exclusive rights to explore and exploit the mineral resources of
the margin out to 200 miles.

The three principal sets of unresolved issues with respect to the economic zone are, first, the question of traditional treatment within the zone;
second, the question of special treatment for highly migratory species and
anadromous species, such as salmon; and third, the question of the delimitation
of the continental shelf boundary in areas where the continental shelf goes beyond 200 miles.

Though it is somewhat early to hazard a prediction on this, it seems
that the direction of the negotiation on traditional fishing is at least to honor
the obligation of conservation that would be binding on the coastal state, and
secondly to accept in general terms the obligation of full utilization, which
would be binding on the coastal state. That is, the coastal state would have the
right to utilize the species that it could utilize at any particular time, something
which would increase as the coastal states' capacity increased, but on the other
hand, as that capacity did not have the ability to harvest up to the maximum
sustainable yield, there would be an obligation to permit others to come in and
fish for that additional increment.

The questions of the priorities within that full utilization obligation
are still much more uncertain and constitute one of the principal areas of negotiation in the Evensen group, which has been holding fairly regular meetings on
these issues.

With respect to the special treatment of both tuna and salmon, I have a feeling that there is at least a general acceptance that there will be some special treatment for highly migratory species and for anadromous species. Precisely what the nature of that especial treatment is at this time is somewhat more up in the air.

Finally, with respect to the question of the edge of the margin and areas where it goes beyond 200 miles, this is still an issue on which there are wide differences of opinion and on which the broad-margin states, particularly Argentina, Canada, and Australia, understandably have very strong views. If I could hazard a guess as to where we are headed on that issue, it seems to me that some accommodation must be found which would meet fairly the concerns of the broad-margin states as well as the concerns of the landlocked and shelf-locked group. The most likely compromise, which seems to be gaining ground, is that in fact jurisdiction in the margin and areas beyond 200 miles would be entrusted to the coastal states. In other words, a 200 mile limit, or alternatively, where the edge of the margin is further seaward, the coastal states would have resource jurisdiction over those margin mineral resources, but would be subject to some degree of sharing of the revenues from mineral exploration and exploitation in that area, and again out to some reasonably objective defined boundary of the outer edge, as Dr. Hodgson will be discussing with this group later in the program.

Shifting to the third major set of issues at the Caracas session, they are the international regime and organization for mineral resources of the deep seabed. This of course is in the areas beyond national jurisdiction. I think there is general agreement that there will be a new international regime and machinery as part of an overall satisfactory agreement. Similarly there is broad agreement that there would be a sharing of revenues from the mining of these resources which would be used for international community purposes, largely for development assistance.

Beyond that, there is very substantial disagreement on the character of the new international organization. In fact, I think that we can say that at Caracas this issue emerged as the most difficult issue remaining in the law of the sea negotiation. There was a very extensive debate, both on the question of the economic implications of what threats if any there may be to developing land-based producers of these minerals and an appropriate way to deal with any such threats, and conversely what threats if any there would be to the interests of consumers on a worldwide basis and how could the interest of the consuming populations of the world be protected as well.

There was also an extensive debate at Caracas on the question of the rules and regulations and general principles of deep seabed mining, particularly the question of to what degree of specificity would such rules and regulations be included in a treaty or in an annex to the treaty. It seems to me that rather than make an effort to focus on each of the operational parameters on the debate on the deep seabeds, which frankly I think has become a rather sterile and nonproductive debate, we might be able to move things along if we shifted to a focus on the underlying concerns that have been expressed by the principal groupings of states in this negotiation.

On the one hand, the developing countries, speaking through the Group of 77 at Caracas, expressed a number of concerns which they have. One of those concerns was certainly that there should be meaningful participation in the financial benefits from deep seabed mining. A second concern was that there should be some protection from any potential threat for developing land-based producers of the minerals from the deep seabed.

A third concern, though less evident than the first two, but nevertheless I feel a real concern, was that somehow the sites that are the best first-generation mine sites might all be taken in the first few years by the companies that are now developing the technology to engage in deep seabed mining. We have not felt that that is the case. In fact all of the evidence that we have is that there are a very large number of first-generation mine sites and that the limiting factor will not be the number of sites but rather the large amounts of capital required to engage in deep seabed mining as well as the ability of the market to absorb the additional increment of minerals to come on stream from deep seabed mining.

Nevertheless, the concern has been expressed and I think it is going to be one issue that we will need to have a look at. In addition to that the members of the Group of 77 have expressed a concern that they have an opportunity to participate in deep seabed mining and that there be some machinery, some technique developed as part of the settlement, which would provide incentives for developing countries to develop technology and engage in mining of the deep seabeds.

On the other hand, the industrialized countries, many of whom have already expended large sums in the development of technology for deep seabed mining, also expressed a number of important concerns. First, they had very strong concerns that there be guaranteed access to the mineral resources of the deep seabed, and particularly in a post-energy crisis or present energy crisis world that they retain the guaranteed access to the important mineral resources of the deep seabeds.

In addition they wanted to protect their interests as consumers and the interests of consumers on a worldwide basis in avoiding price or production controls which would artificially restrict production and hold up prices in a way that could be detrimental to global economic efficiency.

Thirdly, they were concerned that there not be created a large, bureaucratic structure which would be a source of inefficient or efficient sopping up of the funds that would otherwise be available for international community purposes. I think also there was a desire that there be a timely resolution of the issue so that deep seabed mining could proceed in its normal developmental sequence, which has already begun.

I think that the principal task and one of the most important tasks at Geneva is to bridge this gap between both groupings of states and to find creative solutions to those common concerns. Happily, it is my view that this is not something that we should throw up our hands in despair about, despite the difficulty of the negotiation, but rather we ought to shift from the operational level of the negotiation to look at those fundamental concerns and seek available mechanisms to meet fairly the concerns of all groups of states in the negotiation.

Now a fourth set of principal issues at Caracas was the question of protection of the marine environment. Here there are three principal threats to the ocean environment: pollution from land-based sources; pollution from sea-bed mineral exploration and exploitation activities; and vessel-source pollution. As I have indicated, land-based sources are probably the predominant source of pollution of the ocean environment, because of the complexities of the problem, for example, of resolving the question of control of airborne hydrocarbons. You can imagine trying in the complex LOS negotiation to solve the question of automobile exhaust emissions, for example.

The question of land-based pollution is not going to be completely resolved at Caracas. I do think that it is realistic and highly desirable for the international community to agree on a good obligation, binding on all states, to prevent pollution of the marine environment from all sources, including land-based sources.

With respect to seabed exploration and exploitation activities, this is actually a very small portion of the pollution of the marine environment. But on the other hand there is no reason why states should be unwilling to accept at least minimum international standards which would be obligatory on those states in the development of their mineral resources from the continental margin under their national jurisdictions in order to protect the marine environment.

The cost is very low of the pollution control required to prevent blowouts, for example, and other sources of pollution from hydrocarbon drilling in production on the margin. It is a very incremental cost of the overall production itself. In addition to that it is basically a cost that would be borne by the companies and ultimately the consumers that would be engaged in the production and utilization of the hydrocarbons.

Finally, there is a real advantage on a worldwide basis to everyone to having uniform standards for the protection of the marine environment. I have a feeling that the trend is in the direction of accepting these minimum international standards. But I think that it is particularly important for all groups concerned with the marine environment to observe this issue very carefully at Geneva.

Finally, with respect to vessel-source pollution, I think that it is particularly important that there should be high and effective international standards for preventing vessel-source pollution. We have felt that the principal problem in this negotiation is that some states seek coastal state authority over vessel-source pollution within the economic zone. The difficulty we have with this is that there are 120 coastal states. Suppose that each of these jurisdictions had jurisdiction, even residual jurisdiction—in other words, left over even on top of an international system—had jurisdiction to set construction standards throughout this 200-mile area. First, there simply would be anarchy in trying to construct ships that would be able to ply the world's oceans. There would be potentially, not only 120 different construction standards, all perhaps quite reasonable, but in addition to that, since we are talking about jurisdiction, all of those standards could be changed through time. So we really have a situation comparable to placing a house on a railroad flat car on the east coast of the United States, sending it to the west coast and back, and asking that it comply with all building codes en route.

The second problem that we have, with this kind of coastal state authority over vessel-source pollution jurisdiction in the economic zone, is that this is a formula for the regulation of shipping of other states without their participation in the decisions that will affect them. In other words, it is simply not, in any meaningful sense, participatory democracy. This is something that we have felt concerns not only us but frankly ought to be of particular concern to developing countries that would have their shipping and their infant indus-tries potentially subject to the environmental standards and controls of the industrialized nations as well as developing nations around the world, without an opportunity for them to participate in those decisions.

The third problem is of course that, under any such jurisdiction in the economic zone to deal with vessel-source pollution, a majority of all coastal states would be totally zone-locked. That is, 66 out of the 120 coastal states would paradoxically have no access to any ocean on which they face, without going through the potential economic zone of one or more neighboring states. As far as navigation is concerned, in essence the problem is about like that of a 200-mile territorial sea, which would achieve the same effect of a loss of sover-eignity over all shipping in and out of your state. In essence, if there is any such jurisdiction, you become a variety of a landlocked state.

As to how we stand after Caracas on this question of vessel-source pollution, I think there is a very strong trend toward recognition that there should be uniform international construction standards for vessel-source pol-lution and that there should not be even residual competence in coastal states for the setting of such standards.

The issues that are still more disputed in the negotiations concern the question of the extent of such jurisdiction, if any, on a mileage basis, of how the international standards will be enforced, and particularly whether they will be enforced in certain zones within the economic zone, and third the question of the extent of any such jurisdiction, if any, on a mileage basis, and finally the question of whether there would be a special regime for certain limited special areas which may be particularly vulnerable environmentally.

A fifth set of concerns coming out of the Caracas session is certainly the question of marine scientific research. As the experts in this room know full well, marine research has been of very substantial benefit to all of mankind. We could cite for example the developments in plate tectonics and continental drift in recent decades, and other fundamental breakthroughs in oceanography, or we could cite the kinds of assistance that we are obtaining in protection of the marine environment from marine scientific research which is going forward, or frankly, also in terms of permitting more rational utilization of the resource potential of the world's oceans.

We have felt that the principal problem at the Caracas session with respect to marine scientific research is the demand by many states for control in the 200-mile economic zone over marine scientific research, a demand which takes the form of calling for a consent regime that no marine scientific research can be engaged in in the economic zone without the consent of the coastal state.

We have felt that, based on the experience of even the more qualified 1958 Continental Shelf Convention, that kind of consent regime would lead to a variety of real problems, problems of arbitrary denial, for example, of consent, problems of placing unnecessary conditions on marine scientific research, which deters such research, both of which problems have occurred and continue to occur, and problems which perhaps are the most pervasive of simply getting no response when a request for consent is made to the state in question. Sometimes we have referred to this problem as the "in-box, out-box problem," common to all bureaucracies—a request is made and it takes a very long time to move from the in box to the out box, or frankly, ever to arrive at the right box at all.

On the other hand, we recognize that coastal states in the negotiation, particularly many of those that have not until this time engaged in their own marine scientific research, have been concerned with a variety of legitimate concerns that must also be met. Particularly, they are concerned that there not be some kind of unfair mapping of their resource potential in their economic zone without their knowledge, which would then give additional leverage, perhaps unfair leverage, to companies that might be engaged in negotiating resource agreements with the coastal state. It has seemed to the United State and I am happy to say a large number of countries in Geneva which sponsored draft articles that basically attract this proposal that a fair way to meet the concerns of both groups of states was to place a series of obligations on the researching states which were carefully drawn to meet the concerns of coastal states without providing a consent regime with all of its difficulties.

As a result, we have proposed that there should be an obligation to notify the coastal state of research undertaken in the economic zone, that the coastal state be given a meaningful opportunity to participate in that research, for example, to have someone on board the vessel engaged in the research within the economic zone, and third, to permit a sharing of data and samples, in fact, to require a sharing of these data and samples with the coastal state.

Fourth, prompt publication of significant research results should be required, and of course also an obligation undertaken to interpret the results of the marine scientific research in a way which would be useful for the needs of the coastal state. As to where we stand at Caracas on these issues, I think there is very definitely a movement toward at least curtailing a regime of arbitrary consent on the part of coastal states. This was most significantly evident at Caracas in the introduction by a substantial number of landlocked states of articles, and many developing states included in that group, which basically would track the obligation on the researching state approach to the issue.

On the other hand, states are still fairly far apart on this question, and there are still many states that are urging a consent regime for marine scientific research within the 200-mile economic zone.

A sixth issue, and the final principal issue in the negotiations, is the question of compulsory settlement of disputes. Certainly conflict avoidance and stability of expectations are major objectives in the overall treaty process. I think there is wide recognition that we must assure appropriate mechanisms and institutions for fair third-party resolution of disputes arising under the treaty. In this respect, there was a general realization at Caracas of the need for compulsory dispute-settlement machinery, or another way of putting it is dispute-settlement machinery leading to a binding resolution of the issue.

There was a working group, composed of states from all regions, which met very productively at Caracas and my own feeling is that there is a substantial degree of consensus on the need for some appropriate mechanism for third-party resolution of disputes arising under the treaty. The principal differences seem to center on first, the nature of the most appropriate mechanism—should it be a new oceans tribunal as proposed by the United States, or should it be arbitration, or should it be some other mechanism. Second, the question of the scope of the issues which could be submitted to the dispute-settlement process. Or you could consider it in the reverse fashion, which is probably the way the negotiation will focus: that is, what kinds of issues would be excluded from the process of compulsory dispute settlement?, for example, the question of bilateral seabed boundary disputes between adjacent or opposite coastal states.

Now with that overview of the principal issues in the Caracas session of the conference, let me conclude by turning to a few general observations; first, on the areas of emerging consensus evident after Caracas, and second on some actions which I believe are needed if we are to have a useful and productive, or with all the qualifications that Professor Clingan has wisely put on it, a successful session at Geneva.

First, the encouraging areas of general consensus which have emerged after Caracas, and I think they are encouraging. We have never been as close on the basic outlines of where the oceans treaty is going as we are today. They include a strong trend—and one I think essentially not possible to change at this time—of a 12-mile territorial sea, and I believe a substantial trend, though not as clear yet as the question of the breadth of the territorial sea in favor of protection of unimpeded transit of straits used for international navigation.

Secondly, there is very strong consensus on the idea of a 200-mile economic zone which would include at least preferential rights over coastal species of fish out to 200 miles and exclusive rights to explore and exploit the mineral resources of the continental margin at least within 200 miles.

Third, there is agreement on free navigation beyond the territorial sea. Fourth, there is agreement that there should be as part of a comprehensive overall treaty a new international regime and machinery for the resource development of the deep seabed area. Last, I think there is a substantial trend toward acceptance of third-party dispute settlement mechanisms of some sort.

In short, there is progress toward an agreement. It is a rather extraordinary progress. We have never been this close in terms of the overall outlines of what the new oceans law is going to look like. I think it goes too far to say that there is nothing left to be done but to fill in the fine print, because that fine print is rather important. Nevertheless, the broad outlines of the agreement are clearly falling into place. I think the real question is really how long can the negotiation go on without the signature on that final piece of paper that Professor Clingan has talked about before the pressures for unilateral action on the part of all nations, and I am sorry to say on the part of our nation as well, overtake our ability to reach agreement.

That really raises the question of what actions are needed for a successful Geneva session of the Law of the Sea Conference. They are I believe primarily two. First, there must be a genuine will to negotiate and a willingness to take account of the vital interests of all states which must be accommodated for a meaningful treaty. The time for speeches is past. Geneva is a time for negotiation. And the time for confrontation politics has passed. The truth is that there cannot be a law of the sea treaty unless all groups—landlocked, coastal, maritime, developing, industrialized, distant-water fishing, broad-margin states, shelf-locked, et cetera—all of them work to accommodate the concerns of the other groups.

We will go to Geneva in precisely that spirit. We hope that all others will also go to Geneva in that spirit and we are certain that to succeed all of us must do so.

I think two points are particularly important in that connection. What do we mean by a spirit of negotiation? Part of it is certainly a question of maintaining flexibility, particularly on issues that are not of vital importance to one's own nation. And of recognizing that there must be some give and take if one is ever to reach an appropriate agreement.

At the same time it is incumbent upon every nation to make certain and to let other nations know candidly what its own vital interests are that must be accommodated in the negotiation for a satisfactory treaty. For example, we have repeatedly and candidly said to the states participating in this negotiation that we must have unimpeded transit through and over straits used for international navigation if we are to be able to sign a law of the sea treaty. We do not say this out of any sense of threat. Rather we say this out of a candid and honest

need to express clearly one of the vital interests of the United States in the negotiation. We are concerned that unless we do express that candidly and other
states understand that that we could be endangering the success of the Law of
the Sea Conference.

Similarly we feel that it is important that just as we should take into
account and meet the genuine concerns that have been expressed with respect to
the deep seabed negotiation, the United States and other industrialized nations
have important interests in the deep seabed which also must be accommodated
in the overall negotiation.

A second point with respect to the question of the appropriate spirit
of negotiation and what we mean by it is the question of the utilization of groups
in the negotiation. There is nothing per se helpful or harmful in the strong utilization of groups as is very clearly the case today for example throughout the
United Nations system and is certainly being followed in the law of the sea negotiation. On the one hand, if groups get together to consolidate their positions it
can be very helpful in terms of solving one of the great management problems of
how do you negotiate simultaneously with 137 states with differing views in the
negotiation?

On the other hand, if groups get together with a view to adopting a
rigid position and presenting it to other states on a take it or leave it basis, it is
not a formula for negotiation or for concluding a successful law of the sea
treaty. So what must be done I think is for all states, as well as all groupings of
states, to keep before them the importance of genuine negotiation.

The second most important action which I believe is needed for a
successful Geneva session is that early on Geneva must come to grips with its
management problems. This is wholly apart from the question of the will to
negotiate. No one has quite figured out how you do it with 92 issues on the
agenda of enormous importance to the states involved and with 137 to 150
states participating in the negotiation. I think that the answer to that question
first and foremost must mean an early formal focus by the Geneva session of the
conference on negotiating groups on each issue, and of course on the overall
package. We simply cannot make progress by continuing to have sterile debates
in large working groups of the whole in which the differing positions of the
groups pass like ships in the night.

The only way to make progress in those working groups is frankly
to have a negotiation on each of the important issues, in which the states and
the key conference leaders and those principally concerned get together early in
Geneva and negotiate the principal outlines of each of the issues and of course
the overall package as well. I believe that also means a negotiating focus on text,
as the Evensen group indeed is seeking to do at this point, rather than trying to
have simply abstract discussions.

If the conference can deal with those two issues in Geneva I believe
that it can make very substantial progress which will confound the skeptics and

which will clearly demonstrate what I believe to be the case, that the conference leadership from all regional groups is dedicated to a timely and just oceans treaty.

Thank you.

Mr. Clingan: Thank you, John. I am grateful to you for taking time to come down here and be with us. We put you in a difficult position in leading off when you were faced with such a complex of issues and interaction between such a large number of people. Thank you very much.

Joe Warioba has come a long distance to be with us today, another continent, another side of the world, indeed, the third world. We have to be extremely grateful for the immense effort on his part because his nation certainly must be viewed as one of the key participants in this conference and he himself indeed is well recognized as one of the key conference leaders. It is for these reasons as well as the force of his thoughts and his arguments that we are extremely pleased today to have Joe with us.

Commentary

J.S. Warioba
Tanzanian Ministry of Foreign Affairs

Mr. Warioba: Thank you, Mr. Chairman. First of all, I must express my gratitude for the opportunity to participate in the Ninth Annual Conference of the Law of the Sea Institute. Although this is my first time to participate in these conferences, I have had a keen interest in the proceedings and the results of this Institute and, indeed, as it has been said before, it has been one of the pioneering institutions in evolving a new set of rules in the area of international law of the sea.

This morning I will deal briefly with the course of negotiations at the Caracas session of the Third United Nations Law of the Sea Conference. I will not go into the substantive discussions or examine in detail the problems that the session faced. Mr. Moore has shown in his opening remarks the complex nature of the issues that we are dealing with in the conference.

Towards the end of the Caracas session, one of the questions which was frequently asked was, "What has Caracas achieved?" To this question a range of responses was given. There are those who had expected much more than had been done in Caracas and were therefore not satisfied with the results. There were others less demanding in their expectations who were content with what had been done. There are yet others who believed Caracas was a failure and a cause of pessimism on the conference as a whole.

An objective assessment of the Caracas session has, however, to take into account the realities and circumstances which faced the conference. One of the factors is the large number of subjects and issues on the agenda of the conference. There are some thirty omnibus items, most of which carry a number of subjects of various degrees of complexity. These subjects in turn involved a number of issues and interests of many states. Although the Sea-Bed Committee took some three years to prepare for the conference and in the case of the international seabed area it took some six years, the preparation did not go at best beyond the formulation of alternative draft treaty articles reflecting the multi-

18

farious interests involved in the subject. Indeed, it can be said that it was only in respect to the international seabed area that there existed alternative formulations of treaty articles.

In the case of many issues, including the territorial sea, straits used for international navigation, and the exclusive economic zone, there was nothing but an unsystematic collection of proposals reflecting the political positions of individual or groups of states.

Another factor was the large representation at the conference. About 140 states were represented in the conference, as well as observers from liberation movements and international, intergovernmental, and nongovernmental organizations. About a third of the state representations had not had the opportunity to participate in the preparatory work. And Caracas was the first opportunity to record their political stands on many of the issues.

To add to this, many countries had large delegations within which a number of sectorial interests were represented, thus making it difficult for some delegations to determine easily their course of action on any particular issue.

A third factor was the organizational structure of the conference and the method of work. The main negotiating organs of the conference were the three main committees of the whole. The establishment of smaller organs became almost impossible and whenever they were established it became a condition that they remain open-ended so that any delegation could participate, and the amendment invariably did not include decision-making on any issue of substance.

The rules of procedure adopted by the conference, based on a gentlemen's agreement of the General Assembly of the United Nations, included a rule on decision-making with checks and balances that is novel in international lawmaking. The relevant rule, 37, allows voting only when all efforts at reaching consensus have been exhausted and even lays down the procedure to determine when efforts at consensus have been exhausted. This sort of procedure, whatever merits it has, does not encourage speedy decisions.

Fourth, and what really explains what I have said, is the fact that this is not a codification conference. We can say the 1958 conference was a codification conference. But the current one is to a large extent a conference for the progressive development of international law. Besides the attempt to make rules for the international seabed area, there is a serious challenge to the existing rules in other areas. This challenge will not only affect international and national interests, but also sectoral interests within national boundaries.

Last, there are different and conflicting interests and suspicion within national representations which make it a difficult task to evolve national policy positions. As a result of this, the nature of negotiations has become too complex.

The same applies to the organizational structure of the conference, as well as the method of work. No state or representative of any interest group within a delegation is willing to be left out of any serious negotiations, and sometimes leaders of delegations do not have the competence to make decisions and smaller organs of the conference are likewise limited in number and nature of functions.

With that introduction let us briefly look at what happened in Caracas. The substantive work of the conference was done in the three main committees. It may be useful, therefore, to cast a brief glance at the work of each committee, in order to make a somewhat objective assessment of the course of negotiations. The mandate of the First Committee was, and still is, the elaboration of treaty articles to implement the 1970 UN Declaration of Principles on the Seabed and Ocean Floor Beyond the Limits of National Jurisdiction and, as will be recalled, that Declaration of Principles proclaimed that the area beyond limits of national jurisdiction is a common heritage of mankind.

At Caracas, the First Committee spent most of its time on one crucial issue, that is, who may exploit the area? At the end of the session two clear conceptual approaches had emerged and proposals had been formulated to that effect.

One conceptual approach preferred a licensing system of exploitation, by which entities would be given free access to the resources of the area on certain conditions, which include payment of fees to a proposed international authority.

The other approach prefers direct exploitation of the resources by the authority through a joint enterprise.

Broadly speaking, the first approach invokes a laissez faire system, while the second approach prefers a centralized system. The former is supported by the developed countries, particularly those of the Western Hemisphere, while the other is supported by the developing countries.

Having reached that state of logical choices, the First Committee went further to attempt a practical interpretation. Four position papers on best conditions of exploitation were tabled. Three of them—by the U.S.A., Japan, and the EEC countries—pertain to the licensing system and they differ only in matters of time and emphasis on details. The other one, presented by the Group of 77, is faithful to the joint enterprise proposal. As it is now, the stage is clearly set for a hard beginning.

Two best and conflicting proposals are now before the First Committee and the conference must find a solution out of them.

There are other crucial issues to be resolved. For example, the functions, powers, and structure of the international authority, including the establishment and composition of the main organs, but once the issue of who may exploit the area is resolved, it will be relatively easy to deal with those other issues.

The Second Committee has the largest number and some of the most vexing subjects on the agenda of the conference, including the breadth of the territorial sea, the exclusive economic zone, continental shelf, straits, and the rights of the landlocked countries.

The Sea-Bed Committee did not go anywhere near a proper preparation for the conference. What was presented to the conference was a mass of proposals without helpful arrangements and, as I said, these proposals just reflected the interests of individuals or groups of states.

What the Second Committee did during the Caracas session was, in a sense, to conduct prenegotiation talks. In the process, however, the general direction of the negotiations did emerge. In the course of a general debate on each major subject, papers were formulated reflecting the main trends on every issue. At the end of the session, thirteen papers had been formulated and each paper covered the main issues within a given broad subject. These papers include such crucial issues as the territorial sea, straits, exclusive economic zone, archipelagoes, landlocked countries, high seas, et cetera. The issues have already been put in proper focus and, in some cases, one could detect some agreement on some of the issues, or part of the issues. For example, it had become amply clear that a package solution is inevitable if the conference is to succeed.

On the question of the territorial sea, certain trends have become clear. Despite the significant voice of the territorialists who demand a territorial sea of 200 miles, sometimes tempered by the concept of plurality of regimes, and subject to a package that includes the exclusive economic zone, it could be detected that 12 nautical miles of territorial sea was a basis for agreement. It was also evident that the agreement on the question of territorial sea would depend on another two issues, innocent passage and delimitation between the adjustment and other steps.

On innocent passage, two main trends emerged, one favoring complete sovereignty of the coastal state in the area and another restricting that sovereignty and seeking something close to free passage for foreign vessels.

On delimitation between adjustment and other steps, two main trends were discernible, one favoring the median line and another favoring a less precise method, such as delimitation by agreement and/or in accordance with equitable principles.

Despite the absence of agreement in Caracas, it can further be said that the difficult areas have been identified. The same can be said about straits used for international navigation. The attempts at definition of what constitutes a strait used for international navigation clearly revealed that the issue concerns a few straits, special straits in the world, and not the more than 100 straits that had been talked about so much before the conference.

It was also clear that ordinary merchant vessels, doing normal international trade, were not the real concern with regard to the issue of passage and here, certainly, my views slightly differ from that expressed a few minutes ago by Mr. Moore, in that the issue boiled down to the passage of naval vessels and whether rules on passage through straits would be met or supplemented and enforced by the coastal state, or by the international community and the flag states, and further, whether naval vessels should be subject to notification and consent and whether submarines should navigate on the surface when passing through a strait, which is part and parcel of the territorial sea of a state.

On the exclusive economic zone, a clear trend had developed. There was, for the first time, almost complete agreement to the effect that the coastal state had the right to extend its jurisdiction to a belt of a maximum breadth of 200 miles from the base lines applicable to the territorial sea.

The nature of the differences was on the main features of the economic zone and these differences were narrowed down considerably. Indeed, it could be said that there were two broad trends. One trend approached the exclusive economic zone as an area under national jurisdiction, in which the foreign states and the international community had a few specified rights, principally, freedom of navigation, and overflight, and the freedom to lay submarine cables and pipelines.

The other trend approached it as an area of high seas, in which the coastal states had certain rights, limited to resource management.

In discussion of the other issues, such as fisheries, rights of land-locked countries and other geographically disadvantaged states, preservation of the marine environment, marine scientific research, artificial installations, et cetera, the discussions clarified these trends and, in some cases, narrowed the differences and, in some cases, put them in sharper focus.

The Third Committee, whose mandate included elaboration of treaty articles on the preservation of the marine environment, marine scientific research, and the development and transfer of technology, was almost in the same position as the Second Committee in that enough preparatory work had not been done in that committee. Although, through a general debate on the issues, as well as discussion in working groups, there was noticeable movement towards reaching agreement in certain areas, and in conflict areas, the nature of the differences was put in proper focus.

For example, one can say there was broad agreement on the general responsibilities of each state in the preservation of the marine environment and in the furtherance of marine scientific research, as well as the development and transfer of knowledge. There was also broad agreement on the need for global cooperation. In fact, on pollution, the issues boiled down to vessel pollution and the enforcement of regulations.

One group of states, mainly the maritime states, would prefer regulations made by international organizations, such as IMCO, and enforced by flag states, while the other group of states, mainly the developing states, would prefer a zonal approach, in which coastal states would have residual powers to make supplementary regulations and to enforce all regulations in areas under national jurisdiction. With regard to marine scientific research, the crucial issue revolves around the question whether consent is required for carrying out the research.

Briefly, that is what happened in the committees as a whole. The negotiations were not, however, confined to the formal organs of the conference. I am not going to dwell on the dynamics of the conference negotiations. I note that later in the program we will deal with this, but I will say a word or two.

Apart from the three main committees, there was a large number of semiofficial and informal negotiating groups and these groups still exist in the conference. The regional groups of Africa, Asia, Latin America, Eastern Europe, and Western Europe carried on serious negotiations within themselves. In addition, there were other groups, for example, the Group of 77, grouping all the developing countries numbering more than 100 states, the group of landlocked states, the group of coastal states, and many others including a group of political experts. All these groups had plenty of work to do because the subject matter of the conference is so complex that the interests of states are so diverse and one can hardly find two states with similar positions on any issue.

Most of the negotiations, in the same formal and informal groups, took place behind closed doors and it was not easy to know exactly what went on. It can, however, be said that it was in the informal groups that one could find frank talk, shed of most of the diplomatic pleasantries and the deliberate ambiguities. In other words, the real negotiations took place in the informal groups and any group position that emerged was the result of blunt talking. This exercise produced some movement towards a solution on some issues, even on those issues where no clear movement could be seen, much had been achieved behind the closed doors.

Mr. Chairman, viewed in the light of the prevailing realities and circumstances, it is fair to say the Caracas session made some progress. The ten weeks spent at Caracas were definitely too short a time for the conference to achieve widespread agreement on such a complex subject. We can, however, say the session enabled all participants to examine the problem in its entirety and to see things in their proper prospective. In other words, Caracas was an invaluable educational service to the participants. Secondly, the discussions made great strides in the clarification of the issues and presenting them in sharp focus. In particular, the definition of the issues at Caracas revealed, in a clear manner, the nature of the differences. In the absence of adequate preparation for the conference, this was a significant achievement.

The Caracas achievement does not, however, mean the conference did all that it was expected to do. Much more could have been done had there been a will to do so. The mood of many of the delegations was to discuss an issue and then freeze it until the next session. This was due, mainly, to two factors.

First, some delegations lacked the authority to commit their governments on some crucial issues. In addition, facilities at Caracas and time were insufficient for them to consult and receive the necessary instructions.

Second, and more important, men were not willing to agree to anything until an outline of a package had emerged. Be that as it may, had there been a serious determination, I honestly believe greater movement could have been made and at least the essential elements of a package could have been agreed upon.

Furthermore, the crucial element of the Caracas achievement was the narrowing down of the issues, not in the sense of a movement towards agreement, but in the sense of revealing the nature and cause of the conflict. An achievement of this nature does not mean the future work of the conference will become easy. The relevation of the nature of differences, in fact, revealed also that positions were rigid on many of the crucial issues. One way of looking at things is to hope that a clear exposition of the areas and nature of conflict will serve as a guide to governments in their preparation during the intersessional period, so that at Geneva sufficient flexibility will prevail and the deadlock will be broken.

Another point of view is that Caracas has brought disillusionment and there is now considerable lack of enthusiasm on the part of many governments. The conference got off on a high note of expectation, but many governments may now be thinking that it is a waste of time and resources. Should this be the case, and there seems to be some indication that it is, then Geneva will not go at all well.

It is with this background of mixed feelings, of optimism and pessimism, that the next round of talks will open in Geneva of March of this year. The workload is heavy and the problems to be overcome are immense. The need for an agreement is as great as ever, but the danger of failure also looms. However, after a great deal of reflection, many of us still believe there is a chance, but to grasp that chance, Geneva should be approached with certain clear assumptions.

One assumption is that governments will go to Geneva with committed determination, that great need to achieve agreement and thus avoid chaos and disorder in the oceans should be the guiding spirit.

Second, governments should go to Geneva with a clear knowledge that rigid positions will not help. Threats and counterthreats based on majority or national power, threats and counterthreats which have characterized the negotiations so far, will play only a negative role.

Third, the conference should pay little attention to its rules of procedure on decisionmaking. The conference must make tremendous progress at Geneva to insure its survival. It may be too optimistic to expect a clean text of a treaty to emerge from Geneva, but it will not go at all well for the conference if agreement is not reached on the basic issues. Such agreement will be impossible if the conference seeks to use the rules of procedure to the letter.

I believe these assumptions are possible and should that be the case, it becomes necessary for all concerned to approach the next session with extreme seriousness and determination. Each country must commit itself to the goal of contributing to success and must be prepared to be flexible. To that end must also be geared the composition and mandate of delegations. Delegations with insufficient authority will not help and delegates coming as tourists will do nothing but harm. We had too many of this type of delegate who, after a tour of the Caracas negotiations, called press conferences and made statements which were off the mark. One hopes that Geneva will not have that.

Those who have a role to play, different from government negotiators, should also show a more serious sense of responsibility. One of the great disappointments that some of us experienced at Caracas was the role played by nongovernmental groups. There were many representatives of nongovernmental organizations, including the press corps. In many conferences, these groups have been helpful, but at Caracas some of us found many of them rather biased, partisan, and sometimes trivial. Many individuals actually were representatives of this or that organization, but they worked in an individual capacity to propagate the point of view of the country of their nationality, or to look for material for their next article in a magazine, or a book with the same bias.

As for the press, they relished sensation, rather than realistic reporting.

In conclusion, what I can say is that Caracas was not conducive to any trend in the course of negotiations. The session did lay down the groundwork for real negotiations to begin, but it did not do all that it was capable of doing in that session. In the process, the tremendous task that lies ahead was clearly revealed. The goals are well stated for Geneva and, as I said, there is a very heavy workload and there are immense problems to be overcome. The need for an early agreement is more pressing than ever, but time and enthusiasm are running out. We are facing a great test of human determination and it requires the efforts of everyone concerned, including this conference of the Law of the Sea Institute to pass this test.

Thank you, Mr. Chairman.

Mr. Clingan: Thank you, Mr. Warioba, for those extremely thoughtful comments and your analysis of the Caracas meeting. Once again, please accept our gratitude for the immense effort that it took for you to be with us today. Thank you, very much.

Now, I would like to shift hemispheres, again, back to our neighbor to the north, who has problems that are unique and not shared by either the United States or Tanzania and about which I am sure we will all hear.

I want to express, also, my particular gratitude to Paul Lapointe. He is an old and good friend of the Law of the Sea Institute and I say that because he has just proved it again by allowing himself to be pressed into service on extremely short notice to help us out on this panel. My thanks to you, Paul.

Commentary

Paul Lapointe
Department of External Affairs, Canada

Mr. Lapointe: Thank you, Mr. Chairman. Mr. Chairman, as you have just said, I am rather here as a pinch hitter at the moment and we all know that the bases are loaded and I am reminded that pinch hitters have the deplorable tendency to strike out. So, I hope that my contract will be renewed next year, anyway, no matter what I do.

Mr. Chairman, I think that, basically, what I would like to say in the context of the Caracas conference, and the aftermath of the conference, is that it seems to be quite evident that we are going to need time if we want to be successful in our endeavors. I got personally involved in the law of the sea some nine years ago and I would have to agree with all those who say that we have made progress. I do not think there is any doubt about that. I recall, back in 1967, we were arguing as to whether we should say beyond the limit of national jurisdiction, singular, or beyond the limits of national jurisdictions, plural. *S*, apparently, had a lot of meaning for certain countries. Now we have left that. We have gone beyond that.

We also had terrific arguments as to whether we should all support the phrase "for peaceful purposes." Nobody knew what it meant. I do not think that we know yet, today, what it means, but we all accept it. We can put it now in any resolution and everybody applauds.

We were also concerned, a few years ago, about the phrase "the common heritage of mankind." Nobody knew what it meant. I am not too sure we know now what it means, but we are working towards it. We are trying to build up something for mankind, whoever that is. I suppose, as I refer to the program, that we should change the word "mankind" too. Since you are a chairman now, suppose we talk of humanity, or something.

So, I think that we definitely have made progress. I do not think there is any doubt about that. At the same time, I think I do share the guarded optimism, or the cautious pessimism of my friend Joe Warioba as to the prospects of the Geneva session. I am greatly concerned, personally, about the way the organization of the conference provides for our work. I think that Rule 37, for instance, which I personally was involved in drafting in Caracas, was a necessary compromise in order to go over that hurdle and move on with the business of the conference, but I am very concerned that when we do reach a point of making decisions at the conference, Rule 37 might be as much an impediment as an assistance to us. The delays that are provided for in Rule 37 could really prevent progress at some point. The rule was devised basically to protect minority interests, because everybody has a minority interest hidden somewhere in his pockets. It might take us a very long time before we can move ahead.

I noted that John Norton Moore has expressed certain views as to how things are proceeding and of where we have made progress, how he sees things moving on. I do not want to get into the substance of things, obviously my country would have different views as to the direction things are taking, or are likely to take, or which direction is desirable, but we are still a very long way from home and what is of great concern to us at the moment is that apparent trend around the world for unilateral action in the not too distant future. I am referring not only to the United States of America, but to other countries as well. There are urgent problems, pressing problems, arising in all kinds of fields and I would say, perhaps to underline one in particular, in the field of fisheries there are very pressing situations. The same pressures exist in Canada that exist in the United States in this respect and if we do not give the conference a chance, I am afraid that we will never really get around to doing something internationally.

These present trends, I think, are to be controlled to some extent. Just as when we went to Caracas, we made a point of telling our own public, in Canada, at least, that they could not expect a complete success in Caracas. We probably have to face the same situation now. I do not quite see how we can finally succeed, how we can achieve everything in Geneva, either. Of course, I am a bit disappointed that there will be only one session in 1975 and I am not too sure exactly what the position of certain countries will be, following Geneva, if we are not fully successful. My basic feeling is that, even if we were to start voting on the very first day in Geneva, which is rather unlikely, even if we were to do that, I do not quite see how we could manage to finish it in eight weeks. Somebody mentioned, I think it was John Norton Moore, the ninety-two items that we have to deal with and when you add all the subitems, and so on, I do not know, they may run into the thousands, and the formulations that are now on the table, unfortunately, are still quite far apart in many cases.

I have also the feeling that, in many cases, the middle ground has yet to be occupied. If you look at the First Committee business, with respect to the international seabed area, you have two basic views there which are relatively incompatible, and nobody has yet come up with something that is closer to an eventual compromise. John Norton Moore mentioned that we should move to Geneva with a will to negotiate. I certainly agree and I do think that we, in Canada, have that will to negotiate. At the same time, he immediately outlined, just about in the same breath, I may say, an area where he could not compromise, meaning the passage in straits. Now, how do you reconcile this and where is the middle solution? Is there anything between completely free passage and completely coastal control passage? There must be something in between. We have go to to look for that and find it.

John Norton Moore also mentioned the procedural impediments that we have, how we should go about negotiating. I think this is, perhaps, the first task that we should undertake in Geneva, to find a way to negotiate. There have been a lot of informal working groups, discussion groups, and so on. They have contributed to making some progress, but these are not formal groups and the history of the seabed controversy in this conference so far has been that it is impossible to have a working group of a decent size.

Now, you may say, why does not each group designate some representatives to negotiate for it, but I think that I remember having to take that position in Caracas. I could not afford, as a Canadian representative, to let Canada be represented by anybody else in a serious negotiation. We have very serious interests, some of them vital, in this conference. I am not capable of letting even my best friend, be it Australia, or Norway, or anyone, represent Canada in a serious negotiation. I do not think the United States has ever let itself be represented by someone else. They have chosen, for instance, not to be in any group because of their vital interest. I cannot disagree with that. The United States' representative has to defend the United States' interests, but how do we go about negotiating. This is a very serious problem. We have tried, in all kinds of ways. John has mentioned the working group on the settlement of dispute questions. He had one going on fisheries and there were all kinds of groups around the place, but these were never formal groups and, let's face it, the results of these working groups left quite a lot yet to be resolved.

So, how do we do it? We have a Drafting Committee in the conference, which held one brief session to decide that they had met and they were going to separate again and meet some other time, perhaps. How are we going to make use of this Drafting Committee? I am not talking about it just because my friend Alan Beesley is chairman of the Drafting Committee, but there is an official group of limited membership, which we have not used yet. I am not too sure if we will be able to use it in Geneva, but we all know that to negotiate in a formal session in any of the three committees is just about impossible. Everybody keeps repeating his basic position and we have not moved very far away from that.

So, all in all, Mr. Chairman, I have to express a very guarded view of the way things are going, not that I am not prepared to continue. I think we will, but I think we certainly need more time and I would certainly appeal to anybody who has a say in the matter to advise its government to wait it out a bit longer. As Joe has mentioned, this is not a codification conference. We are inventing things as we go along. It will take time and we still need a lot more imagination in order to be able to occupy that middle ground which in many fields, I think, has not been fully explored.

Thank you, Mr. Chairman.

Mr. Clingan: Thank you, very much, for that view, Paul, and thanks again to the entire panel. I think, if you have listened as carefully as I have, you get a pretty good picture of the diversity of views and also the diversity of issues that faced the group in Caracas and I think, probably, the audience is now in a position to begin to make its own judgment on where we stand in the course of negotiations and, hopefully, has some thoughts about how to proceed at this point.

Now, it is time to turn to the audience. I will open the floor for questions or comments. I would ask you to move to the microphones, please, and state your name and your affiliation. You may address your questions to any member of the panel, or the entire panel, except for me. I see some former students in the audience and I know how unmerciful they can be on occasion. So I will keep myself out of the conversation.

Discussion and Questions

Mr. Lee: Thank you, Mr. Chairman. My name is Ted Lee. I am legal advisc to the Department of External Affairs in Ottawa, Canada.

I thought Professor Moore, very courageously at the end of his extremely interesting talk, attempted—I think it is courageous to attempt to list consenses that he saw emerging, or trends that he saw emerging from the Caracas conference. Of the five or six that he listed, I would certainly agree with the 12-mile territorial sea and the economic zone and some sort of a regime for the international seabed area, but I would like to express caveats with regard to two of the trends which he had mentioned. The first is the substantial trend, as he mentioned, towards unimpeded passage through, over, or under straits. I think, as was mentioned by the two other panelists, there really are, here, some serious questions still to be decided and I am wondering whether it is really right to base the view that there is a substantial trend on the fact that more speakers at Caracas spoke in favor of it than spoke against it. I am not sure whether that is really a fair basis on which to judge what he regards as a substantial trend, and it may be that indeed there are other reasons, but this is the one that was mentioned.

It is true, from one optic, on the question of international straits, that, as Professor Moore mentioned, the United States is not asking for anything more than we already have, but that, I think, from another optic, is not really true. I think he would agree that it does really discard the whole principle of innocent passage and here we do have a serious problem that I think that we all recognize and as Paul Lapointe mentioned we hope that we can find some middle way between these two extremes.

The other caveat, Mr. Chairman, that I would like to register is that I believe Mr. Moore said a consensus was emerging towards "free navigation" (I have that in quotes in my notes), beyond the territorial sea. When discussing

30

the question of vessel-source pollution, Professor Moore did mention that there were some outstanding issues. He mentioned the question of who would establish discharge standards and in what area, if it is to be in the 12-mile territorial sea, or out to 200 miles. He also mentioned the problem of enforcement by either flag states or coastal states, as an issue on which there are still many questions outstanding, and also the question of the establishment of special regimes for areas that are highly vulnerable. These are questions which we look forward to discussing, both with Professor Moore quite soon, and with many others. They are issues which affect, very clearly, any trend towards free navigation outside territorial seas.

So, I would express doubts that there is really any trend there, yet. I do not think this is the case.

Thank you, sir.

Mr. Moore: Our Canadian colleagues, both Paul Lapointe and Ted Lee, are highly articulate. I wish that we could get them on our side.

My problem is that when I speak about these things, I have doubts, but when I listen to Paul Lapointe and Ted Lee, I know I am right.

The real problem, with which I agree is that the question of straits is less certain in terms of trend and issues that I lumped it with, for example, the 12-mile territorial sea, or the question of the 200-mile economic zone. Incidentally, one can always say that it is no more or less certain than the straits issue, since it is linked in the thinking of many countries which have accepted it to the straits issue. With that linkage aside, I think, in general, you are right. There is less certainty on straits and there is less certainty on vessel-source pollution, which I am very glad that you linked with the question of free navigation. We have also felt that these are issues that very strongly affect navigational freedom. In fact, that is why the principal source of concern on our part. I do feel, nevertheless, there are reasons that support a cautious statement of a significant trend in the direction of unimpeded transit. It is not solely the indication that more speakers, for the first time, at Caracas supported unimpeded transit of straits, but also the large number of private conversations that we held, as well as a number of other major maritime states. It is very definitely our assessment that there is a decided trend in favor of unimpeded transit through straits.

The real question is why should there be a disagreement on this point between Canada and the United States, or the United States and any other country. We are certainly prepared to consider the questions the coastal states are concerned about with respect to safety, with respect to protection of the marine environment in straits, or especially vulnerable marine areas and, in this connection, we like Ted Lee, very much, to look forward, in all seriousness, to discussion with our Canadian colleagues, as well as all others in the negotiations, but it is our feeling that our position on straits of maintaining unimpeded transit is strongly in your interest as well as our interest and we would like to discuss that in terms of really what is the community common interest on this issue.

One point that Paul Lapointe stressed, I think, is a particularly important one and that is I would like to endorse his focus on the management problems in this conference. I think that he and Joseph Warioba are exactly right, that it is not solely a question of the will to negotiate. That is important. It is indispensable, but there is another element beyond that that is very critical and that really is this management problem of how do you come to grips with moving the parties together on these questions that we have just discussed.

I, too, am somewhat concerned about the rule-making procedure. I do not think anyone is completely happy with that and I do think it has the kinds of dangers that Paul Lapointe indicated. That suggests to me that the only solution to these problems really is an early negotiation in which you do get the conference leaders together on each issue and all the others that would like to participate in a negotiation and you negotiate. You talk about the issues. You work out a package on the deep seabeds that protects the interests of all states, and then you go to your working groups, or your drafting groups and you try to do something with it, but to go the other way around is a sterile exercise and I think that has become abundantly clear to everyone.

The other point I would make is that there are two ways to talk about fairness to negotiate and willingness to negotiate on issues. One is to say that on every issue the outcome has to be a middle of the road compromise. The other is to say that this is a package negotiation and in the real world nations have some interests that are more important to them than other interests. Indeed, they have certain vital interests in which their negotiators will not have flexibility and will not be permitted to reach some, what others may feel, middle of the road solution. What is really needed is a flexibility and an overall sense in terms of the total package of ocean's interest and within that, I think it is unrealistic to expect any nation, whether it is Canada, or the United States, or any others, to reach an agreement which would not take account of its vital interests.

Thank you.

Mr. Clingan: Mr. Warioba, I think, has a comment, and then Mr. Lapointe.

Mr. Warioba: Mr. Chairman, actually my view tends to agree with the view of Mr. Lee on the conclusions that Mr. Moore made. Certainly, I did not agree with his assessment of the consensus that emerged in Caracas and on these particular issues that consensus on unimpeded passage through straits. I think that we can go as far as saying that there might be a consensus on unimpeded passage for merchant vessels, but we cannot say, definitely we cannot say that we are near an agreement as far as military vessels are concerned, as far as nuclear-powered ships are concerned, as far as large tankers are concerned. I think that we are still very far apart and this is the crucial area, whether the actual control with respect to regulation making, whether it is a whole or supplementary, and the area of enforcement is going to be left to the international community and the flag states, or the coastal states that are bordering the straits. I think, here, we still have wide differences.

I was surprised to hear the conclusion of Mr. Moore on the question of free navigation beyond the territorial sea. Here, indeed, is where the difficulty lies with respect to the exclusive economic zone. As I stated in my introduction, his approach is that the economic zone is the high seas, where you have free navigation, but there is the other side and this happens to be the view of the majority. They might not be such very powerful nations, but they are the majority and their view is that the economic zone is not the high seas where you have free navigation. It is a national area. You have the right of navigation, but it is not as free as on the high seas, the approach is that this is a resource-management area, or is it more than that? Now, that is where the difficulty lies and I do not think that we are anywhere near an agreement. Possibly, it might be one of the crucial issues.

Mr. Moore also mentioned another issue which was not touched upon by Mr. Lee, dispute settlement. Certainly, we are aware that in Caracas there was an informal group that worked very hard, with Professor Sohn as secretary, to formulate some thoughts on the question of dispute settlement. To my understanding, this was not an issue which was exhaustively discussed in the conference to the extent of trying to detect a sort of consensus. Certainly, as far as I know, at least in my own group, the idea of third party dispute settlement has not been accepted. The idea of a method of dispute settlement that is acceptable is partially in the nature of third-party dispute settlement, which has not yet been accepted and I think this is an area where you cannot say there is consensus.

I think I will limit myself, at the moment, to this.

Mr. Clingan: Thank you.

Mr. Lapointe: Thank you, Mr. Chairman.

I would like to say a couple of words on this passage issue. It seems to me that we are still hung up on certain terms and concepts which we could very well do away with at this stage of the game. We are using terms that are supposed to help our work, but we are using phrases, for instance, unimpeded passage. Now, I know what the United States means by this theory, but what does it really mean? What is an impediment to passage? Does that mean that there should be no control whatsoever over whatever kind of passage is being exercised through international straits, or any other place? We had the old phrase "innocent passage" and, of course, that does not work, either, because everybody has his own concept of what innocence is. It strikes me that perhaps in the busiest waterway in the whole world, the St. Lawrence Seaway system, the Great Lakes–St. Lawrence Seaway system, we have a completely controlled operation by our two countries and there is no problem. Ships go through, but it is controlled, every step of the way.

Now, it seems to me that we should concentrate on, and it is perhaps the middle of the road solution that we are looking for, that after guaranteeing internationally that all ships of all flags shall have passage, then you can go on and indicate to what extent coastal states, or whatever state is involved, can exercise certain controls on "dangerous" passages. Is it beyond our ken to be able to find a solution where you would have certain controls that would not impede navigation, but would control navigation to the extent that is necessary and not any further?

I think that we are always prejudging the situation, when we start using phrases like "innocent passage" because, for most people, particularly developing countries, and a lot of others, too, that means complete control by the coastal states. You are also prejudging the situation by using a phrase that used to be free transit. Now it is unimpeded passage, but it means just about the same thing, and you are also prejudging the situation because you say you shall not touch that ship because it belongs to somebody else's flag. Is there not a way to guarantee in the first article, when you get to the international straits section of the treaty, to say all ships shall have the right of passage everywhere and then go on to say that in certain situations you can control it to some extent.

I think that then you can negotiate on the extent of the control that you are prepared to accept, but if you say there shall be no control, I think that Joe Warioba could never accept that there should be no control on anything, be it merchantmen or naval ships. But we have to look for something else apart from these too-easy phrases that mean either everything or nothing, depending on who the interlocutor is.

Thank you, sir.

Mr. Clingan: Thank you, Paul.

I think you can see what everybody faced at Caracas. You can see what goes on with a group of three; you can imagine what goes on with a group of 77.

I am going to completely defy the instructions of my chairman and take one more question before we break.

Mr. Ciobanu: Thank you, Mr. Chairman.

My name is Dan Ciobanu, I am a citizen of Romania, and currently affiliated with The Fletcher School of Law and Diplomacy and the Woods Hole Oceanographic Institution.

I have two questions. The first refers to "consensus," and the second to the "common heritage of mankind."

The first question is this: Is there any difference between consensus as it is understood in the practice of the United Nations and consensus provided for in the Rules of Procedure of the Law of the Sea Conference, and if there are any differences, what specifically are they?

The second question refers to the term "common heritage of mankind." In the opinion of Professor Moore, is this term: (1) a figure of speech; (2) a hypothesis of work?; (3) a principle of comity; or (4) a legal principle? If it is a legal principle, what is its specific source in international law? and, secondly, is it a principle of *jus cogens*? Thank you.

Mr. Moore: I think I have the questions, but I will try to briefly restate each one and then try to respond.

The first is the question of what difference, if any, there is between the meaning of "consensus" in the United Nations practice in general and the meaning it has received in the Rules of Procedure of the Law of the Sea Conference.

I think initially I would like to change that question to: What is the difference between "consensus" in normal United Nations practice, and "consensus" as generally interpreted by the United Nations Sea-Bed Committee up until the Law of the Sea Conference, and that difference is rather substantial.

In general, in United Nations practice, it did not mean unanimity; it meant a situation in which basically there was a kind of effort at general negotiated solution, and although there might be a few states that disagreed, they grudgingly went along with the actions of the chairman, who perhaps wielded a very rapid gavel, once this vague thing called "consensus" was reached.

In the United Nations Sea-Bed Committee, it in general came to be interpreted as complete unanimity; that any state participating in the Sea-Bed Committee could, in fact, block any action, and for the most part that happened and the procedures were, I feel, slowed down over what they were in normal United Nations practice.

When it came to adopting the Rules of Procedure, I think there was a feeling on the part of all groupings of states that there were twin horns of the dilemma to avoid. One was premature voting that would result in conference breakdown by failing, frankly, to negotiate the kind of package treaty that was necessary for success. The other is the point that Paul Lapointe has mentioned; that we would get such rigid rules of procedure that we were not going to be able to move forward; that minorities could tie the conference in knots and that, frankly, the solution would be prevented instead of enhanced.

Joseph Warioba was also one of the leaders who was very concerned with that threat as well, and I think the Rules of Procedure which embody the gentlemen's agreement and Rule 37 is an effort to walk a middle ground between those twin horns of the dilemma.

Frankly, I despair of any procedure as a way to resolve the issues in the absence of a genuine negotiation as the first order of business, and once you have that negotiation and there is understanding on the key outlines, then I think all of the other points will follow and we will not be as rigidly concerned with procedure as perhaps all groupings are.

As to the common heritage of mankind, and whether it is a legal principle, and if it is, what the source of the legal principle is, I will not get into the debate among international lawyers concerning the effect of General Assembly resolutions. Ambassador Castaneda has written one of the best books on the point that I am aware of.

But I think as far as our position is concerned, certainly we feel that it is a very important principle. It is a principle that generally will only be implemented when we are able to negotiate the details of the regime for the international deep seabed area. I don't think it means very much in the absence of that agreement, and certainly it is our position that until such time as there is agreement in a comprehensive law of the sea treaty on that point, the question of the potential to mine the resources of the deep seabed continues a permitted high seas freedom under international law.

Part II

Dynamics of Conference Diplomacy

Chairman
Edward Miles
Institute for Marine Studies
University of Washington

Mr. Miles: We are working against rather difficult time constraints.

The idea behind this panel came as a result of some conversations I had with Ambassador Alan Beesley in Geneva in 1973, in which he suggested that there were some rather unique characteristics of lawmaking conferences in the present international system, beginning with Stockholm, and that while the Law of the Sea Conference was clearly a lawmaking one, some people might not have thought so about Stockholm and might not think so about the population and food conferences. Some more thought should therefore be given to the links between these conferences, the ways in which the bargaining was carried on, and whether changes should be made in the way delegations approached these questions.

These are important issues, and my analysis of what went on in Caracas will emphasize the negotiating process aspects; I have asked my colleagues, Professor David Kay, to talk about the intergovernmental dimensions of international conferences generally, and Professor Joseph Nye, to talk about the transnational and transgovernmental dimensions of those conferences. He will explain the meaning of those terms to you.

I listened this morning to the panelists, especially to Mr. Moore, and I must confess that hearing the U.S. had really no problem, or few problems, raised questions in my mind as to whether Mr. Moore and I had, in fact, attended the same conference. I have a very different view of what went on at Caracas and what the implications of those happenings might be, and I have stated this view at some length.

Chapter One

An Interpretation of the
Caracas Proceedings

Edward Miles
Institute for Marine Studies
University of Washington

   The purpose of this paper is to provide a description and interpretation of what happened during the most recent round of negotiations at the Third United Nations Conference on the Law of the Sea held during the summer of 1974 in Caracas. The perspective from which the interpretation is derived is that of an outside observer who was present at meetings of the plenary, Committees I, II, and III, and their working groups throughout the Caracas negotiations. These observations were continually supplemented with information gained in repeated interviews with fifty-four delegates from twenty-nine delegations. At the same time, it should be noted that a great many private, bilateral, and multilateral negotiations were carried on at Caracas to which I had no access and therefore this dimension, which may ultimately have been the most significant, will be largely missing from the paper.
   The paper will begin with a structural explanation of the negotiating difficulties experienced at Caracas and continue with an analysis of the fight over the Draft Rules of Procedure (in both New York and Caracas) and the substantive work done by Committees I, II, and III.

A STRUCTURAL EXPLANATION FOR
NEGOTIATING DIFFICULTIES

The work of the Caracas session can be divided into four phases. The first phase of about one week was taken up with settling the conflict over the Draft Rules of Procedure. The second phase, spanning the next four weeks of a ten-week meeting, was consumed by general debate in both the plenary (two and a half

   Support for this work was provided by the Carnegie Endowment for International Peace and the Institute for Marine Studies, University of Washington. The author wishes to record his gratitude for this support, though the sponsors should in no way be held responsible for the views expressed herein.

weeks) and the main committees (one and a half weeks). The third phase, lasting about two and a half weeks, was one of almost no movement on the major issues in the committees, giving rise to widespread disillusionment openly expressed in the corridors and committee rooms by delegates from all regional groups. The fourth phase emerged in the last one and a half weeks of the conference, when a sense of movement developed in the private negotiations concerning the resource aspects of the economic zone and in the informal working group of Committee II.

During the author's investigations at the final session of the Seabed Committee in Geneva in the summer of 1973, interviews with forty of the ninety-one delegations comprising that committee disclosed a significant split in the perceptions of that group's task. Many claimed that for a committee as large as the Seabed Committee to be asked to prepare for a plenipotentiary conference signaled the start of actual negotiations and that in effect the conference had begun in 1971. On the other hand, many delegates complained to the author that, for their governments, the task given the Seabed Committee did not signal the start of actual negotiations and therefore they had not been given the authority to commit their governments to anything; consequently, their roles were reduced to an unending reiteration of national positions. This discrepancy combined with the number and complexity of the issues to be dealt with by such a large group of countries, seemed to me to be the major factors in explaining the incompleteness of the preparatory work done for the conference, yet, inferentially, it stimulated expectations that significant progress *could* be made at Caracas though a treaty certainly would not be completed there in 1974.

But these expectations turned out to be ill-founded. Many public and informal meetings of the main committees of the Caracas session seemed to be merely a continuation of the unproductive side of the Seabed Committee meetings, an almost unending repetition of national positions in many cases identical with statements made during the first preparatory session in 1971. Why was this so? I would suggest that the extremely slow pace of the conference is the result of a concatenation of at least eight separate factors yielding a lesson of great importance to the international community, to wit: The General Assembly should *never again* convene a conference of the size and complexity of the Third Conference on the Law of the Sea. As a decision mechanism it is absurd and in its size and complexity imposes demands on delegates which in their totality are quite beyond the competence of human beings to manage.

The eight factors referred to are:

1. The size of the conference; as of August 24, 1974, there were 137 participating countries out of 148 invitees

2. The number of issues to be negotiated, covering about 100 separate items

3. The complexity of the issues to be negotiated

4. The structure of the Group of 77 (actually consisting of 110 po-

tential members of whom 103 participated) and its preference for negotiating the entire package of issues simultaneously

5. The failure of Subcommittee II of the Seabed Committee to produce even a few alternative texts on each item within its terms of reference to serve as a basis for negotiation

6. The fact that no deadline for decision was imposed upon the Conference

7. The Rules of Procedure

8. The impact of ideological conflict and system incompatibilities specifically within Committee I

Let me explain these more fully.

Size and Complexity

Factors 1–3, i.e., the size of the conference, the number of issues to be negotiated, and the complexity of those issues yield an unmanageable decision matrix.[1] The response to this burden appeared to be twofold: (a) a marked proclivity to engage in procedural debates almost ad infinitum (Committee III was the worst offender here); and (b) a search for means of simplifying the decision matrix resulting in the insulation of Committees I and II from each other in the negotiation process. This tended to rigidify the bargaining more than was necessary, since it closed off the opportunity for trade-offs on items considered by both committees.

The Structure of the Group of 77 Coalition and Its Negotiating Preferences

Obviously, the difficulties of managing a coalition of 103 countries are enormous. There is considerable diversity of interest among them on many of the substantive issues being negotiated, given their different capabilities, and geographical and biogeophysical endowments. At the same time, the coalition is based on the assumed common interest of all "have-not" states as opposed to all "haves." There is consequently a continuing tension in the group between the ideological dictates of maintaining group unity as the overriding goal and the ways in which representatives perceive their country's interests on the substantive issues under negotiation.

A vivid illustration of this tension was provided in the debates on the economic zone within Committee II on August 6, 1974, in the positions adopted by the Jamaican representative on the one hand and the Algerian representative on the other. In an impressively elegant formulation, the Jamaican representative referred to the concepts of the exclusive economic zone and the patrimonial sea:

> . . . [We] cannot ignore the incontestable fact, that, if these con-

cepts can be a force for the economic good of some countries, then they can also be a force for the economic doom of other countries. The simple fact that we have to face here, Sir, is that nature has not endowed all countries with the same physical, geographical features. With regard to the concept of the Exclusive Economic Zone not all countries have a sufficiently wide expanse of waters fronting their coast, and a sufficient wealth of resources in these waters to warrant the value of a 200 mile jurisdiction. Indeed, some countries, the landlocked, have no coast lines.

The great difficulty facing a Conference on the Law of the Sea is that the problems involved are not necessarily susceptible to solution, as with Conferences dealing with other aspects of international affairs, on strictly political-ideological lines. Here the overwhelming imperatives which call for obedience are the dictates of nature, in the form of the physical attributes of a country, and not the dictates of political ideologies. A country which hopes to get its fair share of the cake from this Conference must first seek to discover its national interest in the light of its geographical endowments by nature, and then, if the dictates of nature permit, align its policy with its political-ideological views. It is this, as it were, defiance of a country's ideological views by nature which makes the problem of the Law of the Sea so intractable.[2]

In contrast, later the same morning, and in an equally enlightening presentation, the Algerian representative argued the opposite point of view. Recognizing, he said, that:

Algeria had no true interests of its own to defend through that concept [the Exclusive Economic Zone], since it bordered on a semi-enclosed sea which lacked a continental shelf and was practically devoid of resources. Nevertheless, it understood the struggle of the peoples of most of the developing countries for the establishment and strengthening of the idea of the exclusive economic zone, and it therefore supported the zone without hesitation. By taking that position it felt that it would contribute to strengthening the solidarity of African countries and of third world countries in general, a solidarity which was not an abstract concept but was based on the desire to make the new rules of international law serve the purposes of development.[3]

This diversity of capabilities, natural endowments, and interests accentuates the difficulty of bargaining within the group on positions to be adopted and consequently much time is consumed. The outstanding success of the group in agreeing on single positions has been in Committee I on the international seabed area with respect to the issues of who may exploit the area and the conditions of exploitation. Perhaps it is no accident that this has occurred, because on these two issues there is a very clear bifurcation of interests between those very few countries possessing the capabilities to exploit the deep seabed and members of the Group of 77. In addition, the group has consistently negotiated on general principles only and has refused to be drawn into negotiations on details, as several members of the Western Group (the U.S. and EEC members in particular) have tried to do.

On the other hand, these conditions do not obtain in Committee II concerning the complex of jurisdictional issues falling under its terms of reference. Consequently the Group of 77 has so far found it impossible, after several years of trying, to arrive at a single position here. The situation in Committee III on the issues of preservation of the marine environment and scientific research and transfer of technology lies somewhere between Committees I and II. Capabilities are concentrated, but not nearly to the same degree as in Committee I. Many members of the group possess potentially quite significant capabilities in different areas of marine scientific research and are assiduously developing these; while many others possess no capability whatever and have little hope of deriving any benefit from extensions of coastal state jurisdiction on this activity. At the end of the session, a considerable degree of restiveness emerged among the landlocked members of the African coalition, who complained that their interests were not taken into account by the Group of 77 proposals, and who cosponsored some rather lenient draft articles proposed by several members of the Western European and Others Group. This led to open conflict among the Africans and India and Yugoslavia, involving several acrimonious exchanges. A similar incident also occurred at the end of Committee II's work.

The Group of 77 has also consistently refused to carve up the package of issues before the Law of the Sea Conference and to negotiate *seriatim*. The Latin Americans have been most adamant on this. They prefer a simultaneous negotiation on all items agreeing finally to none until all issues have been dealt with. In this way, presumably, they wish to minimize their potential losses. But such a stance entails great delays because on every issue the group must at least try to arrive at a common position and this is most difficult when details must be considered.

In addition, this position also tends to proliferate procedural squabbles over the method of work in various committees and the creation of subsidiary organs. Part of the problem here comes from the demands placed on small delegations by a multiplication of working groups in committees. But at least for some members of the Group of 77 there was a certain anxiety that if a lot of separate working groups were created, different parts of the package might be negotiated out of phase with the others because the control problems would be greater. Consequently, they tended to opt for working groups of the whole of each committee rather than smaller, more specialized groups.

The Effect of Inadequate Preparation

The General Assembly reacted to Ambassador Pardo's speech in 1967 organizationally, by creating first an Ad Hoc Committee on the Peaceful Uses of the Seabed and Ocean Floor beyond National Jurisdiction and later making it permanent. In 1971, this greatly expanded committee (to 91 from 35 in 1968) became the preparatory committee for the Law of Sea Conference. This sequence of events maximized the educational effect of the committee on member countries, but in so doing it greatly increased the salience of the ocean issue in the UN and effectively preempted the General Assembly asking the International Law Commission, or any other group of experts, to prepare a set of draft articles which would serve as a basis for negotiations.

The result was predictable. A committee of ninety-one countries cannot "prepare" for an international lawmaking conference when the issues are as multifarious, as complex, and as contenious as those before Committee II. It was possible for Subcommittee I of the Seabed Committee to present the conference with the major alternatives on most issues concerning the international seabed area and authority. But this was not the case in Subcommittee II which generated undigested proposals as if from an assembly line and finally presented the General Assembly with a largely unusable report. Instead of being in a position to begin negotiations, therefore, Committee II had to spend what was left of the summer in Caracas after general debate completing the preparatory work which should have been done within the context of the Seabed Committee. This achievement of Committee II, very firmly and ably guided by Ambassador Andres Aguilar of Venezuela, is in effect the major achievement of the conference at the Caracas session. There now exist a restricted number of alternative texts on every item under the terms of reference of Committee II.

Committee III is an anomaly, or more bluntly an anachronism. There are no substantive reasons for its existence. It is a holdover from the Seabed Committee, created as a mechanism for providing sufficient posts (chairman, vice-chairmen, rapporteur) to meet the demands of the regional groups. There would have been a justification for its existence if in fact the representatives to it were scientific/technical experts. Instead, the people who did the negotiating were largely lawyers who, it was made abundantly clear from the discussions, knew almost nothing about marine scientific research and how it was conducted. Most of the countries which did have experts on their delegations kept them under tight rein; this was as true of developed as of developing countries.

During the last preparatory session in Geneva in 1973, Subcommittee III of the Seabed Committee had produced a number of exceedingly general draft articles on preservation of the marine environment and a few alternative drafts on the conduct of scientific research. Nothing intelligent was said by *anyone*, from any country, developed or developing, on the subject of technology transfer, except by Ambassador Pardo who made virtually this same point to the subcommittee near the end of the summer.

During the Caracas season, Committee III showed a marked preference from the very beginning for wasting a great deal of time in procedural squabbles. This was true throughout the summer. The frequency with which procedural issues were raised by India, Yugoslavia, and Kenya prompted several representatives from the Western European and Others Group to speculate that this was a deliberate tactic to buy time for the Group of 77 to put forward its own position. I found no evidence to substantiate this for the early part of the summer but it may well have been true in the last two weeks of the session when the group was attempting to arrive at a common position but was having a great deal of trouble doing so. Several members of this coalition at this time complained to me that the group meetings were as unproductive as the committee.

By the end of the summer, the exceedingly general articles on the preservation of the marine environment had survived the scrutiny of a special drafting group created for that purpose. The scientific research working group had begun by reopening for discussion everything that had been done in Geneva, but at the end the group presented to the committee a set of alternative formulations to serve as the basis for negotiations. The picture on technology transfer is not much better than it was in Geneva. There were only two very general proposals on the table and one was later withdrawn. It is difficult to see how they can be of much help. Again, nothing enlightening was said by anyone on this subject but at least a useful introductory paper was circulated by the Secretariat.

There is an additional problem which especially cuts across the work of Committees II and III. This was pointed out to me by one astute West European delegate who observed that at these meetings procedures must be relearned on every new occasion because these mechanisms did not possess institutional memories. Moreover, the conference largely took over the procedures of the UN itself, which are more appropriate to forum activities than to negotiating a multilateral convention.

The Effect of No Deadline for Decision

The General Assembly Resolution convening the Law of the Sea Conference did not impose a deadline for final decision. In effect, it left the number of future sessions open. This appeared to reinforce the reluctance to compromise on positions that are strongly held because country representatives generally do not wish to yield until the very last moment. When that would be was never clearly defined, but in Caracas pressures emerged on various sides for making 1975 the cutoff date. For instance, the U.S. Congress appeared to be bent on pushing unilateral action as fast as it could and two U.S. senators made that point belligerently clear to the local press in Caracas and thereby to the conference. The same newspaper also carried reports about similar moves in Norway. Several representatives from developing countries were also privately concerned that their own governments were becoming restive about all the time and required expense when the same fruits could be had by taking unilateral action. At the time of writing, therefore (October 1974), it seems doubtful that the conference could effectively be carried over beyond 1975 without being pre-empted by widespread unilateral actions.

The Rules of Procedure

The fight which occurred in New York, in December 1973, and in Caracas over the draft rules was extremely important because it imposed on the conference a most unwieldy method of making decisions. The bargaining on this issue will be described in some detail in the next section of this paper. Suffice it to be said here that the rules adopted contributed to delays by enshrining the consensus procedure at the heart of the conference and by making voting so difficult and potentially time-consuming that even without contention it would have been difficult to complete the agenda in ten weeks.

The Effect of Ideological Conflict and System Incompatibility in Committee I

This problem will be dealt with more fully when we consider the substantive work of Committee I. It is included here because the emergence of a full-blown ideological confrontation between the U.S. and the Group of 77 on the powers and functions of the International Seabed Authority and the conditions of exploitation is new and is likely to affect all future negotiations on this issue, perhaps thereby increasing rigidity on both sides.

To be sure, this confrontation also includes the EEC countries (minus Ireland) and Japan, but not yet to the same degree as experienced by the U.S.. The reasons for this are idiosyncratic and relate to negotiating style, i.e., a relatively low-keyed approach by France (speaking for the EEC) and Japan as contrasted with a rather flamboyant approach by the U.S. representative, which many members of the Group of 77 found objectionable; in fact, the words used privately were "patronizing," "condescending," and "insulting."

For example, the U.S. representative spoke for two hours on the afternoon of August 8, followed by one hour on the morning of August 9, de-livering what could be fairly characterized as a rather "hardline" speech in defense of the free-enterprise system, extolling its virtues, declaring what issues the U.S. considered nonnegotiable, specifying what kind of convention the U.S. would not sign, and deftly hinting at nonratification and the possibility of un-regulated exploitation of deep seabed mineral resources by U.S. companies, thereby depriving the authority of revenue. This generated a harsh response from the representative of Trinidad-Tobago and an equally strong response from the leader of the Norwegian delegation who thought the U.S. draft articles on rules and regulations related to exploitation absurd and indicative of a late nineteenth-century, early twentieth-century approach to the writing of contracts.

The significance of these exchanges on the conditions of exploita-tion, and earlier on Article 9 of the Draft Treaty concerning the question of who may exploit the area, lies in the fact that the more the emphasis was put on details in Committee I the further the groups moved apart from each other and the more ideology rather than economics was the major variable. Indeed, it seems to me that the groups are now further apart than they were at Geneva; that the U.S. has moved considerably "out on a limb" and that it may be extremely difficult, as a result of the increasingly ideological nature of the dispute and the type of commitments this implies, for both domestic and external constituencies, for it to move back to the point where there are sufficiently significant overlapping interests between the opposing sides to allow resolution.

It is conceivable that other factors that emerged in the private negotiations could be added to this list to explain the disappointing performance of the Caracas session, but I do not see how any international conference could have been more productive given the confluent operation of the eight factors described above.

THE FIGHT OVER THE RULES OF PROCEDURE
NEW YORK, DECEMBER 1973, AND
CARACAS, JUNE 1974

It is not my intention to provide here a detailed textual analysis of the Rules of Procedure adopted by the conference because the scope of such an undertaking is considerable. In any case, this kind of analysis is already being done by others. I will be concerned mainly with the bargaining which took place around Rules 37, 39, and 40, and the major issues which were raised therein. The general significance of this confrontation is explained by the fact that the players without significant marine-related capabilities have a potentially overwhelming coalition, consequently the players with significant marine capabilities precipitated a fight over the method of decision-making to be employed by the conference. In this, they were later joined by at least some members of the Disadvantaged Group.

These events were "convention-breaking" because they constituted a repudiation of the normal General Assembly Rules of Procedure by most of the permanent members of the Security Council. As such, the Rules of the Third UN Conference on the Law of the Sea have become precedents for any future international conference in which similar incompatibilities obtain between substantive capabilities and coalition size.

The New York Round
The first session of the conference was given the task of dealing with all the organizational details of elections, rules of procedure, and the like and it was allotted two weeks (December 3-15, 1973) in which to complete this work. The conference, however, was unexpectedly faced with a major fight in the Western European and Others Group (between the U.S., U.K., and France) and to some extent in the Asian Group over the internal distribution of posts allocated to these groups. This fight consumed the period from December 3-11 and

left only four days to deal with the rules question. The stipulated closure of this session coincided with the end of the General Assembly session and meant that the conference could not be extended since plane reservations were unavailable. This raised two important issues which would not have been raised otherwise.

The major issues surrounding, at that time, Rules 37 (Requirements for Voting) and 39 (Required Majority) were as follows:

1. Which rules were to apply in the interim? This involved a choice between the General Assembly rules and the as yet unspecified rules implied by the "gentlemén's agreement"[4] adopted at the end of the last session of the Seabed Committee and later adopted by the conference itself. The latter further implied four questions: (a) How does "consensus" differ from unanimity? (b) How much of a "cooling-off" period is required before a determination could be made that ". . . all efforts at consensus have been exhausted"? (c) Who is to make such a decision? And (d) by what majorities?
2. How should majorities be constituted? The choice here was again as outlined above.
3. Who is to decide when to vote?
    a) The General Committee?
    b) The main committees and the plenary?
    c) The president of the conference?

As indicated previously, the fact that the conference had insufficient time to complete its work in New York raised two additional issues.

4. Should the rules issue be decided by a vote before Caracas or should it carry over?
5. If the latter, should a working group be created to deal with the issue in the interim?

Though on the surface the fight over representation in the Western European and Others Group was unrelated to the fight on the draft rules that followed, they were linked on at least two points concerning the roles of the General and Drafting Committees. The representation problem arose because the U.S., U.K., and France all claimed dual representation on the General and Drafting Committees thereby drastically limiting the seats available to others in this extremely heterogeneous grouping. (Unlike the other regional groups, the Western European and Others Group is not a negotiating body but a residual category). The same problem conceivably could have arisen in the Eastern European Group over the dual representation of the Soviet Union, but it did not.

In an assumption that the implications of this issue were sufficiently important to determine whether it would continue to participate in the Law of the Sea Conference, the U.S. expended virtually all its political capital in order to prevail against the principle of "one country, one seat" pushed by a large number of members of the Group of 77. A U.S. victory here simply required a defeat for Britain and France.

The two problems are linked because, having expended its capital on the prior issue, the U.S. could not have made credible similar threats of nonparticipation vis-à-vis the roles to be played by the General and Drafting Committees, which were severely restricted by the Group of 77. The General Committee was denied any voice in determining when a vote would be taken and the Drafting Committee, contrary to the stated views of its chairman before he was elected, was denied any authority to negotiate language or to take any independent initiative in resolving conflict over proposals.

The problem that arose over which rules would be applicable for the interim period resulted from one of the very few errors made by the president of the conference on this issue. He had neglected to formalize agreement concerning his proposal, made to the conference on December 7, to use General Assembly rules where applicable. He had the acquiescence of the conference at that time but, in reaction to a Soviet move,[5] it had evaporated by December 11. Indeed Soviet behavior on this item was consistently heavy-handed and was responsible for generating even more controversy than was necessary.

Consensus quickly evaporated when the Soviets moved to tie the current debate to the "gentlemen's agreement" rather than the Assembly rules prior to the adoption of the conference's own rules. The president quickly rejected this interpretation warning that such moves were likely to paralyze the conference. But it was too late, a confrontation developed which did paralyze the conference.

The next day, the Soviets continued to play in the same vein. There was a great danger, they said, of the imposition of majority views on the conference and it was impossible to solve international problems in this way. They therefore proposed a change in Rule 39 to make consensus the method of decision-making. Voting would be allowed only after all attempts at formulating consensus had failed and it would be the responsibility of the General Committee to decide when to vote. Moreover, when a vote was held, majorities should be as close as possible to consensus. Finally, the Soviet delegation warned that its attitude to subsequent stages of the work of the conference would be determined by the attitude of other delegations to these proposals. Not surprisingly, the Group of 77 were adamant in their opposition but curiously, the final result at Caracas was to conform quite closely to Soviet (and U.S.) preferences except for the role of the General Committee.

In reply, Mexico argued that no veto should be given to any group to paralyze the will of the majority and a strong critique was detailed of the Soviet use of the unanimity principle in international conferences. As a result Mexico formally proposed that a vote that arose in any of the three committees should be decided there and not in either the General Committee or the plenary. This was delicately supported by Romania and firmly supported by Yugoslavia, Norway, and Tanzania. Indeed, the Tanzanian delegate, incensed by the Soviet moves and, in particular, by its proposal on the role of the General Committee, later introduced a series of amendments to the draft rules on behalf of the Group of 77 (A/CONF.62/4) and cosponsored by Chile, Colombia, and Madagascar. These amendments specified that the Drafting Committee would not have any authority to initiate texts and that the General Committee would not have the right to decide when a vote should be taken.

The U.S. introduced its proposals on December 13. The required majority for agreement on substantive questions, in its view, should be two-thirds of all states participating in the conference rather than two-thirds of those present and voting. The definition of simple majorities should be in the same view. But the U.S. precipitated another fight by stating that the adoption of the rules of procedure by simple majority was not acceptable since some of the issues involved were of great importance for decision-making by the conference. Japan supported this move while the Group of 77, in particular Tanzania and Venezuela, was pushing strongly for an immediate vote on the basis of simple majorities. Although the president recognized that the invariable international practice had been to adopt the rules of procedure by a simple majority, he was convinced that a vote on the rules would signal disaster for the conference itself, since it would jeopardize Soviet participation and put into question acceptance by the U.S., U.K., France, and Japan of any outcome. He therefore used all means at his disposal to arrive at a compromise in the time remaining (two days).

During the last day, when it became clear that a compromise on the major issues would not be forthcoming, the focus of informal consultations shifted to deciding how the issue should be handled between December 1974 and the Caracas meeting. This implied a retreat by the Group of 77 on its insistence that a vote be held before the end of the first session. On the other hand, the western countries (and presumably the Soviet Union) had proposed the creation of a special working group but the Group of 77 remained adamantly opposed.

The final compromise at this time consisted of an agreement to empower the president to conduct informal consultations with sponsors of all preceding proposals, and a deadline of January 31, 1974, was imposed on all new proposals. While the Group of 77 agreed to let the issue carry over to Caracas, the debate would be terminated by June 27, 1974, and a vote taken at that time if consensus still eluded the conference. On the other hand, Argentina proposed that the General Assembly Rules govern the adoption of the conference rules (i.e., simple majority present and voting) and this was adopted. In this way, the U.S. proposal on this item was defeated.

The Caracas Round

As indicated previously, continued negotiations on the draft rules occupied the conference for the first week of the session. The president began by reporting on the inconclusive consultations which had been held in New York (February 25-March 1) and in Caracas (June 10-12).[6] The deadlock was still holding. Again, he stressed the important moral obligation which the "gentlemen's agreement" embodied and proposed that it be incorporated into the Conference by acclamation. However Chile and Canada did not wish to agree to this until the negotiations had been successfully concluded on defining the "cooling-off" period and the method of voting. Other members of the Group of 77 were opposed to inclusion of the agreement by acclamation and wished to imply the existence of reservation by using the word "consensus."

The plenary was also informed that a certain amount of progress had been made in New York on the definition of the "cooling-off" period, on how to determine when all efforts at consensus had been exhausted, on who was to decide when a vote should be taken, and on what majorities would be required in the plenary and main committees for the taking or deferral of votes. A current suggestion was that, in the main committees, votes would be taken on the basis of a simple majority of those present and voting while, in the plenary, the majority required would be two-thirds. But the president asked all delegations to remember that in the plenary, if less than two-thirds voted to hold a vote, there would be no point in doing so since a two-thirds majority would be required.

Since the deadlock was not yet broken, the president switched to informal consultations among authors of all proposals, chairmen of regional groups, and other interested parties. Not surprisingly, virtually the entire membership of the conference showed up for these negotiations which extended over the weekend and into the next week. It was apparent in these consultations that there was a general willingness to accept the compromise formulation detailed by the president in Conference Room Paper No. 3/Rev. 1 which left a blank space for the required majorities but specified the following provisions:

1. That when a substantive matter came up for a vote for the first time "the President may, and shall if requested by at least 15 representatives" defer such a vote for up to 10 calendar days, but only once.
2. That, at any time, the conference could decide to defer a vote for a specified period if such a proposal were made either by the president or any representative and upheld by a majority of those present and voting.
3. That during the period of deferment, the president, ". . . with the assistance as appropriate of the General Committee," would attempt to facilitate consensus and report to the conference at the end of the period.
4. That if, at the end of this period, no agreement has been achieved, and if there can be no further delay as provided for in paragraph (2) above, a determination that all efforts at reaching consensus have been exhausted shall be made by a majority.
5. That "if the conference does not determine that all such efforts have been

exhausted, the President may propose or any representative may move . . .
after the end of a period of no less than five calendar days . . . that such a
determination be made."[7]

6. That no vote should be taken on any substantive issue less than two working
days after the conference has decided to proceed to a vote.

    Obviously, such a cumbersome procedure would make voting on
substantive matters very difficult, if not impossible, in an eight-or ten-week session and several members of the Group of 77 pointed this out. Others, like Chile
and Cameroon, objected to the length of time of the "cooling-off" period preferring two days and five days respectively.

    With respect to required majorities, there were two alternatives be-
fore the conference: (1) majorities reckoned on the basis of those present and
voting; or (2) majorities reckoned on the basis of the total number of participants in the conference (the U.S. view).

    In a search for a possible compromise, Ecuador proposed that in
committees the majority be a majority of those present and voting provided that
a quorum would be defined as two-thirds of the participants in the conference.
In the plenary, however, the majority would be two-thirds of those present and
voting provided a quorum was defined as two-thirds of the participants. Additionally, two-thirds of those present and voting would have to amount to at least
a majority of conference participants. Neither India nor Australia liked this definition of a quorum, suggesting instead a majority of conference participants, and
Australia in fact made a formal proposal to this effect wherein majorities on substantive issues would be based on two-thirds of those present and voting provided
that this included at least a simple majority of conference participants.[8] This
would provide majorities large enough to ensure a viable treaty.

    Canada, citing the need to avoid a decision-making rush at the end
of the conference as well as the need to provide for sufficiently large majorities,
supported Australia. The Canadian delegation preferred the traditional majority
on substantive issues, but it realized the theoretical need to guard against small
majorities. But it was exaggerated to require two-thirds of conference participants in the plenary, since that would require 100 positive votes when only 75
would be necessary for a quorum. This was insupportable, but the Australian
compromise was acceptable to Canada since it required a minimum of 75 positive votes. A decent compromise for the conference as a whole, therefore, lay
within the range of 75–100 minimum positive votes.

    At this point a large number of states agreed with Canada, among
them Colombia, Iceland, Nigeria, and Cameroon. The Western Group, plus
the U.S.S.R. and Japan, had clearly made major gains in rendering the traditional rules of procedure employed by the United Nations inoperative but they
were losing on the issue of required majorities. In an attempt to salvage something on this issue also, Bulgaria admitted that a majority based upon two-thirds

of the conference participants was a desirable solution but there were other possibilities. The Bulgarian delegate then offered an amendment to the Canadian formulation stipulating that when a final text of the draft convention was to be adopted, a two-thirds majority of conference participants be required and that this would apply in committee as well as in plenary.

Kenya immediately objected to this proposal claiming that all it did was to postpone the veto until the final plenary. The U.S. in response wanted the president to confirm that the final text of the conference would be submitted to the plenary for a separate vote after votes had been taken on its individual provisions. The president confirmed this understanding. Hungary pressed the point that the Australian/Canadian formulation would be acceptable only if a majority of two-thirds of conference participants was required for the adoption of the final text, while Japan preferred requiring such a majority both for substantive matters and for votes to determine whether all efforts to arrive at consensus had been exhausted. As the daily session for June 24 came to a close, deadlock had apparently crystallized around the single issue of required majorities. This, at any rate, was progress.

When the informal consultations were reconvened on June 25, the president outlined a compromise formula on required majorities as follows:

1. For committees, the required majority would be a majority of those present and voting and a quorum would consist of a majority of conference participants (i.e., 76).
2. In the plenary, decisions would be taken on the basis of a majority of those present and voting, provided that this comprised a majority of conference participants. However, a quorum would be two-thirds of conference participants (i.e., 100).

These two provisions had clearly emerged out of the discussions of the previous evening, in particular the Australian/Canadian formulations. With respect to the Bulgarian proposal, on the other hand, there was as yet no solution, so the conference was faced with a choice between procedure (2) to govern the adoption of the final convention or the Bulgarian alternative.

At this point the delegate from Singapore, speaking on behalf of the Disadvantaged Group, introduced a proposal which added to the difficulties of finding a solution. Arguing that the Disadvantaged Group had little chance of securing its objectives unless required majorities were broadly defined, he suggested that in the main committees a quorum should be two-thirds of conference participants (as compared with a majority in the president's formulation) and the required majority should be a majority of those present and voting. For the plenary the same quorum would be required, but the majority would be " . . . two-thirds of those voting 'yes,' 'no' or 'abstention,' including at least a majority of all participants."[9] In addition, he endorsed the Bulgarian proposal for the adoption of the final convention. The major stumbling block here, of course, was the attempt to include abstentions in calculating majorities.

A large number of countries, primarily from the Group of 77, strongly supported the president's formulation but excluding the Bulgarian compromise. These included Norway, Colombia, Thailand, Chile, Argentina, Brazil, Kenya, Mexico, and Iceland. On the other side, the Federal Republic of Germany, Austria, Czechoslovakia, Afghanistan, and France spoke in favor of the proposal made by Singapore. Bulgaria indicated it would accept the president's formulation if its alternative was adopted.

At the end of the evening, the president asked the Singapore delegation to consider seriously whether they wished to press their proposal redefining the quorum and giving special meaning to the words "present and voting." In the face of the previous positions stated by so many members of the Group of 77 and the obvious pressure exerted by the president, the Singapore delegation agreed to yield on the meaning to be given to "present and voting" but "not yet" on the quorum. The meeting was adjourned and two more days were left before a vote would have to be taken. All delegates were aware of this and the president kept insisting that this would be disastrous for the conference.

In the afternoon session of June 25, the confrontation had narrowed to the problem posed by the Bulgarian proposal and the president tried yet another compromise formulation which read as follows:

> Upon completion of its work, the Conference shall adopt the Convention of the Law of the Sea as a whole through a single vote by a majority to be determined, if necessary, in accordance with paragraph 1 of Rule 39.[10]

The Senegal delegate, however, who was chairman of the African Group, confessed to some confusion at this point. What majority, he asked? This had not been decided, the president replied. The representative of Senegal said that the African Group had been given to understand that the majority would be less than two-thirds, but the president declared that this would be left open. The representative of Cameroon, joining Senegal, asked what was the purpose of this new rule? The effect was merely to postpone a decision, this was unnecessary and could lead to grave complications in the end. It was necessary to decide immediately.

Since the hour was late, the question was deferred until June 26, at which time the president declared himself in a quandary since the conference was sharply divided over two remaining problems: (a) the requisite majority for the adoption of the final convention; and (b) whether this should be determined immediately or left for later. There appeared to be no hope of resolving this now, therefore the president proposed an addition spelling out available options as defined by Rule 64.[11] This specified that decisions of the conference on all matters of substance, including adoption of the final convention, would be by two-thirds of those present and voting provided this amounted to at least a majority of conference participants. If this was not acceptable, he said, the conference really had a problem. It took one more evening of private consultations with regional group representatives and others to arrive at a compromise. The president's last formulation was allowed to stand as Rule 39, paragraph 1, and a new paragraph 2 was inserted which read:

> Rule 37 shall not apply to the adoption of the text of the Convention as a whole. However, the Convention shall not be put to the vote less than four working days after the adoption of its last article.

The Rules of Procedure were finally adopted on June 27, the day on which a vote would have been taken had no agreement been reached. The outstanding player of this part of the conference was unquestionably the president, Ambassador Amerasinghe of Sri Lanka. With great skill and imagination he orchestrated a concerted attempt to get agreement without resorting to a vote, producing effective compromise formulations every time the conference bogged down.

The biggest surprise of this phase of the conference certainly was the degree of success achieved by the U.S., the U.S.S.R., Japan, and the EEC countries in changing the traditional rules of procedure. In New York, the hard line adopted by the Group of 77 amply demonstrated that its members knew that their greatest and only strength lay in the size of their coalition and the stand taken by developed countries called for them to nullify much of this capability. On the other hand, the developed countries had recourse to a threat whose credibility even now is not in question: that they would refuse to sign a convention about which they had serious reservations even if it was approved by a two-thirds majority of states present and voting. This would be a pyrrhic victory for the Group of 77.

But even within that coalition there appeared to be problems arising out of the preferences of the landlocked and shelf-locked members in Asia and Africa. In one sense these "disadvantaged" countries were caught between the developed countries and the Group of 77, but this was not without impact on the latter since some attempt had to be made to accommodate the demands of the "disadvantaged" in order to avoid open revolt. The price may also have been quite high for the conference as a whole, since it saddled the meeting with perhaps the most complex and time-consuming method of making decisions ever employed in such a forum and it reinforces the danger that on particularly contentious issues no side will be able to muster the required majorities.

THE SUBSTANTIVE WORK OF THE
CARACAS SESSION

Committee I

Committee I was the only one which had presented the conference with an almost complete text of a treaty containing the major alternatives on each item, except the "rules and regulations" which would govern exploitation of the seabed beyond national jurisdiction.[12] During the preparatory sessions in Subcommittee I of the Seabed Committee the issues which had generated the greatest heat were: (1) the system of exploitation of the international seabed area (i.e., Art. 9 of the Draft: "Who May Exploit the Area"); (2) the degree of control to be given to the authority over all activities in the area; and (3) the composition, powers, and functions of the assembly versus the council in the International Seabed Authority to be established.[13]

As the committee sought to go beyond its preparatory work, the focus of the debate shifted somewhat. Items (1) and (2) continued to generate a great deal of conflict, but almost no attention was paid in Caracas to item (3). Instead, the committee dealt with two additional issues and these also served to increase the amount of conflict to levels that made it seem doubtful that the committee would be able to present the conference with a treaty. These new issues were: (a) rules and regulations governing exploitation; and (b) the economic implications of seabed exploitation.

This change in focus was signaled in the first week of general debate in Committee I (July 10-17, 1974). The chairman of the committee, Mr. Paul Engo of the United Republic of Cameroon, suggested that the two new and most controversial items could not be discussed fruitfully in general debate and should be left for the informal sessions of the working group to be created. The Latin American Group was obviously unhappy about this and put its reservations on record.[14]

Chile, in particular, wanted to say something about economic implications and was supported in this by Peru, who wished the representative of UNCTAD also to take part in the debate since several relevant documents had been forwarded by UNCTAD to the conference.[15] In addition, the secretary-general of the UN had submitted an excellent though controversial report on the same subject.[16] The effect of these developments forced the committee to deal frontally with the issue for a considerable part of the time between July 17 and August 29. It also gave rise to some rather interesting shifts in strategy.

For instance, the move by Chile to force a debate on economic implications was clearly motivated by the desire to give the authority the competence to impose production and price controls on all seabed mineral exploitation in the international area. Indeed, the position of Chile on this, leading the fight on behalf of all land-based producers, was so extreme that it seemed questionable whether Chile wanted such exploitation to occur at all. These fears were echoed by land-based producers in the African Group to the extent that Zaire became the group's spokesman on the issue.

Furthermore, representatives of UNCTAD were clearly in attendance as part of the Group of 77 coalition and received political insulation from that group as they made very forthright recommendations in support of production and price controls to the great displeasure of the U.S., EEC countries, and Japan. (Given this support, the UNCTAD representatives were rather safe. However, Mr. Maurice Strong, executive director of UNEP, found himself in deep trouble in the plenary when he suggested that certain proposals on the economic zone made such a zone indistinguishable from a territorial sea. For this he was severely attacked by the Latin American Group, who appeared to think that Mr. Strong was guilty of conduct unbecoming a Secretariat official. The lesson is clear!)

The emergence of the economic implications issue and the way in which it was handled by the Latin American Group were read by most observers as a tactical attempt to link this issue with the question of rules and regulations, yet to be considered. Moreover, the role of the UNCTAD reports and representatives in the debates, and to a necessarily lesser extent, the role of the UN report and representative, was to raise the possibility of instituting production and price controls as one step in the road of comprehensive commodity price controls. The rationale for this is a potent argument in the Group of 77 and facilitated the submergence of apparent differences in the interests of land-based producers versus consumers in that group.

The tactic appeared to be to increase the complaints about the effects of inflation on poor primary producing countries and, in particular, that payments made to primary producers were not increasing even though the price to consumers everywhere was rapidly increasing. By implication at first, and later explicitly, this linked the seabed issue with other current economic issues of global import, especially the question of raw materials and food. This argument appeared to facilitate the emergence of Zaire as the spokesman of the African Group and was consistently pushed by Zaire and Algeria in Committee I. Significantly, however, the linking of the seabed issue with other economic issues did not include the price of energy. Presumably this was a touchy subject in the Group of 77 and was best ignored.

The opposing strategy employed by the U.S., the EEC countries, and Japan was, first, an attempt to emphasize the difference in interests between land-based producers of minerals who would be affected by seabed exploitation and the vast majority who, as consumers, would benefit from reductions in price as a result of such exploitation. This tactic appeared, at the Caracas session, to have had only a limited success and primarily with those members of the Group of 77, like Singapore, who are also members of the Disadvantaged Group. The second component of developed country strategy was an attempt to link alleged compromises on Article 9 (Who May Exploit) with a rather hardline stand on the rules and regulations thereby effectively emasculating any compromises supposedly made on Article 9.

For a brief moment during the session at Caracas a new issue was raised in the general debate conducted by Committee I and which threatened to disrupt negotiations. On July 17, 1974, the representatives of Venezuela, Mexico, and Tanzania all sought to extend control by the International Seabed Authority over the water column above the international seabed area via control over scientific research, pollution, and living resources. Rumblings among the developed countries, and particularly from the Soviet delegation, warned privately and publicly of dire consequences for the whole conference if this issue was pushed any further. The issue subsided but one doesn't know whether it will surface again. If it does, it could disrupt the conference. Let us now look in more detail at the work on the three major issues in Committee I at Caracas. These are: Article 9; rules and regulations; and economic implications.

Conflict Over Article 9: Who May Exploit the Area.   The informal Working Group of Committee I began a third reading of the draft articles contained in Volume II of the Seabed Committee Report on July 23 and it immediately focused on Article 9.[17] There were four alternatives in this item providing a range of choice between (and including) two extremes.[18] The outer limits of this range were defined by: (1) the U.S. (and others') position which foresaw a weak authority operating on the basis of a licensing system in which the contracting parties would have a predominant role; and (2) the position preferred by many members of the Group of 77 which called for direct control of scientific research, exploration, and exploitation by the authority via the enterprise and through the medium of service contracts.

The movements of this dance between the two extremes had been ritualized in the Seabed Committee and at first, in Caracas, it appeared as if the same old show would go on. But appearances were deceptive because three important variations were added. These were: (1) an imaginative attempt to bypass continuing deadlock by the Jamaican delegation; (2) the negotiation of a single text on Article 9 by the Group of 77; and (3) an apparent willingness on the part of the U.S. delegation to compromise with the Group of 77 on Article 9.

On July 25, the Jamaican representative created a stir in the working group by making a detailed proposal designed to break the deadlock. It was not necessary, he argued, to continue the debate by putting so much emphasis on the alternative texts before the committee; rather, the way out of this impasse lay in focusing on the interests that states would like to see protected and these were five: (1) maximizing the interests of mankind as a whole in exploiting the seabed; (2) ensuring the widest participation on a nondiscriminatory basis in all articles, e.g., provision of goods and services, capital, and direct labor; (3) assuring to consuming countries on a nondiscriminatory basis an adequate supply of mineral products at reasonable prices; (4) securing rational management of the resource by establishing controls over exploration and exploitation; and (5) providing for the equitable distribution of benefits particularly among developing countries.

In suggesting this formulation to guide future negotiations, the representative of Jamaica pointed out that once these interests were provided for the question of who may exploit the area would cease to be contentious, since whoever engaged in exploiting the resource would do so within a framework of conditions imposed by the authority. He also offered such a framework in the form of draft treaty articles.[19]

The chairman of the working group immediately pushed the Jamaican formulation as a courageous compromise that went to the heart of the negotiations. It was the best opportunity yet to make progress, he said, and he urged the group not to let it slip. It appeared to be particularly useful because it did not prejudice the aims of any other group of countries. But the reaction of the working group to the Jamaican proposal was as interesting as it was revealing. The crucial signal here was that the representative of Madagascar (one of the "whips" of the Group of 77 in Committee I) gave a very cautious response to the Jamaican initiative although the normal assumption was that he would have supported a group-member's proposal.

While this was an interesting proposal, he said, there was also another way in which the work could be advanced and this was in letting each delegation be cognizant of all the interests at work in the committee. Could the committee, he asked, allow different groups to consult among themselves? If all went well, then negotiations could go on. This request was echoed by several other delegations, among them Chile, Kuwait, Brazil, Trinidad-Tobago, and Colombia.

It was immediately clear, therefore, that the Group of 77 did not wish to negotiate at that time and that there was some problem of coordination between the Group of 77 and Jamaica. Confirmation of this came later, outside the committee room, when the author was informed that the Group of 77 was indeed attempting to negotiate its own text and that the Jamaican proposal had not surfaced within the Group of 77 before it had been made to the working group as a whole. The implication was obvious that had the Jamaicans done so the group would have prevailed upon them to withhold their own proposal in favor of the single text to be produced on Article 9.

Inferentially, therefore, the Jamaican delegation was obviously in a difficult position since, at the beginning of the conference, Jamaica had made a play for the authority, when it was established, to be located in Kingston. The firm support of the Group of 77 would be needed if this were to become a reality, thereby placing limits on the ability of the Jamaican delegation to take independent initiatives that ran counter to group preferences. This opportunity to negotiate was not pursued and the working group adjourned.

The Group of 77 introduced its version of Article 9 on July 26 and sought to have the negotiations proceed on that basis.[20] In an attempt to get negotiations moving after the weekend, the delegate of Ireland began by asking a number of questions about the text. This procedure was picked up by many other delegations and it was perhaps overdone because it eventually threatened to drown the Group of 77 in a profusion of technical details. Not surprisingly, the group refused to be drawn into a discussion of details, preferring to indicate that there was indeed great flexibility in its alternative under which all interests could be subsumed.

Some of the questions asked were: What are service contracts? How are they to be financed? How can the authority itself conduct research? How will the whole system actually work? Would "other persons" include states? What does "control" by the authority imply? What are the corresponding rights and duties? What means are available to guarantee security of investment to those "natural or juridical persons" actually doing the work?

Among the questioners, the position adopted by the Soviet delegation was perhaps the most revealing. The Soviets objected that the Group of 77 proposal on Article 9 did not reflect previous agreement to allow states to participate in the exploration and exploitation of seabed resources. Does Article 9 refer only to enterprises and companies? asked the Soviet delegate. Does it exclude the rights of states or not? While on the surface this appeared to be a legitimate problem, its use was something of a smokescreen to hide substantive Soviet disagreement with the draft because the Soviet delegation was previously given assurances that the rights of states were not excluded and in the current meeting this was strongly reinforced by Yugoslavia, Romania, and Cuba. An indication of more important objections could be seen in the additional questions asked by the Soviet delegate. Who will actually conduct and pay for scientific research? What is meant by "joint enterprises?" Who will assume the financial risks of exploration?

The opposition of the U.S. and Japan to the Group of 77 text was predictable, though later the U.S. compromised on its original formulation. Japan insisted that the terms of reference of the authority be clearly defined and the relations between the authority and the entities carrying out the exploitation be stablized. There was too much ambiguity in the Group of 77 proposal for Japan's liking; moreover, paragraph 2 of that draft would give the authority unlimited discretion to decide on the kind of participation by states and other entities.

In an attempt to split the difference between the extremes of the original U.S. formulation, which put greatest emphasis on the rights of contracting parties, and the Group of 77 proposal, which vested exclusive and direct control in the authority, the Netherlands delegation suggested the obvious compromise: a mixed system wherein neither states nor the authority would acquire monopolistic control. The degree of supranationality foreseen in the Group of 77 draft was not realistic at this stage of history since those states which would be in a minority in such an organization must have some guarantees that states have the right to explore and exploit the area. The search for this kind of protection through the mechanism of a mixed system seemed to be the intent of a new U.S. proposal introduced on August 1.[21]

In summarizing the debate on Article 9 at the end of this phase the chairman of the working group pointed out that objections to the original U.S. formulation were based on fears that the mineral resources of the seabed would be subject to unregulated exploitation by a handful of countries and he suggested that the proponents of Alternative A deal with these fears. It was also important, he said, that the chairman of the Group of 77, the representative of Colombia, had stated that the language employed in the group's draft was sufficiently flexible to give sufficient guarantees to any entity making an investment. It was significant that several members of the group, in reply to some of the questions addressed, had stressed that the relationship between the authority and the exploiting entities would be contractual and of sufficiently long duration. Furthermore, they had suggested that these service contracts could be financed from the operation itself through the authority's share of revenues or production. While there was no doubt that state enterprises could qualify to contract with the authority, there remained the necessity of specifying how scientific research could be financed if it were controlled by the authority.

With respect to the possibility of a choice between the Jamaican proposal and the draft of the Group of 77, the representative of Jamaica had strongly emphasized on July 29 that the two were not incompatible. That some members of the group had not been convinced that this was so was indicated on August 1 when the representative of the Republic of Korea argued that the Group of 77 text differed from the Jamaican draft on two counts. The first difference was on the issue of scientific research; the group draft specifically called for its direct control by the authority, but it was not mentioned in the Jamaican draft (though it could be subsumed under the words "all activities"). The second difference was over the degree of discretion given to the authority; the authority was supreme in the group's draft, while Jamaica had put the emphasis on rules and regulations. Unless these differences could be eliminated in consultations, he warned, the Jamaican draft would have to stand on its own.

Apparently, the differences were not reconcilable and the Jamaican delegation yielded because, when the report to Committee I on the third reading of Articles 1–21 was being discussed, a rather ironic fight developed. The representative of Jamaica wished to withdraw his proposal, but the delegates of the U.S. and the U.K. insisted that it be retained as a full alternative on Article 9. It appeared that if Jamaica withdrew, and they were pushed far enough, they would be willing to sponsor the draft. Group tactics then shifted to having the Jamaican draft put either in a footnote or at the very end of the report since, they claimed, its focus was much broader than Article 9. They were successful in doing the latter.[22]

The Debate on Economic Implications of Seabed Exploitation.
This issue was handled in the committee rather than in the working group since the major purposes behind the debate were educational as well as political (i.e., to build up support for production and price controls) and there was little drafting to be done. The committee devoted three days and two evenings to the subject. The first day and a half (July 16 and July 30) were devoted to discussions of the UNCTAD reports and the report of the secretary-general. These were very impressive discussions on alternative policies and their implications with outstanding performances by Mr. Arsenis of UNCTAD and Dr. Raul Branco of the United Nations.[23] The evenings of July 31 and August 1 were devoted to so-called "seminars" which were less useful and largely devoted to propagandistic marathons.[24] A formal debate was held on August 7 and 8, but this too was a rather lackluster affair.

In his appearance before the committee, the UNCTAD representative made it clear that developing countries had three objectives on this issue. These were: orderly market development, prevention of major disruptions from a high rate of technological advance, and the equitable distribution of benefits among the developing countries. In addition, the economic implications of seabed mineral exploitation were summarized as follows:

1. Seabed mining primarily would benefit developed countries.
2. There would be an adverse impact on all mineral producers in terms of retardation of growth and perhaps some decline in exports.
3. The effect on producers in developing countries would be very severe since they relied more heavily on this production for export earnings.
4. The compensatory approach to regulation would be unworkable if the authority were confined to disbursing net revenues accruing from seabed exploitation.
5. If producers in developing countries were to be compensated for losses and if other developing countries were to share in the benefits of seabed mining, it would be necessary to establish preventive arrangements in advance of exploitation (i.e., the authority would have to be able to utilize production and price controls).[25]

The U.S., not surprisingly, did not like these conclusions, claiming the evidence was insufficient to support them. Furthermore, the U.S. did not like the assumption made by UNCTAD, and in particular questioned the statement that the benefits of seabed mining would go primarily to developed countries. Benefits would also accrue to users of mineral products everywhere, they claimed, in the form of lower prices. This last statement introduced a theme which was frequently replayed in the following debate but without much effect, since the link between seabed mineral production and lowered prices was seen to be indirect and tenuous given continued inflation. On the other hand, developing country producers successfully transformed their interests into the interests of the Group of 77 as a whole, so that the demands for production and price controls were reinforced considerably.

The presentation of the secretary-general's report on July 30 gave rise to an even more sophisticated and finely nuanced discussion than had occurred at the presentation of the UNCTAD reports, but the drift was the same. The preferred alternative was clearly a preventive approach which again implied production and price controls. As expected, the U.S. returned to the attack.[26]

The U.S. representative began by complaining that this kind of exchange was not the most constructive way to proceed since there was more than one answer to every question. For instance, given currently higher prices for raw materials, was it possible, he asked, to quantify the extent to which the preventive or compensatory alternatives would increase the costs to developing country consumers as opposed to developing country producers? Furthermore, had any analysis been done by the secretariat on the extent to which the preventive and compensatory approaches would benefit *developed* rather than developing countries? There was some possibility of this, he said, on nickel (Canada), and copper (U.S.) *inter alia*.

This introduced a new theme to the debate. Not only would seabed mineral production benefit consumers of mineral products everywhere but production controls were as likely to benefit developed as developing countries. Moreover, would production controls decrease revenues available to the authority? And, finally, to what extent are new technologies needed to take advantage of economic zones and to what extent will they be made from minerals contained in nodules?

The secretariat's reply to these questions was most informative. Concerning increases in the cost of final products given increases in the cost of raw materials, the answer was a qualified yes. The secretary-general's report had referred to impacts in the first decade when only cobalt and manganese were likely to experience price increases. Cobalt was primarily consumed in developed countries, some cobalt was consumed by developing countries but in those cases cobalt was only a small component of the total product. The same could be said of manganese which was used mainly in the steel industry but represented only a small portion of the total cost of the product.

On the question of equipment needed to exploit resources in the economic zone, Dr. Branco agreed that price increases might occur, especially for cobalt and manganese. Similarly, he agreed that production controls could also benefit developed countries since one-quarter of world cobalt production came from developed countries, but this was a small item. Developed countries were also the major producers of manganese and nickel and, to some extent, of copper. It was important, however, to distinguish accounting gains (where a country was both a big producer and a big consumer) from impacts on countries which were either major importers or exporters.

With respect to the trade-off on alternative policies affecting developing country producers and consumers, Dr. Branco suggested that maintaining high prices would benefit developing country producers more than consumers, but the latter could be compensated elsewhere. Production controls would also have the effect of retarding the rate of increase of revenues accruing to the authority. There would consequently be less to distribute if compensation were also to be paid from seabed funds.

The dominant theme in the day and a half debate given to this item in the committee was for a strong authority which would be able to impose production and price controls on seabed exploitation. As stated previously, even more interesting was the response of the African Group to U.S. attempts to split developing country consumers from producers. The representative of Zaire was made the spokesman for the African Group on this issue and in his presentation he stressed that this was only one among many problems in the complex of concerns treated in the Special General Assembly Session on raw materials. U.S. moves had clearly made this a group-unity issue among the Africans and among the more ideologically oriented members of the Group of 77.

The Fight over the Conditions of Exploitation: Rules and Regulations. For the conflict on the last major item before Committee I at Caracas, the scene shifts once again to the working group, and the first player making his way onstage was the U.S. representative, who delivered a two-hour peroration on the afternoon of August 8, followed by a one-hour presentation of draft articles on the morning of August 9. This ignited a general conflagration which dominated the debate on this item.

The entire statement by the U.S. representative was too long to be summarized extensively in this paper, but the major points were as follows: The U.S. objected to the tactics of the Group of 77 insofar as they wished the committee to debate only Article 9 and not the fundamental conditions of exploitation. In particular, the U.S. objected to so little time being allocated to this subject and warned that it would not sign a treaty which did not include articles on such conditions because the U.S. Senate would not ratify it. The conditions of exploitation, and not Article 9, were issues of the highest priority for the U.S. in these negotiations, consequently, the discretionary power of the authority had to be defined precisely before the authority was created.

In particular, two sets of safeguards had to be built into the treaty: safeguards with respect to the structure of the system as a whole and safeguards with respect to the day-to-day operating conditions. Apparently, the most important concern was for stability in the relationship between the authority and a contracting party. There should be no opportunity for capriciousness by the authority, given the numerical superiority of the Group of 77 and its desire to impose production and price controls, once large investments had been made in mine sites. Other operating concerns revolved around criteria for the selection of sites, the area of sites, confidentiality of data, and the like. These are contained in the U.S. Draft Appendix to the Law of the Sea Treaty.[27]

The EEC paper,[28] presented by France, was very similar to the U.S. paper, but did not elicit the response that the U.S. presentation did. The essential difference was one of style. Much of what the U.S. delegate said was in the form of ideological posturing about the free-enterprise system. There was an excessive amount of "noise" in the communication, perhaps engendered by similar ideological posturing in the Group of 77, especially by Peru and Algeria. The point is that the ensuing barrage was aimed as much at the "noise" as at substantive differences in approach, and this was clearly avoidable. The effects also appear to be lasting and, if so, will play a part in determining whether or not there is ultimate agreement on a treaty in Committee I.

The representative of Jamaica, in response to the presentation of the U.S. position, said he was discouraged to find so many nonnegotiable items in it. This, he claimed, showed a total lack of faith in small nations if not in the rest of the world. The U.S. statement, to him, represented the typical speech of the big businessman, but free and unbridled exploitation with raw profit as its motive never provided industrial peace. With respect to the substance of the issue, there appeared to be three alternative conceptual approaches: (1) to elaborate in the treaty all details on conditions of exploitation as in the U.S. paper; (2) to leave the authority free to determine the details in the future, as was advocated by the Group of 77; and (3) to adopt a median line between the two, as was advocated by the Jamaican delegation, by delineating only fundamental norms as a framework for future exploitation. He found the U.S. approach unworkable since it was likely to create a straitjacket of rules and regulations entrenched as a permanent feature of the constitution, thereby having a paralytic effect on technological advance. The Jamaican proposal was an attempt to reconcile both U.S. concerns for stability in the protection of its interests and the pragmatism and flexibility sought by the Group of 77. This was an interesting approach, but to resolve a conflict by splitting the difference between the two sides requires both trust and the perception by both parties that lack of agreement would be worse than agreement on available terms. Both conditions were absent and there were many cues that the U.S., the EEC countries, Japan, and the Soviet Union were quite prepared to exploit manganese nodules outside any internationally defined regime.

The effect of this situation appeared to be to reinforce the intent of the Group of 77 to stand on principle come what may and this is clearly seen in the response to the U.S. statement by the representative of Trinidad-Tobago.

The crucial portions of his statement are sufficiently brief to be worth quoting in detail:

> . . . There was one ineluctable thread running through the whole intervention of the delegate of the United States and that was the predominant role of the free enterprise system with the inevitable presence of the transnational corporations in the economy of his country and the absolute necessity to assure the entrenchment and promotion of this system in the exploitation of the international seabed area. This has been the pivotal point of his intervention and this indeed is the root of my delegation's difficulty . . .
>
> . . . The distinguished representative of the United States raised again the question of ratification of the convention. For delegations like my own we know what ratification means. Indeed, we have already referred to this very question which was formally raised by the distinguished representative of the Federal Republic of Germany. Ratification like consensus in the international arena carries with it a big power connotation. It is easy for the distinguished representative of the United States to say that his government will not ratify a treaty on the law of the sea which does not provide for their interests as they see them. A threat like that by my delegation is of little significance. My government's lack of ratification of a treaty on the law of the sea will by itself be of little significance to its eventual implementation. The value of ratification then means *power* support and *power* agreement. But delegations like my own have a moral position which we will uphold. There are among us countries or groups of countries which by themselves singly or jointly can at any moment exploit the international seabed area in violation of the resolutions of the General Assembly of the United Nations. We would prefer them to do that rather than yield in what we consider a fully just and moral position. My delegation will not be convened here in Caracas at immense cost which we can ill afford merely to sanction a system of exploitation of the international seabed area and certain related procedural guarantees directed at promoting the system of economy of some countries where this is clearly inconsistent with the will and desire of the majority of the international community. The question then before the committee is essentially this: for how long will the international community constituted as it is by a majority of developing countries, continue to accept and support a system of economic order which is clearly inconsistent with its overall interests? For how long will the international community continue to subordinate the interests and desires of the majority to the will and imposition of the few all the more so where the resources of *common heritage* are to be developed and shared in the interest of all?

In the ensuing debate, statements by the representatives of the Federal Republic of Germany and France, *inter alios*, demonstrated quite clearly that most EEC countries and Japan, as potential exploiters of the international seabed area, shared the U.S. view. In fact, the EEC countries (minus Ireland) later introduced their own detailed statement on conditions of exploitation[29] and, like the U.S., objected to items V and VI of the Chairman's Working Paper,[30] arguing that processing, marketing, and scientific research were not to fall within the domain of the authority. Japan also made similar statements.[31]

The position adopted by the Soviet Union in this exchange was especially interesting. Concerned primarily with protecting the positions of state enterprises and agencies and historically opposed to creating strong international organizations, the U.S.S.R. could not possibly support the Group of 77 on this item. China, however, could and did, ideologically making the most of the situation. The Soviets chose not to reply to China's charges and innuendoes, restricting themselves to a careful analysis of their interests in the items under consideration. Consequently, the Soviet representatives argued that they had to know what laws and conditions would govern the participation of state enterprises in the expensive and complex exploitation of the seabed. The Soviet Union, they warned, could not accede to the convention until it was clear that the convention was acceptable and this meant that the details had to be worked into the convention and not left for the authority to determine.

As the Soviets continued, it became clear that their position was identical with the EEC position, and they later gave strong support to the EEC paper rather than putting in one of their own. Like Italy, the U.S.S.R. objected to the contention of the Group of 77 that domestic law not apply to exploitation of the international seabed area. Those questions had to be decided immediately and, from their point of view, the essence of the problem lay in the duties and obligations of the exploiter and of the authority. In particular, those who wished to establish a strong authority needed to spell out clearly what these rights and duties would be.

At this stage of the proceedings, the Group of 77 was in a difficult position. The focus of the debate had in fact shifted from Article 9 to conditions of exploitation. The U.S. had introduced a detailed paper which threatened to render nugatory all of the group's gains on Article 9. It was also clear that the EEC, Japan, and the U.S.S.R. were much nearer to the U.S. than to the group and the strategy of the former was continuously to pressure the latter for details. Under the leadership of Peru the group began internal negotiations on its own statement on basic conditions. The intent here was to establish the supremacy of the authority (Article 9, paragraph 2) in the rules and regulations governing the exploitation but to do so while staying at the level of general principles, thereby avoiding drowning in a welter of technical details which exceeded the competence of most of the group's delegations. These principles would constitute a framework or general guidelines under which the authority would exercise its discretionary rulemaking and contracting powers.

In this, the group succeeded, but these informal negotiations graphically illustrated the difficulties and time-consuming nature of achieving consensus within the group. The negotiations began prior to the weekend of August 10–11 and continued through the morning of August 15. The work of Committee I simply came to a halt during this time. Delegates would show up at the appointed times each day but there would be no meetings since the group had been unable to conclude its work. Within the group, apparently, the negotiations were equally as exasperating as between the group and the rest of the world. For instance, at the beginning only about ten delegates were involved, but after every draft they could not secure general agreement and the size of the drafting group increased eventually to about twenty-five countries. At the end, however, the group managed to agree on a draft of twelve articles[32] and, given the difficulties, this was a remarkable achievement, but it cost the committee almost a week when there was very little time left.

The debate at this point took a rather surprising turn when the prestigious leader of the Norwegian delegation suddenly appeared in the working group to deliver extremely harsh criticism of the positions advocated by the U.S. and the EEC countries and to support the draft articles and approach proposed by the Group of 77. According to the Norwegian representative, the U.S. and European drafts had embarked on an impossible attempt to produce detailed regulation of the conditions of exploitation simultaneously with the negotiation of the treaty itself. Moreover, both papers reflected concepts of former times, adopting provisions from mining and other contracts utilized in the early decades of the twentieth century.

There were three particular provisions which appeared to have generated this attack. First, Article 3 of the U.S. draft and Article 3 in the European draft, which provided for automatic licensing. This, claimed the Norwegian delegate, would reduce the authority to a mere registry of the rights of prospectors, while the authority would have no possibility of evaluating whom they wanted to do the work, what they wanted the exploiter to do, etc. Second, the duration of mining rights (Article 5 in the U.S. draft and Article 8 in the European draft) were defined much too extensively: for the U.S. it was 55 years, while for the EEC it was 50. This was contrary to all recent events in mining and petroleum concessions. And third, the size of the area to which the exploiter would have exclusive use rights was also much too large (Article 4 of the U.S. draft and Article 7 of the EEC draft). The representative of Norway objected, as contrary to all modern trends in oil and mining concessions, to the claims that a concessioner would have the right to exploit 54,000 km^2 of the international seabed area for petroleum and 360,000 km^2 for hard minerals when current practice in the award of concession blocks was 500 km^2 in Norway, 250 km^2

in the U.K. and 400 km^2 in the Netherlands. Finally, objections were made to the definition of working conditions only in terms of money rather than in work fulfilled.

Not surprisingly, this attack caused public and private reverberations in the U.S.-EEC camps not only as a result of what was said and its significance in the current confrontation but also, and perhaps particularly, as a result of who had said it. Jens Evensen, Norwegian minister of commerce and shipping, is seen by most delegations in the Law of the Sea Conference to be one of the very influential players in the game, especially in the role of mediator. At the same time, he has a considerable reputation as a negotiator of mining and offshore petroleum concessions and both dimensions came into play in delivering this blast. This raised tension both within the Nordic countries group and the EEC since Denmark is now a member and Norway is not. (Denmark would also be placed in a difficult position in the event of Norway establishing an exclusive economic zone of 200 miles). In any event, the EEC group, and especially France as the leader, greatly resented the Norwegian attack. The Group of 77, not surprisingly, was delighted. The Soviets, presumably, were unhappy also, given their support of the EEC position. China was obviously pleased and reiterated warnings that the "common heritage" should not be allowed to fall into the hands of the superpowers and others with advanced technology.

The U.S. chose to treat the attack seriously, responding in a preliminary way immediately following the Norwegian statement and continuing in greater detail in the afternoon. Responding to the charge that the U.S. proposal was not consistent with modern principles of mining contracts, the U.S. representative claimed that the Norwegian delegate had not adequately considered that seabed mineral exploitation in the international area would occur in 15,000 feet of water in the middle of the ocean. This had never been done before and the world was therefore at the same stage relative to seabed exploitation at which it had been seventy-five years ago relative to mineral extraction on land. In such an early stage of development, regulations must not overload a prospective miner with administrative requirements that would stifle production.

Turning to the Chinese charge that under the U.S. and European drafts those with the technology would gain control of the authority, this, said the U.S. representative, was a matter of interpretation. The U.S. did not want control, it wanted a system that would allow its participation on a fair and equitable basis. The fact that the U.S. possessed the financial and technological capacity to exploit was not inconsistent with control by the authority. It was therefore possible to produce a treaty which encouraged production while maintaining control by the authority.

These two themes were developed more fully in the afternoon. The U.S. argument continued to focus on the inapplicability of extrapolating from experience gained in land-based hydrocarbon exploitation to deep seabed mineral exploitation. Much larger block sizes, for instance, were required in the ocean because manganese nodules were found in a very thin layer on the seabed. A large surface area was therefore required if a miner were to have an economically viable site. Concerning the Norwegian statement that the authority should be able to choose who and what it wanted, the U.S. thought this an extreme position, inappropriate at that stage of the negotiations. There was a need to set out in the treaty itself the criteria which the authority was to use in entering into legal arrangements.[33]

By the end of the day on Friday, August 16, the working group had concluded a third reading on Articles 1–21 of the Draft Treaty, conducted an extensive debate on Article 9 and, for the first time since the Seabed Committee was turned into a preparatory committee for the conference in 1971, had met head-on the entire range of issues involved in regulating conditions of exploitation. In addition, Committee I, under the leadership of its chairman, Paul Engo of the United Republic of Cameroon, and with the support of all land-based mineral-producing developing countries, had conducted extensive debates on the economic implications of seabed mineral exploitation. At this time, the question arose of what to do in the last week of committee work scheduled by the conference. It gave rise to an immense and often embarassing procedural squabble.

During the Committee I session on August 5, at which the chairman of the working group had presented a report on the group's work on Articles 1–21, the Brazilian representative had suggested that the chairman of Committee I, Mr. Engo, assume responsibility for conducting informal discussions within the committee on how best to proceed with further negotiations on Article 9. At that time it seemed like a good idea and there was general agreement. But obviously this procedure was rather quickly overtaken by events as the confrontation on the conditions of exploitation emerged. As the connection between Article 9 and the rules and regulations was made clear, there appeared to be no chance that the U.S., the EEC, Japan, and perhaps the U.S.S.R. would agree to a sequential treatment of these items. Mr. Engo's attempt therefore died a-borning.

During the session of Committee I on August 19, at the conclusion of Mr. Pinto's third and last report of the work done by the working group on conditions of exploitation, the Brazilian representative made another proposal in the light of these changed circumstances. This proposal was that the committee create a single negotiating group under the chairmanship of Mr. Pinto. The task of this new group would be to negotiate on Articles 1–21, especially Article 9, and the conditions of exploitation. This negotiating group would be composed of delegations *appointed* to it from regional or interest groups, but it would also be open-ended in membership.

The Brazilian proposal was seconded by Tanzania, the representative of which gave effusive support to Mr. Pinto as the best possible individual to chair this group.[34] Thereupon the proposal was *unanimously* accepted by the committee.

During the session on the afternoon of August 20, the representative of Barbados asked whether it would be possible to review the decision of the previous day on the negotiating group, since it seemed to him of questionable utility given its expansive mandate with so little time left. Furthermore, once negotiations had begun, a certain sequence of events was envisaged by Rule 37. As a result, there appeared to the Barbadian delegate a certain constitutional indelicacy in the creation of this negotiating group. A more propitious course would have been to ask the chairman of Committee I to undertake this task, but the mandate of the group should be restricted to Article 9. There was apparent within the committee an inability to agree on representatives to a small negotiating group, especially among the membership of the Group of 77. Given its mandate, therefore, the group would have to be of the whole since too many diverse interests were involved.[35]

The chairman of Committee I replied that in response to an earlier proposal he had already begun negotiations on Article 9, yet the previous day another proposal had been made to create a group under Mr. Pinto's direction. This put him in a difficult situation and he refused to rule on the issue, leaving it to the committee to decide. He did complain, though, that he had not been consulted about the proposal made on August 19. The ensuing debate degenerated into a most unseemly squabble among the membership of the Group of 77, thereby demonstrating the difficulties of negotiating important details within that group when the issues were major and interests of individual members diverged.

At issue here was the mandate of the group, its composition, its tenure, and its chairman. Mali, Colombia, Tanzania, Mauritania, Guinea, Ghana, Zaire, Chile, and the Republic of Korea were strongly in favor of maintaining the decision of the previous day, only Barbados, Uruguay, and Nigeria were opposed, and the meeting adjourned inconclusively.

At the beginning of the session on August 21, the chairman of Committee I reported on the results of informal consultations designed to get the committee out of this difficulty. It was decided that: (1) the negotiating group would be created and that it would be chaired by Mr. Pinto; and (2) that the group would be limited to fifty members, though it would be formally open-ended and would consist of nine representatives from each region plus the authors of all proposals submitted. The representative of Barbados, however, returned to the attack. His delegation, he insisted, did not delegate to either the Latin American Group or to the Group of 77 the right to negotiate on its behalf beyond the Caracas session. The life of this new negotiating group, therefore, did not extend beyond the Caracas session. If, in the next session, a decision was made to continue in this way, it must be within a group of the whole chaired by the chairman of Committee I.

The representative of Brazil disagreed. It was not his understanding, he said in response, that all this effort had been made only for two days. The group must have a longer life. It would be dissolved only when its terms of reference had been fulfilled or when Committee I decided. The U.S. and Spain supported the Brazilian interpretation and Barbados urgently called on the chairman for clarification, reiterating that no one but Barbados could negotiate for Barbados on its proposal concerning Article 8 of the Draft Treaty. This elicited a flood of requests for the floor with, *inter alios*, Uganda, Liberia, and Turkey echoing Barbados' fears concerning the representativeness of this group and seeking to eliminate the possibility of any intersessional meetings.[36]

In an attempt to surmount this problem of representativeness as it evidenced a lack of trust between members of the Group of 77, the Brazilian delegate made yet another proposal. He proposed that: (a) Committee I recommend that the negotiating group not vote; (b) the negotiating group would exist during the time necessary to complete its mandate; and (c) the negotiating group would meet only during sessions of the conference. He denied that equitable geographical representation was an issue, since on Article 9 and the conditions of exploitation the Group of 77 held common positions. Barbados immediately disagreed with the second of Brazil's proposals, stating his intention to ask for a vote if necessary. This was avoided when both contestants accepted the chair's reformulation that the negotiating group would exist as long as Committee I thought it necessary. This implied that the committee would periodically request reports from the chairman of the negotiating group and make decisions as required.

The negotiating group was thereafter constituted as follows:

African Group—Egypt, Nigeria, Tanzania, Mali, Morocco, Ghana, Madagascar, Algeria, and Lesotho
Asian Group—Iran, Kuwait, China, India, Pakistan, Yugoslavia, Singapore, Afghanistan/Nepal (shared), Philippines/Indonesia (shared)
Latin American Group—Brazil, Bolivia, Chile, Honduras, Jamaica, Mexico, Peru, Trinidad-Tobago, and Venezuela
Western European and Others Group—Austria, Canada, Federal Republic of Germany, Italy, Netherlands, Norway, Sweden, Switzerland, and U.K.
Eastern European Group—U.S.S.R., Ukraine, Byelorussian S.S.R., Poland, Hungary, Czechoslovakia, Romania, Bulgaria, German Democratic Republic
Plus *Authors of Proposals*—U.S., Japan, Colombia (for the Group of 77), France (for the EEC), and Australia.

On August 27, the chairman of the negotiating group reported to Committee I that the group had held six meetings and had decided to begin with Article 9 and the conditions of exploitation. Beyond this he could say no more since it was necessary to protect the confidentiality of discussions. From the perspective of other members of that group, however, who informed the author on the pace and content of negotiations, there was in fact nothing substantive to report. Constituted so late in the session with a second round to follow, there was absolutely no incentive for anyone to negotiate seriously. Consequently, several members predictably indulged their penchant for long ideological rambles. The six meetings of the negotiating group, from this perspective, merely represented the continuation of general debate with no changes in position evidenced.

Committee II

The pattern of work adopted by Committee II was necessarily quite different from that of Committee I. Committee II, as stated previously, was faced with the task of completing preparatory work left unfinished by Subcommittee II of the Seabed Committee. The mechanism utilized by the chairman, Ambassador Aguilar of Venezuela, was, in committee, to hold debates on every item of the Agenda falling within the Terms of Reference of Committee II. Once the debate on an item was concluded, the chairman, with the assistance of the secretariat, prepared a listing of trends in the form of alternative draft articles, seeking to restrict these to the lowest possible number. These texts, called Working Papers, were revised twice, the usual pattern to revision being an attempt on the part of each country to see that its position was clearly stated in the alternative draft articles. While the series of Working Papers will constitute the basis of negotiations in future session, there are also eighty-four individually or jointly sponsored sets of draft articles on particular items which represent the desire of each country to protect its position on the details. It would be too large an undertaking to analyze carefully all of these proposals here. I will therefore confine myself to only a few of the major items: (1) territorial sea/straits; (2) the economic zone, preferential rights, and the continental shelf.

Territorial Sea/Straits. There was a striking degree of agreement on the subject of the territorial sea. There was virtually unanimous agreement on a twelve-mile territorial sea once certain other items relating to straits used for international navigation, the economic zone, and the delimitation of the continental shelf were satisfactorily resolved. The group opposing this trend was, of course, those Latin American countries preferring the establishment of a 200-mile territorial sea: Peru, Brazil, Ecuador, Panama, and Uruguay. The major stumbling block most directly related to the territorial sea is the issue of transit through straits used for international navigation and the possibility of unimpeded passage for vessels through straits which would be affected in the event of agreement on a twelve-mile territorial sea.

With respect to the proposals introduced by individual countries, almost the entire range of interests is encompassed with three of these. The first is the proposal introduced by the United Kingdom (A/CONF.62/C.II/L.3) which seeks to balance the interests of both a major maritime participant and a country bordering the most heavily traveled strait in the world—the Straits of

Dover. The crucial ingredients of this view recognize free passage through straits (including overflight) for vessels of all nationality; prohibit the coastal state from promulgating regulations which affect ship design and construction and place this competence, along with the enactment of measures to control ship-generated pollution, in an appropriate international organization (IMCO). Presumably, this formulation would also be entirely satisfactory to the U.S., U.S.S.R., France, and Japan.[37]

The other extreme, which may be regarded as representing the view of a large number of countries in the Group of 77, is contained in the proposal of Oman (A/CONF.62/C.II/L.16). The heart of this proposal is Article 6 which allows the coastal state to regulate, *inter alia*: the installation, utilization, and protection of navigational facilities and aids (though the article does not specifically say so, this clearly implies regulation of ship design and construction); the control of marine pollution; the passage of ships with special characteristics (i.e., nuclear submarines, supertankers, etc.); and allows only innocent passage of vessels through the straits. It is important to realize that this position reflects both the general ideological thrust of the Group of 77 in significantly increasing the authority of the coastal state and the special interests of Egypt in its conflict with Israel vis-à-vis the Straits of Tiran; and the special interests of Iran vis-à-vis the straits of Hormuz. This makes it doubly difficult to deal with.

Lying between these extremes is the proposal by Fiji (A/CONF.62/-C.II/L.19), constituting a revision of an influential paper by the same delegation on the subject of territorial sea (A/AC.138/SC.II/L.42 of July 19, 1973). This compromise formulation would allow coastal states to regulate passage but these regulations could not be more restrictive than relevant IMCO conventions on the subjects of ship design, construction, manning, or equipment. Submarines would be required to navigate on the surface except when prior notification is given to the coastal state. However, no mention is made of overflight.

The debate on this item in Committee II was instructive in clarifying the interests that were underlying positions taken and in illuminating the difficulties of resolution. Speaking for coastal state regulation of passage, Iran argued that the need for passage through straits should not prejudice the legal status of the territorial sea if those straits happened to be in the territorial sea of a state. The only way out of this difficulty was to apply existing law in the form of the right of innocent passage.[38] This kind of argument characterized the line adopted by "straits states" with substantive interests to protect. The more symbolic position is amply illustrated in the line of argument followed by Tanzania. Upholding the right of the coastal state to regulate passage through straits, the Tanzanian delegate claimed that in areas of heavy traffic, it would be highly dangerous to allow submarines to pass secretly, warships must therefore give prior notification. "Why the secrecy anyway, if passage is peaceful," he asked.

The interests of the opposing side were strongly argued by the U.S., among others. In fact, on this and two subsequent occasions, the U.S. insisted that there could not be a successful conference unless this question was resolved and that the question was of the highest priority for the U.S. Denying that unimpeded transit imperiled the security of the coastal state, the U.S. representative claimed that such a right of transit did not imply a right to engage in activities harmful to the coastal state. In any event, straits were most unlikely places from which coastal states could be threatened, their waters being so confined.

With respect to safety of navigation and prevention of pollution, internationally derived regulations would have to be predominant though, in the case of prevention of pollution, states bordering straits would be able to recommend special requirements to appropriate international organizations. To be valid, however, these requirements must be generally accepted. Rights of over-flight of these straits would also have to be protected, since territorial seas would be extended.

In addition to the special interests of the Arab states, the global security interests of the major maritime players, and the ideological preferences of some members of the Group of 77, there is another major set of interests which are entangled in this issue. These concern shipborne trade, not so much relating to bulk cargo but primarily relating to the shipment of petroleum and petrochemical products. Apparently for this reason, the delegate of Sri Lanka had suggested that a distinction be made between commercial and military vessels in which unimpeded passage would be accorded the former, though they would have to conform to pollution regulations enacted by the coastal state. On the other hand, the coastal state would have to be accorded some safeguards relative to the passage of military vessels.

The U.S. and others appeared much troubled by this argument and Czechoslovakia, speaking for the Eastern European Group, denied that the security of the coastal state was an issue at all in this debate. He warned that restrictions on freedom of transit would benefit only a few coastal states though they would be detrimental to the interests of all developing countries as well as most others dependent on trade. In terms of substantive interests, this problem appeared to be potentially more significant than the issue of security because it affected every participant in the conference, though not in the same way.

For instance, unimpeded transit was of high priority to *all* the major maritime players, primarily for economic reasons involving the transport of oil. This affected national security in the broadest sense. The narrow issue of passage of warships, particularly submarines, was of high priority to only a few countries within the major maritime group. The economic dimension was also of particular importance to developing countries everywhere and to all landlocked developed countries since increased charges stemming from diverse coastal state regulations on ship design, construction, equipment, and manning would obviously be passed on to the consumer. But even granting this assumption, some countries, Canada in particular, found "gunboats much less threatening than loaded oil tankers" and consequently pushed for the primacy of coastal state rights and responsibilities in managing passage through straits. This position dovetailed quite nicely with the interests of the ideological leaders of the Group of 77 to close the circle.

The special interests of the Arab states vis-à-vis Israel, perforce put them at the other extreme from the U.S. *et al.* but a hidden dimension to this confrontation lay in the significance of the Straits of Hormuz for control of the transport of oil. In this light, an exchange between the representatives of Egypt and the U.S. on July 23 was particularly interesting.

In response to the original U.S. intervention on July 22, the representative of Egypt declared himself happy that the U.S. had put all three elements on the table, i.e., security, control of pollution, and freedom of navigation. However, he failed to understand why the U.S. rejected the applicability of the regime of innocent passage to straits which would require prior notification of all vessels. Moreover, since it was clear that the U.S. refused to have its submarines surface when transiting straits, how was the coastal state to ensure that these vessels were observing the obligations against utilization of weapons of any kind? The fact was that the area in question would be within the territorial sea of the coastal state. This appeared to have been denied in the U.K. proposal (L.3), the thrust of which was to treat the straits in question as being some sort of a high seas area in which the coastal state would exercise only occasional, special jurisdiction. This was clearly inadequate since, from the perspective of maintaining national security, the fundamental issue at stake was how the coastal state would exercise its supervisory capacity. This question could not be brushed aside and no agreement was possible without its resolution.

Obviously, this position was 180° opposed to the position adopted by the U.S. In order to protect local interests vis-à-vis a neighboring adversary, Egypt insisted on a principle that would safeguard the regulatory supremacy of the coastal state in managing passage through straits. In contrast, intent on preserving rights of passage for submarines, other warships, and oil tankers, the U.S. insisted on a principle that could give the coastal state no credible guarantees at the level of principle. The only guarantee possible was between the U.S. and the rest of the world: i.e., that straits were areas of confined waters from which no master would choose to threaten a coastal state. (Another point, which in the circumstances could not have been made with grace, was that the U.S. clearly did not need to pass through straits in order to threaten anybody.)

This guarantee, while credible in the abstract, could give no solace to Egypt, since it was Israel they were worried about and not the U.S. Conducted at the level of principle, however, the Egyptian position merely added fuel to the Canadian claims and the ideologists of the Group of 77. If this analysis is correct, it is difficult to see how any compromise formulation is possible. The opposing positions appear to be mutually exclusive and splitting the difference between them is therefore not an available option. Furthermore, any compromise would have to go largely in the direction of those who wish to see coastal state regulation of passage, *vide* the Fijian proposal (L.19), and this is characterized as unacceptable by the opposing side. This is a clear confrontation in which each side leaves the other only the possibility of capitulation. This is yet another rock on which the conference can falter unless trade-offs are not calculated on this single dimension alone, but are widened to include the economic zone and perhaps the deep seabed regime.

The Economic Zone, Preferential Rights, and the Continental Shelf. These are the major economic issues which were at the heart of the negotiations in Committee II. *The U.N. Comparative Table of Proposals Related Directly to Living Resources* (A/CONF.62/C.II/L.1), based on the work of Subcommittee II of the Seabed Committee, succinctly summarizes most of the subitems in question. These may be characterized as follows:

1. Whether or not an economic zone will be established
2. If so, the nature of coastal state jurisdiction to be exercised therein
    a. sovereignty (jurisdiction) over living and nonliving resources, scientific research, and the control of marine pollution
    b. sovereignty (jurisdiction) over living and nonliving resources only
3. The spatial extent of the zone and methods of delimitation
4. Regional sharing in the economic zone, including access for neighboring landlocked or geographically disadvantaged states
5. Coastal state preferential rights over living resources beyond the territorial sea (as an alternative to the economic zone)
6. The nature of coastal state obligations concerning full utilization of living resources under its control ("shall" versus "may")
7. The allocation of authority over anadromous species
8. The allocation of authority over highly migratory species
9. Settlement of disputes
10. Inspection and enforcement
11. We can add to the above, the continental shelf: definition, limits, and delimitation criteria

Since the scope of these issues covers so large a number of items, I have attempted to catalog state positions on the economic zone, preferential rights, and the continental shelf. This catalog is included as an appendix to this paper and is based on positions stated in the debate as well as formal proposals, singly or jointly submitted. There is a certain amount of slippage in the two since delegations change their positions over time. I have included the entire range of positions adopted in each case even though, as has occurred with the delegations of Lesotho and Liberia, they may be contradictory. Table 1-1 summarizes the distribution on the economic zone and preferential rights.

Of 120 positions indicated by 110 delegations, 73 (61 percent) have

Table 1-1.   Economic Zone Positions of Delegations in Committee II

Position	Frequency	Totals
200-mile territorial sea	8	
200-mile economic zone, including science and pollution	21	
200-mile economic zone, including science and pollution, but landlocked access to living resources and region access to living resources by geographically disadvantaged developing countries in region	34	
200-mile economic zone, including science and pollution but also including obligation for full utilization, living resources	6	
200-mile economic zone, including science and pollution, but global access to living resources for developing countries	1	
A regionally defined 200-mile economic zone, including science and pollution	3	73
200-mile economic zone, including pollution but not science	5	
200-mile economic zone, including science but not pollution	1	6
200-mile economic zone, excluding science and pollution but including full utilization, living resources	9	
No economic zone, pref. rts. living resources, full utilization	9	
No economic zone, contiguous zone natural resources, landlocked access living and nonliving resources, reg. shar. living and nonliving resources for geographically disadvantaged	21	
No economic zone, 12-mile territorial sea, international regulation living and nonliving resources	2	41
Total		120

Source: Appendix
Note: 110 countries indicated preferences; multiple positions are possible.

as their common denominator a comprehensive 200-mile economic zone, including not only living and nonliving resources but scientific research and control of marine pollution as well. Only a very small group of delegations has added either scientific research or pollution, but not both, to coastal state jurisdiction in the economic zone, but a significant number, 41 (34 percent), adopt positions which either erode or clearly oppose the concept of our economic zone. The situation is actually more complicated than this because, within the group supporting the economic zone, there is considerable variety. Some would like to see obligations for full utilization of living resources imposed on the coastal state (e.g., Canada, Australia, New Zealand, Spain, Portugal, and Ireland), others will support an economic zone only if guarantees on regional access to living resources for developing countries within the region are written into the convention (e.g., Trinidad-Tobago, Jamaica, Barbados). Finally, some would prefer the establishment of regional economic zones only, failing that they appear to opt for a position quite opposed to the concept of such a zone (e.g., Bolivia and Paraguay).

With respect to the Continental Shelf, the polarity is not quite as marked but there is still cause for concern. Of 61 delegations stating positions on the issue as catalogued in Table 1-2, 35 (57 percent) prefer a distance limit of 200 miles while 19 (31 percent) wish to see the continental margin as the definition.[39] Not surprisingly, this latter group contains almost all the countries with margins greater than 200 miles, so the underlying interests are unmistakably clear. Only two countries, the U.S. and Ghana, still talk about revenue-sharing beyond 200 miles if the margin is adopted as the criterion. This is certainly a long way from 1970–71.

It does appear then that the thrust is for a comprehensive economic zone and against both "full utilization" obligations for the coastal state and limited jurisdictions in the economic zone, but the battle is far from won since, if these are final positions, *no faction seems capable of garnering a two-thirds majority*. Admittedly, the author did not have access to private bilateral and multilateral bargaining on these issues, and some participants have expressed a certain amount of optimism as to the outcome, but the probability seems to me high that the conference can fail because no side can muster the majorities required for decision. This subjective assessment of probability is reinforced when one looks at the pattern of negotiating behavior in Committee II.

Though there was a virtual orgy of proliferation in the number of

Table 1-2. Continental Shelf Positions of Delegations in Committee II

Position	Frequency
200 miles	35
Continental margin	19
200 miles or margin with revenue sharing	2
200 meters depth or 200 miles if economic zone established	2
500 meters depth or 200 miles	1
4000 meters depth or margin	2
	61

negotiating groups, the paucity of output is astounding. There were simply very few proposals containing large numbers of cosponsors coming out of these efforts. Even when groups did produce papers, the length of time it took, coupled with rumbling dissatisfaction from group members, did not augur well for the Conference. For instance, it is well known that the EEC still does not have a coherent policy on fisheries, yet it was reasonably assumed that the nine could agree on a position opposing the economic zone. Eight members eventually did cosponsor a paper on fisheries (L.40), but it took two and a half years and at the last moment the United Kingdom did not go along. Yet another example lies in the fate of the Coastal States Group, organized by Canada, containing all of the strong supporters of a 200-mile economic zone and many of the influential players in the conference. This group was composed of about eighteen delegations and it attempted to produce a complete compromise package to present to the conference as a focal point for general agreement,[40] but even though this group met for two years only nine of the eighteen members agreed to cosponsor the paper. The reaction of the plenary to L.4 was even more instructive.

Since the proposal of the Coastal States Group constructed a comprehensive package on most of the major issues before the conference, its cosponsors[41] attempted to introduce it before the plenary on the grounds that its contents went beyond the mandate of any single committee. This caused an uproar because a large number of delegations thought that such a proposal would skew the course of negotiations in favor of the Coastal States Group. Turkey therefore objected to the introduction of L.4 in plenary instead of in Committee II, but the president explained that, because of its scope, it was merely to be introduced in the plenary without any substantive discussion. The Canadian representative, who would introduce the paper on behalf of the cosponsors, also argued that he wished to avoid a similar procedural wrangle if the paper was introduced before Committee II where states could object precisely because it went beyond the mandate of that committee.

The president clearly had expected a challenge to his ruling that any delegation had a right to choose the forum for the introduction of its proposals, but though Turkey continued to object, the Turkish delegate was most reluctant to move a formal point of order. The representative of Tunisia, however, objected to the chair's ruling and called for a vote, the results of which were most surprising. The president's ruling was upheld by a narrow majority (38-50) and the number of abstentions (39) was quite large. Apparently, many delegations resented the president's ruling because they thought he supported the package proposed by the cosponsors of L.4. The president in turn said that the narrow vote caused him "grave concern." His ruling merely reflected what was legally permissible, but if the current attitude prevailed the position of the chair would be untenable.

L.4 was significant because it was the only comprehensive package presented to the conference in an attempt to move the negotiations along. But even though it moved in the direction of the dominant trend, many delegations had objections to all or parts of it. Since no other group was able to put forward a different package, many delegations did not want it introduced at all. The difficulty of engaging in serious negotiations rather than continuing the skirmishes to protect a variety of national positions continues to plague the conference and this underscores the absence of sufficiently large majorities to allow any other outcome but failure.

At the same time that this fight was going on, another contentious issue was injected into the proceedings by the president, when he suggested that the conference seek to achieve agreement on the basic issues at Caracas and to make this the major official statement of the session.[42] Obviously, this proposal could never have secured widespread agreement, given the dynamics I have just described. For many delegations, this raised more serious questions than L.4 since whatever was agreed to at Caracas would constrain them in the future, even though the president denied that this was the intention. Significantly, the U.S., U.S.S.R., and Japan all opposed this suggestion, claiming that existing differences on the major items precluded agreement on general principles unless the details had been successfully worked out. The fear was that agreement on general principles at Caracas could serve only to emphasize coastal state rights without delineating correlative duties and that this would remove any incentive for the majority to negotiate on the details. The president's proposal was eventually withdrawn.

During the course of the Caracas session, one authoritative observer suggested to me that the conference, given its size and complexity, could not get out of deadlock unless delegations first agreed on a general concept. I agreed with this but clearly positions on the major issues before Committee II and the sequence of events generated by the attempt to introduce L.4 in the plenary and by the president's proposals demonstrated beyond a doubt that there are still fundamental differences between delegations on which general concept will be adopted. Since no agreement is possible until the details are worked out and since conflict on the details is widespread and high, delegations appear to prefer the *danse macabre* of reiterating national positions to negotiating and it is very difficult to break out of this.

Committee III

The Preservation of the Marine Environment. Earlier in the paper I dealt with the major structural problems of Committee III, its penchant for engaging in procedural squabbles and the constraining effects of its overlapping responsibilities with Committee II. There is not much to be said about the output of the Working Group on Preservation of the Marine Environment because, except for the regulation of ship-generated pollution, its task is an impossible one. The Law of the Sea Conference can do little or nothing about pollution from land-based sources (the major problem of ocean contamination), pollution via the atmosphere, etc. On all these subjects the working group could have produced no more than pious platitudes in the form of general obligations not to pollute, to cooperate regionally, and the like.

The Canadian delegate, declaring that preservation of the marine environment was the most important Canadian objective at the conference, provided an excellent summary of the major problem areas facing the committee on this item.[43] They were four:

1. The effect of differing levels of economic development on the duty of combating marine pollution (i.e., how will costs be apportioned?)
2. Adoption of rules and standards for the prevention of ship-generated pollution
3. Enforcement of rules and standards for the prevention of ship-generated pollution
4. The basic zonal approach to the adoption and enforcement of measures for the prevention of marine pollution

The Law of the Sea Conference cannot deal effectively with the first issue but it can with the other three, all of which really relate to ship-generated pollution. The debate this time generated less heat than in 1973 in the Seabed Committee, primarily because the IMCO Conference had been held in October 1973 and this removed the immediate cause of contention between Canada on one side and the U.S. and U.K. on the other. But the basic questions remained concerning the authority to regulate against ship-generated pollution.

A certain willingness to compromise was apparent on the part of the advocates of coastal state rights. For instance, emphasizing that his delegation was still opposed to the exclusively international approach to allocating responsibility for this problem, the Canadian delegate appeared to find a Norwegian compromise formulation acceptable.[44] This approach made a distinction between coastal states' rights relative to discharges, dumping, and traffic separation as opposed to coastal states' rights relative to ship construction, design, equipment, and manning. But, from the point of view of those advocating the exclusively international approach, the problem still remained, since Canadian proposals would allow coastal states to regulate ship design and construction in specified cases. This issue was clearly stated by the Canadian delegate:

> The solution to this problem does not lie so much in restricting the exercise of Coastal State rights to particular areas of jurisdiction. In the view of the Canadian Delegation the solution was rather in restricting their exercise to cases where they are strictly necessary and are applied, under appropriate safeguards and on a nondiscriminatory basis, in response to particular geographic, navigational or

ecological situations not adequately covered by international rules and standards.[45]

Obviously, the debate had undergone a subtle shift since summer 1973; it was no longer a simple confrontation between the exclusivists on both sides. The draft articles submitted by Canada, Fiji, Ghana, Guyana, Iceland, India, Iran, New Zealand, the Philippines, and Spain[46] are particularly interesting in this regard. This approach assumes the existence of an economic zone which gives to the coastal state rights and duties in respect to protecting and preserving the marine environment (Article VI). Generally, coastal state regulations on ship-generated pollution are to conform to internationally agreed-on rules and standards (Article VII), but:

> Where internationally agreed rules and standards are not in existence or are inadequate to meet special circumstances, Coastal States may adopt reasonable and non-discriminatory laws and regulations additional to or more stringent than the relevant internationally agreed rules and standards. However, Coastal States may apply stricter design and construction standards to vessels navigating in their zones only in respect of waters where such stricter standards are rendered essential by exceptional hazards to navigation or the special vulnerability of the marine environment, in accordance with accepted scientific criteria.

This position appeared to appeal to most delegations except those major maritime countries with large merchant marine and tanker fleets. Its potential appeal to states bordering enclosed or semi-enclosed seas may be even greater in the long run. Phrased in this way, the zonal approach to pollution control may well garner a two-thirds majority, but those maritime countries primarily affected still appear firm in their determination to reject these provisions, and there are two proposals, by the Federal Republic of Germany[47] and Greece,[48] which still stipulate flag state jurisdiction in enforcing pollution-control regulations.

Scientific Research and Development and Transfer of Technology. The basic issues of the debate on scientific research have not changed significantly since the work of the Seabed Committee.[49] The Group of 77 continues to demand the inclusion of scientific research within the range of activities expressly controlled by the coastal state in the economic zone. This line of argument frankly underscores a high degree of mistrust of the purposes served by scientific research and rejects all distinctions between pure, applied, and military research. While the group insists that the costal state must control research, its members deny that they intend to place unreasonable restrictions on research and proclaim themselves open to cooperation and mutual assistance.

The nature of the new relationship between the coastal state and developed countries seeking to carry out research in the economic zones of other states was most clearly defined by the representative of Mexico.[50] The coastal state would now have the right to participate in all stages of research in zones subject to their control, i.e., the territorial sea, patrimonial sea, and continental shelf. These stages are defined as the planning, execution, analysis, and interpretation of research projects and results. Consent would also give the coastal state a right to share samples, to have access to raw and processed information, to require that the results be published, and to supervise the conduct of research. Presumably, control would also imply the right of the coastal state to change or add to the very nature of the research project itself.

The opposing view, as stated explicitly by the United States, would not require consent of the coastal state, but would allow research once certain obligations are met by the researcher. Most of these are remarkably close to those elaborated by the delegate of Mexico.

1. Advance notification of the proposed research, including a detailed description of the research project
2. The right of the coastal state to participate directly or through an international organization of its choice
3. Sharing of all data and samples with the coastal state
4. Assistance to the coastal state in interpreting the results of the research project in a manner that is relevant to the coastal state
5. Publication as soon as possible of the significant research results in an open, readily available scientific publication
6. Compliance with all applicable international environmental standards; and
7. Flag state certification that the research will be conducted by a qualified institution with a view to purely scientific research[51]

Obviously, items 6 and 7 conflict with the Group of 77 approach. In addition, these obligations do not require coastal state participation in the planning of the project and thereby preclude coastal state competence to change the direction of the research project. But the crucial difference here—as in the case of straits and pollution control—is in the scope of coastal state authority to prescribe and the adverse implications of this perceived by those opposed. In the words of the chairman of Committee III, Ambassador Yankov of Bulgaria, the main issue is the proper determination of the scope and extent of the rights and obligations of the coastal state in the zone adjacent to the territorial sea, and the rights and obligations of others undertaking research in this zone.[52]

By the end of the session, the Working Group on Scientific Research and Transfer of Technology had agreed on the following alternatives to serve as a basis for negotiations concerning the right to conduct marine scientific research and the consent, participation, and obligations of coastal states:[53]

1. A proposal by the Group of 77 that stipulated the exclusive rights of coastal states in the economic zone and of the international authority, directly or through service contracts, in the international seabed area.
2. A proposal, originally jointly sponsored by Ireland, Mexico, and Spain but later without Mexico, which provides for a consent regime, but declares that consent shall not normally be withheld if specified obligations are met.
3. A proposal put forward by the Netherlands, the Federal Republic of Germany, and a group of disadvantaged states, which closely resembled the U.S. proposal described earlier.
4. A proposal jointly sponsored by the U.K., Denmark, U.S.S.R., and Switzerland which provides, *inter alia*:

> States and appropriate international organizations have freedom to carry out marine scientific research in areas where coastal states enjoy economic rights over marine resources . . . except that marine scientific research aimed directly at the exploration or exploitation of the living and non-living resources shall be subject to the consent of the coastal state. Requests for consent shall be submitted well in advance and shall be answered without undue delay.

Without a doubt, the most exciting portion of Committee III's work occurred on the very last day left to the committee, August 23. At this time a proposal on scientific research was dramatically introduced by its cosponsors, which included several landlocked countries, several developed West European maritime states, plus Lesotho, Liberia, Uganda, Upper Volta, and Zambia. The significance of this was largely symbolic in that the cosponsors of A/CONF.62/-C.3/L.19 had succeeded in splitting both the Group of 77 and in particular the African Group. This proposal did not provide for a consent regime and it sought to protect the interests of landlocked and other geographically disadvantaged countries. As such it elicited harsh responses from India and Kenya.

In the ensuing debate a clear coastal state–landlocked split emerged within the Group of 77. In particular, the Kenyan delegate demanded to know what "rights" landlocked countries possessed concerning marine scientific research. How did these "rights" differ from those of coastal states: How were the landlocked countries to get access to the sea? How could they avoid bilateral negotiations in order to do so? He was surprised to note, he said, that some Group of 77 colleagues supported L.19, which was diametrically opposed to the group's proposals contained in L.13. What kind of game was being played here? he asked. For reasons peculiar to the South American continent, Argentina then intervened to reject any right of landlocked states to carry on scientific research in the economic zones of coastal states.

In replying to the charges, the delegate of Singapore asserted that L.19 reflected a sincere attempt to realize common ground between coastal, research, and landlocked states. He was dismayed, he said, at the purely bilateral trend to the discussion in which the interests of landlocked countries were totally ignored. All members of the Group of 77 were not obligated to be bound by every article in L.13, he said, and Singapore's interests were not adequately reflected therein.

The exchange between the Africans was particularly acrimonious and the delegate of Lesotho heatedly rejected the charges leveled by Kenya as demonstrating contempt and intrusion upon Lesotho's national sovereignty. The Liberian delegate contented himself with supporting the explanation given by Singapore but after the conference adjourned I was told that Liberia had withdrawn its support for L.19. Just before adjournment, also, a new proposal on the economic zone was introduced in Committee II by the African Group.[54] This proposal provided for a consent regime on scientific research, yet it carried as cosponsors the names of Lesotho and Liberia. This episode merely demonstrates the significance of a point made much earlier in the paper; as negotiations focus on substantive interests and details, the pressure intensifies on the Group of 77, and within the African Group in particular, given the relatively large number of landlocked countries in the coalition. As this pressure continues, these groups are likely to break down at certain points but not necessarily on all items. It depends on the ways in which packages are constructed and the extent to which the interests of landlocked countries are accommodated therein.

CONCLUSIONS

The thrust of the argument developed in this paper is clearly pessimistic. It seems to me that if the style of negotiating characteristic of the Seabed Committee and carried over to Caracas is again employed in Geneva the conference will fail in the sense that no treaty will be produced. It will fail because no faction appears to possess the required majorities. In addition, even if a treaty including all of the preferences of the Group of 77 is concluded, this is unlikely to provide the world with a viable ocean regime since the countries with the capabilities are unlikely to sign and ratify.

Admittedly, bluffing, posturing, and threatening are behavioral ingredients of most negotiations and it is always difficult to assess from the outside what a player's minimum acceptable conditions might be. These perhaps have become clearer to those engaged in the private bilateral and multilateral discussions. But if each group refuses to make major concessions early in the Geneva meetings, the tendency will be to continue as they have in the past and there simply will not be the time to resolve all the important issues. Failing this, the conference will be overtaken by events, with the increased probability of multiplying points of conflict over resources and navigation in the future. If this occurs, the danger that these tensions will increase world conflict levels is real, with the potential that these tensions can at times infect non-ocean-related issues. Yet one more opportunity of creating effective regimes within which the activities of the world can be fruitfully conducted will have been lost.

Table 1-3. State Positions on Economic Zone and Related Issues

Country	1 200-mile T.S.	2 200-mile E.Z.; C-S control S.R. & P.	3 Regional E.Z.; S.R. & P.	4 200-mile E.Z.; S.R. not P.	5 200-mile E.Z.; P. not S.R.	6 200-mile E.Z.: no control S.R. and P.	7 No E.Z.; pref. rts. for C-S over L.R.	8 No E.Z.; contig. zone for all N.R.	9 No E.Z.; 12-mile T.S., int'l regulation L.R. & N-L.R. beyond 12 miles	10 Access to L.R. for N.L.S.	11 Access to M.R. for N.L.S.	12 Regional sharing of L.R. for devel. geograph-ically disadvan-taged states	13 Global access to all L.R. for devel. countries	14 Full utiliza-tion	15 Conti-nental shelf
New Zealand		X								X				X	margin
Honduras		X													200 mi
Nigeria		X										X			200 mi
Portugal		X												X	4000 m
Mexico		X													margin
German Democratic Republic						X									
Yugoslavia														X	200 mi
Upper Volta					X			X		X	X				200 mi
Madagascar			X							X					200 mi
Paraguay					X			X		X	X				200 mi
Zaire										X		X			200 m
Congo		X								X		X			
Cyprus		X								X		X			
Barbados		X								X		X			
Dahomey	X														
Mauritania		X								X		X			200 mi
Israel	No firm preferences indicated														
Trinidad-Tobago		X			X							X			
Switzerland								X						X	
Ireland								X			X				
Sweden						X				X					
Finland	No global 200-mile E.Z.; regional decisions only.														
Bangladesh		X								X		X			200 mi
Tanzania		X								X		X			200 mi
Kenya		X								X		X			200 mi
Liberia		X				X									200 mi
France							X							X	
Sri Lanka		X								X		X			
China		X								X		X			

(continued)

Table 1-3 continued

Country	1 — 200-mile T.S.	2 — 200-mile E.Z.: C-S control S.R. & P.	3 — Regional E.Z.: S.R. & P. not P.	4 — 200-mile E.Z.: S.R. not P.	5 — 200-mile E.Z.: P. not S.R.	6 — 200-mile E.Z.: no control S.R. and P.	7 — No E.Z.: pref. rts. for C-S over L.R.	8 — No E.Z.: contig. zone for all N.R.	9 — No E.Z.: 12-mile T.S., int'l regulation L. & N-L.R. beyond 12 miles	10 — Access to L.R. for N.L.S.	11 — Access to M.R. for N.L.S.	12 — Regional sharing of L.R. for devel. geograph-ically disadvan-taged states	13 — Global access to all L.R. for devel. countries	14 — Full utiliza-tion	15 — Conti-nental shelf
El Salvador		X								X					
Togo		X								X					200 mi
Ghana		X								X		X			200 mi or Rev. sh.
Greece				X											margin
Iceland		X								X		X			
Western Somoa		X								X		X			
Tonga		X								X		X			
Nicaragua		X				X									200 mi
United States														X	margin with Rev. shar.
Burundi		X								X		X			200 mi
India		X								X		X			margin
Federal Republic of Germany							X								200 m or 200 mi If EZ
Cuba										X		X			margin
Thailand	X									X		X			
Peru						X?									200 mi
Romania						X?				X		X			
Pakistan		X								X		X			
Italy							X								
Republic of Korea		X											X		200 mi
Argentina		X								X					margin
Ivory Coast		X													margin
Uganda					X			X		X		X			200 mi
Malaysia		X ,								X	X	X			
Bolivia			X							X	X	X			
Senegal		X						X		X		X			
United Kingdom					X	X									200 mi
Ukr. SSR														X	
Bhutan								X						X	
Poland							X							X	margin
Brazil	X														

No clear preferences indicated

(If EZ, one in which coastal state exercising functionally determined rights, subject to international duties)

Country	(final column)
Chile	margin
Tunisia	200 mi
Egypt	
Australia	margin
Byelo. SSR	
Nepal	
Belgium	margin
Albania	margin
Indonesia	margin
Guyana	
Uruguay	
Democracy of Yemen	
Somalia	
Singapore	Limited (If EZ est.)
South Africa	margin
Khmer Republic	200 mi
Panama	
Turkey	
Libya	200 mi
Ecuador	200 mi
Haiti	
Democratic-Republic of Korea	
Afghanistan	margin
Spain	Limited if EZ est.
Guatemala	
Japan	
Netherlands	200 mi
Jamaica	
Guinea	
Bulgaria	
Denmark	200 mi
Venezuela	
USSR	500 m or 200 mi
Lebanon	200 mi
Algeria	200 mi
Austria	
Burma	
Canada	margin
Colombia	margin
Iraq	
Mali	
Botswana	
Laos	

(continued)

Table 1-3 continued

Country	1 200-mile T.S.	2 200-mile E.Z.; C-S control S.R. & P.	3 Regional 200-mile E.Z.; S.R. & P.	4 200-mile E.Z.; S.R. not P.	5 200-mile E.Z.; P. not S.R.	6 200-mile E.Z.; C-S control S.R. and P.	7 No E.Z.; no pref. rts. for C-S over L.R. and P.	8 No E.Z.; contig. zone for all N.R.	9 No E.Z.; 12-mile T.S., int'l regulation L.R. & N.L.R. beyond 12 miles	10 Access to L.R. for N.L.S.	11 Access to M.R. for N.L.S.	12 Regional sharing of L.R. for devel. geographically disadvantaged states	13 Global access to all L.R. for devel. countries	14 Full utilization	15 Continental shelf
Lesotho		X								X	X	X			200 mi
Luxembourg							X	X		X	X	X			
Swaziland								X		X	X	X			
Zambia								X		X	X	X			
Sierra Leone		X						X		X		X			200 mi
Sudan		X								X		X			200 mi
Cameroon		X								X		X			200 mi
Morocco		X								X					200 mi
Norway		X													margin
Gambia	No position on zone indicated														200 mi
Republic of Vietnam	No position on zone indicated														200 mi
Mauritius		X													margin
Malta	Previous position changed														200 mi

Sources: A/CONF.62/C.2/SR.21-29 (economic zone); A/CONF.62/C.2/SR.11-14 & 20 (continental shelf); A.CONF.62/C.2/SR.30 &31 (preferential rights); A/CONF.62/C.2/L.4; A/CONF.62/C.2/L.17; A/CONF.62/C.2/L.21; A/CONF.62/C.2/L.35; A/CONF.62/C.2/L.38; A/CONF.62/C.2/L.39; A/CONF.62/C.2/L.40; A/CONF.62/C.2/L.47; A/CONF.62/C.2/L.60; A/CONF.62/C.2/L.65; A/CONF.62/C.2/L.82.

Explanation of abbreviations in column headings:

T.S.   Territorial sea
E.Z.   Economic zone
C.S.   Coastal state
S.R.   Scientific research
P.   Pollution
N.R.   Natural resources
L.R.   Living resources
N-L.R.   Nonliving resources
N.L.S.   Neighboring landlocked states
M.R.   Mineral resources

NOTES

1. *See* Robert L. Friedheim, "A Law of the Sea Conference—Who Needs It?" *International Relations and the Future of Ocean Space,* ed. Robert G. Wirsing (Columbia, S.C.: University of South Carolina Press, 1974), pp. 44–66 and especially p. 62.
2. Text of Jamaican statement to Committee II: August 6, 1974. For a summary, *see* Doc. A/CONF.62/C.2/SR.28, pp. 6–9.
3. Ibid. pp. 18–19.
4. *See* Doc. A/CONF.62/WP.2, June 25, 1974. The Gentlemen's Agreement reads:

> Bearing in mind that the problems of ocean space are closely inter-related and need to be considered as a whole and the desirability of adopting a convention on the Law of the Sea which will secure the widest possible acceptance,
> The Conference should make every effort to reach agreement on substantive matters by way of consensus and there should be no voting on such matters until all efforts at consensus have been exhausted.

5. The formal record of the first session of the conference is contained in Doc. A/CONF.62/SR1.13, February 22, 1974. This analysis, however, is made from the detailed notes of the author who was present at every session.
6. Doc. A/CONF.62/SR.15, June 26, 1974, pp. 5–7.
7. A provision was later inserted which suspended this requirement during the last two weeks of a session. *See* Conference Room Paper No. 3/Rev. 2, June 25, 1974.
8. Doc. A/CONF.62/L.1, p. 23.
9. Conference Room Paper No. 5, June 25, 1974.
10. A/CONF.62/SR.16, June 27, 1974, p. 8.
11. With the adoption of a new Rule 40, this became Rule 65. It reads:

> These rules of procedure may be amended by a decision of the Conference taken by the majority specified in paragraph 1 of Rule 39, after the General Committee has reported on the proposed amendment.

12. *See UN Report of the Committee on the Peaceful Uses of the Seabed and the Ocean Floor beyond the Limits of National Jurisdiction,* Vol. 2 (New York: United Nations, 1973).
13. *See* the excellent summary by the representative of Sri Lanka, Dr. Christopher Pinto, chairman of the Working Group of Subcommittee I to Committee I, July 11, 1974. A/CONF.62/C.1/SR.2
14. *See* the Summary Record for July 10, 1974. A/CONF.62/C.1/SR.1

15. For a list of UNCTAD documentation, *see* Doc. A/CONF.62/26, June 6, 1974.
16. *See* Doc. A/CONF.62/25 of May 22, 1974: *Economic Implications of Sea-Bed Mineral Development in the International Area: Report of the Secretary-General.*
17. The procedure employed in the working group was an interesting one. The three most controversial items were always tackled in the working group as a whole, but the third reading of the relatively noncontroversial items, Articles 1–8 and 10–21, was done in another small group which met generally after lunch before the working group as a whole convened. This obviously allowed efficient dispatch of a considerable amount of work while the working group went from confrontation to confrontation on the three most controversial items.
18. *See* UN Report of Committee on Seabed, Vol 2, pp 57–58.
19. First Committee, Informal. Conference Room Paper No. 3, July 25, 1974.
20. First Committee, Informal, C.1/CRP.4. The text reads:

> All activities of exploration of the area and of the exploitation of its resources and all other related activities including those of scientific research shall be conducted directly by the Authority.
>
> The Authority may, if it considers it appropriate, and within the limits it may determine, confer certain tasks to juridical or natural persons, through service contracts, or association or through any other such means it may determine which ensure its direct and effective control at all times over such activities.

21. First Committee, Informal: CRP.5/Add. 2, Alternative D:

> All activities of exploration and exploitation in the area shall be conducted in accordance with legal arrangements with the Authority pursuant to this convention, regulations included in this convention and those promulgated by the Authority pursuant to this convention.
>
> The Authority shall enter into legal arrangements for exploration and exploitation with contracting parties, groups of contracting parties and natural or juridical persons sponsored by such parties, without discrimination. Such parties or persons shall comply with this convention, regulations included in this convention and those promulgated by the Authority pursuant to this convention.

22. *See* Doc. A/CONF.62/C.1/L.3, August 5, 1974: *Draft Articles Considered by the Committee at its Informal Meetings,* pp. 6–7, 19.
23. *See* Doc. A/CONF.62/C.1/SR.5, pp. 9, 10.
24. This was especially true of the representative of Chile who, it appeared, wanted to forestall completely mineral production from the seabed.
25. *See* also, UNCTAD, *The Effects of Production of Manganese from the Sea-*

Bed . . . , Doc. TD/B/483, April 23, 1974; *The Effects of Possible Exploitation of the Sea-Bed on the Earnings of Developing Countries from Copper Exports,* Doc. TD/B/484, May 28, 1974; and *Exploitation of the Mineral Resources of the Sea-Bed beyond National Jurisdiction: Issues of International Commodity Policy,* Doc. TD/B/449/-Add. 1, June 26, 1973.

26. Doc. A/CONF.62/C.1/SR.9, pp. 15–16.
27. Doc. A/CONF.62/C.1/L.6. This was originally presented informally to the working group as Conference Room Paper 6, August 8, 1974.
28. Doc. A/CONF.62/C.1/L.8, originally Conference Room Paper 8, August 15, 1974.
29. Doc. A/CONF.62/C.1/L.8.
30. First Committee, Informal. Conference Room Paper No. 6, August 7, 1974, pp. 2–3.
31. Doc. A/CONF.62/C.1/L.9.
32. Doc. A/CONF.62/C.1/L.7, originally introduced as Conference Room Paper No. 7, August 15, 1974.
33. While no record of these debates appears in the documentation of the Conference, a characteristically excellent and detailed summary of the positions of groups on all items can be found in the third report of the chairman of the working group to the chairman of Committee I on August 19, 1974. *See* Doc. A/CONF.62/C.1/SR.14, pp. 4–11.
34. *See* Doc. A/CONF.62/C.1/SR.14, p. 15. (This is an inadequate summary of what was said.)
35. *See* Doc. A/CONF.62/C.1/SR.14.
36. Doc. A/CONF.62/C.1/SR.16.
37. *See also* the proposals introduced by Bulgaria, German Democratic Republic, Poland, and the U.S.S.R. (A/CONF.62/C.II/L.26) and all Eastern European States (A/CONF.62/C.II/L.11).
38. For this debate, *see* the Summary Records for July 22–23, 1974. A/CONF. 62/C-II/SR. 11–14.
39. This includes Argentina and Portugal declaring a preference for the 4000 m isobath.
40. This Coastal States Group was created before the "Evensen Group" or the Committee of Jurors under the chairmanship of the leader of the Norwegian delegation, in an attempt to bypass deadlock within Subcommittee II of the Seabed Committee. The difference here is that while it also included opponents of the economic zone concept the Coastal States Group did not. So far the Evensen Group has not formally presented any "packages" to the Conference.
41. Canada, Chile, Iceland, India, Indonesia, Mauritius, Mexico, New Zealand, and Norway.
42. *See* Press Release SEA/C/80, July 29, 1974.
43. Text of the statement of Leonard H. Legault to Committee III, July 16, 1974.
44. Statement of the representative of Norway in Plenary, July 2, 1974. Doc. A/CONF.62/SR.5, pp. 19–23.

45. Text of Canadian statement, p. 12.

46. Doc. A/CONF.62/C.3/L.6, July 31, 1974.

47. Doc. A/CONF.62/C.3/L.7, August 1, 1974.

48. Doc. A/CONF.62/C.3/L.4, July 23, 1974.

49. *See* John Knauss, "Developing the Freedom of Scientific Research Issue of the Law of the Sea Conference," *Ocean Development and International Law Journal,* Vol. 1, No. 1 (Spring 1973), pp. 93–120.

50. Statement of July 19, 1974. Doc. A/CONF.62/C.3/SR.8, pp. 5–7.

51. Text of the statement of the U.S. representative to Committee III, July 19, 1974, pp. 2–3. *See also* Doc. A/CONF.62/C.3/SR.8, pp. 2–5.

52. Summary of general debate, July 19, 1974. Doc. A/CONF.62/C.3/SR.9, pp. 23–24.

53. Doc. A/CONF.62/C.3/L.17.

54. Doc. A/CONF.62/C.2/L.82.

Chapter Two

Intergovernmental Dimensions of International Conferences

David A. Kay
International Organizations Research Project
American Society of International Law

Mr. Miles: Our second speaker is Professor David Kay, currently Director of the International Organizations Research Project, American Society of International Law.

Ed Miles has asked me to speak on the intergovernmental dimensions of international conferences. What I would like to do is to really give you a series of rules of thumb, rules of thumb of how one observes international conferences, and leave a considerable amount of time, really, for discussion as to whether these rules—rules really derived from looking at conferences other than LOS—have any application at all to the dynamics of LOS's negotiating process.

The first rule of thumb is, despite Ed's, I think, very well-founded advice that the General Assembly never again create an intergovernmental conference of the type that LOS is typical of, the advice is not likely to be taken. We are in a period of endemic international intergovernmental conferences, partly because of what I read in the *Wall Street Journal* took place at Caracas, but partly because I think it also tells us something about this endemic.

The range of international organizational activity in terms of these conferences really spans an area far larger than that. Ed mentioned that it started with the Stockholm conference on the environment. Really it goes beyond that. It started much earlier. You can think of the UNCTAD conferences on trade and development, the conferences on the peaceful uses of outer space for atomic energy, going down through environment, population, food, LOS, resources.

This year not only will you have a conference in Geneva on LOS but you will also have "The Year of the Woman," that is being celebrated with a conference on women's rights.

There is a story that occurred last September when the new Bolivian president arrived in New York. He met the secretary-general. In the course of his discussions, the secretary-general congratulated him on Bolivia's fine move of agreeing to host the conference of "The Year of the Woman."

The president was more than slightly disturbed. He had never heard of this commitment by his government. He immediately after the meeting raised the issue with his foreign minister. The foreign minister hadn't heard it. Sure enough, it was a commitment made by the previous government, not communicated to the present government, but "Yes, Virginia, there will be a conference on women's rights scheduled for this year more or less at the same time as LOS."

This endemic nature of intergovernmental conferences is something I am afraid we, as academics, and others as government representatives or representatives of private interest groups more or less are going to have to live with, Ed, despite your really very sound advice.

A second rule of thumb, the first being that these things are going to be around and we might as well get used to them, is that for large governments, governments the size of the United States and our European allies, the important international conference really takes place before the international conference.

The important LOS negotiations for the U.S.—important in terms of working out a detailed position—took place not at LOS, but took place, as I assume all of you know far better than I, before LOS. This is true of almost every one of these conferences, whether it be food, whether it be environment, whether it be population or UNCTAD. The important negotiations for a large government take place prior to the conference because of the number of bureaucratic interests mobilized within the government on any one of these thematic topics.

You take the recent food conference. The battle between Agriculture and State, for example, was fairly well documented in the press as a battle, although it wasn't entirely a battle, between Butz and Kissinger, was a battle of major proportions for contending U.S. interest groups.

As a result of this, another rule of thumb is that the U.S. really doesn't like, or at least most people in the U.S. government do not like, these conferences, these interbureaucratic bargaining relationships—whether it be food, or LOS, or population. They are really very difficult. They expend a lot of bureaucratic capital, a lot of blood, and a lot of time, and you would prefer to dump them.

With only one or two exceptions, these conferences have been opposed by the U.S. when first proposed in the U.N. General Assembly, and almost right down to the day on which they were convened the U.S. has stood against them.

Food is one example of an exception to this, and it is an exception that points up another rule of thumb about large government behavior; that is, within large governments, some bureaucracy, some large bureaucratic group, sees some interest in having intergovernmental conferences if it is a way of their getting some domination, some policy space in an area which is otherwise controlled by another domestic bureaucratic group. In the case of food, it was a way in which the State Department had an opportunity for exercising some control because of its believed monopoly over international relations in an area in which the Department of Agriculture was contending that it had the sole prerogative of setting U.S. policy in that area.

This turns out almost in every one of these areas. A bureaucratic group that is contending for domestic power may at times see advantage to taking it to the international route as a way of extending its control or contending for control.

Another rule of thumb that flows, really as a subdivision of this, is big governments almost always behave as dinosaurs at intergovernmental conferences. They are too locked into positions by the preconference that takes place back home to have much flexibility. This means that more often than not, influence flows to states that otherwise would not be very likely to have very much influence at these conferences as compared to the United States, the European states, or even the Soviet Union.

Stockholm is a good example, although I know you can think of many examples out of LOS. But in the environmental negotiations, the U.S. was so locked into so many positions—vis-a-vis Department of Defense, vis-a-vis the Council on Environmental Quality, the Environmental Protection Agency—and it had to defend those positions because it was committed to them by previous treaties agreed to at home that it could exercise very little influence on major issues that developed during the conference because it was too busy fighting issues it was already committed to. Consequently, a number of states exercised far greater influence at Stockholm than one would have expected from external circumstances for those states to have exercised.

Another rule of thumb is that traditional intergovernmental diplomatic methods and skills really are very difficult to apply at most of these intergovernmental conferences, and this is also, I think, a reason that most departments of state, external affairs, foreign affairs, really do not like these conferences. They are difficult to apply because first the subject matter tends to be thematic, and thematic outside of the normal foreign affairs range of issues. There are very few foreign affairs officers who feel completely at home with things like the law of the sea, food issues, population issues, peaceful uses of outer space and atomic energy. It brings a lot of people in with technical expertise which is not well understood by traditional foreign affairs officers and they feel lost. The subject matter itself disorients them.

A second reason is that it mobilizes interest groups, and this is particularly true of nongovernmental interest groups, which foreign affairs officers feel uncomfortable with. In environmental discussions as well as in LOS, one major group has been, for example, scientists. Foreign affairs officers in most foreign affairs bureaucracies simply do not mix very well with scientists.

Scientists tend to view politics as getting in the way of real science. We scientists could settle all these issues if only the politics would keep out. The foreign affairs officer tends to view a scientist as naive; if they don't watch what they step on, it is going to turn out to be the German Democratic Republic or the People's Republic of China, or South Africa, or what have you, or they are going to screw up our relationships with the Israelis. You have these scientists mucking around. Non-governmental organizations as a general lot which are brought into almost all of these thematic conferences tend to be viewed as very close enemies by most departments of state, foreign affairs, type of bureaucrats.

A third reason that the traditional methods do not seem to apply very well is often the objectives are not the normal objectives that one sees as being the end of the diplomatic method. Quite often the objective for a thematic conference such as food or population or environment is really mainly consciousness raising, bringing an issue to attention, mobilizing domestic concern for it.

That is not the traditional objective of the diplomatic method, and it is one that most foreign affairs bureaucracies feel very uncomfortable with.

Very seldom in these conferences—and I think LOS is an exception here—have the institutions and lawmaking procedure been the major objective of the conference itself. This is an objective that is better suited, by its very nature, to the foreign affairs officer.

Let me briefly say a few things about the operational aspects dimensions of these intergovernmental conferences that I think is true on a comparative basis.

In terms of lifestyle, they typically follow a three-part existence. About 90 percent of the conference itself is sluggish, sluggish to the extent of looking even from the inside as being a case of nonactivity. The last 10 percent of the conference, 5 to 10 percent, is one of a real rush to completion, of getting everything done before the hotel throws us out. We run out of our per diem. Our wives demand that we return home, or whatever the excuse that you can hear around these conferences, and it is amazing, as you go to various ones, the excuses one has for why you have to be home at X date really do start to sound very similar.

Here, again, knowing what went on at Caracas only from the *Wall Street Journal,* maybe there are some other reasons why people had to get out of Caracas in the end.

But I think this rush to completion aspect is really an aspect of the decision-making process of all of these conferences. It reflects the need of large governmental bureaucracies for flexibility in negotiations, and if you are in a department of state or foreign affairs or external affairs and you are locked in by domestic treaties, alliances with other bureaucracies, as to what your position has to be.

You can only claim exception from those treaties under the most dire of circumstances, and one of the most dire of circumstances is that we have to conclude something by 12:00 midnight on the 22nd of May or we get kicked out of the hotel and you can appeal for exception from normal rules. All good members of foreign services know how to write those telegrams justifying the action taken because something had to be done and we couldn't get full explanation back to you or wait for your concurrence.

That seems to be a recurring theme. It started in the first UNCTAD conference, really, in which the whole UNCTAD institution was designed literally in the last thirty-six hours under the threat that something had to be done before we get to Geneva.

If I were to be at all optimistic about what is likely to take place this spring in Geneva, the only source of optimism I can find is not the assurance of the Department of State that everything is right with the world, but the assurance that if something is not done by the day on which you get kicked out of the Palais or the Intercontinental, nothing is going to be accomplished. In many ways, I think that is the truest way of getting something accomplished.

The third aspect of this is the follow-up. Almost all of these conferences have left a large amount of activity to be done after the end of the conference. It is amazing, when you look at them, that you can almost plug them into exactly the same boxes when the same things are pushed over either to the next Assembly section, the next ECOSOC session, or some other interim group. In really no case that I can think of can you find a conference that has completed its full agenda in the time in which the conference was held.

So it has almost this peaking lifestyle. With regard to the politics of them, I think there are some similarities here. One of the first is that issues tend to get interconnected by these conferences, which is another reason that foreign affairs bureaucracies in general do not like them.

There are two sorts of interconnections. One is the interconnection with issues outside the normal subject domain of the conference itself. These are issues like Israel, South Africa, the German Democratic Republic question, what used to be the People's Republic of China question, issues that arise from conference to conference on every occasion, and they are interconnected regardless of what is the connection between population and whether or not Israel is within or without the group of the Middle Eastern states, or Israel's policy with regard to the West Bank.

Those sorts of issues always arise, and the very nature of the conference, having to decide on what its rules of procedure are, who are its members who get entitled to credentials, allow those types of interconnections to be made.

There is another type of interconnection that is made within conferences and these are subject matter interconnections, interconnections between, for example, nuclear pollution in the environmental conference, between nuclear pollution and creating a bureau on human settlements, in which, in order to trade votes, Country A is interested in a human settlements fund, Country B is

interested in having nuclear pollution as or not as a rival aspect of the environmental program, so you trade those sorts of issues.

The very nature of a conference in which you have a package of
issues put together, you take votes on them, allow these types of interconnections to be made, and they are present in every intergovernmental conference of
this type.

A second type of political relationship that runs out is the one of
group politics. Group politics is an aspect of parliamentary diplomacy. It is
certainly found within the UN, and even in normal General Assembly sessions.
It tends to be more present in intergovernmental organizations, and partly,
I think, in intergovernmental conferences. I think this has been a learning
experience.

Starting with UNCTAD, where the Group of 77 got its original
name, they learned that there was a certain advantage to holding together, certain
natural leaders arose, the conferences tended to come every year or every two
years, the same people appeared, the same governments instructed delegates in
the same way, so you got really a group dynamic.

It is not just the Group of 77, or 105, however you want to count
them now; it is other groups as well, the Western European group, the Common
Market group now has more or less a formal procedure in approaching these conferences which assures a type of group politics.

There is a transferrability, also, of rules and procedures. Ed mentioned the voting procedure at LOS. There are precedents for this, at least within
UNCTAD. But from looking at the two, what goes in UNCTAD is a conciliation
procedure that looks remarkably similar to LOS, and I would almost be willing to
bet that if you were to look at these closely, you would find that some secretary
member indeed had before him at some time the conciliation procedures for
UNCTAD and was prepared to step forward with draft rules that directly related
to UNCTAD's experience in this area.

It would be interesting to hear Ed's comments. My view in looking
at the UNCTAD conciliation procedure, though, is that if, in fact, this is what is
followed at LOS, one's hope of having anything substantive accomplished is not
very good because those procedures have not proved to be, at least in my view,
very workable.

Another aspect of the politics of these types of conference is that
the skill of the secretariat tends to prove decisive. This is partly because the
natural leaders, the large states, tend to be immobilized.

I might as well dash out my last rule of thumb under politics, and
that is that at most of these conferences, the U.S. tends to be inept, and "inept"
is often too polite for the conduct of U.S. diplomacy in these intergovernmental
organizations. It is inept because the domestic treaties that bind its policy positions allow little reasonable room for flexibility and for leadership. It depends on
who is there at what time speaking on what issue.

The comic opera performance that took place at the World Food Conference at Rome is just one example, and you can find it in almost every one of these intergovernmental conferences, inept U.S. diplomacy caused by conflicting bureaucratic groups in the U.S. domestic process.

But this immobilization process of the United States means that the secretariat is often the broker and performs the most crucial function in putting together what is to emerge at the end of the conference.

A final aspect I would like to mention in terms of rules of thumb is really the objectives of these conferences, and what can be said about the intergovernmental dimensions of them.

I think the most common theme that runs through all of these conferences is that if they are successful at all, and I think there is a great deal of legitimate dispute as to whether they, in fact, are successful at all, it tends to be in the education and consciousness-raising category. They mobilize people to thinking about aspects of issues that they might not otherwise have thought about.

Without a Rome conference, it is, I think, reasonable to contend that the secretary of state probably would not have thought about, or certainly not have thought as much as he has about food. It tends to provoke things onto the agenda of people who otherwise would not be there, and that is true not only with secretaries of state, but I think with average newspaper readers as well. The Rome Food Conference was rather successful in that area.

In terms of institution-making, the history of these conferences is not at all encouraging. The institutions, by and large, that they have created have not long survived the initial momentum of them. UNCTAD, I would say, is hardly in existence as a vital institution today. I think the environmental conference, the mechanism of UNEP, is in serious disarray now. The chaos around Nairobi and the Nairobi operation in general is not one to encourage one about the capability of building governmental organizations at these conferences.

We will have to wait to see what comes out of food, but my guess is that the lesson here is that it is not likely to be much better than what came out of UNCTAD or UNEP.

In terms of lawmaking, few of these conferences have attempted this task, and I think that is one reason LOS is so difficult. It is not just the complexity of the issues, although I certainly agree with Ed and Bob Friedheim that the decisional matrix of something like this is staggering in terms of the calculus of how one would work it out, but it is also just the very procedure itself.

Large conferences of this type, as distinct from other smaller lawmaking conferences, are not a form likely to do this very well.

The final function and objective often aspired to but never successfully done, in my view, is in terms of wealth distribution, and to accent that that tends to be a part of LOS, here there is absolutely no reason to be encouraged by this. Intergovernmental organization conferences of this type simply have not been successful in their very minor attempts at creating mechanisms for distributing global wealth or changing patterns of distribution of wealth, and for reasons that should be rather obvious in terms of the mechanisms, the structures, that underlie wealth-distribution patterns. They are simply not easily tapped by global conferences of this type or easily changed.

So what I have attempted to do here is lay out some rules of thumb which I hope later will provoke some discussion from those of you who know far more than I do about LOS, as to whether they are typical of LOS negotiations, or whether there are reasons to believe that, for example, the U.S. is not inept in LOS but is a shining diplomatic leader of the community, able to fix on an objective and move flexibly toward it.

Chapter Three

Transnational and Transgovernmental Dimensions of International Conferences

Joseph S. Nye, Jr.
Center for International Affairs
Harvard University

Mr. Nye: David Kay has described power in conference diplomacy. It is worth going back before the era of conference diplomacy to have some idea of what rulemaking used to be like. After all, the rules that we are now talking about amending at the Law of the Sea Conference are essentially derived from the days when the British made the rules and the British navy enforced them. Rules were made by the strong, and strength was roughly equivalent with military strength.

This traditional way of rulemaking has been affected by two very long-run changes, since the days of British hegemony. The first change is in the role of force in international politics, force being somewhat less acceptable and somewhat more costly for large countries to apply than it used to be. A second change is the increased use of multilateral diplomacy for a whole variety of issues. This stems from two sources (1) the complexity of issues and the large number of players involved, and (2) the emphasis on democracy and participation as a basic norm which is embedded in world political culture today.

I think this is worth stressing, because the trends that Ed and Dave described, the trends that we see in the UN conferences on ecology, or population, or food, and of course LOS, are not new, they have deeper roots. After all, the 1930s conference on the law of the sea at The Hague was an interesting departure from tradition and one in which, although there was almost agreement on a 3-mile limit, in a sense seriously undermined the 3-mile limit. The very fact of allowing states to bring the issue into question weakened the ability of the hegemonic power to enforce the rules. As Swartzrauber has put it, it was quite a change from tradition when a landlocked state like Czechoslovakia could have a say on where the limits in the sea would be.

This political process we are involved in, the process of conference diplomacy, reflects some deeper, underlying trends. It is not merely a recent aberration or misuse of power by the less developed countries, as Ambassador Scali has implied.

The politics of conference diplomacy are a special political process. They are politics in which influence in the conference is not the same as power outside the conference. This has been well described for the '58 and '60 conferences by Bob Friedheim. Ed Miles has just given us, I think, a very excellent description of it for the current LOS.

In some studies I did on the UN Conference on Trade and Development, I looked at an index of power inside of UNCTAD and an index of power outside of UNCTAD. One of the interesting things was that the United States turned out to be the most powerful country both inside and outside of UNCTAD, but its influence inside of UNCTAD was primarily negative in a blocking sense. Power in the conference diplomacy on trade which UNCTAD represented was very imperfectly related to power in the outside environment, whether it be military power or economic power. In a correlation which ranges from minus 1 to plus 1, the correlation was .4. In other words, there is a relationship to power in the outside world, but a very imperfect relationship. To put it another way, conference diplomacy is a power game played with a very special set of rules. The more specific the institution in its functions, usually the less discrepancy there is between power inside and outside the organization.

One of the dimensions of conference diplomacy is transgovernmental interactions. We do not want to ask merely, "What is the power of a state inside and outside a conference?" We should also ask the question, "What is a state in the first place? What does it mean that there is a national position?" Many states and many national positions are composites of a variety of interests. Ed Miles describes in his paper very clearly the conference within a conference that goes on in the U.S. delegation in Caracas, and presumably will continue in Geneva. What the conference diplomacy does is bring together similar parts of different states that would otherwise be kept quite separate, and this allows the possibility of what we call transgovernmental relations, or interactions between subunits of different governments acting with some degree of autonomy.

One can think of the world, then, as composed of a whole variety of potential coalitions, some of which cross national boundaries. For example, American farmers had much more in common with European consumers than they did with European farmers in the 1960s, and the U.S. secretary of agriculture really had more in common with the European finance ministers than with European ministers of agriculture in terms of the types of coalitions they might form. But national sovereignty usually prevents these coalitions, in fact, from being formed. They are regarded as disloyal in some cases, and there are just not chances to interact in others. Institutions are usually set up along common lines, not across them.

What conference diplomacy in international organizations does is provide two things. It provides physical proximity and an agenda where ostensibly separate units have a chance to come together, and it provides, to some extent, an aura of legitimacy for the interactions that do occur.

The United States government sends delegations to some 600 conferences a year. It is interesting to note that less than half the staff of those conference delegations comes from the State Department. There are many other agencies which are involved and have direct interaction with counterparts abroad. Similarly, there is a high degree of involvement of the private interests on these delegations, or as observers.

This is not necessarily a bad thing in the sense that this type of interaction between subunits of governments is probably necessary to manage complex interdependence, particularly among the more advanced industrial societies. These transgovernmental interactions, in a sense, are part of the essential machinery of government for interdependence. But at the Law of the Sea Conference there is a different type of effect because of a third major change in the long-term politics of international rulemaking.

The third change is that the interests of the maritime powers today are far more complex than they were in the era of the British leadership in the ocean area. The Law of the Sea Conference is not just the conference of national positions, but one which is crosscut by a number of potential coalitions in which functional groups share information and coordinate responses to opportunities, whether it be the navies which keep each other closely informed, or scientists, or different types of fishery people, or ecologists, or whatever the various clubs which characterize and crosscut national positions at the conference. This crosscutting of interests and sharing of information has an effect upon negotiations. In a sense, there is a tension between these functional interests and the national positions in the negotiations.

There are different degrees of transgovernmental interaction, and such interactions are limited by the amount of attention paid by top political leadership. This varies in several ways. It varies with the type of government. There are some governments which are not very permissive about this. There are other governments which are quite permissive. It also varies over time. As top political attention is focused on or away from an area, transgovernmental interactions go up or down. This is clearly demonstrated by studies that have been done in the international monetary area.

Transgovernmental interactions are also related to the functional specificity of the organization. The more functionally specific or narrow the organization, the greater the opportunities for these transgovernmental interactions. But they also occur in large conferences, and one of the things that we can ask is, "What effect do they have on Miles' basic question of whether you have successful negotiations coming out of such conferences?"

They probably have a rather odd effect. I think they tend to reinforce the tendency of conference diplomacy to redistribute political influence toward the less-developed countries. It has often been said, for example, that international organizations have an effect of overcoming the world's feudal communications pattern. Johan Galtung, a Norwegian sociologist, has likened the traditional communication patterns among nations to a structure in which the top countries deal separately with different parts of the bottom, but the bottom countries do not deal with each other. Conference diplomacy tends to overcome that. Look at the efforts of a number of the Latin American countries or Iran to extend their jurisdictions in the 1930s. Each of them had to suffer the efforts of the large countries to push back their extensions separately, whereas, in the current period of international conferences, they are able to reinforce each other's position.

But there is another aspect besides the national positions, and that is the way that conference diplomacy, through transgovernmental interactions, allows the poor states to some extent to penetrate the richer states and stronger states. In other words, you don't find the usual pattern of the rich states penetrating the poor, but the poor penetrating the rich. This is related to the increased complexity of the positions of the interests in the rich states and, in fact, the usually much simpler range of interests in a number of the weaker states.

The poorer states can use conference diplomacy to get allies in and among the richer states. Less developed countries could see, and indeed were told, that the U.S. oceans policy position in 1970 was not fully fixed; that they had potential allies within the rich societies for their view of how they wanted ocean space to be organized.

One of the implications of this is that there is certain danger that these transgovernmental interactions will reinforce the incongruence between power inside and outside of the conference diplomacy, and that too great an incongruence in power inside and outside of the conference diplomacy leads to large risks of failure.

From the global point of view, one could argue that conference diplomacy is not a bad thing if it gives a certain amount of assets for influence to the weaker states of the world. After all, it is not such a bad idea to let the poorer or weaker have a few more chips in playing the game. But presumably there is a danger if the chips are stacked too differently from outside the conference chamber in that the strong may either quit the game or, indeed, even overturn the board. Force does still exist. There still are residual elements of traditional ways in which rules are established. Unless there is a sense of the limits that are necessary for moderation in the use of the various aspects of conference diplomacy, the great danger is that there will be a loss of any achievements from conference diplomacy.

The trend toward large conference diplomacy can become quite a dangerous game, as Ed Miles has suggested, and the transgovernmental interactions that occur at large conferences act to reinforce rather than to countervail these dangerous aspects. In a sense my presentation is a footnote to very able descriptions you have heard about the government-to-government positions in these conferences. My conclusion is that the transgovernmental interactions reinforce these dangerous aspects rather than countervail them.

Discussion and Questions

Mr. Hosni: My name is Hosni, and I am presently with the Woods Hole Oceanographic Institution.

I attended the Caracas convention in the capacity of advising a number of Middle Eastern countries, and I represented the state of Yemen. I state these qualifications not to justify my intervention in trying to reflect a different point of view about the Group of 77, a different point of view from what has been advanced by the first speaker. I certainly do not intend to do that or torture you with such a different one.

I only want to point out that there was a particular trend regarding straits that has never been brought out, in the morning session or in this afternoon's session, and the trend hinged on a differentiation between the uses and the regime of the straits that control entrance into enclosed seas, and others that do not.

Of course, I am well informed about the position advanced this morning by a certain speaker about the difficulty of definition of what is a strait that is used for international navigation and what is not. Also, I am informed about any position that hinges on whether certain uses are acceptable or not for states controlling straits.

I only want to say that some of the uses of straits that control entrance into semienclosed seas have not been fully appreciated and have not been fully discussed. This was a trend which had actually been advanced in Caracas, but not very strongly, only because there was not so much paperwork that has been produced on it.

Mr. Yalkovsky: My name is Yalkovsky and I am a marine geologist at Buffalo State. I would like to make just one minor comment before I ask my question.

The comment is that some dinosaurs were very fleet of foot, no more than two feet high, very agile and maneuverable, but the question of Israel and the common heritage of mankind has come up both this morning and this afternoon.

What I am concerned about is some aspect of what happened with regard to UNESCO in November and its relationship to the nature of the seabed treaty beyond the limits of national jurisdiction. It used to be said that the great strength of the United Nations was in the technical agencies, UNESCO, ICAO, IMCO, and other agencies of this sort; that its weaknesses were in the political aspects in the General Assembly.

In November the United Nations denied archaeological funds to Israel from UNESCO, despite the fact that even United Nations observers said there was no justification for this. Apparently it was done on the basis of Realpolitik. If a seabed treaty is agreed upon, whether it is a treaty dealing with licensing or whether it is an exploration and development unit under international or intergovernmental control, what assurance is there that these other agencies cannot be manipulated politically. A large nation, as Professor Nye pointed out, is certainly not going to be frozen out. It has the clout to prevent this. But what about unpopular smaller nations, not only Israel, but any other nation that falls outside of the group of—it may be 77 now—but by the tyranny of those who have the votes?

What assurance is there that when agreement is reached upon some sort of treaty that any particular nation can have confidence that it will benefit later; that it cannot then be frozen out?

Mr. Kay: I think there are two answers. One is an easy answer that there is no assurance. I think that is the correct answer.

I think the more fundamental answer is that—and it goes beyond what we can do here, although I would be glad to discuss it with you later—I think what we are currently witnessing in the international organization system is what is really a civil war, and its foot is at the foot of most civil wars, really, and that is the relationship between power, representation, and the division thereof between them, and we are currently seeing that take place in the international organization network.

But it is a subject that goes way beyond here, and in effect, what happened to Israel, what happened at the recent UN General Assembly session as well, was in many ways that type of maneuvering and civil war between what is the proper relationship between external power, internal power, and representation in the organs, and the sniping and shooting that goes with any civil war is going to take place.

It really is a breakdown in many ways of the fabric and the substructure of an international organization created in a very different world, in the period right after 1945, and it means that on issues like Israel, like South Africa, you can give no assurance that what may be viewed by one group or another group as an injustice is not going to take place.

Mr. Miles: Paul, did you want to speak to this point?

Just let me make a comment here about assurances. Just to finish it up, with respect to the law of the sea treaty, obviously one set of questions that is consistently being addressed by all participants, and most consistently perhaps by the U.S. and the EEC countries, the Group of 77 and the Committee I on the seabed regime is what assurances we will have for the future that the conditions will not change at will, will not change capriciously, et cetera, and obviously it is very difficult to give assurances if what you focus on is purely voting majorities.

But I must ask you to remember that in most of the history of the United Nations, it has, in fact, been the United States which has controlled the majority, and what is currently happening is a shift in the distribution of influence within large deliberative assemblies and the fact that the United States and the EEC countries no longer do so.

This raises the question, then, of what is the response or what probable responses are there to minorities in these organizations which object to governmental decisions. In the case of the Soviet Union around Korea, it would have been withdraw, but the Uniting for Peace Resolution was never worked out in detail, as had been implied at that time, precisely because the cost would have been too high.

In today's world, I think the cost of the response of the minorities, since they are the ones with the capabilities, would probably be to withdraw resources from organizational programs, and that if these organizations cannot then garner other means of support from the traditional ones, there will be increasingly difficult situations with regard to the programs to be carried out. There are no effective, automatic assurances that one's interests in the future will always be taken into account. One is playing a game, in effect, on the basis of second-best solutions for limited periods of time.

Even if there were a law of the sea treaty this year, it would not settle the question for another generation. I think the point that this raises is that the international system as a whole, and organizations like the United Nations, must seek to include within regimes that are created some provisions for continuous review; otherwise, they quickly become inoperative and result in more conflict than they are designed to solve.

There have been three individuals I saw previously. First, Paul Lapointe, second, Don McKernan, and third up here.

Mr. Lapointe: Thank you, Mr. Chairman.

Mr. Chairman, I would just like to interject a little note of controversy perhaps in this procedure.

Mr. Miles: Good.

Mr. Lapointe: Directing my comment really to Mr. Kay, who described a very strange kind of being which he calls a diplomat or foreign service officer, or something like that, who seems to be pursuing objectives of his own without any relation whatsoever to the facts of life or anything. He doesn't like scientists. He cannot stand for certain things. I am not too sure how he can justify this in light of my own personal experience at Caracas.

Could he tell me, perhaps, how he views a foreign service officer, a diplomat, or whatever he calls it, and what kind of a role is that person supposed to play, if it hasn't got anything to do with fisheries or with mining or petroleum, or what have you.

I was a bit shocked. I know that diplomats are in the minority here, although we are a majority of the conference. I don't want to defend only a minority cause, but I am a bit struck by this sort of concept, which I have heard in other places, describing diplomats as people who have nothing to do with reality, pursuing their own objectives in the conference, playing their own little procedural games, and apparently doing things which have nothing to do with their national interests.

Mr. Kay: That sounds like we met the same person.

What I was describing I don't think is a myth. What I was describing was an empirical composite, really, of having looked at at least half of the last twelve international conferences and the foreign service representatives there.

I don't think I described it as being out of touch with reality, because I think it is in touch with what they view as reality, the reality created by their own bureaucratic establishments. I am not really sure how we reconcile two different empirical bases, your base which sees foreign service officers as being in touch with and friendly with scientists, et cetera, and my own. We obviously both touch different parts of the beast, and you notice that he has a trunk and I notice that he has a tail. Maybe it is the same elephant, or maybe it is not.

My description certainly was not of someone who is out of touch with reality, but of someone who has his own objectives defined by his own bureaucratic organization, which makes it very difficult for him to deal with a different set of objectives in other bureaucratic organizations.

Mr. McKernan: Thank you, Mr. Chairman.

First I want to agree with Paul Lapointe. I take exception to the remarks of Dr. Kay.

As I have seen them, at least, in the United States government, where I participated in events leading up to the Law of the Sea Conference, it seems to me a great deal of effort was made to make it possible to negotiate and to bring together the various elements of the United States government.

I think he may be right that this is much more difficult in large governments, but I can tell him and the rest of the conference that a great deal more time is spent on it in large governments as well.

What I really wanted to say, Mr. Chairman, I wanted to chide you, my colleague, Dr. Miles, by pointing out that on the first page of your 92-page opus you start by talking about the meager results of the conference, and yet you take 92 pages to analye these meager results. I would rather remind you and some of my colleagues of some of the remarks made by Mr. Warioba this morning that, in fact, there were a number of things accomplished at Caracas, not in final negotiating results, but at least in identifying the issues rather clearly, as your paper does very well, indeed, I might say.

I hope you would agree with me that it would not be possible to draw up such a comprehensive and interesting and important table as you have drawn up without a Caracas conference.

The other serious question I wanted to pose to Dr. Miles was that in his paper he does not address the question that I suspect he discussed in his role as a nongovernment person in Caracas, and that is the question of how various players in this game see the alternative to failure at the conference.

To some of us who have been involved, one of the things that keeps us going is that when we look at the other side of the coin—that is, when we look at failure—it looks so bad and really so awful for the world in the decade or two to come, that this keeps us going, keeps our hopes up, although I think my views on the discussions thus far would be more along the lines of Ambassador Warioba than John Norton Moore of my own delegation; that is to say, I am not as optimistic that we have crossed the mountain and are going down the other side.

But at the same time, looking at the alternatives to failure, it seems to me important that my own country and other countries at the conference try with renewed vigor to reach agreement. I would appreciate your comments on that very important question. Thank you.

Mr. Miles: Those are fair questions, Don. The meager results refers to what Dr. Johnston calls the official goals of the conference; that is, the negotiation of a treaty or treaties establishing a regime for the oceans. On that score, I think the results were meager.

On the argument, which is not dealt with at any length or systematically in the paper, on what other contributions there might have been at Caracas—and I frankly did not do so because just describing what did happen led me to 92 pages, and I was a little scared of what my colleagues would say if I wrote any more—this is admittedly a very serious and important question on which the conference then comes out much better. I would give it a much higher score.

With respect to clarifying the issues on a number of items—in particular items in Committee 1, in Committee 3, and even also in Committee 2—the conference Committee 2, and Ambassador Aguilar in particular, deserve high marks for finishing the preparatory work of the Sea-Bed Committee. I regard the Sea-Bed Committee, the Subcommittee 2, as having performed miserably, and

it therefore delayed the work that could have been done in the course of substantive negotiations by having completed that preparatory work last summer in
Caracas.

But on the score then of clarifying the issues, pointing out exactly
where the differences lie, identifying what needs to be done, one would have to
say the results were not meager.

There are still in my mind many questions about whether one can
move from the clarifications of Caracas to more substantive results as defined by
the official goals of the conference, given the dynamics of that international
conference. I think this remains to be demonstrated, and that is where my pessimism lies.

With regard to the alternatives—and we will get to this in some detail
with Doug Johnston's paper, and I deliberately did not deal with them in mine
because Doug had been assigned that for Thursday morning—I am not sure, Don,
that this view that failure, the production of no regime, is a disaster worse than
that reflects the attitude of a large number of delegations at the meetings.

I think people make very hardheaded calculations about what their
interests are, how much they will gain in the short run and how much they may
lose. When you begin to look at it that way, no treaty may not be so bad for a
number of people, including certain interests in the United States. So I am not
sure that we ought to be sanguine when we begin, as we will on Thursday, to
discuss the question of alternatives to failure.

I am not sure that failure presents sufficient incentive to a sufficient
number of delegations, including the delegation of the United States, to make
them change positions rather drastically. I think this may be the difference
between us.

Mr. Sacco: My name is Sacco. I am from the University of Siena in Italy.

I am puzzled because two words are used synonymously while they
are not. Sometimes we say that the object of the Caracas conference was a new
law for the ocean. Sometimes we say a new law for the seas. From my point of
view it is not exactly the same thing, because I happen to come from a country
which has something like 10,000 kilometers of coast without touching any ocean.

This poses a problem, because there are seas like the Red Sea—and I
am grateful to Mr. Hosni for raising the point—which totally depend on straits.
In the Mediterranean, my country depends on the one side on Gibraltar and on
the canal, of course, for all of its traffic. There are other countries which are
dependent. Yugoslavia, for instance, is dependent on Italy, and the Eastern Mediterranean is dependent on Italy and Tunisia.

The problem of innocent passage through straits, or unimpeded transit, is for us quite an important problem. The definition itself is quite an important problem. The type of regime that is being sought reminds me of certain
things that happened in the European Economic Community. There is a kind of

supernational, in that case, body that established regulations and characteristics over what can be done and what cannot be done, and this is sometimes very dangerous.

I think we should discuss that. I was very negatively impressed by Mr. Lapointe's definition of what unimpeded transit is, because once established, then every ship of every flag has a right to pass through straits which come into territorial waters within that definition. That is not enough.

If I might tell you a story, you were never able for years to buy any gas kitchen made in Italy in any country of the Community because there was an officer in charge to check if that kitchen could pollute and kill people. They took two or three years to check that thing, and this was a way of discriminating against the Common Market through a technical device, which is very similar to the control that the coastal state could impose on tankers, for instance, to see if they can pollute or if they cannot pollute.

If we give discretionary power to national bureaucracies of the coastal states to check if the passage is innocent or not, or if it is to be impeded or not, just by mere bureaucratic delay this can become very dangerous. So I would like to know if, in the opinion of the people who were at Caracas, the problem of the definition of what innocent passage is has been sufficiently discussed, and also who has to prove innocence? Is the ship to prove that it is innocent, or is it up to the coastal state to prove that it has not been innocent after it has passed through?

Mr. Miles: I am in great difficulty here. You have raised a question which exercises delegations at great length, and I just received a note from the director of the Law of the Sea Institute that I am to call a coffee break right now and to announce that small discussion groups will begin at 3:30 and that sheets showing group assignments are available on the registration desk.

But I have incurred a further obligation because I recognized a gentleman here to ask a question before the break, and this is not a ploy, but we just do not have time at the moment to respond to the very difficult question that you raised. Perhaps it can be continued in whatever group you attend, or on successive days. At least it is in the record.

Please, one last question.

Mr. Finlay: My name is Finlay. I just raise a point that I think should be discussed in the small groups or elsewhere.

I am a bit disappointed that in a discussion on the dynamics of conference diplomacy there would be no discussion of the dynamics of existing rights under the international law as it now stands.

I have prepared a table on the basis of State Department reports which shows that 50 percent of the coastlines of the world are held by seven coastal nations, and 75 percent by twenty-five coastal nations. Ninety-two of the smallest countries in the United Nations control two-thirds of the voting, with less than 10 percent of the population of the United Nations, and those ninety-two nations control only a very small percentage of the coasts of the world and, correspondingly, of the continental margins.

I think it is perfectly obvious that unless the majority considers the existing rights of the countries that have the extensive coastlines, you will have no viable convention coming out of the conference.

Another point, of course, is the decision of the International Court of Justice in the Iceland fisheries case, which said that Iceland's unilateral action of extending its fishing jurisdiction fifty miles was contrary to international law. That presents a dynamic which protects the existing rights of the distant water fisheries nations, which I do not think can be ignored in a determination of the rights of the coastal states within the economic zone. Thank you.

Mr. Miles: That, too, obviously would give rise to a considerable and spirited discussion, and I remain in the position which I have described.

I may add that it is suggested that in the discussion groups, among questions raised, perhaps participants might give some attention to the following three questions:

First, what organizational changes might be considered which would speed up the progress of negotiations in Geneva.

Second, if it is true that there is high conflict on the details of a settlement, as well as on the general concept which should guide it, how do we go about negotiating the entire package simultaneously? Is it possible to break up the package? How? With what consequences? And in what order should issues be considered?

Finally, how should public and governmental expectations be handled in the event that the Geneva meeting will not be able to produce anything near what was officially described as the objectives of the Third United Nations Conference on the Law of the Sea? How do we deal with the problem of declining confidence in the UN and the Law of the Sea Conference as a result of what will be perceived to be failure, given the rather high-flown propaganda with which this activity was sold to governments initially?

Thank you for your patience.

Part III

Ocean Resources Issue at the Law of the Sea Conference and Beyond

Chairman
Francis T. Christy, Jr.
Resources for the Future, Inc.
Washington, D.C.

Mr. Christy: Good morning, everyone. Today we turn to the session of the conference dealing with the natural resources in the oceans.

I have the feeling that the Law of the Sea Conference itself has been somewhat misleading. There has probably been an excessive amount of focus on and attention paid to the Law of the Sea Conference itself. This tends to create a belief, on the one hand, that if the conference is a successful one it will resolve all of our problems, and then we can go home and do our own things, or to believe, on the other hand, that if the conference is a failure, we will end up in ultimate and absolute chaos.

Neither of these views is correct. Even if the conference is highly successful it will still not resolve many of the problems of the management and the distribution of the oceans' wealth, and if the conference is a failure, it will not necessarily lead to chaos and not perhaps to much greater conflicts than we might likely have with a successful conference.

The problems of the management and the distribution of the oceans' wealth are extremely complicated, and we should not expect to be able to resolve those problems in the brief span of years that we have had available for the preparatory sessions and for the UN conference itself.

We are really just on the threshold of a major transition regarding the law of the sea, a transition, to put it somewhat simplistically, from the principle of the freedom of the seas, in which there was no satisfactory authority or jurisdiction, to a period in which we will have established some kind of authority and jurisdiction over the oceans' resources.

And this is not an easy transition to make, by any means, and not one that can be resolved in the space of the ten years or so in which we have been dealing with the issues.

We are really in the process of dismantling the principle of the freedom of the seas, which after all, took something like 100 years to become established. And we cannot really expect to dismantle that principle and arrive at a substitute in the very immediate future.

The problems are really too great to be resolved fully by the Law of the Sea Conference. Now, this does not mean that the conference cannot have some value, at least value in terms of educating the people with regard to the kinds of the issues that are important and in their interests. This is what we are turning to today, to try to elucidate a little more clearly and a little more carefully some of the problems and the complexities that exist with regard to the management and the distribution of the seas' wealth, with the hope that by doing so we may be able to arrive at some kind of improved understanding, which will in the long run help to facilitate rather than to impede the eventual achievement of better systems for the management and distribution of the seas' wealth.

So today we turn to the natural resources themselves, which are the major cause of some of these conflicts and difficulties. In the morning we will deal with the minerals of the seabed, and in the afternoon, we will open with the discussion of the seabed margin and then turn to fishery matters.

Now, this morning, we will briefly set the stage for a debate, and then engage in a debate among various interested parties, trying to focus on the major points of disagreement and the major difference in interests, and to be as precise about these as we can.

To open the sessions, we have Dr. Roy Lee, who has a Ph.D. in international law from London University, a Chinese who is currently with the UN Secretariat in the Oceans Economics and Technology Office, and who has been working very closely with the UN Conference, particularly as the Secretary of Committee I.

Chapter Four

Machinery for Seabed Mining: Some General Issues Before the Geneva Session of the Third United Nations Conference on the Law of the Sea

Roy Skwang Lee*
United Nations Secretariat
Deputy Secretary of the First Committee of
the Third United Nations Conference on the
Law of the Sea

INTRODUCTION

The purpose of this paper is to point out some of the general issues relating to certain specific questions concerning the international seabed regime and machinery: the scope of treaty application, accommodation of different interests and activities in the ocean space, the location of the executive power, financial requirements and operational efficiency, the exploitation system and the conditions of exploitation. Whenever appropriate, suggestions are made with a view to eliciting responses to some proposed solutions to these questions.

The law of the sea is, perhaps, one of the most interesting and challenging frontiers in international law and relations. The Third United Nations Conference on the Law of the Sea is unprecedented in terms of the manifold and complex problems to be solved,[1] the enormous amount of material with which it has to deal, as well as its size and procedure. The mere fact that within sixteen years three conferences were convened illustrates the importance which the international community attaches to the subject and the complicated nature of the problems with which the community is confronted.

The First United Nations Conference on the Law of the Sea, in 1958, adopted four conventions dealing, respectively, with the territorial sea, the high seas, fishing and conservation of the living resources of the high seas, and the continental shelf. It did not, however, succeed in settling the questions of the breadth of the territorial sea and of fishing limits. The second conference was thus convened in 1960 to deal with these questions. By a margin of one vote, the second conference failed to reach any agreement.

The 1958 conference was of a manageable size, with eighty-six participating countries (ninety were invited). But 150 governments have been invited to participate in the present conference. In 1958, the decisions at the

*The views expressed are put forward in a personal capacity.

committee level were taken by a simple majority and in the plenary by two-thirds majority. For the present conference, this classic rule was considered inadequate and the General Assembly has adopted a "gentlemen's agreement" to the effect that the conference should proceed by consensus on substantive matters, and there should be no voting on such matters until all efforts at consensus have failed. The first organizational session, held in December 1973, failed to find a way to implement this "gentleman's agreement." At the Caracas session, agreement was reached on this issue and is reflected in Rule 37 of the Rules of Procedure of the Conference. According to this rule, consultations and cooling periods of up to ten days are required before any major decisions can be taken.

The first conference had before it seventy-three concrete draft articles prepared by the International Law Commission over a period of seven years. The present conference did not follow the usual United Nations' practice dealing with international law items, i.e., through the Legal Committee and the International Law Commission. From the outset the problems involved were considered predominantly political. The Committee on the Peaceful Uses of the Sea-Bed and the Ocean Floor beyond the Limits of National Jurisdiction was in fact the preparatory committee and only in 1971 did it embark on the task. Unlike its predecessors, this conference does not have a basic text to work on: it has before it a comprehensive list of twenty-five subjects and issues relating to the law of the sea which it should deal with, and a mass of material in the form of numerous conflicting proposals, alternatives, and amendments, amounting to a total of six volumes. The mandate of the present conference is twofold: (1) to review and revise the existing law of the sea; and (2) to establish an international legal regime with an appropriate machinery for the area of the seabed and the ocean floor, and the subsoil thereof, beyond the limits of national jurisdiction— substantive rules for the regulation of this area not being provided by the existing legal regime of the high seas.

Regarding the review and revisions of the existing law of the sea, the conference will have to deal not only with those questions that the first conference failed to resolve, but also with those issues that need to be reformulated in order to reflect the needs and realities of the contemporary world. These issues include navigation through straits, the concept of the economic zone, problems of special interests groups (e.g., the landlocked and geographically disadvantaged states), pollution, transfer of marine technology, and scientific research.

The question of establishing a regime and machinery for the international area entails the drafting of new laws. In 1967, the UN General Assembly expressed the anxiety of a large sector of the international community over the competitive exploitation for military purposes of the strategic potential of the seabed and the ocean floor beyond the limits of national jurisdiction. To divert this trend, a 35-member ad hoc committee was established to study the question of peaceful uses of that area. This ad hoc committee was transformed in 1968 into a standing committee, whose membership over a period of five years was expanded three times from forty-two to ninety-one to accommodate the divergent interests. When in 1970 the General Assembly decided to convene a third conference, the Sea-Bed Committee was again transformed, in effect, into the preparatory committee for the conference.

On the basis of the work of the Sea-Bed Committee, the General Assembly in 1970 adopted unanimously[2] the Declaration of Principles governing the seabed and ocean floor. Some of the major points may be summarized as follows:

1. the seabed and ocean floor, and the subsoil thereof, beyond the limits of national jurisdiction, as well as the resources of the area, are the common heritage of mankind; the area is not subject to appropriation and no state may claim or exercise sovereignty or sovereign rights over any part thereof; no state or person shall claim, exercise or acquire rights with respect to the area or its resources incompatible with the international regime to be established and the principle of this declaration;
2. the area is open to use exclusively for peaceful purposes;
3. the exploration of the area and exploitation of its resources are to be carried out for the benefit of mankind as a whole;
4. states shall act in the area in accordance with the applicable principles and rules of international law, including the UN Charter, and in the interests of maintaining international peace and promoting international cooperation and mutual understanding.

The General Assembly also expressed the view that an international regime and machinery should be established as soon as possible by an international treaty of a universal character generally agreed upon, to govern all activities involving the exploration and exploitation of the resources of the area and other related activities.

It is the first time in history that the concept of common heritage has found expression in an international instrument. It is perhaps even more significant that an area of at least 225 million square kilometers[3] is reserved for mankind as a whole and will be administered by an international organization on its behalf.

Ambassador Amerasinghe, chairman of the Sea-Bed Committee and now president of the conference, stated on the occasion of the adoption of the Declaration that:

> With the caution that is customarily reserved for official pronouncements by sovereign states on anything that rises above the level of the mundane . . . we can all agree that its [the Declaration's] conspicuous merit is its daring originality and its real virture is its moral force.[4]

One might also add its political force and from this standpoint, one could say that the Declaration is perhaps even more binding than treaties. In the three years following the adoption of the Declaration, Subcommittee I of the Sea-Bed Committee embarked on the elaboration of a convention on the regime and machinery on the basis of the declaration and submitted what it had accomplished in 1974 to the Third Conference on the Law of the Sea.

Another important decision of the General Assembly, commonly known as the moratorium resolution, should be mentioned in this connection. Prompted by the fear that states with the requisite technology and finance might initiate operations for the mining of mineral resources, the Assembly declared in 1969 that, pending the establishment of an international regime in the area, states and persons were bound to refrain from all activities of exploitation of the resources of the area, and no claim to any part of the area or its resources was to be recognized. Although most of the industrialized and Eastern European countries voted against this resolution, it was adopted with a majority of thirty-four votes and was further strengthened by the unanimous adoption of the Declaration of Principles a year later. Although the Declaration did not restate that states and persons were bound to refrain from all activities of exploitation of the resources of the area, this is implicit in paragraph 3 of the Declaration in which it is stated that "no state or person shall claim, exercise or acquire rights with respect to the area or its resources incompatible with the international regime to be established and the principles of that Declaration."

The Third United Nations Conference on the Law of the Sea held its first substantive session in Caracas, June–August 1974. The substantive work of the conference is divided among the three main committees. The establishment of an international seabed regime with an operational machinery is assigned to the First Committee. Unlike the other committees, the First Committee has before it a draft convention containing fifty-two articles prepared by Subcommittee I of the Sea-Bed Committee on the basis of proposals and working papers submitted to the subcommittee.[6]

The draft convention has two parts: Part I, entitled "Principles," relates to the status, scope, and basic provisions of the international seabed regime (Articles 1–21) and Part II relates to the functions and powers of the proposed international authority (Articles 12–52). The Sea-Bed Committee had completed a second reading of Part I and Articles 33–44 of Part II dealing with powers and functions of the assembly and council; it had only completed a first reading of articles dealing with the institutional aspects (Articles 22–32), the secretariat (Article 45), the subsidiary organs (Articles 46–56) and the miscellaneous provisions (Article 52). Different positions under each draft article were set out in the alternative texts and whenever necessary brackets were used to indicate disagreement within an alternative text. A glance at the texts of the draft articles shows clearly that tremendous efforts must still be made if the numerous issues are to be ironed out. Indeed, hardly any draft article has been completely agreed upon. Every draft article contains two or three, or even more alternative texts; this includes the first twenty-two articles dealing with the basic principles governing the regime. This is because, even at the present stage, members of the committee still hold diametrically opposed views on the fundamental issues: for example, the nature and character of the regime, the basic exploitation system, and power and functions of the authority envisaged. Unless the fundamental differences are resolved, a series of alternative texts is inevitable.

At the Caracas session, the First Committee met in various forms and on different levels in order to have the flexibility to enable it to tackle, in the most appropriate manner, different subjects and problems. Thus, it held general debates to enable those thirty-odd new members who did not participate in the Sea-Bed Committee to express their views; only eleven of them spoke. At its informal meetings Draft Articles 2–21, dealing with the regime, were considered and changes were made in several articles. While most of the modifications were formal or stylistic, some are indications of substantive development. For example, the deletion of brackets from the provisions of Draft Article 21 on settlement of disputes is an indication of a general agreement on the need for such machinery. The discussions on Draft Article 9, relating to the exploitation system and on conditions of exploitation, generated great interest and controversy. A working group was established to conduct negotiations on these issues. The committee did not have time to consider in substance the draft articles relating to the international authority, though some minor editorial changes were made during the informal discussions. In response to a request from certain Latin American and African countries, general discussions and seminars were held on possible effects of seabed mining on land-based minerals.

Before turning to the issues before the conference, it is important to note that the present negotiation on the seabed regime and machinery is influenced by a number of considerations which bear the seeds of controversy. Some of them may be mentioned here to illustrate the circumstances.

First, for an overwhelming majority of the participants, the proposed seabed regime and machinery must be a faithful implementation of the concept of the heritage of mankind declared by the United Nations General Assembly in Resolution 2749 (24) of 1970. Many members also place particular emphasis on the principle that the exploration of the area and the exploitation of its resources must be carried out for the benefit of mankind as a whole, irrespective of the geographical location of states and bearing in mind the special interests and needs of the developing countries. The exploitation system must consequently be capable of fulfilling this fundamental objective. A licensing or regulatory system, as proposed by some members of the committee, was, in the view of some members, inconsistent with this objective.

Second, according to the secretary-general's study, depending on the limits of national jurisdiction to be defined by the conference, valuable resources such as petroleum and natural gas are primarily to be found in areas within national jurisdiction.[7] Among the mineral resources to be found in the areas beyond national jurisdiction (e.g., phosphorite deposits, hot brines, and metallized muds), mining of manganese nodules is presently considered the only resource of commercial interest for at least the next two decades. As a result, nodule mining becomes the central issue of the whole negotiation. These nodules contain mainly manganese (24%), nickel (1.6%), copper (1.4%) and cobalt (0.21%). Since the value of nodules prior to the extraction of these minerals represents only 6–10 percent of the ultimate value, the proposed authority must have, in the view of many delegations, overall control of the industry, including processing and marketing.[8]

At present, only 3 percent of the seafloor of the world has been extensively surveyed. It is reported that the highest nodule potential is situated in the north equatorial center of the Pacific Ocean in water depths between 10,000 and 18,000 feet, at least 1000 miles from shore.[9] While most of the nodule deposits lie in areas beyond national jurisdiction, reports have indicated that some rich deposits may also be found within national jurisdiction, for example, near the French Polynesian Islands, Tonga Platform, and Western Samoa. It is possible, therefore, that the international seabed mining system might have to compete with national undertakings.[10]

Third, even among the leading experts on nodule mining, opinions differ significantly as to the complexity of the technology required and the magnitude of investment needed. On the one hand it is generally maintained that nodule mining requires not only advanced technology and the expertise of many disciplines, but also large and long-term investments with returns possibly delayed for several years. The construction of a commercial-scale hydraulic nodule-mining system and differential-precipitation processing plant would cost in the region of $184 to $200 million.[11] According to this view, probably only a dozen or so states have both the financial and technological capacity to exploit seabed resources. On the other hand, it is claimed that a relatively simple and inexpensive way exists, involving about $10 to $20 million of capital investment from mining to processing.[12] This system would, however, sacrifice overall metal recovery and would be less efficient. At present, the necessary technology and know-how have been developed largely by a small group of companies operating on a multinational basis.[13] Many important decisions, such as what the future exploitation should be, which must be taken now require knowledge and information pertaining to nodule mining. For example, if the financial and technological requirements were beyond the capability of the international authority, the exploitation conditions would have to be attractive to those companies in order to obtain their finance and expertise. But if the technical know-how and investment were within reach, the authority could then conduct exploitation directly, which is wished by many developing countries. Because of the very nature of the subject, this prerequisite knowledge cnnot be adequately met.

As has been reported, nodule mining could be operated on a large

commercial scale beginning 1985. The possible effects on land-based production
have become a major concern of some developing countries whose national
economy is based on the export of these minerals. What would be the effects
and how to regulate them are other controversial issues before the committee.

Fifth, in the view of many delegations, the present negotiation on
the seabed regime and machinery constitutes an integral part of a package deal
upon which the whole treaty on the law of the sea is to be constructed. Once the
constituent parts of the package deal are agreed upon, it is reasonable to expect
that many of the divergent positions might be withdrawn.

Sixth, two events in the United States demonstrate the importance
of the outcome of the conference. There has been before the United States
Senate, for the last three years, a bill which, if passed, would authorize the U.S.
government to issue licenses for deep-sea mining.[14] It is reported that the action
of the Senate will be influenced particularly by the outcome of the conference.
The second event is that, on 14 November 1974, Deepsea Ventures filed with
the Department of State a notice of discovery and claim of exclusive mining
rights over an area of 60,000 sq. km. in the Pacific Ocean.[15] It also requested
diplomatic protection and protection of investment. The U.S. Department of
State has not yet replied to the company directly, though it issued a public
statement that the exploitation of the seabed is governed at present, pending
the outcome of the Law of the Sea Conference, by the 1958 Convention of the
High Seas. This may be interpreted as in favor of Deepsea Ventures' claim.

ISSUES RELATING TO THE SCOPE OF
TREATY APPLICATION

The first issue relates to the application of the treaty to third states,
i.e., noncontracting parties. In the alternative texts of a number of draft articles,
references are made at different places both to "contracting parties" and to
"states."[16] Sometimes there is a clear indication of the sponsor's intention, other
times the intention is not clear. Some members argued that since the area beyond national jurisdiction and the resources of the area are the common heritage of mankind, the treaty must be prepared on the basis of universality. In
their view, the seabed regime must apply to "all states." The general feeling was
that this question should be left open at this stage of negotiation and returned to
when the general framework was completed.

According to Article 34 of the Vienna Convention on the law of
treaties, the general rule is that a treaty cannot create obligations or rights for a
third state without its consent. Accordingly, if it is intended to confer benefits
on noncontracting parties, the actual exercise of the rights by the noncontracting
parties would require acceptance of any conditions and obligations laid down
in the treaty (Articles 35–38). The pros and cons of extending the treaty applications to noncontracting parties should be fully considered. From the practical

point of view, to permit a third state to benefit from the regime (e.g., to exploit its resources) might raise difficult questions of implementation and enforcement. Also, it would be unfair to those states which took the trouble to become contracting parties to the Convention.

One basic issue which is reflected in the alternative texts of several draft articles[17] relates to what types of activities are to be governed under the regime and regulated by the authority. A large number of delegations favor a comprehensive approach and consider that all related activities taking place in the international area should be governed by the convention and that the convention is not required to specify these activities. As illustrations, such activities include scientific research, exploration of the area and exploitation of its resources, preservation of the marine environment, prevention of pollution, processing and marketing of commodities recovered from the area, conservation of living resources, and the protection of archaeological and historical treasures. On the other hand, some members consider this approach too general and prefer that the convention specifies the activities (i.e., activities relating to the exploration of the area and exploitation of its resources) which come within the scope of the convention; the authority would then only have functions with regard to those specified therein.

The divergent opinions on this question reveal the existence of two distinctive groups in the committee regarding the competence of the authority: one favors empowering the authority with an all-embracing jurisdiction, and in case of doubt, the authority is to decide whether it has jurisdiction over a particular activity; the other seems to prefer to limit the authority's powers to those required for the exploration of the area and exploitation of its resources. In the light of the spirit of the General Assembly Declaration and in particular, paragraph 4,[18] it seems desirable that the authority should have the power to deal with all activities affecting the legal regime of the international seabed. Moreover, since the 1958 High Seas Convention does not provide adequate substantive rules in this regard, the new convention must remedy this shortcoming. But for the purpose of clarity and to avoid potential disputes, the scope and nature of the activities covered by the convention should be clearly defined.

Limits of the area is another important issue. At the Caracas session this question was not discussed on the understanding that the landward limits of the international area would coincide with the seaward limits of the coastal state's jurisdiction and that this question was to be settled later in the light of the decision taken by the Second Committee regarding the economic zone and continental shelf of the coastal states. Since the distribution of mineral resources and their exploitability are closely related to the depth and distance from shore, the location of the boundary of the international area has significant and particular bearing on the economic value and purposes of the international regime and machinery. An examination of the proposals before the Second Committee seems to indicate that the international area is likely to begin somewhere 200 miles seaward of the coastline.[19] Two of the four proposals on limits of the area before the First Committee specify the figure of the limits: one criterion is 500 meters isobath and, when the isobath is less than 200 nautical miles, the distance of 200 nautical miles; the other uses the outer lower edge of the continental margin and, when the edge is less than 200 nautical miles, up to that distance. As mentioned earlier, in all likelihood, manganese nodules are to be the main resource to be exploited in the area in the next two or three decades. There may still be a hope that states may agree to sharing the resources or revenues beyond the 200 nautical miles.

Finally, there is the question of the legal status of the waters superjacent to the area. Presently, there seems a general agreement that only the seabed, ocean floor, and the subsoil thereof will be governed by the new legal regime. The existing legal status of the waters superjacent to the area and that of the air space above those waters will not be affected.[20] How to accommodate the different interests and activities in the ocean space is an important issue to be resolved.

ISSUES RELATING TO THE ACCOMMODATION
OF THE INTERESTS AND ACTIVITIES IN
THE OCEAN SPACE

Seabed mining activities could affect or might be in conflict with activities of the coastal states (Draft Article 15), activities in the water column, or other activities in the seabed area (Draft Article 17). The major issues are how to reconcile the different interests and uses, and whether it is possible to establish some priority among them.

So far as the relationship between the activities of the coastal states and those of the area is concerned, a majority of members seem prepared to accord a primacy to the coastal states: activities should be conducted with due regard to the rights and legitimate interests of the coastal states in the region; consultations are required with the states concerned in order to avoid possible infringement of such rights and interests. Some members favor, however, an equal treatment which requires all activities of exploration and expoitation to be conducted with due regard to the rights and interests of both the coastal states and the authority, since it is also necessary to safeguard the area and the rights of the authority. Although the second view carries only minority support, it has more pursuasive power than the former. Be that as it may, several minor points remain to be clarified: whether only "states" should be addressed, or the provision should cover "activities in general" or "the exploration and exploitation activities"; whether this provision should apply to activities in the whole area or only to activities taking place adjacent to its boundary or limits.

One controversial issue which is considered fundamental to the coastal states relates to the conditions under which a coastal state may take emergency measures to prevent, mitigate, or eliminate dangers of pollution or other hazardous incidents or acts which all members seem to agree that such dangers must be "grave and imminent." Some members suggest that the conditions (such as reasonableness and proportionality) limiting a state to take emergency measures under customary international law should additionally be introduced. Others prefer not to introduce such limits; they question the validity and general acceptance of such conditions. They accept, however, that the measures must be justified by the "necessity" of the circumstances.

Since some resources (such as an oil field) can be depleted from one side of the boundary, concern was expressed that a special provision is needed to cover exploitation of resources lying near or across the boundary between the area and a coastal state. Under the present proposal, the resources lying across limits of national jurisdiction cannot be explored or exploited unless with the agreement of the coastal state or states concerned; where such resources are located near the limits of national jurisdiction, consultations are required and where possible, exploration and exploitation through the state or states concerned. While it is debatable whether this proposal is justified for resources such as hydrocarbons, it seems unnecessary insofar as manganese nodule deposits are concerned. It would seem that a more general provision, giving equal status and requiring full cooperation between the coastal state and the authority is called for.

Activities in the marine environment and in the area could give rise to at least two types of conflicts: conflicts between different seabed activities (e.g., nodule mining, research activities, laying of cables and pipelines, harvesting of sedentary species) and conflicts between seabed activities and activities in the water column (e.g., navigation and fishing).[21] Under the present proposals, it is clear that exploration and exploitation activities would be under the jurisdiction of the authority. It is not clear, however, whether laying of cables and pipelines for communication purposes and harvesting of sedentary species are to be included under the authority. The basic issue is whether any preference should be given to any activities and if so, to which activity.

In this connection, it may be useful to mention here the position under the 1958 Geneva conventions. Freedom of navigation, freedom of fishing, freedom to lay submarine cables and pipelines, and freedom to fly over the high seas are recognized by the 1958 Convention on the High Seas (Article 2) and must be exercised by all states "with reasonable regard" to the interests of other states, in the exercise of the freedom of the high seas. Under the 1958 continental shelf convention, the rights of the coastal state to exploit resources on the continental shelf is given a primacy over other activities in the high seas (Article 5). Thus, by analogy, one might argue that the exploration and exploitation activities on the international seabed should take priority to other uses on the high seas in case of conflicts.

Draft Article 17 contains two paragraphs of broad principles; each deals with the question of accommodation of activities in the area and in the marine environment. Each paragraph has two alternative texts: one requires that all activities in the marine environment be conducted "with reasonable regard" for the exploration and exploitation activities in the area; the other that such activities not result in any "unjustifiable interference." In other words, one tends to give primacy to activities in the area; the other, primacy to activities in the marine environment. The existence of two very different views perhaps indicates the need for a new approach to these problems.

In view of the very different interests of the parties involved, it is normal that each claims priority over the others. The solution perhaps does not lie in determining the priorities but in stressing the importance of the need for consultations in the event of conflicts. The likelihood of actual conflicts is minimized by the vastness of the area. The theoretical value of possible conflicts should not be overstressed.

ALLOCATION OF THE EXECUTIVE POWER

The international authority, as presently conceived by members of the committee will include at least four principal organs: an assembly which is composed of all the contracting parties, a council which is a smaller organ, an operational organ, and a secretariat. The assembly and the council have overall responsibilities. In addition, proposals have been submitted for the establishment of a variety of subsidiary organs in the form of commissions to deal with economic, technical, and legal aspects of the seabed activities. There are also proposals for setting up a system for the settlement of disputes.

Various proposals have been made to the committee on the powers and functions of the assembly and of the council. Because of the divergent views of the members, some being diametrically opposed, the committee is faced with an extremely difficult problem in assigning the powers and functions of these two organs.[22] The major issue is the location of the executive power. There are two basic approaches in the proposals. On the basis that the assembly is the representative body, it should be the organ empowered to deal with any questions within the competence of the authority, to give directions and recommendations to other organs and to member states, and to review the decisions of the subsidiary organs in order to ensure the ultimate authority on all matters. The council should be under its supervision and perform those functions assigned to it by the assembly and manage the day-to-day business.

The second school, favored by many industrial countries, advocates maximum autonomy between these two major organs and holds the view that hierarchical order is unnecessary. Their functions and powers should be clearly defined and distributed in the interest of efficiency. The assembly should be given only general recommendatory power, leaving the other organs with more limited membership to take the necessary economic and technical decisions.

Furthermore, the relationship between the assembly and the council should not be predetermined but left to practice. While endorsing this approach, some members also hold the view that certain technical regulations and basic guidelines (e.g., those relating to exploitation) should be provided in the convention itself or in the annexes attached to it in order to ensure stability.

When it came to the formulation of the substantive powers and functions of the two organs, a spectrum of views emerged and was reflected in the alternative texts on each and every one of the powers and functions proposed for the assembly or for the council, whether with respect to the sharing of benefits, establishment of rules, standards and practices, prevention of pollution, participation of developing countries, scientific research, or exploitation activities. It should be mentioned here that as Ambassador Christopher Pinto, chairman of the informal committee, pointed out, one possible way to reduce the difficulty of the allocation of the executive power may lie in the structure of the council.[23] If the council could be constituted in such a way as to be a miniature assembly reflecting truthfully the different interest groups of the full membership and their respective voting strengths, it would not matter if the executive power were assigned to a smaller organ, i.e., the council. Such a system would have the advantages of efficiency and economy. Indeed, two proposals are formulated along these lines[24] and can be adapted to the need.

The divisions between the developing and developed states on the one hand and the five regional groupings[25] on the other need to be reflected in the structure of the council. It is important, however, that the special interest groups should also be given recognition in the composition. Such groups include those member states having both the technological and financial capability to exploit seabed resources, the landlocked[26] and legally defined geographically disadvantaged countries, the major producers and consumers of copper, cobalt, nickel, and manganese,[27] the least-developed states,[28] and other special interest groups.

The following examples are intended to illustrate the extent of the divergence on the question of location of the executive power. It is believed, however, that once the ground rules regarding the structure of the council have been established, the question of allocation of powers and functions becomes easier. It is submitted, therefore, that the committee should first settle the structures of the council, the role of the assembly and its relationship with the council, and then the question of powers and functions.

On the question of benefit-sharing

Six alternative texts have been proposed respectively for the assembly and for the council.[29] Four approaches may be identified. Some representatives propose that the assembly should be the organ to adopt the precise criteria and rules for the equitable sharing of benefits derived from seabed resources. Other representatives consider that the "criteria" should form part of the convention itself and that the assembly would merely adopt supplementary guidelines for implementing the criteria. Another alternative prefers the adoption of a general provision empowering the assembly to approve proposals by the council for the equitable sharing of the net income of the authority in accordance with criteria specified in the convention. Still other representatives suggest that the whole matter of benefit-sharing should be dealt with by the council or by a subsidiary organ.

Establishment of rules, standards, and practices

Eight alternative texts have been proposed for the assembly, and four texts for the council.[30] The main approaches are mentioned here. Some members suggest that the assembly should be given the power to adopt, on the recommendation of the council, international rules, standards, and practices relating to a variety of technical and operational subjects dealing with the exploration of the area and the exploitation of its resources, and noninterference with the freedom of the high seas. Those who consider that the council should have the primary role in the adoption of operational rules prefer to empower the council to do so, or to transfer a part of such rules to it. Some members feel strongly that rules relating to the noninterference with freedom of the high seas is a subject outside the competence of the authority.

Another approach is similar to the International Civil Aviation Organization, created under the 1944 Chicago Convention on International Civil Aviation: i.e., the technical and operational rules, standards, and practices should form part of the text of the convention itself, and there should be established a procedure for their implementation through technical annexes containing specific regulations to be prepared by the council or a subsidiary organ. Such technical annexes would come into force after being submitted directly to the contracting parties and approved by them. The amendment of these annexes would follow the same procedure. Some members, while agreeing with this approach, feel that the assembly should have an opportunity to examine these annexes and submit recommendations to member states on the matter.

Prevention of pollution and contamination of the marine environment[31]

In the view of some members, the assembly should have the power to adopt general principles and recommendations concerning the prevention of pollution and contamination of the marine environment, resulting from or caused by exploration and exploitation of resources, while others consider that such power should be extended to cover pollution from all activities in the area. Some also consider that the assembly should be empowered to take measures to prevent, mitigate, or eliminate pollution or the threat of pollution, as well as other hazardous occurrences. Some members argue, on the other hand, that such powers should be given to the council or perhaps to a specialized subsidiary organ. A proposal has also been made to empower the council to issue emergency orders for preventing serious harm to the marine environment arising from any activity connected with resource exploitation, and to approve nondiscriminatory nominative principles dealing with a variety of matters concerning the uses of the marine environment. Other representatives prefer to omit such a provision on the ground that the proposal goes beyond the competence of the authority as they conceive it.

Participation of developing countries

Several alternative proposals have been put forward relating to the power of the assembly in connection with the question of the participation of developing countries in exploitation of resources.[32] The proposals deal with arrangements for the training of personnel of those countries, provision of technical assistance, employment of qualified personnel from such countries, and recognition of a certain priority for such countries in specialized activities connected with exploration of the area and exploitation of its resources. On the other hand, some members feel that these powers should be assigned to the council or to the operational or subsidiary organ.

Scientific research

Several proposals have been submitted on scientific research; they deal with the encouragement of research, the promotion of international cooperation in research on resource exploitation, exchange of scientific and technical information, exchange and training of scientists and experts, application of scientific techniques, and acquisition of facilities, plants, and equipment.[33] One or more of these measures is supported by members of the committee, but no one group of measures commands general support. In particular, opinions differ on the steps to be taken to accomplish those tasks. For some members, the assembly should take measures to achieve them; some only agree to the assembly's adoption of principles or making of recommendations, while others prefer not to direct the assembly to adopt any particular mode of action at all. Some members assign the provision of services, equipment, and facilities to a subsidiary organ, while others suggest that the training of personnel should be the function of a different organ.

Exploitation activities

The distribution of powers and functions between the assembly and the council also differs according to the resources-exploitation system proposed. Some of those members who are in favor of a licensing system are inclined to empower the assembly to adopt, upon the recommendation of the council, rules regarding the entire licensing system, while others give the council or a subsidiary organ the power to carry out operations in the area, the assembly having no direct role in the matter.[34] According to this view, the assembly should be limited to the consideration and determination of general questions and conditions relating to the exploration and exploitation activities.

Those who envisage an entirely different exploitation system contemplate in this regard a different distribution of powers and functions. They prefer to assign a regulatory power to the executive organ, while leaving the operational organ, i.e., the enterprise, to deal with the day-to-day business under the guidelines established by the former.[35]

According to the system proposed, a different organ was to undertake the actual operation. Thus, those favoring the pure licensing system proposed either the operations commission, the permanent board, or the exploitation commission. Those envisaging a range of possible means (e.g., service contracts, joint ventures, or licensing) proposed the management and development commission, international seabed operations organization, or the exploration and production agency to carry out such functions. The Group of 77 members support the creation of the enterprise as the organ of the authority responsible for carrying out all technical, industrial, and commercial activities relating to the exploration of the area and the exploitation of its resources. The enterprise would have legal personality to carry out its activities and to be held liable, the power to conclude contracts, financial autonomy, and competence to acquire necessary movable and immovable property.

Regulation of production

There are two distinctive approaches to this issue. On the one hand, some members considered that seabed mineral production could affect the economic interests of those states whose national incomes are primarily based on the export of nickel, copper, manganese, or cobalt. It is important in their view that the international authority should be empowered to deal with this question. Opinions differ as to what kind of functions and powers should be assigned to the assembly and the council. Some members proposed that the assembly should be empowered to decide from time to time areas which are open to or free from exploration and exploitation.[36] Other members proposed additionally that the council should have the power to take measures to regulate the production, marketing, and distribution of raw materials from the area in consultation or collaboration with the competent organ of the United Nations or with the specialized agencies concerned.[37]

On the other hand, some members felt that the power to reserve areas could impede resource development of the seabed. Instead of regulation of production, they argued for the stabilization of commodity prices on a global basis, taking into account the production of raw materials from the area.

The difficulty in agreeing on a solution to this problem is further complicated by the fact that any attempt to assess the possible impact of seabed mining on world markets and on the exports of developing countries requires forecasts of metal production both from nodules and from land-based sources, as well as an estimate of demand for manganese, nickel, copper, and cobalt. Since certain essential information needed for the projections of seabed production can only be obtained at present from sources of private companies involved in nodule-mining activities and cannot objectively be verified, an accurate assessment of possible impact becomes very difficult.

On the assumption that the nodule industry may become an important source of supply of minerals by 1985, it has been estimated that the prices of cobalt and manganese are likely to be reduced by then respectively by 60 percent and 50 percent, though the impact on the prices of nickel and copper is to be slight.[38] Although members of the committee have recognized the importance and difficulty of this issue, agreement on the appropriate measures is yet to be reached. Perhaps, all that is needed at present is that the assembly should be given competence to deal with the question in the light of future development: the secretariat may be entrusted to keep a close watch of the situation and be required to report regularly to the competent organ on the development; the executive organ should have power to take the appropriate action whenever necessary.

ISSUES RELATING TO THE FINANCIAL REQUIREMENT AND OPERATIONAL EFFICIENCY

In the light of the proposals before the committee, there seems a general assumption that the authority would be self-supporting, though member states might have to provide financial support to the authority in the initial period. Opinions differ on when such support might be necessary and how it might be provided. Some members consider that such financial support should be assessed only in relation to administrative expenses and would limit such assessment to the initial stage until the revenue received is sufficient to support the authority itself; others support financing through borrowing.[39]

The financial aspects of the authority need to be carefully studied. For example, according to the Secretary-General's study on the *Economic Implications of Sea-Bed Mineral Development in the International Area*[40] , and based on the assumptions given therein, revenues from nodule minining per unit could be expected in 1985 in the range of $104 million to $193 million.[41] From this would have to be deducted the administrative expenses and the shares of contractors contributing the finance and/or the technology. Thus, financial support for the authority would be necessary from its creation until 1985 and after 1985, the authority would have income presumably from nodules. Estimations of the total annual expenses of the authority could be very different depending on, *inter alia,* the size of the organization, the number of subsidiary organs, and the scope of its activities.

The international authority might require a budget higher than the medium-size international organizations for several important reasons. The first is that, according to the proposals before the conference, besides the principal organs, up to six functional commissions[42] might be created as subsidiary organs. While some of the proposals have received a certain amount of support, there is no general agreement on the creation of all. Each proposal for a commission is accompanied by an alternative statement for its omission on the ground that some other organs of the authority should perform the functions contemplated or that the authority should not have such functions at all. In the interest of economy and efficiency the creation of these commissions should be carefully examined. The total administrative expenses for running these organs could be very high and the creation of a tribunal would be an additional expense. Second, it is reasonable to assume that the authority would need an inspectorate and supporting equipment, such as ships, airplanes,[43] and a communication system, in order to exercise effective control over the international area and the activities taking place therein. Third, if the authority were to have the regulatory power to control the supply of minerals from deep-sea mining, as proposed by some members, the authority might have to store such minerals.[44] No doubt these are all worthwhile and meaningful activities but they are very costly. There is a need to look into these financial aspects of the authority at this stage so that appropriate action can be taken if necessary. At least, the negotiation would not proceed on the basis of wrong assumptions or misunderstanding.

Should the conference decide to reduce the number of the subsidiary organs, it would be appropriate to consider whether some of the proposed functions might not be assigned to the secretariat. Under the proposals before the committee, the secretariat is primarily an administrative organ. Opinions of the members of the committee differ on the substantive functions of the secretariat. For example, some members were inclined to give the secretary-general certain functions in scientific and technical matters (e.g., to promote scientific research, to issue notice to mariners concerning dangers to navigation, to maintain a register of the disposal of radioactive and toxic materials in the area, etc.), whereas other members considered either that such functions were unnecessary or that they should be assigned to another body.

One of the most important functions which has been proposed is that within the secretariat there would be established, when needed, an inspectorate which would be responsible for dispatching inspectors to examine operations conducted within the area and to report to the executive organ any noncompliance with obligations established by the authority.[45] Care has been taken regarding the necessary procedures for appointing inspectors, their responsibilities and obligations[46]; most of the provisions have been proven adequate and satisfactory through the practice of the International Atomic Energy Agency.[47]

In connection with the possibility of the operation of ships by the authority, mention should be made of Article 7 of the 1958 Geneva Convention on the High Seas, which envisages the operation of ships employed for official services of an intergovernmental organization flying the flag of that organization. Presumably, one of the purposes of the operating of ships by the authority would be to ensure effective and direct control of the activities taking place in the international area. To this end the authority would need to inspect any ships or installations which might be suspected of violating its regulations or of illegal operation. Under the High Seas Convention, only warships under specific circumstances may board a foreign ship on the high seas (Article 22). Express treaty provision would be necessary, if inspection is envisaged.

It would seem that other similar functions requiring objective evaluation might also be entrusted to the secretariat. So long as the secretariat is under the supervision of the executive organs, as it is, there is little danger that the secretariat may be *ultra virus.* The secretariat would be required to report to that organ and it would be the function of the executive organ to make the necessary decision. In this way, the secretariat would remain an organ for implementation and the authority would be spared the financial burden which would otherwise be imposed by the creation of the subsidiary organs.

An effective machinery for the settlement of disputes can increase operational efficiency. Disputes of a different nature and at different levels could occur among the member states, the authority, and the entities contracted with the authority. The nature of disputes could also be of various kinds: e.g., treaty interpretation, contractual relationships, application of rules and regulations promulgated by the authority, and conflicts among the activities on the seabed.

At the Caracas session, there appeared to be general agreement that a dispute-settlement machinery would be needed. The substantive provisions, however, remain to be worked out. A number of proposals are before the committee and some of the basic approaches to this question may usefully be mentioned here.[48] There is one comprehensive proposal which envisages the setting up of a permanent juridical organ with comprehensive and compulsory jurisdiction and the power to make binding decisions; amendments have been made to modify this approach. Other proposals put forward methods of settlement other than a permanent tribunal. These proposals envisage either an ad hoc tribunal whose members would be chosen by the parties from a panel of persons, or submission to the International Court of Justice. Another proposal, which was formulated on the basis of the enterprise concept, contemplates settlement of disputes between the enterprises and entities that have entered into service contracts or joint ventures with it. There was also the suggestion that before submission to the tribunal, the disputes should first be submitted to the council with a view to reaching an agreement. Failing agreement, then the dispute would be submitted to the tribunal.

It seems that various procedures should be made to suit different kinds of disputes. For example, a dispute between two contracting parties on the interpretation of a specific treaty provision should follow a procedure different from a dispute arising from a service contract. While all disputes should be settled expeditiously, the nature of the latter requires a much more simplified and efficient procedure. In general, it would seem desirable to provide a simplified procedure for disputes between the authority and the entities, and between the entities.

ISSUES RELATING TO THE EXPLOITATION SYSTEM AND CONDITIONS THEREOF

The exploitation system

At the very early stage of the negotiations in the Sea-Bed Committee, there were principally two kinds of proposals: exploitation under license to be issued by an international body and direct exploitation exclusively by the international authority. Later, the idea of resource exploitation through service contract or joint venture was introduced. As the negotiations continued, a number of mixed systems have emerged with variant degrees of emphasis on the three basic positions. A mixed system seems to represent the present trend of development. The central difficulties are: how to construct this mixed system, which position is to be taken as the basis, and what the exploitation conditions are.

The question of the exploitation system is dealt with in Draft Article 9, entitled "Who May Exploit the Area." Four alternative texts have been put forward. Under the first alternative text, all exploration and exploitation activities are to be conducted by the contracting party or parties, or natural or juridical persons under its or their sponsorship. The conduct of the operation is subject to regulation by the authority and in accordance with rules set out in the convention. The second alternative provides a slight but important variation of this position by adding the possibility that the authority may decide "within the limits of its financial and technological resources to conduct such activities." These two approaches seem to have the support largely of the European countries and Japan.

The third approach, favored by the United States, is that the exploration and exploitation activities are to be conducted in accordance with "legal arrangements." The international authority is required to enter such arrangements with a contracting party or parties, or natural or juridical persons under its or their sponsorship. Such legal arrangements, which obviously include both licensing and contractual arrangements, are to be made pursuant to the convention and regulations of the authority.

The fourth alternative is proposed by the Group of 77, now having over 100 members. This approach is also supported by China. Romania, and Spain. The text of the Group of 77 reads as follows:

> All activities of exploration of the area and of the exploitation of its resources and all other related activities including those of scientific research, shall be conducted by the Authority.
>
> The Authority may, if it considers it appropriate, and within the limits it may determine, confer certain tasks to juridical or natural persons, through service contracts, or association or through any other such means it may determine which ensures its direct and effective control at all times over such activities.

The basic concept of this text is that the seabed authority should be the sole representative of mankind for the carrying out of exploration and exploitation activities in the area. While it requires that all these activities are to be conducted directly by the authority, it also has the flexibility that the authority, at its discretion, may also confer certain tasks to other entities under contractual arrangements so long as "direct and effective control at all times over such activities" is ensured. The discussions ensuing in Caracas revealed two major issues of general concern: the interpretation of the term "juridical or natural persons" and the discretionary power of the authority. The legal nature of service contracts and joint venture was also briefly discussed.

Some members of the committee considered that the system proposed by the Group of 77 was too vague and general to provide the stability required by interested entities and that it gave the authority too much discretionary power, either implied or explicit in the text, in selecting the entity, the task, the arrangement, and in making the decision of whether or not to exploit the area. The sponsors maintained that all the guarantees that could be reasonably expected by those entities currently possessing the technological and financial means to explore and exploit the seabed would be met and would be the subjects of future regulations to be issued by the authority.

The term "juridical or natural persons" was interpreted by some members as prejudicial to those whose economic system only permits state or public enterprises. The sponsors explained that the term included not only corporations under a private enterprise system but also states and states' enterprises, and that the ideological background of an applicant would be taken into account by the authority in selecting contractors for seabed operations.

Some members also argued that the contractual entities with the authority should be restricted to states and states' enterprises on the ground of their accountability. In this connection, the question was raised whether states and states' enterprises would be entitled to immunities. The general opinion seemed to be that once a state or state's enterprise had entered into a service contract or a partnership with the authority, the former could no longer resort to immunities to which it would otherwise be entitled under international law. In any event, it seems that for all practical purposes, the waiver of immunities by a state or state's enterprise could be stipulated explicitly in the contract so as to leave no room for other interpretation.

The question was also raised that if private persons or enterprises are permitted to engage in seabed exploitation activities, they must be sponsored by a contracting state or a group of contracting states and the sponsor would ensure their financial and technological accountability, be responsible on their behalf, and guarantee the confidentiality of the technical information and data submitted. It was maintained on the other hand that this was inconsistent with the concept of the heritage of mankind and that with careful planning and regulations the authority could be relied upon to deal with private persons and enterprises directly. Be that as it may, there is much to be said for using the state as a referee or guarantor and for purposes of enforcement and sanction. It seems desirable that such possibilities should be explored by the committee.

At a certain stage of the committee's work, the relative merits of joint venture and service contract should be assessed to determine which is more suitable to the need. Some of their respective characteristics may be briefly noted here.

Joint ventures, which are often called "multinational public enterprises," are widely employed in different fields such as air transport, industry, power, navigation, telecommunications, roads, railways and research.[49] In the oil industry, joint ventures (or participation contracts) and service contracts (or work contract) are extensively used and can take different forms.[50]

A joint venture can be created pursuant to an agreement between participants which, by nature, may include states, juridical or natural persons, as well as private or public enterprises. The fact that it is created by a special agreement between the participating parties permits flexibility in organization, financing, operations or marketing, according to what would best suit the functions to be performed. By nature, it is more insulated from political pressure and therefore it can minimize the influence of political considerations in its decision-making. Such a joint venture or enterprise is in a better position to attract the required managerial skills and to allow the necessary initiation, expediency, and flexibility. The fact that it has juridical personality and financial autonomy as well as certain privileges to facilitate its operations ensures the carrying out of its tasks. Shares may be issued to the partners and payments for shares may be made in different forms, such as cash, machinery and equipment, resources, technical data and know-how, or other services. A joint venture may be structured similar to a private corporation, i.e., general shareholders' meeting, the board of directors and general manager, etc.

A service contract, like a joint venture, is also constituted by an agreement between the parties, though the legal relationship changes from partner to contractor. As partners, the risks and benefits are shared, whereas in a service contract, the contractor assumes all the risks and only when the service is accomplished receives a valuable consideration which could be cash or a share of the product or profit. The contractor supplies all necessary information and data technology and know-how, as well as all industrial properties necessary for

fulfillment of the specified service. Unlike a joint venture, there is no institution to be created; from the point of view of the authority, little is involved in
the case of a service contract, except perhaps inspection and supervision. Service
contracts are flexible and can be used either for a specific task (e.g., to design or
construct a nodule recovery system or a processing plant) or to accomplish a
whole phase (e.g., evaluation) or an entire operation (e.g., the production of X
millions of tons of nodules from a designated mine site). The more specific the
performance is, the more knowledge and experience are expected on the part of
the employer, i.e., the authority, since it would have to decide what is to be done
at a particular stage and to supervise the implementation of the specific tasks
in the light of the overall operation.

The advantage of a joint venture is that the authority would be able
to participate in all phases of the operation and that is an ideal situation for
acquiring the necessary experience and management skills. To achieve this, a
carefully designed control and regulatory system is indispensable in order to
ensure that the joint venture would serve the intended purpose. Up to now,
the experience in controlling multinational cooperation from extracting revenues
has not been very successful. Moreover, as a partner, the authority would have to
be equally equipped as the counterparts in terms of experience and knowledge.
This may be difficult at the early stages of the authority. In addition, the operation of such a joint venture also requires presumably large expenditures in over-
heads and administration, which can be burdensome to the authority at the
early stage when it has no income at all. The merits and demerits of a service
contract are the opposite. It does not involve the vital question of control or
detailed regulations, nor does it entail creation of additional institutions (e.g.,
shareholder assembly, board of directors, managers, executives, and auditors).
The important shortcoming of technology transfer can be remedied by making
training an obligation of the contractor.

As mentioned earlier, the relative merits of joint ventures and service contracts should be investigated. It is important that all options should be
kept open at this stage.

Conditions of exploitation

The deliberations on the divergent exploitation systems seemed to
indicate at the time that there was no possibility of reconciling the different
points. There was a feeling that a breakthrough might be possible if the committee were to consider the conditions of exploitation. It was hoped that the
differences in concept might be bridged through examination of the operating
conditions underlying these concepts. While certain members remained uncon-
vinced, in the absence of a better solution, the committee decided to consider
the question of conditions of exploitation.

Draft proposals on the conditions were submitted to the committee
by the United States,[51] the Group of 77,[52] the EEC countries[53] minus Ireland

and Japan.[54] The sponsors of these proposals have stated that these conditions are preliminary in nature and are intended to reflect concepts rather than final detailed provisions. Indeed, it is known that some of the sponsors have already started revising the conditions in the light of the views exchanged in Caracas.

The proposals of the United States, the EEC countries, and Japan were fairly similar except in certain aspects which will be mentioned later. There are significant differences between the proposals submitted by these industrial countries and those submitted by the Group of 77. Some of the differences reflect the basic exploitation system envisaged. The proposals submitted by the industrial countries chose to spell out not only certain general principles but also technical details.[55] The text of the Group of 77, on the other hand, contained only general principles. Several considerations may have contributed to this approach. In the first place, the Group of 77 holds the view that the treaty should not contain detailed rules and regulations which are to be dealt with later by the authority itself. It suffices to state only the basic essential principles to guide the authority in establishing detailed rules and regulations, and to provide it with sufficient indications of of the kind of policy that it should follow so as to assure to the entities interested in seabed mining. Secondly, it is possible that the Group of 77 felt that it did not possess the necessary technical knowledge and know-how to deal with such conditions as size of the mine site or duration of the contract. On the other hand, the industrial countries considered it essential to define the discretionary power of the authority in precise terms, regarding both the structure of the exploitation system as a whole and the day-to-day operating conditions (e.g., selection of sites, area of sites, protection of data and information). They stress the importance of building a stable relationship between the authority and the entity so as to avoid alteration of conditions once large investments have been made.

Some members felt that the approach and conditions submitted by the industrial countries were too rigid to meet technological changes in the future and preferred a pragmatic and flexible approach. The size of the mine sites[56] and the duration of the arrangement[57] proposed by the industrial countries were considered by some members too large and too long. In this connection, comparison was made to the experience in offshore oil operations. Although the Group of 77 text did not specify the size or the length of the contract, the sponsors made it clear that this and other considerations would be met so as to guarantee efficiency and optimum yield.

One of the essential differences between the Group of 77 proposal and those of the industrial countries is that the former divides the complete cycle of the activities involved into ten stages,[58] beginning with scientific research and ending with processing, transportation, and marketing, whereas the latter provides for two stages: prospecting, and evaluation and exploitation. The industrial countries objected strongly to the inclusion of processing, transportation, and marketing on the ground that these activities are beyond the competence of the international authority. It should be noted that these differences represent not only basic conceptual preferences but also economic considerations. As mentioned earlier,[59] the value of raw manganese nodules represents only 6-10 percent of the total value of the minerals recovered after processing. This explains why the Group of 77 insisted on the inclusion of these important stages.

As mentioned earlier, the Group of 77 text envisages the possibility that the authority may confer certain tasks to juridical or natural persons through service contracts, joint ventures, and any other such forms of associations. It is clear that the form of the arrangements is contractual and licensing is excluded, whereas the United States text uses the term "legal arrangements," which include, by interpretation, licensing as well. Both the EEC and Japanese texts refer to award of contracts, and that represents a significant departure—presumably licensing would not be included. According to the Group of 77 text, contractual arrangements may be concluded for any of the ten stages, whereas under the texts of the industrial countries, no arrangement is needed for prospecting, except notification of or registration with the authority.[60] Upon such notification or registration, the authority is to issue either a prospecting certificate or a registration valid for two years, renewable and nonexclusive. The EEC and the Japanese texts require certain contractual arrangements to be made for the phases of evaluation and exploitation and such contracts confer exclusive rights. It should be noted here that prospecting is not subject to any area limit, whereas contracts for evaluation and exploitation are subject to specific limits of the area.

Another important difference is that according to the Group of 77 proposal, the rights or obligations arising from a contract may not be transferred except with the authority's consent, whereas the other texts either permit free transfer, subject to the transferee's undertaking to comply with the convention and tribunal's orders and decisions, or merely require notification of the authority.

With respect to the qualifications of the entities, the United States text requires the sponsoring party to provide assurances that a natural or juridical person is financially and technically competent, whereas the Group of 77 proposal empowers the authority to establish precedures and to prescribe qualifications in this regard. The Japanese draft specifies that, in the case of an exploitation contract that is separate from the general survey, the applicant must be conducting or have conducted evaluation activities under a contract.

On the question of selection of entities, there seems to be general agreement that the applicants should be selected on a competitive basis. The Group of 77 text further specifies that account be taken of the need for the widest possible direct participation of developing countries, particularly land-locked countries. The EEC countries text permits a maximum number of contracts which may be awarded to a particular entity of six contracts in respect of each category of minerals.

The United States proposal provides that an applicant has "the right to mine" upon satisfaction of specified conditions, whereas the Group of 77 text provides that satisfactory performance entitles the contractor only to priority in the award of the contract for further stages of the operation.

Performance requirements are considered necessary by practically all members; some texts provide such requirements in considerable details (e.g., the United States and the EEC texts).

While there was general agreement on the need for inspection and supervision, opinions differed as to who should carry out such tasks. While the United States text suggests that the sponsoring party is responsible for the performance of any duties and obligations imposed on persons it sponsors, other proposals seem to envisage that the authority should carry out inspection and supervision in accordance with the terms of the contract. On the question of application of operational rules, standards and practices, the Group of 77 text envisages that the authority should take the necessary measures, whereas the other three texts contemplate such measures being taken by the contractor or the party making the legal arrangement with the authority.

It is specified in the Group of 77 text that the applicable law is solely the provisions of the Convention, the rules and regulations laid down by the authority, and the terms and conditions of the relevant contract entered into by the authority; no national law is applicable. The main purpose obviously is to exclude national law. One might argue that these instruments cannot possibly contain rules so detailed that they could cover all possible contingencies. On the other hand, once the application of national law is permitted, even on a subsidiary basis, it could bring conflict between the constituent instruments and national legislation. It is preferable to avoid this possible conflict by giving the constituent instrument exclusive jurisdiction. The assembly or the council should have power to remedy any lacunae in the main document or to submit it to the tribunal which is contemplated.

Under the United States proposed conditions of exploitation, the right to mine is to be suspended if the tribunal finds that the miner has grossly and persistently violated the convention or that he has willfully failed to comply with a decision of the tribunal. The text of the Group of 77 states that "in case of a radical change in circumstances or 'force majeure' the Authority may take appropriate measures, including revision, suspension or termination of the contract." Some members considered this provision not specific enough to promote a stable relationship between the authority and the contractors.

The basic concept of the Group of 77 is expressed in the requirement that the title to the area and its resources are to be vested in the authority and that its title to minerals is not to pass to other entities except in accordance with the authority's rules and regulations, and the terms and conditions of the relevant contracts. This is to ensure, *inter alia,* its direct and effective control. Another special feature is that the authority is to determine areas available for exploitation activities. The idea is to ensure that some of the best known mine sites would be reserved for future exploitation or for those members who at present do not have the finance or technology to participate in the activities.

CONCLUSION

Many important and fundamental questions remain to be settled before an international seabed regime and machinery can be established. Though the ultimate outcome is, to a large extent, dependent on the negotiations on the law of the sea as a whole, the various positions in the First Committee need to be consolidated. To achieve this, it is of paramount importance that the regime and machinery must reflect in an effective manner the underlying considerations and basic objectives of the different interest groups. First, a large number of developing countries would like to ensure that the revenue derived from the exploration and exploitation of the international area will not be consumed by a few, but will be distributed to all, particularly those needing it. Second, there is the concern for technology transfer and conservation of resources. A group of countries, including some of the landlocked and geographically disadvantaged states, have a keen interest in acquiring the technology and in participating in the exploitation activities. They want to ensure that incentives are provided to encourage the acquisition of technology and that, when they have acquired it, there will still be sufficient resources for them to exploit. Third, the land-based mineral producers amongst developing countries are worried that their future national incomes could be jeopardized by minerals produced from the international area. They want to ensure that there will be a built-in mechanism to forestall such a possibility. Fourth, some industrial countries have repeatedly emphasized that they must have guaranteed access to the minerals produced from the international area in order to meet their industrial needs. Flexibility and ingenious solutions are required to tackle these issues: unless they are dealt with adequately, no significant breakthrough can be expected.

It is suggested that, instead of proceeding article by article, the committee may wish to consider examining together all provisions relating to a particular set of issues, whether they relate to the principles, the structure, or the powers and functions of the organ. Thus, with respect to the set of issues connected with the question of exploitation, it is possible to identify the exploitation system (Draft Article 9), the exploitation conditions on which four proposals have been submitted, the operational organ (Draft Articles 38–44), and other related issues (e.g., equitable sharing, rules, standards and practices, reservation of areas). Irrespective of the differences between the proposed exploitation systems, one important common element is that they all accept "contractual arrangements" as one of the means to be employed by the authority for resource exploitation. The exclusion of licensing and inclusion of direct exploitation by the authority are yet to be agreed upon. An early agreement on the exploitation system is essential since it determines the nature and character of the authority and functions and powers of the different organs.

Similarly, all the provisions in different parts of the draft convention dealing with the question of possible effects of deep-sea mining on land-based minerals should also be dealt with together. An early agreement on this issue would serve to consolidate the different positions in the committee on other issues. Thus, the question of general norms regarding exploitation (Draft Article 10), safeguarding the interests and needs of mineral-producing states (Draft Article 34, paragraph 32), regulation of production (Draft Article 36, paragraph 40) and the planning/price stabilization commission (Draft Article 47) may be identified.

Another important subject, which has not yet been dealt with by the First Committee, is the assignment of the executive power between the principal organs of the authority. A great deal of conflict arising from overlapping competence and repetition of functions could be avoided if this basic issue were given priority consideration. As suggested earlier, the heart of this problem is the structure of the council. If the council can be so constructed as to reflect accurately the respective interests and the strength of the different groups, the assembly should then be concerned solely with policy matters, leaving the council to deal with the day-to-day matters. Once this is settled, the detailed powers and functions of the various organs fall into place. In dealing with the powers and functions of the assembly and the council, it is suggested that they should be examined side-by-side to avoid repetition and inconsistency. For that purpose, a comparative table may be particularly useful.

On the basis of the proposals submitted to the First Committee and the estimated revenue from nodule mining, the possibility exists that the new organization's expenditures could be substantial, hence reducing the total sum for development assistance. Moreover, the organization would have to be financed during the initial years before income from nodule mining could be expected (in or about 1985). This and other questions relating to the financial requirement and operational efficiency of the international authority should be carefully examined so that appropriate action can be taken, if necessary. At least misunderstandings or wrong assumptions can be avoided.

It is possible that the Geneva session could be the last chance for agreeing upon the skeleton of a multilateral treaty. If this much is not achieved, it might be too late to forestall unilateral action.

Mr. Christy: Thank you very much, Mr. Lee, for a clear elucidation of some of the numerous difficulties that boggle the mind as to how and in what way we can reach decisions on many of these issues.

NOTES

1. See H.S. Amerasinghe, "The Third UN Conference on the Law of the Sea," C.A. Stavropoulos, "Procedural Problems of the Third Conference on the Law of the Sea"; special UNITAR publication, *UN and the Sea,* April 1974; the publication also contains an unofficial classification of proposals relating to the law of the sea, prepared by the author.
2. United Nations, General Assembly Resolution 2749 (XXV) was adopted by 104 to nil. Most of the Eastern European countries abstained.
3. The total area of the ocean is about 361 million square kilometers. The area under 200 n.m. is about 133 million square kilometers.
4. United Nations, General Assembly, *Summary Records* (A/PV.1933), 17 December 1970.
5. General Assembly Resolution 2574 (XXIV) of 15 December 1969 adopted at its 1833rd meeting by 62 to 28, with 28 abstentions.
6. The following proposals or working papers were submitted: (1) United States: Draft UN Convention of the International Sea-bed (A/AC.138/25), 1970; (2) United Kingdom: International Regime (A/AC.138/26 and 46), 1970 and 1971; (3) France: Establishment of a Regime for the Exploration and Exploitation of the Sea-bed (A/AC.138/27), 1970; (4) Tanzania: Draft Statute for an International Sea-bed Authority, (A/AC.138/33), 1971; (5) USSR: Provisional Draft Articles of a Treaty on the Use of the Sea-bed for Peaceful Purposes (A/AC.138/43), 1971; (6) Poland: Working Paper on an International Organization on the Sea-bed and the Ocean Floor, and the Subsoil Thereof (A/AC.138/44), 1971; (7) Chile, Colombia, Ecuador, El Salvador, Guatemala, Guyana, Jamaica, Mexico, Panama, Peru, Trinidad and Tobago, Uruguay, and Venezuela: Working Paper on the Sea-bed Regime (A/AC.135/49), 1971; (8) Malta: Draft Ocean Space Treaty (A/AC.138/53), 1971; (9) Afghanistan, Austria, Belgium, Hungary, Nepal, Netherlands, and Singapore: Preliminary Working Paper (A/AC.138/55), 1971; (10) Canada: International Sea-bed Regime and Machinery Working Paper (A/AC.138/59), 1971; (11) Japan: Outline of a Convention on International Sea-bed Regime and Machinery (A/AC.138/63), 1971; (12) Italy: Articles on Composition of the Council (A/AC.138/-SC.I/L.24), 1972; Preliminary Draft Articles Concerning Basic Principles of the Regime and Regulations for the Granting and Administration of Licences for the Exploration and Exploitation of Minerals (A/AC.138/SC.1/L.28), 1973; (13) Turkey: Articles on Archaeological and Historical Treasures (A/AC.138/SC.1/L.21), 1973; (14) Greece: Draft Articles on Protection of Archaeological and Historical Treasures (A/AC.138/SC.1/L.25), 1973.
7. For further details, see Report of the Secretary-General, *The Economic Significance, in Terms of Sea-bed Mineral Resources, of the Various Limits Proposed for National Jurisdiction* (A/AC.138/87), 1973.

8. See Report of the Secretary-General, *Economic Implications of Sea-bed Mineral Development in the International Area* [hereinafter referred to as 1974 report of the Secretary-General] (A/CONF.62/25), 22 May 1974, pp. 11 and 29.

9. 1974 Report of the Secretary-General, p. 5, and D.R. Horn, B.M. Horn and M.N. Delach, *Ferromanganese Deposits off the North Pacific,* Technical Paper No. 1 (Wash. D.C.: National Science Foundation, 1972). This area lies between 6°N and 20°N latitude and extending between 110°W and 180°W longitude, stretching from over 200 miles west of central America to southwest of Hawaii.

10. The reports of the UN Economic Commission for Asia and the Far East indicated that several states in that region were interested in developing the deposits lying within their jurisdiction. See two reports issued by that organization relating to Tonga platform and Western Samoa in UN document E/CN.11/L.343.

11. See, for example, Rothstein et Kaufman, "The Approaching Maturity of Deep Ocean Mining - the Pace Quickens," Offshore Technology Conference Preprints, Vol. I, 1973 pp. 323–344, and Chapter 12 of this volume by J. Flipse.

12. See, for example, J.L. Mero, "Potential Economic Value of Ocean Floor Manganese Nodule Deposits," Conference on Ferromanganese Deposits on the Ocean Floor, 1972, Washington, p. 191 and Chapter 12 of this volume by Mr. Mero.

13. These include, for example, Summa Corporation (formerly Hughes Tool Corporation), Kennecott Copper Corporation, DeepSea Ventures, Inc. (an affiliate of Tenneco), International Nickel Corporation, Summitomo Group/MITI, Arbeitsgemeinschaft Meerestechnischewinnbare Rohstoffe (AMR) of the Federal Republic of Germany, Centre National pour l'exploitation des oceans (CNEXO), and Societé de Nickel of France.

14. The bill is generally known as S.1134 which is before the Committee on Interior and Insular Affairs of the Senate. Amendment No. 946 to S.1134 was submitted at the 93rd Congress. It is reported that the bill will be resubmitted to the 94th Congress for consideration. For details of the bill and hearings before the committee, see Committee on Interior and Insular Affairs, Hearings before the Subcommittee on Minerals, Materials and Fuels 93rd Congress, 2d sess., 1974, part 2, pp. 770–791.

15. The claim lies between latitude 15° 44'N and 15° 16'N and longitude 124° 20'W and 124° 46'W on the abyssal ocean floor in water depths ranging between 2300 to 5000 meters. The claim stated that DeepSea would commence commercial production within fifteen years for a period of forty years. It asserts the exclusive rights to develop, evaluate, and mine the deposits and to take, use, and sell all of the manganese nodules in, and the minerals and metals derived therefrom.

16. For example, Draft Articles 10, 11, 12, 18.

17. For example, Draft Articles 3, 15, and 23.

18. Paragraph 4 of the Declaration states that "all activities regarding the exploration and exploitation of the resources of the area and other related activities shall be governed by the international regime to be established."

19. See Provisions 68 and 81 contained in the Working Paper of the Second Committee (A/CONF.62/C.1/WP.1), 15 October 1974.

20. During the general debate at the Caracas session, three delegations, however, spoke in favor of extending the new regime to cover the water column. (A/CONF.62/C.1/SR.6.)

21. It may be noted here that manganese nodules are extremely rare in areas where there is rapid sedimentation or those parts of the sea floor underlying areas of high biological productivity in the water column. Accordingly, nodule mining is unlikely to take place in the same area where there are extensive fisheries resources.

22. As the present proposals stand, the assembly has thirty-four items of powers and functions and the council, forty-seven items. Thirty are items common to both.

23. See Summary Record A/AC.138/C.1/SR.67, 1973.

24. See Draft Article 35, alternatives A and D.

25. According to UN practice, there are five regional groups for purposes of consultations and other matters (e.g., distribution of seats): Africa, Asia, Eastern Europe, Latin America and Western Europe, and others.

26. The geographical location of states classified according to regional groups is as follows:

Region	Coastal	Landlocked	Total
Africa (including Namibia)	30	13	43
Asia	35	6	41
Eastern Europe	7	4	11
Latin America	24	2	26
Western Europe and Others (including the United States)	26	6	32
Total	122	31	153

27. The major copper, nickel, manganese, and cobalt exporters and consumers are as follows:

1. *Major exporters*

Copper	*Cobalt*	*Manganese*	*Nickel*
Chile	Zaire	Gabon	Canada
Zambia	Zambia	South Africa	France
Canada	Cuba	U.S.S.R.	Australia
Zaire	Morocco	India	Cuba
Peru		Brazil	Dominican Republic

2. *Major consumers*

Copper and Nickel

A. U.S.   B. China
    Japan   Brazil
    U.S.S.R.   Mexico

Germany, Federal Republic of   India

U.K.   Argentina

France

28. According to the UN Committee for Development Planning, the following countries are classified among the least developed among developing countries:

    Africa (16):   Botswana, Burundi, Chad, Dahomey, Ethiopia, Guinea, Lesotho, Mali, Malawi, Niger, Rwanda, Somalia, Sudan, Uganda, Tanzania, Upper Volta.

    Asia (8)   Afghanistan, Bhutan, Laos, Maldives, Nepal, Western Samoa, Yemen

    Latin America: Haiti

    See UN document E/4990, 1971, p. 19.

29. See Draft Article 34, paragraph 24 and Draft Article 36, paragraph 27.

30. See Draft Article 34, paragraph 28, and Draft Article 36, paragraph 36.

31. See Draft Article 34, paragraphs 21 and 23, and Draft Article 35, paragraph 23.

32. See Draft Article 34, paragraph 25, and Draft Article 36, paragraph 28.

33. See Draft Article 34, paragraph 27, and Draft Article 36, paragraph 30.

34. See Draft Article 36, paragraph 39.

35. See Draft Articles 38–44.

36. See Draft Article 34, paragraph 31.

37. See Draft Article 36, paragraph 40.

38. *Report of the Secretary-General* (A/CONF.62/25), 22 May 1974, p. 41. See also list of major exporters of these minerals contained in footnote 27.

39. See Draft Article 34, paragraphs 8 and 9, and Draft Article 36, paragraphs 7 and 8.

40. A/CONF.62/25, 22 May 1974.

41. Ibid, p. 71.

42. Proposals have been submitted for the creation of: (1) a Rules and Recommended Practices Commission which would consider and recommend the adoption of international rules, standards, and practices relating to a variety of technical and operational subjects dealing with the exploration of the area and the exploitation of its resources; (2) a Planning/Price Stablilization Commission whose principal function would be to investigate or review current trends of supply and demand and prices of raw materials obtained from the international area and to make recommendations regarding the price rates at which seabed minerals from the area may be sold and the quantities of such materials to be made available at any given time; (3) a Scientific and Technological Commission which would undertake directly scientific investigations of ocean space and the development of technologies for the exploration of the area and its resources; (4) a Legal Commission whose functions would be to promote harmonization of national maritime laws and the development of international laws relating to ocean space and, in particular, to the area; (5) an international Seabed Boundary Review Commission, which, as the title

suggests, is designed to review the delineation of boundaries submitted by contracting parties and to negotiate differences and to make recommendations in this regard to the parties concerned; (6) an Inspection and Conservation Commission which would review, approve, and inspect all work programs carried out in the international area whether undertaken by an appropriate organ of the authority itself or under arrangements authorized by it.

43. Draft Article XXV provides that "The Authority may move vessels under its flag and may, exclusively for peaceful purposes, emplace installations in the sea and on the sea-bed beyond national jurisdiction."

44. This is reflected in a report prepared by the United Nations Conference on Trade and Development. See *Implications of the Exploitation of the Mineral Resources of the International Area of the Sea-Bed: Issues of International Commodity Policy, Report by the UNCTAD Secretariat* (TD/B/C.1/170), December 1974.

45. See Draft Article XLV.7.

46. For example, since industrial secrets and other confidential information might come to the knowledge of the staff by reasons of their official duties, proposals have been made to introduce the necessary protective measures. Any breach of confidence would be considered a grave offense and any disclosure would entail not merely action by the organization but also personal liability for damage. Proposals have also been made prohibiting the secretary-general or any staff member, either during or subsequent to his service, from being associated with or having financial interests in any enterprise concerned with the exploitation activities of the area. This provision was considered necessary in order to avoid possible conflict of interests.

47. See Articles III, XI, XII, and XIV of the Statute of IAEA. P. Szasz, *The Law and Practices of IAEA,* IAEA publication, Legal Series no. 7, pp. 531–658; and M. Willrich, (ed.) *International Safeguards and Nuclear Industries,* 1973.

48. Draft Article 37.

49. C. Fligler, *Multinational Public Enterprises* (International Bank for Reconstruction and Development, 1967); W. Friedman and G. Kalmanoff, *Joint International Business Ventures* (Columbia University Press, 1961); L. Franko, *Joint Venture Survival in Multinational Corporations* (Praeger, 1971).

50. See Van Meurs, *Petroleum Economics and Offshore Mining Legislation* (Elsevier Publishing Company, 1971), Chapter IX.

51. United States: Draft Appendix to the Law of the Sea Treaty Concerning Mineral Resource Development in the International Sea-Bed Area (A/CONF.62/C.1/L.6), 13 August 1974.

52. Text prepared by the Group of 77 and circulated in accordance with the decision taken by the Committee at its informal meeting on 16 August 1974 (A/CONF.62/C.1/L.7).

53. Belgium, Denmark, France, Federal Republic of Germany, Italy, Luxembourg, Netherlands, United Kingdom: Annex to the Law of the

Sea Convention: Conditions of Exploration and Exploitation
(A/CONF.62/C.1/L.8), 16 August 1974.

54. Japan: Working Paper on Conditions of Exploration and Exploitation
(A/CONF.62/C.1/L.9) 19 August 1974.

55. For example, size of the mine site, maximum number of contracts, duration,
fees, and categories of minerals.

56. The maximum mine site proposed respectively by the United States, the
EEC countries (minus Ireland), and Japan were 30,000 sq. km.,
60,000 sq. km., and 60,000 sq. km. The EEC text requires relinquishment of one-third of the site upon exploitation, though one
contractor may hold up to a maximum of six contracts (i.e. 240,000
sq. km.). The Japanese text requires a relinquishment of one-half
of the mine site. Neither the U.S. nor the Japanese text mentioned
the maximum award.

57. A total of fifty-five years in the case of the U.S. proposal, fifty years in the
EEC proposal and thirty years in the Japanese proposal.

58. These ten stages are: scientific research, general survey, exploration, evaluation, feasibility studies, construction, exploitation, processing, transportation, and marketing.

59. A/CONF.62/25, p. 62, *op. cit.*

60. The EEC countries' text uses the word "declaration."

Panel Discussion

Mark Coler
U.S. Department of Treasury,
Office of Raw Materials and Oceans Policy

Mr. Coler: I am going to try and keep my speech to the ten minutes, and my relative ignorance of the area, compared to the other distinguished panelists up here will certainly assist me in that endeavor.

I think I will talk a little about what the U.S. experience has been with commodity agreements. I will speak about that because the resources of the seabed agreement, certain specified minerals, in many ways, as Mr. Lee pointed out, will be the main product from the seabed for the next twenty years, and in that very generalized sense it does have certain aspects of a commodity agreement.

I think the most notable thing about the U.S. experience with commodity agreements is that we don't have any. At least, there aren't any into which the U.S. government has entered formally at this time—agreements of a binding nature, concerning the transfer of commodities. There are, of course, companies with long-term contracts, but there really have not been any governmental agreements.

I believe there have been such agreements occasionally in the past, the Coffee Agreement about two years ago lapsed, but at this point the nature of U.S. agreements has been very—well, the two that come to mind are the Wheat Council and most recently, the World Food Council. These have been agreements of a general and consultative nature, providing for extensive consultative mechanisms and exchange of information. They have not provided for any specific type of regulation of the product, the exchange of product, or the prices of those products.

I think this is particularly striking when you compare the activities of some other governments, but this contrast between the U.S. attitude, what historically has been the U.S. attitude, and that of other governments, I think is of rather long-standing nature. And those of you who are familiar with the Tin Council Agreement are aware that for some twenty years that agreement, which is a buffer-stock arrangement, set up between producer and consumer countries in order to stabilize volatile movements in the tin market, the U.S. I think is the only major industrialized country which is not a member of that agreement.

So that the rather striking contrast and uniformity with which the U.S. has taken this attitude towards commodity agreements demands some explanation, and clearly it is not accidental.

I suppose a cynic could say that the U.S. has been an importer of raw materials, that agreements may tend to raise the average price of such raw materials, and that a raw-material importing country may be reluctant to enter into such agreements.

But that explanation really does not hold water. It has—I think there are two things you will find wrong if you try to take that seemingly rationalistic and cold approach. First of all, the U.S. is not—it is a major exporter of raw materials as well as an importer of raw materials.

You are all aware that in the agricultural area, the U.S. position is rather comparable to the position of the Persian Gulf states in the petroleum area. It has a very high percentage of the trade, both in wheat and the feed grains, and some of the other agricultural products. It is also an exporter of phosphates and coking coal, and, in the oceans' area, of nickel scrap, and has, at times, exported copper, although it is not, at this point, a net exporter of copper.

And the other area, in which I think that the simple view that an importing country does not want to enter into such an arrangement doesn't hold up, is that this contrasts with the view of the other European countries, and of Japan, who on average import far more raw materials than the U.S., and who have participated in such buffer agreements, and some of them feel that these have worked out well, as is evidenced by the Tin Council.

So I think we have to look elsewhere to say why this attitude has developed, and why it has persisted so long. I think it really goes back to the very basic view, that has been held in the U.S. for a hundred years, that from the standpoint of both the producer and the consumer it is best to let the market allocate resources, the feeling being that you can't fight the market, that you may make short-term changes in it, but ultimately both parties are losers.

This is a rather general and perhaps seemingly philosophical view, but it had a rather concrete, specific implementation in the form of the anti-trust laws, and those laws have rather strong teeth. As you know, these were— the first one, in 1890, was the Sherman Anti-Trust Law. That was specifically directed toward the cartel, a delivered agreement to raise prices.

And antitrust laws have been probably the longest standing and most persistent of the U.S. economic laws. I think the sincerity with which the conviction has been held that the market is the best allocator is evidenced by the fact that the antitrust laws are directed against U.S. companies. They prevent

U.S. companies from getting together and making any sort of agreement, whether they are selling to the domestic market or to a foreign market, any sort of agreement that would tend to fix or raise prices, the price of commodities.

This atitude has persisted even in very recent years. I think the question has come up in East-West trade rather frequently since it opened up in 1972. U.S. companies have been faced more frequently with nonmarket economies, with single purchasing agents, what we would call "monopolistic," but clearly are not viewed that way in many of those countries. And the question has come up, shouldn't there be an exemption for U.S. companies? Why can't U.S. companies get together when, if you go over to Moscow and you want to sell a product, there is only one buyer there, and you have to deal with one buyer, why can't U.S. companies get together and reach some sort of agreement to prevent or at least to reach balance of power between the buyer and the seller? And the answer has been no. At least so far, the Justice Department has not allowed exceptions, even in this rather extreme case.

I think this attitude, and its roots are manifest in the antitrust laws, explains two things, the first of which is rather strong American reaction to cartels. I guess all of you who read *Business Week* are aware of Mr. Kissinger's views on cartels, but this has been a rather strong concern in all parts of the government.

I think the possibility of cartels developing in other areas has been viewed with alarm, and a study recently appeared that deals basically with nonfuel minerals, a study of critical imported commodities that came out about two weeks ago, in which it was indicated that the U.S. government had been looking at the possibility elsewhere, and it was a matter of real concern. It has been a matter of great concern in the legislative branch. The recent trade bill has specific provisions that would deny certain preferences to less developed countries in the event that they join in producers' associations which disrupt the market.

No one is quite sure which associations will ultimately fall under that denomination. At this point, the only one seems to be the OPEC cartel.

Finally, though, I think it is the specific development of the U.S. antitrust laws, and the very strong influence they have had, that explains why the U.S. has been reluctant to enter into any kind of administrative price agreements.

Back about fifty years ago, the question came up as to whether an agreement could be justified it it were shown that the intent of it was to stabilize prices within the market, to prevent unreasonably low prices from developing; a number of other justifications were offered to show why the full effect of this agreement was desirable and should be supported and perhaps should even be encouraged. And the Supreme Court, at that point, threw out the argument and it has never been raised since, at least not in that form.

They simply decided that any type of agreement to set prices, any kind of agreement to set production levels, whether or not that agreement was intended to stabilize the market or create desirable side effects, was unreasonable per se. And that is the term that, I think, persists right up to today.

Of course we are talking about history at this point, and there are many changes going on. It is very difficult to say whether this type of attitude will persist in the future, but I think the antitrust laws, if they are any indication, are enjoying a resurgence, at least domestically, in the U.S. economy, and this attitude has been held with great tenacity and with great sincerity for nearly some eighty years. So I don't know what the implications will be for the future in commodity agreements. I certainly don't know what the implications will be for the oceans, which is far more than a commodity agreement, but perhaps these comments may be useful to you in looking at the resources parts of the oceans agreements.

Mr. Christy: Thank you, Mark. I think we ought to consider whether we want a Sherman Anti-Trust Act to apply to the oceans, not so much perhaps with regard to the developing countries' production controls, but to the controls of the cartels, the oligopoly that might be created by Tenneco, Kennecott, and a few of our producers. But we can discuss that in the later period.

I now turn to Alvaro de Soto who is the delegate of Peru to the UN Sea-Bed Committee, and who has been there since the beginning of the discussions. Currently he is Chairman of the Drafting Committee on Sea-Bed matters of the Group of 77.

Panel Discussion

Alvaro de Soto
Peruvian Mission to the United Nations

Mr. de Soto: Thank you.

I should perhaps begin with a couple disclaimers. The first is that any similarity between the views that I express and those of my government is purely coincidental.

The second is that if I seem to have a tendency to speak on behalf of the developing countries, it is on the one hand because I am the only member of the panel who comes from a developing country, and on the other because I can't resist playing the role.

I want to deal first of all with one issue which was referred to fairly frequently in yesterday's meeting, which is the question of the ideological input, particularly on the part of the developing countries, which I might also call the theological factor in the negotiation.

This factor arises not only on the extrajurisdictional, or international issues, such as the seabed beyond national jurisdiction, but also on the issues of a more jurisdictional nature, such as when representatives from developing countries insist on assertions of sovereignty, and resist the more functional approach to which they are encouraged by representatives from developed countries.

The fact is that certain concepts such as sovereignty, for instance, are not considered outmoded by developing countries, because they have not yet been properly affirmed. They have not yet been absolutely asserted vis à vis developed countries. It is all right to forsake sovereignty and to forsake other essentially national notions if you have already clearly established that what you own is beyond dispute. That is to say, interdependence is all right so long as you have, as a prerequisite, independence.

Now, the ideological input in the negotiation has been frequently blamed yesterday on the conference mechanics; that is, the tendency of delegations to bunch together because it seems to make their point of view clearer. It also has been referred to as the UNCTAD approach. Of course the Group of 77, which is the reunion of developing countries, did arise at UNCTAD.

This ideological factor has, of course, been referred to, in a way which I would not describe as disparaging, but rather as something which should not be there, an extraneous factor which is not helping the negotiation at all.

The fact is, however, that certain notions, such as common heritage, are extremely important to developing countries as a group. I am sure that here I would not claim false pretenses in saying that I am speaking on behalf of developing countries on this particular issue.

There was one speaker yesterday who felt that we should shift the focus of the negotiation in the First Committee to what he referred to as the "underlying concerns." And he managed, I believe, to expose what the underlying concerns of developing countries are in the negotiation without any mention of the principle of common heritage.

Now, the principle of common heritage is extremely important to us, and we are wedded to it by the declaration of principles that was adopted by the General Assembly. We think that it is extremely important because it uproots and sets aside other notions such as those deriving from the principles of the freedom of the high seas, and the idea of res communis. Common heritage does have a meaning.

I am not going to go into the issue of whether it is a principle of international law. That is not important at this stage, because we do not, as yet, have any practice by states of such a principle.

The common heritage principle does imply to us, first of all, peaceful purposes, though that is more in the line of a premise, than the idea of nonappropriation by anyone of any part of the area, and also that no claims of sovereignty should be made over the area. It implies the notion of a proxy, that is, of trusteeship and trustees, which means international machinery; and implies also the notions of equitable sharing and, perhaps most important, equitable participation, joint participation.

Now, this common philosophical approach by developing countries toward the idea of common heritage has been possible, even though there exists, and there does exist, a certain variance between developing countries as to what the extent of the area should be, that is, where the jurisdiction of coastal states should end.

The question, though, is that it is not really terribly relevant to the principle itself what the value of the area is, what the contents are. You do not change your principles because of the amount of money involved. It may vary once we get down to certain details of implementation of the principles, and it may lead to certain variations when we are concerned with, for instance, the size of machinery or even the nature of the machinery, but whether it is oil, gas, manganese nodules, or whatever it is, the principles continue to be the same. There should really not be any need for a change in this.

It seems that there is a difference of point of view, of approach, between developing countries and representatives of developed countries, because the latter essentially are defending interests of private firms whose constituencies are composed essentially of stockholders whose only notion is that they should make a certain amount of money, whereas the others are representing governments, and governments—at least we must assume—are trying to represent the points of view of all the people.

The common heritage, as I was saying, means that it must be a joint operation. Exploitation of the resources of the seabed beyond national jurisdiction must be a joint operation. That means that the title to the resources must remain in mankind, and it is mankind, through whatever agency it decides to appoint, which has the right to dispose of the resources one way or another.

Now, this means that we have rejected the licensing or concessions approach, which Mr. Lee referred to very lucidly. The reason for this is simply that licensing carries the notion of giving up rights, real rights, property rights. An illustration of this problem is in the conflict that arose with regard to Article 4 of the regime, which refers to nonappropriation, that no state or person, natural or juridical, shall claim, acquire, or exercise any rights. The dispute was whether it should be over the resources or with respect to the resources.

The conflict arose because if we are saying "over" the resources, we are talking about property rights, whereas we don't want to talk about property rights. We want to say "with respect to" resources, because the rights will be of another nature. The property of the resource is held only by mankind through an appropriate authority.

Now, Article 9 represents perhaps the first written agreement by the Group of 77 on the seabed area. The first paragraph of that Article represents the ideal: that all activities should be carried out by an authority on behalf of all mankind.

One reason why the developing countries want this is because they do not have the means to undertake the activities themselves, and so they have to have an appropriate proxy. They can't just hand it over to a few firms. Now, an operational authority is an ideal and it is an aim. But developing countries have not lost their minds, and they realize that they will not be able to exploit the seabed solely by means of an authority, because it would not be able to do so, not having either the money or the equipment to start with.

And so we have a second paragraph in Article 9, which is an exception to the principle in paragraph one: that the authority may confer certain tasks upon others. It is clear that it means conferring certain tasks on private or state firms. Obviously, that will have to be the practice, at least, in the early stages. We will have to avail ourselves of the services of companies that at present have the finance capital, the equipment, and the technology.

Now, yesterday a reference was made, I believe it was by Edward Miles, to an attempt by the developing countries, by the Group of 77, to enshrine in the basic conditions, paragraph 2 of Article 9.

This is, of course, true in a sense. But I would go even further. I would say that the basic conditions that were elaborated by the developing countries were based entirely on, and even derived from, paragraph 2 of Article 9. They are the framework for rule-making by the authority as to the indirect modality of exploitation by the authority foreseen in paragraph 2 of Article 9. I say "framework for rule-making" because I think developing countries made it fairly clear that, in their view, there should not be a mining code or detailed conditions of operation set forth in the convention itself, but rather that the authority should be given considerable leeway to lay them down itself.

The criterion behind this is that the authority, as a resource manager, must have considerable, wide discretion. I feel that this approach—that the resource manager needs wide discretion—is not entirely different from the point of view contained in the Metcalf bill, through which the mining companies would also have quite wide discretion.

I believe that my time is almost up, but I would like to say a little word about the economic implications of exploitation of the area. I think that the fact that the developing countries—all developing countries—have been able to agree on something like Article 9, which, as I say, summarizes the system to be applied to the area, as well as the basic conditions, makes it fairly clear that the point of view that the authority should exercise considerable control over all activities in the seabed is not merely a conspiracy or a plot by a few land-based producers who essentially do not want any exploitation to be carried out at all.

I think that here we have a Lincolnian adage which is perfectly applicable, that you just can't fool that many consumers all at the same time and for such a long time. The land-based producers are simply not that powerful.

Now, I think that on economic implications, the focus at Caracas shifted somewhat, from the issue of what the damages to certain land-based producers are going to be to what powers the authority needs in order to counteract any possible damage to some land-based producers.

I think that it should not surprise us that the developing countries agree that what is for the benefit of all should not lead to damage for a few. And if the argument, set forth constantly and consistently by the representatives of many developed countries, that no damage is actually going to occur in the foreseeable future to a few land-based producers, is true, if that argument is true, I say, well then, there does not seem to be any harm at all in giving the authority the proper machinery to resolve the problems, because it will never have to be used.

On the other hand, if it is true that there is going to be damage, well let us simply give the authority the means to do so. It is clear that if the land-based producers are in the minority that they are said to be, then it is very unlikely that they will be able to control the international authority in the way that some fear that they might.

Thank you.

Mr. Christy: Thank you, Alvaro. We have a nice distinction between the two approaches as mentioned by the two past speakers, and I hope we will return to this later on in the discussion period.

We now turn to someone who is actually out there intending to do some of the mining, Dick Greenwald, who is the Secretary and Special Counsel of Deepsea Ventures, which recently submitted what is referred to here as "a notice of discovery and claim of exclusive mining rights and request for diplomatic protection and protection of investment by Deepsea Ventures, Inc."—this to an area somewhat the size of Ireland out in the Pacific Ocean.

Panel Discussion

Richard Greenwald
Special Counsel
Deepsea Ventures, Inc.

Mr. Greenwald: Thank you. I thought that I was invited to this conference as the skeptic in the broad spectrum of invited perceptions, but after listening to yesterday's discussion, I found it hard to be more skeptical or pessimistic than any of the speakers, other than John Norton Moore.

And I thought maybe I was invited as the optimist, but that obviously is not right.

When talking to many of the participants yesterday, I found that a great number, if not most, were not aware that Deepsea had filed the mining claim that Francis Christy just described to you. I thought I would take just a few minutes to make a few general comments, and then read to you extracts from the claim so that you will know what we will be talking about probably for the next hour.

First I would like to comment on Alvaro de Soto's comments of just a minute ago. I don't know whether it was intended or not, but it is my perception that the basic conditions of the Group of 77, if implemented, would result in the suppression of ocean mining. One of the reasons that we filed the claim was to provide knowledge of ocean-mining operations and the technical requirements of ocean mining to decision-makers, so that they did not make decisions that inadvertently prevented the efficient and effective development of the mineral resources of the seabed.

I can illustrate one of the problems in the basic conditions of the Group of 77 by saying that the basic conditions contemplate that if there are arrangements between the authority and a contractor (or a venturer), the contractor is required to provide all of the funds, all of the talent, all of the know-how, and all of the equipment. He is expected to be under the total control of the authority at all times for whatever portion of the operation he has contracted for, and yet he takes all of the responsibility, assumes all of the liability, and all of the risk, even as to losses and damages arising as a result of instructions from the authority that has total control over him. This is not realistic. No corporation (state or private) would sign such a contract.

I would like, before reading you extracts from the claim, to give you some of the perceptions that Deepsea had before we filed that claim. The first perception was that the international negotiations at the Third Conference on the Law of the Sea were more or less wandering into a permanent state of confrontation, without a great deal of willingness to resolve the basic issues at the conference in Caracas or the conferences coming after Caracas.

The second perception was that the company could not long survive in the waiting mode that we had been in for a year and a half, waiting for these international negotiations to arrive at some conclusion. We were not stopped dead. We were doing a lot of process research, we were doing some marine-science studies, but we were not operating and doing engineering development on the mine site to the extent that our operations were planned in the late sixties and early seventies. Of course, the LOS Conference was originally scheduled to begin in '73, and there was great hope back in those years that it would be concluded in '73. We are now in 1975, without a great prospect of resolution in '75, and perhaps no great prospect of resolution of conferences in '76 and beyond. The next (delayed) activity on the "critical path" of the company plan was the detailed mapping and development of our chosen mine site. We chose that mine site some years ago. Now, that development and evaluation would make use of several ships at that mine site, plus a lot of coming and going of ships, men, and messages to and from that particular mine site. We would be very obvious in the location of the mine site. Our investment in that mine site thus would be threatened because many people would gain knowledge of where the mine site was.

The third perception was that decisions were being made, or positions were being taken, in the international negotiations that had little relationship to the technical facts of ocean mining. We needed to disclose those facts. In order to disclose some of those facts (for example, environmental data) in a way that would be credible, the facts would have to be confirmed by government authorities. In order for the work-product of government authorities to maintain that credibility, they would have to be based upon some knowledge of conditions at our mine site. That meant the government authorities probably would have to know the location of our mine site, and do actual work at that mine site. Again, the location of our mine site would be thus compromised without a timely legal solution.

The fifth perception was that the Lord helps him who helps himself. No sense sitting, with nothing happening in Caracas. We had better start looking to our own protection. Under the theory expounded by the U.S. delegation, ocean mining is a legitimate exercise of the Freedom of the Seas Doctrine, that is, the law that exists now. If we could make our claim in a way that did not do violence to that doctrine, we would not be at cross purposes with the U.S. administration. I want to emphasize at this point that when we filed the claim with the State Department, that was the first knowledge that they had of that action. There was no, and I repeat, there was no collusion between the State Department and Deepsea Ventures. They were shocked, I think, or surprised.

Let me now paraphrase some sections of the claim. I will submit the whole claim for the record if the Chairman thinks that will be helpful. In fact, I will submit not only the claim, but the supporting legal opinion.

Mr. Christy: Without objection, it is so ordered.

Mr. Greenwald: This claim was filed with Secretary Kissinger on the 15th of November, 1974. It was recorded in the Office of the Clerk of the Circuit Court of Gloucester County on the same day. We requested that Secretary Kissinger make it available to the public. It is also available for public inspection at the Clerk's Office in the County Circuit Court of Gloucester County, Virginia. There was no attempt to make a secret claim. We realized that one of the purposes of making a claim is to put other ocean users on notice as to the type of activities at the mine site, in order that the chances of conflict at that mine site may be minimized and that other actual users of that area have a chance to come in and seek accommodation of any conflicting uses.

Deepsea Ventures, Inc., in the claim, gives public notice that it has discovered and taken possession of, and is now engaged in developing and evaluating, as the first stages of mining, a deposit of seabed manganese nodules.

The deposit is illustrated in a sketch attached to the claim, and the coordinates of the deposit are given.

The deposit lies in an area approximately 60,000 square kilometers for purposes of development and evaluation of the deposit, which area will be reduced to 30,000 square kilometers upon expiration of a term of fifteen years, absent force majeure, from the date of the claim, or upon commencement of commercial production of the deposit, whichever occurs first.

The deposit lies on the abyssal ocean floor in water depths ranging from 2300 to 5000 meters, and is more than 1000 kilometers from the nearest island, and more than 1300 kilometers seaward of the outer edge of the nearest continental margin. It is beyond the limits of seabed jurisdiction presently claimed by any state, and the overlying waters are high seas.

The general area of the deposit was identified in August 1964 by the predecessor in interest of Deepsea, and the deposit was discovered by Deepsea on August 31, 1968.

Deepsea, or its successor in interest, will commence commercial production from the deposit within fifteen years of the date of the claim, and will conclude production within forty years from the date of commencement of commercial production, whereon the right shall cease.

Deepsea has been advised by counsel, whose names appear at the end of the claim, that it has validly established the exclusive rights asserted in the claim under existing international law, as evidenced by the practice of states, the 1958 Convention on High Seas, and the general rules of law recognized by civilized nations.

Deepsea, in the claim, asserts the exclusive rights to develop, evaluate, and mine the deposit claimed and to take, use, and sell all of the manganese nodules in, and the minerals and metals derived therefrom. It is proceeding, with appropriate diligence, to do so, and requests and requires states, persons, and all other commercial or political entities to respect the exclusive rights asserted herein.

Deepsea did not assert, nor did it ask the United States of America to assert, a territorial claim to the seabed or subsoil underlying the claimed deposit.

Deepsea, in the claim, respectfully requested the diplomatic protection of the United States government with respect to the exclusive mining rights described and asserted, and any other rights which may hereafter accrue to Deepsea as a result of its activities at the site of the claimed deposit, and similar protection of the integrity of its investments heretofore made, and now being undertaken, and to be undertaken in the future.

This request was made prior to any known interference with the rights being asserted, and prior to any known impairment of Deepsea's investment. It was intended to give the Department immediate notice of Deepsea's claim for purpose of facilitating the protection of Deepsea's rights and investment, should this be required as a consequence of any future actions of the United States government or other states, persons, or organizations.

The protection requested accords with the assurances given on behalf of the Executive Department of the Congress of the United States, including those by Ambassador John R. Stevenson, by Honorable Charles Brower, and Honorable John Norton Moore, one of which is:

> It is certainly the position of the United States that the mining of the deep sea bed is a High Seas Freedom, and I think that would be a freedom today under international law. Our position is that companies are free to engage in this kind of mining beyond the 200 meter mark, subject to the international regime to be agreed upon, which we recognize, and of course assured protection of integrity of investment in that period. [Statement of John Norton Moore before the Senate in 1973.]

Deepsea has used its best efforts to ascertain that there are no pipelines, cables, military installations, or other activities constituting an exercise of the freedom of the seas in the area encompassing the claimed deposit, or in the superjacent waters with which Deepsea's operations might conflict.

So far as known, no claim of rights has been made by any state or person with respect to the claimed deposit, or any other mineral resources in the area encompassing that deposit, and no state or person has established effective occupation of the area.

Initially, approximately 1.3 million wet metric tons of nodules will be recovered by Deepsea from the deposit per year. In accord with market conditions, this may later be expanded to as much as 4 million wet metric tons per year recovered.

Deepsea's processing and refining technology, successfully demonstrated in its pilot plant, will recover copper, nickel, cobalt, manganese, and other products, depending on the market situation and competitive conditions.

The recovered weight of the major four metals that the initial 1.35 million wet metric tons of nodules will yield per year, will be: copper, 9150 tons; nickel, 11,300 tons; cobalt, 2150 tons; manganese, 253,000 tons.

Mr. Christy: Dick, it might be helpful if you could open that up to the map, and leave it on the desk so that people might take a look at it.

I was interested in Mr. de Soto's use of the term "theological" instead of "ideological" and to find this echoed by Dick Greenwald, when he says, "The Lord helps him who helps himself."

We only have 15 minutes left before lunch, so we ought to begin with the discussion, to be initiated by Giulio Pontecorvo, who is Professor of Economics at the Columbia University School of Business, and a fellow board member of the Executive Committee of the Law of the Sea Institute.

Giulio.

Panel Discussion

Giulio Pontecorvo
Graduate School of Business
Columbia University

Mr. Pontecorvo: Well, sitting here between Alvaro's moving statement about
the common heritage, and Dick Greenwald's claiming, like Balboa, the Pacific
Ocean, suggests the difficulty I have in following these two acts, particularly in
the five minutes allowed by Francis Christy.

All I can hope to say is the few things that appear to me to reveal
the economic reality of the deep-sea mining industry, and, I assure you, this is a
poor offering when compared to the emotional content of the other two statements that we have had today.

I think I would like to begin by making one point that was made by
Dr. Coler. I will put it a little differently, rather than on the basis of the American
Anti-Trust Act, though that approach is just as good.

In the Middle Ages, the acts of engrossing, regrading, and forestalling
were crimes punishable by death. They were punishable by death in order to
provide the village with protection from the predatory merchants who threatened
it with starvation by cutting off and monopolizing the supply of foodstuffs.

In this context, then, to the world community, controls on output
pose a very special problem, and really threaten in many ways the whole concept
of improvement of the conditions of human life. I think we want to keep that
particular point very much in mind.

The second point is that one way you could maximize the benefits
from the sea mining industry is to start with the concept that the world is a collection or set of individuals. In this context, given certain conditions, which I will
mention in a moment, the introduction of sea mining will, in fact, act to maximize the gross national product of the world, gross world product, and to raise
on the average the standard of living of all.

If, however, you complicate the problem of optimization by the
introduction of national states, and by the introduction of other institutional
entities, corporations primarily, the optimization problem gets very messy
indeed, and this is where, of course, we are at the moment.

164

In regard to the conditions under which we wish to engage in sea mining on a large scale, I am assuming two things about which I have no real knowledge: that the environment is not seriously threatened by sea mining, and that the costs of production in the ocean are lower than they are on land, both in average and marginal terms.

This implies or raises a question as to who may engage in sea mining. Now, the report of the secretary-general on the question of the structure of the industry made it very clear that the capital costs involved are relatively low, and that the technology is relatively simple. By this I mean we are not dealing here with something like the computer industry, but rather with something more analagous to the automobile industry. Low capital costs imply that if a large number of firms and nations are currently developing this technology, then in the future the technology will be for sale. Where the technology is available, large numbers of states, including many developing states, will be able to engage in sea mining. We may envision, therefore, an open industry with many participants throughout the world.

However, the point to be made, from the view of economic analysis, is that if you have a large number of producers, what in fact you will get is the output from the oceans at the cost of production. In other words, the price level of the output will be at a minimum.

Now, if we get outputs from the large number of producers at minimum cost, this creates a rather cruel paradox for the Law of the Sea Conference. It has been my assumption for a long time that one of the essential ingredients in that conference has been the question of income redistribution between rich and poor nations, and that this condition is implicit in the concept of the common heritage.

It is quite clear that if you get significant output from the oceans, and you get it at minimum cost, this will benefit the developed states as well as the developing. In the initial stages of development the industry will benefit the developed states more. To a limited degree in the short run, but extensively in the long run, the new industry will benefit the developing states who are able to take advantage as consumers of low-cost raw materials. This is because the growth rates of certain developing states will, on average, be higher than those for the already highly developed states.

However, we must be aware that there will be some developing states which don't do much developing, and who will not benefit directly, and only very indirectly from the output from the oceans.

This, however, is not an argument that can be used, it seems to me, to restrict output from the oceans. The effect on both developing states and developed states of restriction of petroleum output is currently a good illustration of the depth of the problem and the impact that monopolistic restrictions on output have on states in all stages of development.

In order to achieve, therefore, a more equitable distribution of income from the output of the oceans, particularly if in the initial stages there should be significant earnings on private account, the appropriate vehicle is a tax of some sort, not restrictions on output or regulations that establish a minimum price level.

Next we must consider the question of how to compensate those who will lose as a result of the operation of the new industry. There is a well-established principle called the Compensation Principle, which allows transfer payments, which would be the transfer of a portion of the revenues raised by taxation to the losers in this game.

I submit that this process of taxation and revenue showing is very complicated. It requires detailed knowledge of capital values, rates of production, and costs of production in both land-based and sea mines. I will come back to these complications in a moment.

In my mind, a great deal of the confusion and the disruption caused by the sea-mining issue at the Law of the Sea Conference stems from the uncertainty with respect to what is involved in this industry, what the implications of it are, what the capital costs are, what the costs of production are. Failure to have any of this information in the public domain means that the negotiators are in total ignorance of the crucial economic variables, and, therefore, they must resort to very complex legalistic devices to protect their countries in the face of the high level of uncertainty.

The more that the level of uncertainty with respect to the industry can be reduced, the simpler will be the legal and political problems associated with working out compromise solutions for the social control of the industry.

This implies, as a final point, that the international authority, whatever its political or legal form, must have the capability to perform a number of economic functions, i.e., it must be able to understand the processes involved in exploration and exploitation, it must be able to cost these functions, it must be able to engage in research with respect to these activities, if it is going to manage, regulate, and tax the industry efficiently.

This suggests that the authority has got to be an economic entity in order to provide a defensible basis for compensation, if it should in fact be decided that compensation is necessary. The compensation question may come out quite differently than we expect, particularly if the time horizon, over which sea mining is to proceed in any significant amount, is stretched out a little bit. There is a very important distinction to be made between entry, and the startup of this industry, and the rate of production some twenty years down the road. Since the time horizons for most private producers are extremely short, extended time horizons for increasing output will, in fact, reduce the need for compensation.

I don't know how long that took, Francis, but that is what I have to say.

Discussion and Questions

Mr. Christy: I would like to thank the panel very much for their various presentations. I find that there are a number of various points on which there are significant disagreements. One of those that interests me is the apparent disagreement in defining the wealth that is constituted within these manganese "noodles" as a friend of mine calls them. And it would appear that, for some, the nodules are sources of economic revenue or consumer benefits in economic terms, whereas for others there are sources of participation in decision-making, an international kind of decision-making process.

Now, when there are such disparate values, there is very little in the way of a common denominator upon which one can make trades and negotiate. Perhaps it might be useful to think in terms of how much a unit of participation, if you can have such a thing, is worth in terms of a unit of revenues foregone, or consumer benefits, and try to arrive at some basis for reaching decision through that kind of technique.

In other words, one might say "What price theology? What is the value of a unit of theology in arriving at these decisions?"

That is just one of many kinds of disagreements that I detect from the discussions so far.

What I would like to do now is to have a discussion among the panelists themselves, before turning to the audience. And I will lay down another tyrannical rule, and say that in the discussion by the panelists, they should keep their remarks short and succinct.

Who would have the first go among the panelists?

Mr. Greenwald: I'll start it off. I am not sure this is going to address your question, but it will address my question.

We're talking about units of participation in a pioneering industry, and we should be talking about units of contribution. The industry is new, the technology is just being developed, the risks are high. Any participation in an ocean-mining project has to be judged just by the nature of the thing, by what the participant can contribute.

Mr. Christy: You are not willing to undertake a contractual arrangement, whereby your costs are fully covered, so that you don't bear the risks? The international agency bears the risks.

Mr. Greenwald: I haven't seen any proposals to that effect to respond to. Every proposal that I have seen tends toward the technologically capable organization taking all of the risks and getting damned few of the benefits.

Mr. Christy: Mr. de Soto.

Mr. de Soto: Just a word. The authority, as a participant in this operation, puts up as its part, the resources which are the common heritage of mankind.

Mr. Christy: Giulio.

Mr. Pontecorvo: I must say, Chris, that I find the notion that the authority should, in fact, bear the market risk here pretty horrifying. The authority starts bearing the market risk, and then the authority begins to immediately assume, quite correctly in those circumstances, controls with respect to output. And I would have to say that I agree with Alvaro, that the resource base is available. I want the resource available on a competitive basis. I want the risks borne by the entrepreneurs in the marketplace.
 The correct remedy for the public interests in these circumstances is competition, and also the imposition of the tax regime necessary to provide compensation, if in fact compensation is deemed necessary, but also to redistribute income if in fact there should be windfall gains and losses here, any noncompetitive price situation initially, at least in the industry.

Mr. Greenwald: I would like to make a comment on that. I am speaking now just in the context of U.S. commercial practice. The only reason for the existence of a corporation, a private corporation, is to assume risk, and the motivation for assuming that risk is that the corporation will get a decent share of the benefits, the return of capital and a little profit over and above that, or a lot of profit over and above that, depending on your expectations and your capabilities.
 I think all of us recognize that there is an international content to manganese nodules. And I think everybody recognizes that there are existing and valid international aspirations, and that the manganese nodules do contain some value to be allocated for the purposes of development in the developing countries.

The question is how much of that value should go for those purposes, and who will assume the risk entailed in producing that value? I think that is really the basic issue. I don't think the views of this panel are as divergent as they sound on this issue.

Mr. Pontecorvo: I think that there is a real fundamental question, Dick, there however. If you give the authority power with respect to taxation, this does require an international agency that has capability that no international agency has that I can see at the present time. And that, in fact, is a novel and unique condition that the conference and the world will have to face. And I think that most sovereign states are not particularly anxious to face it.

Mr. Christy: Mark.

Mr. Coler: I may be missing the point, but it seems to me that in the early years, the first ten or fifteen years, there is not much choice about who would bear the risks, since the authority would not have the funds to bear the risk in any event. So I think it is necessarily forced on the corporation during that period.

At some later point, either through agreement with the constituent states or through independent funding, it might be able to take on the risk-bearing function. But I don't see any alternative in the early days. I guess this is what some of the others here are saying.

Mr. Greenwald: One of the things that has dismayed me in the last seven years of UN seabeds activity is the inability of the Sea-Bed Committee and the Third Law of the Sea Conference to face the international revenue issue squarely.

The method and measure of the production of international revenues and the method and measure by which those revenues will be allocated to those countries which have an aspiration or a right to a share in the revenues has not been faced. It has not even—the approach has not been made. There has been only some conceptual thinking about it.

Some of you may know that the ocean-mining industry sponsored legislation before Congress four years ago, seeking an interim solution to the ocean-mining problem. The original bill was written by representatives of several mining companies, of which I was one. In that legislation, we wrote a provision for the sharing of a portion of the revenues for international developmental purposes.

As far as I know, that is the only time that those international aspirations for a sharing of the revenues have been actually addressed in the form of draft legislation, or specific articles, or anything. Curiously enough, of course, those provisions were struck out of that legislation, not by us, but by people testifying against the legislation on internationalist grounds.

But the point is that that issue needs to be addressed. There can be no resolution of the Law of the Sea Conference without addressing it squarely in both senses: the method and measure to be applied in the production of revenues, and the method and measure of their allocation.

My personal feeling is that it is difficult to set up a revenue system which will be applicable to all ocean miners. For instance, if a U.S. corporation and (separately) a state agency of the U.S.S.R., by some means, exercised rights to mine in the ocean (and I'm just using this as an example) and both recognized that part of the revenues produced or the benefits produced should be allocated to the international community, if those revenues to be extracted were to be a percentage of the profits of the organizations, problems would arise based upon the different accounting systems in the Soviet system of commercial accounting and the U.S. system.

How do you bring those into a common scheme? It is very difficult. It has been my feeling that we should seek a two-tier revenue system in which states should obligate themselves to any international authority that is created to pay a portion of the benefits on a generally accepted method, perhaps based upon square miles or square kilometers or something like that, and then each state could tax its own miners on a different system if it wanted to, or not tax them at all if it wanted to, just so long as its obligation to the authority was the same as everybody else's.

Taking the other question, the allocation of benefits, my personal feeling is that once those benefits are produced and put in the hands of the international authority or some other international agency, then the developed countries should have nothing else to do with the allocation. Let the developing countries allocate them among themselves. Let the potential recipients compensate those developing countries that think they have been injured by ocean mining, let them come before their peers and in some way determine the extent of their injury, if any.

Mr. Christy: Mr. Lee, Mr. de Soto, and then Mr. Coler.

Mr. Lee: Just a small point, Mr. Chairman. I think we might have to bear in mind that it is not only the economic considerations that are the primary criteria for the whole negotiations. One should perhaps look at it in a much broader perspective. It is the first time that a piece of property will be administered by an international organization, and here within this administration then the countries will try to live together, and some of the theoretical bases, Mr. de Soto has pointed out, are in the minds of many delegations.

To some internationalists, this future administration of this property is some kind of functional integration towards an international community. I think if you look at it from that point of view, perhaps you can see why the issues are broader than just merely how to make money and how to share a few dollars which might be shared from the mining system.

Mr. Christy: Alvaro.

Mr. de Soto: The problem of distribution of benefits is a very difficult and complex one. There are myriad criteria which you can apply to it: the degree of development, the poverty of a country, whether it is coastal, whether it is land-locked insofar as it affects its degree of economic development, etc.

You could go on and on. There was one proposal to apply the inverse ratio of contributions to the U.N. regular budget, which is based on the capacity to pay of members. But in any case, the question of revenues, I think, is one of distribution among states, particularly developing countries.

I don't think there is any question here of distributing between the companies that actually do the operating and the countries, parties to the treaty, or the members of the international community. That's not it. They will make their profits, but the revenues will be for the members of the international community.

Mr. Christy: Mr. Coler, and then we will turn to the floor for questions.

Mr. Coler: I just sort of wonder sometimes, I guess when you are talking about the ocean, it's awfully big, and there is a natural tendency to speak in very large terms when you are talking about the seabed revenues and 100 million square miles of seabed. But I wonder how big the revenues we are talking about really will be in the near future.

After all, we have to have an agency set up, we have to have funds for administration. And we are talking about an industry which does not look that big. According to the UN report, maybe $400 million by the mid-80s. If you tax it too heavily, you won't have an industry at all, so you can only tax at some reasonable rate, and I wonder whether the amounts that issue in the end will be that large. Certainly they will be large at some point, but I wonder if they will be that big in the next ten years.

Mr. Christy: Thank you.

There are some people from the floor who would like to ask questions.

Mr. Kolodkin.

Mr. Kolodkin: Thank you, Mr. Chairman. Allow me to express my views and to make only three comments.

Mr. Christy: Excuse me. Would you identify yourself, please first?

Mr. Kolodkin: Kolodkin is my name, from the Soviet Union.

Mr. Chairman, the Caracas Conference showed some new trends, which concern the powers and competence of the future international authority. These trends showed the attempts, which go, it seems to me, far beyond the original goal of the creation of this authority and of the legal nature of its powers, to deal only with the exploitation and the exploration of the mineral resources of the seabed and its subsoil.

One of these attempts shows the trend to give to the authority the power to regulate scientific research and to grant licenses, not only for seabed activity, but for scientific research in the high seas, including water column.

At the same time, I can see then that the right to conduct scientific research beyond the limits of the national jurisdiction is the right of every sovereign state. I base this conclusion on the principle of the Freedom of the High Seas, which is recognized now as an element of the *jus cogens* principle.

I consider the freedom of scientific research on the high seas to be an indispensable element of the freedom of the high seas. I also believe that the functions of IOC-UNESCO, as to coordination of scientific activity and scientific research, quite satisfy the needs of insuring scientific research and the freedom of scientific research.

Of course, we can examine the possibility of broadening the function of the IOC, in accordance with the well-known resolution VI–13. In any way, it is difficult to adopt the proposal that gives the power to the international authority to grant licenses and to conduct other activities in regard to scientific research.

My second remark concerns the question of the following problems. Who will have the right to conduct the exploration and exploitation, which was mentioned by Mr. Lee, and Mr. Lee mentioned some alternatives.

I am in favor of the mixed system, keeping in mind that not only the international authority, but also the states, not the legal persons and physical persons, but states will have the right to explore and exploit the ocean's mineral resources.

It is my reasoning, based on the generally accepted principles of contemporary international law, that the state enjoys a legal personality and is the main subject in public international law.

The Soviet doctrine recognizes also that the international-intergovernmental organizations are also the subjects of international law and have legal personality. But we cannot deprive the state of its indispensable right to explore and exploit the mineral resources of the seabed.

And at last, my third remark is on the problem of the conflict between different types of ocean use. It seems to me that we cannot forget the existence of the specialized agencies of the United Nations. The problems of coexistence, seabed acitivity, and navigation could not be solved without the IMCO powers. These powers, as you know, concern the safety of navigation. The existing IMCO practice concerns the operation of the Collisions Regulation, and the scheme of dividing traffic shows the reasonableness of these considerations.

I should like to emphasize again that we cannot go beyond the main aim of the establishment of the international seabed authority to deal with the exploration and exploitation of mineral resources.

Thank you, Mr. Chairman.

Mr. Christy: Thank you very much.

Would any of the panelists like to comment on that?

Mr. Greenwald.

Mr. Greenwald: I would like to endorse Mr. Kolodkin's first remark having to do with the initiative in Caracas to extend the authority of the seabed authority over scientific research. Such an extension would be "creeping jurisdiction" of the international authority. That particular initiative was a major factor in our decision, in our corporate decision-making process, as to whether Caracas and its following conference were going to reach any resolution, with issues like that being raised so late in the conference. That tended to confirm our feeling that nothing could be expected in the near future from this conference.

His remarks about making use of existing intergovernmental organizations are also very important. I have in mind the Federal Aviation Authority in the United States, where 40,000 bureaucrats exercise jurisdiction over 30,000 planes. If the seabed authority duplicates bureaucracies by ignoring competent agencies already in existence it may make the FAA look like a relatively lean and hungry organization.

Mr. Christy: Let's not impose U.S. inefficiencies on the rest of the world.

Mr. Greenwald: Well, that's a good idea. I endorse that.

Mr. Christy: Mr. de Soto.

Mr. de Soto: Thank you. Just a word about scientific research. The IOC has been unable to come up with a definition of scientific research which would distinguish it in any acceptable way from exploration for commercial purposes.

It has not been possible to do so in IOC. Now, I don't wish to alienate the scientific community. It is not the purpose, and my government, I don't think, has done it. Quite the contrary, we have been fairly liberal about it. But scientific research relates to commercial operations and it is very difficult to establish a distinction. Commercial exploration is a source of knowledge, and if the authority is not able to control the research in such a way as to know what is going on, and so those of us who do not have the knowledge or the means to carry out the research ourselves can, through the authority, begin to acquire that knowledge, then we have no access to that knowledge. And so we must have at least some sort of supervision of what is going on, in order to be able to have some appropriate participation.

With regard to participation of states, I think the Group of 77 made it fairly clear that states would also be able to participate in activities in the sea-bed through appropriate state enterprises. I don't think it is advisable that states be allowed to shield themselves behind the immunities accorded to states in international law, because it would not be fair vis à vis the international authority to oppose it to states.

Thank you, Mr. Chairman.

Mr. Christy: Any other questions from the floor?

Mr. Lee: Thank you, Mr. Chairman. My name is Ted Lee, Chairman of the Interdepartmental Committee for the Canadian Government on Law of the Sea.

I think that the timing of the action of Deepsea Ventures as described by Mr. Greenwald, was particularly regrettable, coming prior to the most important session of the Law of the Sea Conference, namely, the Geneva session.

The Caracas session was not, as he just mentioned, the main substantive session of the conference, it was the beginning, it was the groundwork session. You had over forty countries that had never been in the Sea Bed Committee, that had no exposure to the issues at all. They had to be brought along, and many of us, contrary to much of what you heard yesterday afternoon, those of us who were directly involved in the conference, look forward to significant developments at Geneva, and to substantial progress which will, if not at Geneva, certainly at a third session early in 1976, result in some very clear developments on the law-of-the-sea issues.

Therefore the timing, I think, was very unfortunate.

The claim of Deepsea Ventures has been written into the record, submitted this morning, and I would like, with your permission, to read out and put in the record a five-sentence response, which the Canadian government submitted to Deepsea Ventures on December 6th. It reads as follows, and then I would like to ask two questions of Mr. Greenwald.

> It is the policy of the Canadian Government to seek, through the development of international law in appropriate fora, the establishment of a legal regime to govern the exploration and exploitation of the resources of the deep sea bed beyond the limits of national jurisdiction.
> Indeed, this is the task that is now being pursued by the third U.N. Law of the Sea Conference to which Canada attaches the greatest importance. Canada subscribed at an early stage in the work of the United Nations in this respect, to the concept that the exploitation of these resources should be carried out for the benefit of mankind as a whole. The Canadian Government, therefore, does not accept the assertion by Deepsea Ventures, Inc. that it has exclusive mining

rights or some priority in time over that portion of the international sea bed area, as described in the notice to the Secretary of State, or that it has acquired any rights to that area or the resources thereof, through its activities.

The Canadian Government reserves its position concerning the legal rights of states and their nationals with respect to the area of the sea bed beyond the limits of national jurisdiction, pending the outcome of the third United Nations Law of the Sea Conference.

I would be interested in knowing what has been the response from the United States government, and also from other governments that Deepsea Ventures kindly notified on November 15 that it was making this claim. And that is how it came to our attention.

Secondly, I am wondering how is Deepsea's claim to exclusive, and I underline "exclusive," mining rights reconciled with the principle of freedom of the high seas? Is it really based, as we heard earlier, on the principle that the Lord helps them that help themselves?

Thank you.

Mr. Christy: In response to your first question, we are very fortunate in having within the audience a high official of the U.S. government who might be able to answer that. And I will ask Tom Clingan, who is Deputy Assistant Secretary of State, to tell us what the response is of the U.S. government.

Mr. Clingan: Thomas Clingan, State Department. I thought you would never ask.

Let me say this about that. The State Department, of course, has made no formal response to Deepsea Ventures, and not being as alert, intelligent, and quick as our Canadian colleagues, we have the matter under study and will make an appropriate response.

We have, however, issued a public statement regarding the claim, since the claim was made public, in which we said that we neither grant nor recognize exclusive rights in the deep seabed.

Thank you.

Mr. Christy: Thank you, Tom.

And the second question, I think Dick Greenwald should be able to answer.

Mr. Greenwald: No, I think I'll first answer the first question by giving Deepsea's official response to the Canadian government. I am going to use their language and change the word "Canada" to the word "Deepsea."

It is the policy of Deepsea to seek, through the development of international law in appropriate fora, the establishment of a legal regime to govern the exploration and exploitation of the resources of the deep seabed beyond the limits of national jurisdiction. Indeed, this is the task which is now being pursued by the Third United Nations Law of the Sea Conference, to which Deepsea attaches the greatest importance. Deepsea subscribed at an early stage in the work of the United Nations in this respect to the concept that the exploitation of these resources should be carried out for the benefit of mankind as a whole.

Deepsea, however, reasserts its continuing position concerning the legal rights of Canada and its nationals with respect to the area claimed.

Mr. Christy: But, Dick, you have not responded to the second question with regard to whether you can have exclusive rights, or whether you can operate only the rule of capture.

Mr. Greenwald: Under the Freedom of the Seas Doctrine, as it existed before the concept of the continental shelf (or before the Doctrine of the Continental Shelf) arose in 1945, there were many examples of effectively maintained exclusive claims to the deep seabeds beyond the territorial seas of nations. We have used those claims and associated state practice as sufficient precedents for our legal action. We recognize that the area of law is rather thin, but we are very confident of our precedents, and believe them sufficient to our purposes.

Mr. Christy: Any other comments from the panelists on that interpretation of international law?

Mr. de Soto.

Mr. de Soto: Mr. Chairman, I have heard many times the fear expressed that the authority was turning into a state. Now we have a case, I think, of a firm trying to assume the attributes of the state, and I think that this is rather sensational.

Mr. Christy: Other questions.

Yes, back there.

Mr. Finkle: My name is Peter Finkle, Memorial University of Newfoundland, Canada.

Mr. de Soto, in your comments you stressed the importance of the sovereignty to developing states. Then, in your later comments, you stressed the concept of mankind and its common heritage.

There appears to be a contradiction in terms. Could you comment?

Mr. Christy: Could you reidentify yourself? I don't think we caught your affiliation. And could you expand a bit on the question?

Mr. Finkel: Peter Finkle, Memorial University in Newfoundland, Canada. I don't think I would like to expand on the question. It was a contradiction that Mr. de Soto—it appeared to be a contradiction in his statement, where he stressed the terrible importance of sovereignty to the developing states, and then in the closing comments, stressed the importance of the common heritage of mankind. I think the question speaks for itself, and I would like you to explain the apparent contradiction.

Mr. de Soto: The only way I could see a contradiction is perhaps in the size of the area. Or are you suggesting that all sovereignty by coastal states be rolled back to the coasts, and the entire ocean be the common heritage?

      I don't think that anyone has seriously proposed that. The common heritage of mankind begins where national jurisdiction ends.

Mr. Christy: I think it is the question of the limits.

Mr. Vargas: My name is Jorge Vargas—

Mr. Christy: Excuse me. Ladies first, Jorge.

Ms. Mariani: Thank you. My name is Georgette Mariani. I am from the Centre Pour L' Exploration Des Oceans, Paris, France.

      I want to comment on Mr. de Soto's remarks about marine scientific research, when he said that IOC was not able to make a distinction between scientific research and exploration.

      First, I would say that no formal request has been made to IOC, and I think that would be an opportunity of asking IOC, especially this group of legal questions, the mandate of which was renewed under the proposal of Brazil at the last IOC Executive Council, and that could be an interesting task for this group.

      Second, this distinction is absolutely necessary, coming to us between my incentive to research and exploration, because otherwise such research would be interfered with unnecessarily, and it would be the end of scientific research. There is a great difference in objective character, means, and so on, between scientific research and exploration. We have had the opportunity during the conference to explain these differences.

      My second question applies to Mr. Greenwald. I would like to ask him to elaborate on the precedent he quoted for granting of exclusive rights under national law. I would like to have some precise examples of these exclusive rights. Thank you.

Mr. Christy: Mr. de Soto.

Mr. de Soto: Yes, I agree that a definition of fundamental scientific research would be most useful. I am not myself an expert on scientific research, nor do I participate in IOC, but I have it from sources in IOC that this is essentially the stumbling block from the legal point of view.

Thank you.

Mr. Christy: Mr. Greenwald.

Mr. Greenwald: Would you like for me to read the precedents relating to exclusive rights recognized beyond the limits of national jurisdiction?

Mr. Christy: Briefly mention them, I think. It is almost lunchtime.

Mr. Greenwald: Ms. Mariani, I will give you a copy of the legal opinion, if you wish. It has been supplied to CNEXO and, through the French Embassy in Washington, to the French government. The precedents flow from the various pearl-fishery histories through the Tubantia case, having to do with salvage on the international seabeds, into various whale fishery cases (Ghen versus Rich, Swift versus Gifford, etc.) and on to practice in Spitzbergen . . . there are a number in here, and I think it would be better to just hand this opinion over to you. Most were recognitions of exclusive use of resources in nonsovereign areas prior to 1945.

Mr. Christy: Thank you.
Giulio.

Mr. Pontecorvo: The question of scientific research has come up a couple of times, and the question of a distinction between exploration and exploitation has been mentioned as an important legal question.

I submit that this is a semantic difficulty of not much substance, maybe legal substance, but it does not seem to me to be substance, either with respect to science or industrialization. Scientific research is an investment in knowledge, and it is a capital investment like any other capital investment, and the question is who can use the knowledge that is obtained?

The answer is that all can use the knowledge, and that the knowledge benefits all. That, however, begs the underlying issue, which has been raised by a number of the developing states with respect to this question, in that the marginal value of the knowledge is much greater to developed states than it is to developing states, and therefore the implication of it in the short run at least is to acerbate the question of income distribution throughout the world, and I think this is the substance of the issue with respect to scientific research, again, that it reduces to an income distribution problem.

Mr. Christy: I have time for one more question.
Jorge Vargas, I think.

Mr. Vargas: My name is Jorge Vargas, from the National Council for Science and Technology in Mexico. Being in an academic and scientific environment, I would like to be enlightened with some clarification with respect to some comments made by both the U.S. representative in the panel, Mr. Greenwald, as well as the U.S.S.R. speaker.

There are three points. The first one—

Mr. Greenwald: May I correct you for a second? I am not the U.S. representative. I always represent myself and, at some times, I represent my corporation but those are the limits of my mandate.

Mr. Christy: He represents the nation of Deepsea Ventures.

Mr. Vargas: Okay. The first question is, there has been some talk about marine scientific research as a freedom. I would like to know where is the basis, the legal basis, for this so-called freedom of scientific research? As far as I recall, I think the Convention of the High Seas does not expressly recognize the existence of this so-called freedom of scientific research.

Number two, if there is such a freedom, how does the U.S.S.R. speaker define such a freedom of scientific research?

And number three, expressly again with the participant from the U.S.S.R., how does he reconcile his statement with the proposals submitted to the Third Committee at the Caracas Conference by the U.S.S.R. delegation in the sense that the government of this country is willing to seek the consent of the coastal state in connection with marine scientific research activities that they call fundamental research?

Thank you.

Mr. Christy: Dick, do you want to comment?

Mr. Greenwald: I would like to defer temporarily to Mr. Kolodkin while I read up on my Article II of the High Seas Convention.

Mr. Christy: Mr. Kolodkin, would you like to respond to those questions?

Mr. Kolodkin: Thank you, Mr. Chairman.

On the first comment of my Mexican colleague, I should like to refer to the discussion of the United Nations International Law Commission and to remember that Professor François from the Netherlands pointed out that besides the four freedoms which are indicated in the Geneva Convention on the High Seas, we have also two freedoms to explore and exploit the seabed resources on the high seas. These are the comments of the report of the Commission of the United Nations.

On the second, we have Article II in the existing Geneva Convention on the High Seas, which states that besides four freedoms which are mentioned in this article, the states may enjoy the other freedoms recognized in contemporary international law.

On the third, I should like to refer to the draft Article of the Convention on Scientific Research in the World Ocean, which was proposed in the Sea-Bed Committee by some delegations, including the Soviet delegation, on the 15th of March, 1973. In Article I, we can find the following definition of scientific research: "Scientific research in the world's oceans means any fundamental or applied research and related experimental work conducted by states and their juridical and physical persons, as by international organizations, which does not aim directly at industrial exploitation, but is designed to obtain knowledge of all aspects of the national processes and phenomena occurring in ocean space on the sea bed and sub-soil thereof, which is necessary for the peaceful activity of states, for the further development of navigation and other forms of utilization of the sea and also utilization of the earth space about the world oceans."

I should like to add that the remark of my Mexican colleague concerns the economic zone. But we do not now discuss the problem of the powers of coastal states in the economic zone. We are discussing the situation beyond the limits of national jurisdiction as to the activity on the seabed.

As far as my Mexican colleague touched the problem of scientific research and the attitude of Soviet Union to scientific research in the economic zone, I'd like to recall the Soviet draft, which was proposed on 5 August 1974 at the Caracas Conference; I should like to quote from Article V:

"Within the limits of the economic zone, each state may freely carry out fundamental scientific research unrelated to the exploration and exploitation of the living or mineral resources of the zone.

Scientific research in the economic zone related to the living and mineral resources will be carried out with the consent of the coastal state."

In this connection, it would be useful to remember that the Scientific Council on Ocean Research (SCOR) in 1971 elaborated the criteria which give us the possibility of dividing fundamental or scientific research and industrial scientific research.

Thank you, Mr. Chairman.

Mr. Christy: Thank you very much. I am quite interested in the fact that this discussion has gotten involved in the scientific research aspects, which indicates really the importance of this matter. I wish we had more time for full discussion of this and the other matters we discussed this morning.

National Maritime Limits: The Economic Zone and the Seabed

Chairman
Lewis M. Alexander
Department of Geography
University of Rhode Island

One of the elements in any law of the sea negotiations, along with the various processes and dynamics, is the idea of the limits of national jurisdiction. And unfortunately here one has to be precise, particularly if one is going to put lines on a map. It is fine to talk in the abstract, but at some point, a line may have to be drawn; one of the problems we have been running into for many years now is where the limits of national jurisdiction will be, both in the water column and on the seabed.

Things have been changing a great deal. At one point we had the exploitability criterion, which seems to have gone by the board before it was ever officially put into practice. Now the other problems come up about seabed boundaries, and we have two people to talk on this; another problem which comes up, which we will be talking about at the end of this session concerns archipelagoes.

Our first speaker this afternoon is Robert Hodgson, the Geographer of the Department of State, who will talk about seabed limits.

Chapter Five

National Maritime Limits: The Economic Zone and the Seabed

Robert D. Hodgson
The Geographer
U.S. Department of State

INTRODUCTION

The 1958 Geneva Convention on the Territorial Sea and the Contiguous Zone dealt with two types of national control over the oceans: the sovereign territorial sea, of an unspecified breadth; and the jurisdictional contiguous zone, defined as not exceeding 12 nautical miles from the national baseline. The latter zone permitted the coastal state to exercise jurisdiction over customs, immigration, fiscal, and other matters without the sovereign rights of the territorial sea. The Convention on the Continental Shelf established a third zone—an area for the economic exploitation of the resources, both living and nonliving, of the seabed and its subsoil adjacent to the coastal state.

The Third United Nations Conference on the Law of the Sea (LOS III), after eight years of preparatory work by the U.N. Seabeds Committee, has begun the labor of modernizing, revising, and/or augmenting these and the other two conventions on fisheries and the high seas that constitute modern, conventional international law of the sea. It is not yet apparent, at least to me, the form which the new convention(s) will take. LOS III may build on, i.e., amend the existing conventions or, as seems more likely, replace them either in their entirety or by incorporating certain parts of the existing law directly or in an amended form into a new, comprehensive treaty. The four existing conventions will probably become one—quite different in substance and in scope.

One of the major and most vexing problems being faced by LOS III involves the limits of national jurisdiction in, on, and under the sea and the nature of the coastal states' jurisdiction within this zone. I will address only

This paper has not been cleared by the Department of State and does not necessarily represent the official policy of the United States government.

the question of the first issue—the boundary—although the two are, to a large measure, almost inseparable in the minds of many people and for many states.

A NATIONAL ECONOMIC ZONE VERSUS AN INTERNATIONAL SEABED ZONE

It is obvious from the first session of LOS III in Caracas that the final treaty will establish a national zone of economic control in the sea adjacent to the continents. The zone will be a broad area of jurisdiction for the exploitation of resources—living and nonliving. Some states, primarily Latin American, are attempting to territorialize the zone by increasing the rights of the coastal state and its exclusivity and even sovereignty within the zone. If carried to an extreme, the economic zone would become a territorial sea with certain navigational rights guaranteed. The desire for territorialization will be resisted by the majority of the participants in LOS III, but in the consensus negotiations of the UN forum, the ultimate, substantive nature of the zone remains unclear.

Most states, coastal and landlocked, have spoken in favor of the concept of a 200-nautical-mile economic resource zone for all coastal states. In fact, in the opening plenary sessions in Caracas, 96 of the approximately 116 states speaking on the issue endorsed the concept or noted the need for the treaty to include such a zone.

We must realize, however, that this support is not identical in character or in degree. Some states demanded greater territoriality; others accepted the concept only with limitations on state jurisdiction. Many landlocked states demanded the right of access to the economic zone(s) of adjacent states, while some, e.g., Denmark, favored the zone for nonliving but not for living resources of the water column. The 96-state group, although sufficient to carry the day, does not constitute a homogeneous or monolithic entity. Many important issues still divide the members, and these problems will have to be resolved before the 200-mile boundary becomes a fact of conventional law.

Of the 20 states which spoke against the broad economic zone concept, nine are landlocked states and the remainder are shelflocked.

The major support for the 200-mile economic zone, as a sole limit to national jurisdiction on, in, and under the sea, appears to be centered among the Organization of African Unity (OAU) states and the northern Latin American States, which constitute a majority of the Group of 77. The OAU will probably meet in mid-February on LOS and other matters, with the decisions reached bound to have a profound effect on the spring negotiations in Geneva. The limit of national jurisdiction is likely to be a major point in any OAU meetings on law of the sea. A change in position, or a break in African solidarity, in favor of the 200-mile limit as the sole limit for maritime jurisdiction could have a decisive effect on the outcome of the boundary question.

Although little has been said on the issue, a 200-mile economic zone boundary presumably would be developed by the arcs-of-circles method generally utilized in the delimitation of the territorial sea under current convention practices. Several other important issues, however, have also received little public attention:

1. The limit of national jurisdiction for the economic zone should be established quickly and permanently. Unlike the territorial sea limit, the economic zone boundary will mark the line of separation between national and international activities. Problems of delimitation between adjacent states, moreover, can serve only to delay the development of this important line. As noted, once established, the boundary should not be subject to change, in order to grant the permanence of tenure important to petroleum or mining concessions.

2. The 200-nautical-mile zone may or may not be measured from the same baseline as the territorial sea and the existing contiguous zone. The present Convention on the Territorial Sea and the Contiguous Zone permits the drawing of straight baselines under certain geographic conditions of the coastline, and a similar concept may develop for mid-ocean archipelagic states.

Straight baselines over the years have become longer and more extensive, encompassing wide areas of the world's seas. Many of these longer straight baselines have been developed to extend national control over resources rather than for strategic or sovereignty reasons. The narrowness of the band of territorial sea did not permit the coastal state to extend its economic jurisdiction over important areas of the sea.

With the new economic zone concept, the raison d'etre for extensive straight baselines becomes much less pressing and valid. Furthermore, the greater the distance measured from a baseline, the less influence will be exerted by the straight baselines. Such systems will extend a 3-mile territorial sea disproportionately more than a 12-mile sea. The influence on a 200-mile economic zone, in contrast, will be very small, barring the use of very extensive lines. On the average, the gain of area for the economic zone, depending on the nature of the system, appears to be in the 1 to 2 percent range.

3. Whatever the baseline system, the seaward limit of national jurisdiction should be a mathematically definable and recoverable line measured either by computer or on accurate charts defined on the proper projection. Mercator charts should be avoided for most areas of the world, owing to the distortions inherent in the projection. Arcs of circles meet this criterion, as would "straight lines" parallel to a system of straight baselines. "Straight lines" drawn on a chart (particularly on a Mercator projection chart), however, will not be "straight" on the earth. Many different methods exist to define a "straight line" between two fixed points on a spheroid such as the earth. The most precise and perhaps best line would be a geodetic line, or geodesic.

Any one of the various mathematical lines would be acceptable if the treaty specifically requires the nature of the line to be made known. However, since differing lines may work to the advantage of adjacent states, leading to possible disputes in delimitation of lateral lines, it would be advisable for the treaty to specify the exact type of line to be utilized. In the narrow confines of the territorial sea and contiguous zone, the problem is not very great; however, as distances increase with an economic zone so will the size of potential disputed areas. As noted, the geodesic would be the most precise, but should the treaty fail to specify it, rhumb lines, great circles, small circles, grid lines, etc., would be acceptable if properly specified and defined.

"Straight lines" would be easier to recover than arcs of circles, and perhaps the outer limit of the 200-mile economic zone should be expressed by chords and/or tangents to the arcs measured from the national baseline. To prevent misuse of the system, a maximum length of straight line should be prescribed in the treaty. Chords will obviously reduce the area of national jurisdiction while tangents will increase it. Depending on the length of line permitted, the "loss" or "gain" of area could be held to a minimum.

The 200-mile economic zone would enclose within national jurisdiction approximately 37,750,000 square nautical miles, leaving 67,517,000 square nautical miles in the international zone. Roughly one-third of the seas (35.86 percent) would be national economic zones and two-thirds international.

SEABED JURISDICTION BEYOND AN ECONOMIC ZONE?

As noted before, the Convention on the Continental Shelf provides for the economic jurisdiction of the coastal state over a zone of the sea floor and its subsoil. The existing definition of the outer limit of the continental shelf, however, possesses so many elastic clauses and phrases as to constitute a meaningless definition of a "limit." Questions arise immediately: since petroleum has not yet been exploited beyond the 200-meter depth specified, does this depth mark the prevailing legal limit of national jurisdiction on the seabed? However, certain creatures of the shelf are harvested at depths of 500 to 600 meters well beyond the "magical" 200-meter depth. Does their exploitability provide a greater depth as *the* limit of national seabed jurisdiction or just *a* limit? Do we have, as a result, several limits on the seabed, with functional parameters, i.e., one for nonliving and one for living resources of the shelf?

The situation obviously could prove to be hopeless. As a result, certain individuals and states have taken a different approach to the definition of the Convention, interpreting the language much more broadly. They claim that the Convention grants to an adhering state the right to exploit the resources of the adjacent seabed and its subsoil to the edge of the submerged continental margin.

This concept may be interpreted in differing ways. The Convention obviously refers to the "continental shelf," the nearly flat extension of the coastal surface of the continent under the coastal sea. The shelf varies geologically in depth from a few meters to about 550 meters in depth, depending on world location. The 200-meter figure was chosen merely as an "average" depth, really about 130 meters, for the feature. Should this narrow interpretation prevail, only a few states—Australia, Canada, Mauritius, the United Kingdom, the United States and the Soviet Union—could have seabed limits beyond a 200-mile economic zone for the seabed and its subsoil.

The concept clearly is too restrictive. As a consequence, many have claimed that the intention of the Convention was to grant to each coastal state the entire submerged portion of the adjacent continental block. This definition would include the flat shelf and the steeper slope extending simplistically to the ocean floor. In many places in the world, however, in particular along the rim of the Pacific basin, the foot of the slope lies well within 200 nautical miles of the coastline. Furthermore, faulting and other complex geological activities have created situations which depart radically from the simple model. In either event, the 200-mile economic zone would enclose the entire national shelf and slope of the continental block.

To further complicate matters, the foot of most of the world's slope is covered with unconsolidated sediments known as the "continental rise." These sediments largely stem from the erosion of the continental block and hence may be said to be a part of the block. The seaward limit of the rise may, however, contain primarily marine sediments or a mixture of continental and marine. In areas of expansive deltaic formations, the rise may extend for more than a thousand kilometers seaward or to the mid-oceanic ridge province.

Obviously, as the definition of the "continental shelf" extends into deeper waters, a greater number of states will be encompassed by the definition. Depending on the criteria, approximately 44 coastal states may qualify under an extensive seabed/subsoil criterion, such as the foot of the slope—an increase of 38 states over the narrower continental shelf definition noted previously.* It should be noted, however, that no two lists of these states have proven to be identical; the question of definition of the seabed and the problem of boundary delimitation with adjacent or opposite states obviously affect the listings. In any event, no more than 50 coastal states would qualify as broad-margin states.

Immediately one asks if such a definition of certain coastal states' rights beyond 200 miles could be deemed equitable. Less than 40 percent of the coastal states or about one-third of all independent states would qualify. The question may be answered that such a seabed limit would not be equitable since it applies to such a small minority of states. However, the number 50 is close to a "blocking third" in any voting arrangement requiring more than

*See Table 5-1.

two-thirds majority. It would appear that a compromise will have to be evolved, if all broad-margin states remain in a cohesive bloc and the conference wishes to avoid a deadlock. It is by no means clear that such cohesion does and will exist. A second answer to the question gives an entirely different solution: existing conventional international law has already granted these broad-margin states this resource zone for its exploitation; the new convention cannot take away these preexisting rights. A prediction of the outcome in LOS III is not possible with existing data.

If we assume, however, that the new LOS III convention will extend jurisdiction for the broad-margin coastal states in these cases where the continental margin extends beyond 200 miles from the baseline, how may one define the boundary of this seabed/subsoil zone? Obviously, to be accepted by 150 states, the boundary definition will have to be simple, i.e. nontechnical, containing a certain degree of clarity, and yet be deemed equitable to all states concerned as either a right or a compromise. It should be permanent.

The simplest definition to negotiate would be the most general one, which unfortunately would contain the greatest chance for misinterpretation and dispute. The language, for example, could merely state that the coastal nation has jurisdiction over the resources of the seabed and subsoil of the continental margins contiguous to its territory which extends/prolongs beyond the 200-mile economic zone. The terms or parameters would not be defined.

This definition, however, would probably not prove satisfactory since it is open to the widest degree of interpretation. The clause could be made more specific and restrictive by adding the phrase "including the continental shelf, slope and (perhaps) rise" to qualify "continental margin." These terms have certain geological meanings, which are generally if not universally accepted. As a result, the definition could prove to be more acceptable to a greater number of narrow-margin states.

Lack of a precise definition, however, would inhibit the use of such language unless the concept were to be coupled with a boundary commission and dispute settlement provisions within the section of the treaty. These two elements may prove to be necessary under any boundary formula, although the problem of dispute settlement over "territory" could be difficult to negotiate.

A third simple definition would select, as in the shelf convention, a predetermined isobath as the limit of the continental margin. The problem is that, as with the continental shelf, no single depth figure would satisfy all states. The existing 200-meter figure would be too restrictive and little support could be gained for its adoption. Portugal, in Committee II in Caracas, proposed a 4000-meter isobath. This would be a disastrous selection and would create jurisdictional havoc. The figure, depending on the treatment given to isolated islands as basepoints, could include all mid-oceanic ridges of the four main oceans and would create a segmented, isolated, and small international zone.

Only the North Pacific Ocean would not be divided into detached pockets of international jurisdiction. To be accepted, a depth criterion shallower than 4000 meters would have to be selected, which would leave many areas of geological continental margin excluded from a national seabed zone.

Other suggestions have been advanced, formally and informally, for a limit for a seabed zone. In the original treaty advanced by the U.S. for discussion in the Seabeds Committee, a gradient concept was proposed as the seaward limit of the national trusteeship zone. Gradients, however, are often very difficult to determine; the continental margin and the seafloor do not resemble the nice smooth lines we draw on our diagrams to represent the principle involved. It would be difficult, although not impossible, to establish gradients on rough surfaces mathematically. This type of complex formula has always been hard to negotiate because most laymen do not understand the principles involved in the mathematics.

Gradients are also subject to manipulation depending on the angle of the line in relation to the direction of the isobaths. To be "true" the two lines should be held perpendicular to each other to the greatest degree possible. A second question involves the values to be chosen to mark the "slope" and the "rise" limit. The map published by the Office of The Geographer based on the research of Heezen and Tharp used 1:40 for the slope and 1:1000 for the rise edges. These figures represent arbitrary selections and may be difficult to rationalize scientifically. The latter, of course, would be very difficult to measure with any degree of precision and hence to locate with an accuracy of plus or minus 20 to 25 miles. The inclusion of the entire margin would add approximately 5,000,000 square nautical miles to national jurisdiction.

Professor Hedberg, the Princeton University marine geologist, has suggested a method whereby the seaward edge of the geomorphic continental slope would be determined as a "baseline." Then the coastal states could establish "straight line" boundaries with a zone measured seaward of the slope base. He suggested three alternatives: 100, 200 or 300 kilometers.

In this proposal, however, Hedberg discounted any 200-mile economic zone boundary as an alternative. The greatest width—300 kilometers— would allocate to narrow-slope states a sea area of roughly 200 nautical miles in breadth. Thus his morphological boundary would be the sole boundary for national jurisdiction. The suggestion would be very practical and worthwhile were the resources of the seabed, in contrast to the water column, the most important or the sole criteria for a national zone. However, many coastal states look upon the living resources of the water column as of more immediate value than those of the seafloor and subsoil. Furthermore, the concept of a 200-mile zone has become so much a part of the negotiations that it would be impossible at this time to change the direction of the concept.

I am afraid that many scientists, including myself, have become enamored of the concept of a natural boundary, i.e., the shelf, slope, or rise.

In fact, nature rarely, if ever, changes its character abruptly along a "line" boundary. Rather, natural changes invariably occur through zones or frontiers. Moreover, the negotiations constitute political/legal acts, and things "natural" may have little or nothing to do with this type of negotiating process. They may form a basis for discussion but should not be deemed so important as to affect the political processes.

The best boundary, on land as on the sea, is one which is accepted by the states concerned. The 49th parallel boundary between the United States and Canada is a "natural" monstrosity, but its acceptance by the two states makes it an excellent boundary. Thus the best boundary for LOS III will be one which will be acceptable to the vast majority of the states involved in the negotiations. The boundary must be simple, have at least the appearance of equity and be easily determined and recovered.

As a result, it appears to me that a Hedberg-type boundary would be the easiest to determine and to negotiate, the simplest in concept and the least likely to cause a seeming inequity by granting the coastal state too extreme a zone of national jurisdiction on the seabed and subsoil beyond the economic zone. The boundary would, of course, apply only beyond the 200-mile economic zone.

Unfortunately, this type of formula will not completely satisfy states which have large deltaic fans associated with the adjacent seabed areas. Examples of these fans are those of the Ganges and Indus deltas in the Bay of Bengal and the Arabian Sea, large parts of which would be excluded by Hedberg's formula. The areas of thickest sediments, i.e., those most likely to contain hydrocarbons, however, would be included within areas of national jurisdiction. Beyond this area the cost of hydrocarbon extraction could be prohibitive because of both the distance from land and the depth of water factors. The National Petroleum Council, in its 1974 paper, estimates the percentage of recoverable hydrocarbons beyond 200 miles to the seaward edge of the rise to be between 1 and 5 percent of the total marine potential. Thus this type of formula would exclude perhaps only 1 to 2 percent. We have not yet been able to measure the areal effects of these formulae, but they would definitely include less territory than the 5,000,000 square miles of the entire margin.

Professor Hedberg has wisely stated that we should all preface these types of discussions with the qualifier "we don't know." We don't know, for example, how much it would cost to extract a barrel of petroleum from even a giant field in water depths of 3500 meters in an area 400 miles from land. However, even if the environment were not hostile, as it would be in the Arctic and the Antarctic, it is logical to assume that the cost would be 2–5 times or more than the present cost of a barrel of oil. How may we use petroleum if we have to pay $40 to $50 for a barrel of it?

Consequently, a conservative application of the Hedberg concept appears to be a reasonable economic and political compromise for the limit

Table 5-1. Potential Wide-Margin States

Argentina	Mauritius
Australia	Mexico
Bahamas, The	Netherlands (Surinam)
Barbados	New Zealand
Brazil	Norway
Canada	Oman
Denmark (Faeroes, Greenland)	Pakistan
Ecuador	Papua New Guinea
Equatorial Guinea	Portugal
Fiji	Senegal
France	Sierra Leone
Gabon	Somalia
Ghana	South Africa
Guinea	South-West Africa (Namibia)
Guinea-Bissau	Spain
Iceland	Sri Lanka
India	Tanzania
Indonesia	United Kingdom
Ireland	United States
Kenya	Uruguay
Liberia	U.S.S.R.
Madagascar	Yemen (Aden)

of national jurisdiction on the seabed beyond 200 miles. In the original concept, he mentioned 100 kilometers, which closely approximates 60 nautical miles, for the zone in which the boundary could be drawn. This figure has been mentioned by certain states in other contexts and does not appear to be radical. Logically, the slope/rise break can be determined by echo soundings with relative ease and at not too great an expense. Professor Hedberg has already determined, by use of bathymetric charts and echo sounding profiles, the slope break for much of the world. If this concept is deemed too complex, an isobath approximating the break—2500 or 3000 meters—might be chosen as the baseline. The boundary of national seabed jurisdiction could then be determined in the 60-mile zone measured seaward of this "legal" slope edge.

The final limit of national seabed jurisdiction, of course, should be determined by straight lines, i.e., geodetic lines or other specific lines, within the zone. Obviously most coastal states will opt for the maximum territory and will draw chords to the arcs measured from the baseline. The resulting limit would appear to be reasonable and equitable for the newly developing convention as well as for the existing Convention on the Continental Shelf.

The ultimate decision—200 miles or 200 miles plus a formula for determining the limit of jurisdiction on the seabed—will be made within the arena of the UN Conference, which is negotiating the most complex treaty yet undertaken by the world community. The limit of national jurisdiction is but one of many issues to be faced and solved. The boundary question, however, must be one of the first items to be resolved, for without a limit, it will be difficult if not impossible to determine the nature of national jurisdiction within the zone. Furthermore, many of the developing countries are delaying decisions on other vital issues until the question of the economic zone—vital for national development—is settled in an equitable manner.

Mr. Alexander: One of the points which you mentioned at the end of your paper concerned the potentially wide margin states, that is, those countries which might have their continental margins go more than 200 miles offshore. There are forty-four of them listed in Table 5-1, which is just under one-third of the nations of the world. One of the countries so listed is Canada, and we are pleased to have as our second speaker Don Sherwin from the Canadian Department of Energy, Mines, and Resources.

BIBLIOGRAPHY

Alexander, Lewis M. "Alternative Methods for Delimiting the Outer Boundary of the Continental Shelf." Unpublished paper, done for the Office of External Research, U.S. Department of State.

——. "Tabulation" of Provisional Summary Records of Plenary Meetings, 28 June–15 July 1974 (A/CONF.62/SR 21–42). Unpublished compilation for the Office of The Geographer, U.S. Department of State.

Garcia Amador, F.V. "Latin America and the Law of the Sea." *Occasional Paper No. 14,* July 1972. Law of the Sea Institute, University of Rhode Island.

Hedberg, Hollis D. "National-International Jurisdictional Boundary on the Ocean Floor." *Occasional Paper No. 16,* 1972. Law of the Sea Institute.

Johnston, Douglas M. and Gold, Edgar. "The Economic Zone in the Law of the Sea: Survey, Analysis and Appraisal of Current Trends." *Occasional Paper No. 17,* June 1973. Law of the Sea Institute.

U.S. Department of State. "Composite Theoretical Division of the Seabed" (map). Office of The Geographer, 1973.

——. "Major Topographic Divisions of the Continental Margin" (map). Office of The Geographer, 1970.

——. "Theoretical Areal Allocations of Seabed to Coastal States . . . ." *Limits in the Seas No. 46,* August 12, 1972. Office of The Geographer.

U.S. Geological Survey. "Summary Petroleum and Selected Mineral Statistics for 120 Countries, including Offshore Areas." *Geological Survey Professional Paper 817,* 1973.

——. "The Worldwide Search for Petroleum Offshore—A Status Report for the Quarter Century, 1947–1972." *Geological Survey Circular 694,* 1974.

U.S. National Petroleum Council. *Ocean Petroleum Resources, An Interim Report of the National Petroleum Council, July 4, 1974.*

Commentary

Don Sherwin
Department of Energy, Mines, and Resources
Canada

Mr. Sherwin: Thank you, Mr. Chairman. I am a geologist, so I must warn you, I don't have the gift of expression that members of the legal profession, so many of whom are represented here, have, so I am going to have to resort to visual aids.

The subject of my talk today will be the continental margin of Canada, how we determine its outer limit, and its economic importance to Canada.

The Canadian margin is one of the largest in the world, second only to that of the U.S.S.R. Including Hudson Bay, it covers an area of almost 2,000,000 square nautical miles, of which over 1,000,000 square nautical miles is comprised of physical continental shelf, with the remainder split between the slope and the rise.

The physical shelf is deeper than most shelves in the world. In fact, 35 percent of the physical shelf lies beyond 200 meters of water depth. This is because our shelf has been glaciated to a great extent, and has not recovered from the weight of Pleistocene ice. The shelf is also very broad, particularly off the east coast, where the Grand Banks extend to 265 miles from the coast, and the total margin that you see in green, to the edge of the rise, extends to as much as 650 miles from the southeast tip of Newfoundland.

In contrast, on the west coast margin, which is what we call a "subducting" or "consuming" margin, as is most of the Pacific rim of the Western Hemisphere, the physical shelf averages less than 20 nautical miles in width, and nowhere does the continental margin itself extend beyond 120 nautical miles.

In the Arctic Ocean, the physical shelf averages about 60 nautical miles, and the total margin extends beyond 200 miles in several places, so that 75,000 square nautical miles of margin in the Arctic Ocean lie beyond 200 miles.

193

This is the east coast continental margin of Canada. It is a classic type of margin. It is what we call a "passive" or "trailing" margin. It has suffered no severe tectonic activity in the past 200,000,000 years.

Again, there are three elements of the margin, the continental shelf, the slope, and the rise. The continental shelf edge is near the world's average of 140 meters as far north as the feature called the Flemish Cap, at the north end of the Grand Banks, and then the edge of the shelf drops to 400 to 500 meters north into Baffin Bay. The continental slope dips at about two to three degrees, and extends to water depths of 2000 to 4000 meters, and then the continental rise dips more gently away to the abyssal plains of the North Atlantic Ocean at water depths of 3400 to 5400 meters.

Now I am going to run through an exercise to show you how we actually determine the physiographic elements of the continental margin of Canada.

First of all, we take detailed bathymetric charts like the one you see here off Nova Scotia, which have been prepared from closely spaced hydrographic surveys, and we draw a series of profiles across the margin at 50- to 100-mile intervals, as shown on these lines.

This is typical bathymetric profile across the shelf, slope and rise in the vicinity of Sable Island, off the east coast. The vertical exaggeration is times 25, in order to show the topographic elements of the sea floor. The shelf break is very easy to recognize. The base of the slope is picked geometrically where the inclination on the sea floor becomes less than 1 in 40. The base of the rise is picked where the inclination becomes less than 1 in 400, where the sea floor merges with the flat abyssal plains of the North Atlantic.

Now, a fourth point on this cross section is determined by the projected base of the slope which some scientists believe is representative of the geological limit of the margin. This is picked by extending a line from the edge of the shelf, through the geomorphic base of the slope to the level of the abyssal plain. These four points are then joined up on all the profiles to give the edge of the shelf, the geomorphic base of the slope, the projected base of the slope, and the base of the rise.

The projected base of the slope, is a more normalized line, and does not have the fluctuations of bathymetry of the geomorphic base of the slope, and this is why we have selected this line in this particular section.

The same exercise was carried out for the Grand Banks and Flemish Cap, and for the margin off Labrador. As you can see, the edge of the shelf, the geomorphic base of the slope, the projected base of the slope, and the base of the rise are shown.

Now, complementary to the bathymetric surveys, for the past twenty-five years, we have had a number of geophysical programs run across the Canadian continental margin, including seismic reflection and refraction and gravity and magnetics.

The composite results of some of the geophysical profiles carried out in the surveys off Nova Scotia across the margin in the vicinity of Sable Island illustrate the various crustal layers which are identified by their velocity signatures, that is, the velocity of the seismic energy passing through the rocks. This is complemented by the density of the rocks given by gravity surveys.

The continental crust, the very thick area, consisting of lighter, moderate velocity rocks, granites, and sediments in the upper part, grading down to denser rocks in the lower part, floats like an iceberg on the denser higher velocity rocks of what we call the "mantle."

Beneath the Atlantic Ocean, what we call the "oceanic crust" is only about five kilometers thick, compared with forty kilometers of continental crust. Now, the oceanic crust consists, again, of very dense rocks, gabbro and basalt, and as you can see, the mantle rises some thirty kilometers to compensate for the density loss created by the five kilometers of sea water.

Now, the transition from continental crust to oceanic crust starts at about the edge of the shelf, and is all over with by the base of the continental rise. This transition is how we map the geophysical limit of the continental margin and, as you can see, it coincides very closely with the bathymetric or physiographic limit of the continental margin, that is, the base of the continental rise.

In practice of course, neither one of these criteria would be used to delimit the actual edge of the margin itself. However, we would propose straight base lines, as Bob Hodgson suggested, drawn perhaps just within the base of the continental rise, connecting points defined in geodetic coordinates of longitude and latitude.

Another criterion for identifying the limit of the continental margin is the thinning of the sediments of the coastal plain sedimentary wedge, that you can see at the first layer below the blue water of the sea. The coastal plain sedimentary wedge off eastern Canada is the northern submerged extension of the Atlantic coastal plain of the northeastern United States.

Now, the shelf, the outer shelf particularly, the slope, and the rise are all underlain by sediments of Mesozoic, Tertiary, and Quaternary age. These sediments are mainly terrigenous, what we call terrigenous clastics, derived from erosion of the continent. They are part of the continent, and they reach their thickest development approximately beneath the continental slope, near the base of the continental slope and the upper part of the continental rise, where they reach thicknesses of ten kilometers. Then they thin rather gradually out to the western edge of the mid-Atlantic ridge, where they taper out to nothing, but beneath the base of the rise they are still between two and three kilometers in thickness.

The coastal plain sedimentary wedge is based on seismic reflection carried out by the petroleum industry, and also the results of exploratory drilling. I won't go into the details here. They are obviously pretty complex, but the coastal plain sedimentary wedge off Canada includes all the elements necessary to create a favorable habitat for hydrocarbons, that is, firstly, thick reservoir rocks, including deltaic sandstones and coarse carbonate banks. We have excellent source rocks in the form of shales, which interbed with and overlap the reservoirs, and above all, we have suitable traps for the pooling of hydrocarbons; they have already accounted for some small discoveries.

A map of the continental margin shows the drilling that has been carried out by the oil industry since exploratory drilling began in 1966. There have been 104 wells drilled off the east coast of Canada, including these two most recent ones on the Grand Banks. One of these wells was over 200 nautical miles from shore. There have been eight discoveries made, oil and gas discoveries, on the Canadian east coast continental margin, six small ones in the vicinity of Sable Island, and two more significant gas discoveries off the Labrador shelf.

The aerial geology of the east coast continental margin illustrates that the most prominent feature is the submerged Atlantic coastal plain, and in this area it is entirely submerged. It does not crop out on shore at all, as it does in the northeastern United States. And this constitutes the single largest sedimentary basin in all of Canada.

Beneath the Gulf of St. Lawrence, we have older rocks of the Paleozoic age. Basement rocks outcrop on the inner portions of the continental shelf.

The thicknesses of sediments beneath the coastal plain sedimentary wedge vary dramatically. The thickest sedimentary areas actually underly the slope, the lower part of the continental slope, and the upper part of the continental rise. There are roughly four thick sedimentary basins beneath the outer continental margin.

Now, the thickness of sediment in any sedimentary basin is generally considered to be one of the better indicators of hydrocarbon potential. In fact, in sedimentary basins in which there has been very little exploration, the estimates of hydrocarbon resources, potential hydrocarbon resources, which might be recoverable, are often determined by multiplying the volume of sediments times a yield factor, in terms of hydrocarbons per cubic mile of sediment. Now this hydrocarbon yield factor is usually based on the results of drilling in other basins which have similar geological characteristics.

Using this technique as well as what we call stochastic or probabilistic determinations in areas where drilling has been carried out—for instance, on the shelf—we have determined that some 35 percent of the remaining recoverable hydrocarbon resources in Canada, that is, potential hydrocarbon resources, underly the Canadian east coast continental margin in the area shown on this map.

The potential for minerals other than hydrocarbons is also thought to be great as well. However, very little is known about this yet, because there has not been too much demand by industry in this field.

Examining the continental margin beyond 200 miles, one can see that one-third of the east coast continental margin actually projects beyond the 200-nautical-mile line. This includes part of the Grand Banks, and all of Flemish Cap, one-half of the east coast continental slope, and two-thirds of the continental rise. This is an area of one-third of the total east coast continental margin, or 250,000 square nautical miles.

The hydrocarbon potential of this area beyond 200 miles is thought to be substantial. We have some estimates that 16 percent of the total recoverable hydrocarbon potential of the east coast continental margin may lie beyond 200 miles. Three of the four thick sedimentary basins extend beyond and across the 200-mile zone, and are well developed in the area beyond 200 miles. These include reservoir rocks, source beds, and above all, some domal and anticlinal structures which have excellent possibilities for trapping hydrocarbons, major accumulations of hydrocarbons.

This is supposed to be a technical discussion this afternoon, so I am not going to talk about the Canadian position regarding the outer limit of the juridical shelf. However, perhaps these illustrations may describe better than words the lack of logic in the use of a fixed 200-nautical-mile line in determining the outer limits of jurisdiction over the shelf.

The 200-mile line, as you can see, has no respect for natural boundaries, either physiographic or geological, since it lops off great portions of the shelf, the slope, and the rise, and it cuts major sedimentary basins in two.

So I think perhaps you might understand the Canadian position that coastal states should be able to exercise sovereign rights over seabed resources, not only out to 200 miles, but over the whole of the submerged continental margin, that is, out to the limit of the continental rise.

Thank you.

Commentary

Mochtar Kusumaatmadja
Indonesian Ministry of Justice

Mr. Kusumaatmadja: As a nongeographer, I am rather at a loss in this distinguished company, but I think my function is to relate to you how a non-technician looks at geography.

My views would be based on my experience in negotiating six continental-shelf boundary agreements, three territorial-sea boundary agreements, and in the process also settling one land-bound agreement with Australia, now with New Guinea.

I must start by saying that, as a lawyer and negotiator, I find geography, geology, and geomorphology very helpful elements in settling boundary questions. In all the boundary agreements we negotiated with our neighbors, geographical, geological, and geomorphological arguments or factors were always put forward, at least in the beginning stages.

I am saying this because in our experience when negotiations proceed, then we found that ultimately we had to decide matters by other means, and that is that in the end, it is really a question of reaching a solution between the two parties that is equitable, reasonable, and politically acceptable.

I am saying this because although we recognize the importance of geology and geography and geomorphology in these things, one should not exaggerate their importance or ability to settle these questions only on these factors. The reasons are many.

One is that the geographical realities are just too diverse to be able to come to solutions that would have a general meaning, and this hindrance becomes more serious when one goes beyond bilateral settlements towards regional settlements, and even more so of course, when one projects this on a global scale. Then it becomes almost impossible.

So I would say that, speaking now about the global attempt to fix •
a boundary between the national seabed and the international seabed, I think

that there the greatest chance for a successful outcome would be to base it on a numerical kind of solution, like the 200-mile economic zone, because if one uses a geographical or geological solution, it is obvious that many countries which do not have geological features that would justify their part of the argument, would not find such a solution acceptable.

Ever since March 1971, when, in the UN Sea-Bed Committee, the 200-mile economic zone limit was supported by Ambassador Pardo, I think the concept has gained strength. I am not saying that it should be so on this numerical concept alone, because it still leaves the question of those countries that have a margin beyond the 200-mile limit. I think that is the remaining question.

But I would hesitate to go back and use another criterion like the Hedburg solution, because that would go to a limit that is less than what seems now to be generally acceptable. It would be less than acceptable to many of those that already support the 200-mile economic zone limit, and the other drawback is still there. It would not cover those that would not be able to rely on geological arguments. So how do we resolve this remaining problem? There are various ways.

Those countries that have a wide margin could help a solution by just foregoing that claim. That is one possibility. Or those that do not have a margin, and are content with the 200-mile limit, say to those that have a margin, "Look, why do we stop at a 200-mile limit?" Or, they say, "All right. There are not so many anyway who have a margin, let's adopt the principle of 'live and let live' and you can have the margin."

There is yet another solution that sounds reasonable—I don't know because we happen not to be involved, and then you can afford to be reasonable about these things—and that is that you adopt a middle way perhaps, and then it would be a—I hesitate to use the term because it has a certain connotation—a kind of "intermediate" zone under the administration of the coastal states, but one in which the international community would participate in its benefits.

There are all kinds of solutions, but the problem now is that we have to come to a solution of some kind because it would be a pity if the Geneva experience were repeated, I mean here the Geneva experience with respect to the territorial sea of 12 miles.

At that time there was a chance that if nations had agreed on the territorial sea, then that would have been settled. It was not settled, and another thing was also left open, the continental shelf definition, with the so-called exploitability criterion, which at that time seemed a very reasonable solution, but which proved to be a Pandora's box.

So there is every reason I think to adopt a limit of some kind, and I don't know what limit, and everything is helpful, geography and all that, but I think the message is that it comes down really to just agreeing on a limit.

I really do not know the answer, and I think that is the more honest and straightforward answer that one could give to this problem. There are alternatives. I have just given three alternatives, but I am speaking on behalf of nobody, and I don't know whether the alternatives sounded as reasonable as they do to me.

I hope that the OAS Conference which will take place before the Geneva Conference will come to a recommendation on this score, because the resolutions of this body will carry very great weight.

In conclusion, I do not agree that nothing has been achieved. I think a lot has been achieved. It took a long time, but I think the 200-mile economic zone limit is in the process of firming up, and just a few problems remain, affecting not too many countries.

That's all I have to say as a nonlawyer. I only want to caution not to rely too much on geographical factors, because I found out in my negotiations, for instance, that it is very difficult to find two geologists who agree with one another. They are worse than lawyers, I might say. Thank you.

Discussion and Questions

Mr. Alexander: Thank you very much, Mochtar. I am sorry to hear you attack geography, the mother science, but—

I am enjoined by Chairman Christy, who has returned from poolside, that we should wrap this thing up shortly. However, I think we have time for a couple of questions.

Mr. Yalkovsky: One of the things that seems not to have been enumerated in the 1958 Geneva Law of the Sea Convention was the freedom to do research at sea, scientific research.

Now it may not have occurred to a lot of people, but the Law of the Sea Conference in 1958 was probably not chosen because that was a period of sunspot high, but there was another activity at that time that was. It took place in 1957 and 1958. It was the greatest single cooperative, peacetime venture in the history of the human race. It was called the International Geophysical Year, or the IGY.

There seems to have been no protest raised about that particular activity, not even when the Russians fired Sputnik I into orbit to initiate the space age. In fact, most of the nations in the world issued postage stamps to commemorate that event.

Now, sunspot highs have been correlated with a great many other things, including the good and bad vintage years of the wines of France, but in 1960, there was another Law of the Sea Conference, and this gave the legal community or the world community two years to protest. The IGY gave us a quantum jump increase in our knowledge of the oceans.

Another three years passed without substantial protest against scientific research at sea. That was 1963, a period of low sunspot activity, the so-called "Year of the Quiet Sun." The world oceanographic community took that opportunity to study the least known ocean—The Indian Ocean and it set

201

forth the Indian Ocean Expedition. There seems to have been no protest raised about the right of scientists to study the Indian Ocean. In fact, the interesting thing about both of these expeditions, both of these years, was that all of the various nations that participated paid for the publication of the particular research that they did and freely distributed it throughout the world. This material has now been published freely and openly. This information too is now the common heritage of mankind and it was four years before Arvid Pardo used the phrase.

The data that have been acquired from these two particular scientific years have been of great benefit to mankind. Now, the notion that if one wants to do research in the deep ocean, he would have to submit his material to some kind of international seabed authority is a bit ludicrous because there are now a substantial number of articles in journals that are unread except by the editor and the men who wrote the papers, but if the Committee of 77, or anyone else, would like to start to read all of the scientific data that have been accumulated since the International Geophysical Year, I would suggest that they would be very busy for a very, very long time.

But despite the fact that so many data have been accumulated, we need to know much more. We still know less about the depths of the sea than we know about the surface of the moon. In fact, we know more about the moon's backside than we know about the ocean's bottom. It has sometimes been said that it is probably not more interesting.

So I would suggest that since the 1958 Geneva Conference on Law of the Sea did not include the right to do scientific research, it must have been guilty of a slight oversight.

Mr. Nweihed: I am Kaldone Nweihed from Universidad-Simon Bolivar, Caracas.

Listening this afternoon to this panel on the boundaries of the continental shelf, I would like to pose a question to geographers, geologists, and lawyers here represented. It might be actually the opposite of the Canadian point of view, as brought to us by Mr. Sherwin.

During the Caracas conversations, the African bloc especially thought of replacing the juridical criterion of the continental shelf with the new (economic zone) concept. It would amount to exactly the opposite side of the Canadian argument.

I wish to hear something about this African trend.

Mr. Hodgson: That is a question which is really loaded for bear. There is no doubt in my mind that within the negotiating process, there are two different concepts of our approach to the problem. One is that there is existing conventional law in the form of the continental shelf convention, which has already granted to certain states certain rights.

I recognize, and it is in the initial part of my paper, that there are differences of opinion as to what was granted by the continental shelf convention; possibly because the exploitation of petroleum has not yet exceeded the 200-meter depth limit—the 200-meter limit is more or less a sacrosanct line, which is not to be exceeded by any new convention.

The second concept is that the various provisions of the convention really intended to grant to each coastal state its entire margin. Now, I recognize that a very small number of states in the world community have signed the continental shelf convention, and, hence, feel themselves bound by it. I recognize also that the Law of the Sea Convention is writing what is called a new law of the sea. It is not at all clear to me whether the outcome of the Caracas-Geneva-Caracas Convention will be a complete obliteration of the existing Convention on the Continental Shelf—in other words, a replacement of it by only a 200-mile zone—or whether the rights that are granted under some interpretations of the continental shelf will continue to prevail.

I have no strong opinions myself as to the legal rights under the existing continental shelf convention. Being a geographer, I can hide behind the fact that I don't know anything about the law, but there are a sizeable number of states, somewhere around forty to fifty, that have continental margins which extend beyond 200 miles.

They represent a sizeable bloc of votes in the UN conference. Presumably, the negotiations will be a political compromise. To eliminate that size minority may not be acceptable. I don't know.

But there is no question that there are two particular viewpoints. One is that the existing convention grants some rights, the second is that the new convention may replace those rights. What the answer will be, I hope we will know in 1975 or '76.

Mr. Alexander: I think we have time for one more.

Mr. Hosni: My name is Hosni, and I am with Woods Hole Oceanographic Institution.

I think I only heard one speaker about the question of extending the seabed area to 200 miles but not beyond, being the criterion that is most acceptable. And also I heard another speaker, including the last one, saying that there might be some sort of compromise that would eliminate, but not totally, the interests of some of the states involved.

I am only wondering if any compromise that might ever come would bring out a certain big exception, that might be along the lines of the theory of special circumstances that have obliterated totally the theory of the median line. I am only hopeful that, and I would like to hear some comments on any possible compromise that might bring out some ambiguity in terms of either special circumstances or—I don't know what it could be otherwise, but if there is ever going to be something like this, I am wondering what value would be given to such a compromise. If I may hear anything about this, please.

Mr. Kusumaatmadja: We found that the median line concept is very helpful, but it can only operate when you have a situation where it can be applied, and that is, where you have either adjacent countries or countries lying opposite each other.

But the situation with the national versus international seabed area problem is one in which the median line might not be operable. That is the difficulty. So we are left with the only test available under such circumstances, and that is the test of reasonableness, of whatever that means.

The Role of FAO and of the Regional Organizations after the Conclusion of the Third United Nations Conference on the Law of the Sea

Chairman
Francis T. Christy, Jr.
Resources for the Future, Inc.
Washington, D.C.

Mr. Christy: Can we get started please?

We have a long program this afternoon. We are running a bit late. I had, myself, a 92-page paper, but I will forego reading it in the interests of time. In fact, I will make my introductory remarks very brief.

We are on the subject of fisheries, and particularly on the problems that will persist in the management and distribution of fisheries' wealth after the Law of the Sea Conference, whether the Law of the Sea Conference is a success or a failure.

And to open up the discussion, we have Fred Popper, who is the Assistant Director-General for Fisheries of the Food and Agriculture Organization of the United Nations.

Fred.

Chapter Six

The Role of FAO and of the Regional Organizations after the Conclusion of the Third United Nations Conference on the Law of the Sea

F.E. Popper
Assistant Director-General (Fisheries)
FAO

When Francis Christy asked me to come and speak to you about the role of FAO and of the regional organizations after the conclusion of the Third UN Conference on the Law of the Sea, I accepted with both pleasure and apprehension. Pleasure, because I knew I would be among friends—both old and new; friends moreover who were knowledgeable about this and other related subjects so that I would undoubtedly learn much that is new and useful. I also felt—and still feel—apprehension at having to speak about matters that are still at some distance in the future, that to some extent are controversial and about which one has to make a lot of assumptions. Depending on what assumptions one makes, one is likely to arrive at very widely differing conclusions. I shall try to make my assumptions as objectively as I can, but they will inevitably involve a great deal of personal judgment. I must emphasize therefore that when I draw conclusions or express views these will be my own personal ones and not those of my organization. Of course, I shall also have to refer to, and quote from views already expressed by the governing bodies of FAO and its Committee on Fisheries, as well as to relevant comments or proposals made so far by governments regarding my subject matter, but I shall endeavor to keep these references and quotations distinct from my own thoughts and views.

INTRODUCTION

Having made these necessary reservations, let me start, Mr. Chairman, with a brief look at the present role of FAO and the regional organizations vis-à-vis the LOS Conference and its preparatory committee. In this respect there exists what seems to me a notable difference between the present conference and the previous United Nations conferences on the law of the sea. The 1958 and 1960 conferences were preceded, in 1955, by an International Technical Conference on the Conservation of the Living Resources of the Sea, to which nearly all

207

then-existing regional fishery organizations made important contributions. And those organizations were the central theme of that conference. The situation is quite different in the present case! With the single exception of the Permanent Commission for the South Pacific, fishery bodies did not participate actively in preparations for the present conference and all technical and scientific documents relating to fisheries were requested from FAO, including a report on the basic features, activities, and achievements of the fishery bodies themselves.

The basic explanation for this difference that comes to mind is that on the earlier occasions governments in general were not seriously contemplating a regime under which the bulk of marine fisheries would be within national jurisdiction. As regards fisheries, governments were therefore preoccupied with the problem of management in international waters. Today, on the contrary, the main concern is with the extent and nature of national jurisdiction over fisheries; the possible role of international organizations is, at least at first sight, of less importance. In parentheses, let me remark that in 1955 FAO would hardly have been in a position to furnish authoritative information on the subject, whereas in recent years we have been able to supply the Sea-Bed Committee, to its satisfaction, with the information it requested.

While, in the present discussions on the law of the sea, less emphasis has been placed on the role of regional bodies, the point has not been ignored altogether. On the one hand, several delegations have criticized fishery commissions and considered them not useful. The shortcomings or weaknesses usually referred to in these cases include the lack of adequate powers as regards the adoption, implementation, and enforcement of management measures. It has also been argued that regional bodies are sometimes dominated by a few states which use these bodies to maintain their quasi monopolies and to prevent other states from developing their fisheries.

On the other hand, a number of delegations, from both developing and developed countries, have expressed the view that regional bodies are indispensable and that, where necessary, action should be taken to strengthen them. It is this view which coincides with the constant policy of the FAO Committee on Fisheries, as endorsed by our governing bodies. In fact, at its very first session in 1966, the committee set up a subcommittee which it entrusted with the task of developing cooperation with international organizations concerned with fisheries. One of the terms of reference of that subcommittee is to suggest steps to increase the efficiency of existing fishery commissions.

What then, have the regional bodies themselves been doing in recent years? First of all, over the past two years, two new regional commissions have been set up, namely the International Baltic Sea Fishery Commission and the Western Central Atlantic Fishery Commission. Then, at least five existing fishery bodies have taken steps to widen their powers or strengthen their activities.

Thus, the General Fisheries Council for the Mediterranean decided in March 1974 to undertake without delay a revision of the 1949 agreement under which it was established and, in the light of the experience acquired by other regulatory fishery bodies, to recommend such amendments to the agreement as would make the council better adapted to the new tasks it may be called upon to perform and more effective as regards, in particular, the adoption, implementation, and enforcement of conservation measures. Another body established within the framework of FAO, the Indo-Pacific Fisheries Council, also agreed, in November 1974, that the time had now come to undertake a thorough review of its functions and responsibilities. In its own words, the objective of this review is not only to correct existing shortcomings but also to enable the council "to meet new challenges." In this respect, I should mention that at a session held shortly thereafter, the FAO council requested that we consider speeding up the modification of the statutes of existing FAO bodies so that they could take a more active role in dealing with the interlinked problems of fishery management and development.

The International Whaling Commission has also been looking into its own achievements and limitations. At its last meeting, in June 1974, it noted the changes which have occurred in whaling and stocks of cetaceans since the 1946 International Convention for the Regulation of Whaling was signed. Bearing in mind the necessity of strengthening the mechanism for the international conservation of whales and their rational management, it decided to establish a working group of interested member nations to review the convention and to consider convening a conference of plenipotentiaries.

There are two other recent cases in which important existing fishery bodies are strengthening or widening their powers or at least have this matter under consideration. In 1974, the North-East Atlantic Fisheries Commission was empowered to recommend measures for catch and effort limitation and also national catch quotas. In the same year, the International Commission for the Northwest Atlantic Fisheries decided to propose an extension of the convention area and agreed to discuss further amendments suggested by the U.S.A. to provide for speedier entry into effect of conservation measures recommended by the commission.

In this context I should perhaps also mention that the Committee on Fisheries, meeting in Rome in October 1974, requested that the Secretariat submit to its next session a paper offering suggestions on ways of changing the present status and composition of the Fishery Committee for the Eastern Central Atlantic. One of the purposes of that request is to consider under what conditions the committee could have wider powers.

As regards FAO itself and its Committee on Fisheries, their future has been discussed on several occasions by the committee and by its governing bodies. The most recent of these discussions took place at the October 1974 Session of COFI in response to a recommendation by the Conference of FAO that COFI should review its own ability to discharge all the responsibilities that could be bestowed upon it in any new régime governing the oceans. But, after a variety of views had been expressed, the general agreement was that no final conclusions on the future structure, status, and functions of the committee could be reached before there was at least a clear indication of the outcome of the Conference on the Law of the Sea.

Having considered, by way of introduction, the recent past I must now turn to the more difficult task of looking into the future. I shall do so by concentrating on two aspects; the implications of a substantial extension of national jurisdiction over fisheries and the implications of alternative institutional arrangments in the field of fisheries in the world as a whole.

THE IMPLICATIONS OF THE EXTENSION OF NATIONAL JURISDICTION OVER FISHERIES

General

Since I am speaking to a gathering of distinguished specialists, there is no need for me to dwell upon the biological characteristics of fish and the complex migration patterns of many species, either inshore-offshore or laterally along coasts. You are also fully aware of the need to apply management measures throughout the migratory range of these species. For biological reasons alone, the management of the greatest part of the marine stocks, if it is to achieve its objectives, will still require close and effective collaboration between at least the coastal states concerned and in some few, but not unimportant, cases with others capable of fishing those stocks beyond the limits of national jurisdiction, even though these may be very considerably extended.

But there is, in my view, another important reason for effective international collaboration, which in many cases will have to go beyond the group of states directly concerned with a particular stock. That is that fishermen from different countries may not only compete for a share of the yield from a particular stock but also for a share of the market for their catch. It is difficult and, in practice, often impossible to subject one group of fishermen fishing one stock to onerous restrictions while another group fishing a different stock but selling in the same market is free of them.

The extension of national jurisdiction, say to 200 miles, will therefore not remove the necessity for international cooperation in management. Collaboration is, moreover, needed not only in management proper, i.e., the formulation and enforcement of regulation, but is indispensable in providing the scientific and statistical basis for management. Such collaboration will often, for practical reasons, have to be organized for an area encompassing a number of individual stocks.

While I then foresee a continuing need for international collaboration in management and associated statistical and scientific work, it seems clear also that there will be substantial changes in the extent and nature of such collaboration in consequence of a general extension of fishing limits. Now will these changes be uniform throughout the world? It is obvious, for instance, that not all coastal states will benefit equally from an extension of national jurisdiction over fisheries and that even their interests may differ considerably. A quick glance at a world map will show that in many areas a simple 200-mile limit will be scarcely relevant and that complex problems of boundaries will have to be solved. Moreover, the position of individual coastal states will depend on other factors, such as the uneven occurrence of living resources.

In this connection, a few figures recently compiled in FAO may be of interest. In 1972, of the total marine catch (excluding whales) of 55.8 million tons, nearly three-quarters, i.e., 40.5 million tons, were caught by vessels fishing off the coasts of their own country, divided almost exactly equally (20.4 to 20.1 million tons) between developing and developed countries. Of the remaining 15.3 million tons a good two-thirds (10.6 million tons) were taken by developed countries off the coasts of other developed countries and a little less than a quarter (3.6 million tons) off the coasts of developing countries. The developing countries themselves caught a little over one million tons away from home, half off other developing countries' coasts and half off developed countries'.

I would propose to take these figures as a basis for hazarding a guess at what the distribution of management responsibilities would be after a general extension of jurisdiction on the basis of the 200-mile principle. I believe I am justified in this because, with the exception of some tuna, amounting to perhaps 600,000 tons, and comparatively small catches of some other species, all the fish included in our statistics is at present caught well within 200 miles of some coasts. Assuming then for the moment that each coastal state would be responsible for the management of all the fish caught off its coast, the developing countries as a group would be responsible for catches about 4 million tons (or 20 percent) greater than those they now take off their own coasts. This global figure, however, conceals the very great differences between the individual positions of developing countries in relation to the fishing grounds. While some would be responsible for catches many times greater than what they now take themselves, there will be no significant changes for many others, and a few, who have developed fisheries off other countries' coasts, will become more dependent on the management efforts of those countries. To complete the picture, let me mention that for the developed countries as a group responsibilities for catches off their own coasts would increase by about 11 million tons or 55 percent.

These figures provide, of course, only a first indication of the order of magnitude of the increased management responsibilities, and incidentally of increased opportunities for development of their fisheries, that might result from a general adoption of wide limits of fishery jurisdiction. If potential as well as actual catches were taken into consideration, not only would the absolute figures be higher, but the emphasis would shift somewhat in the direction of the developing coastal states.

As regards management, while most of the developed countries concerned will perhaps have no great difficulties in adjusting their own institutions and the relevant international ones to the new allocation of responsibilities, it is to me apparent that a substantial number of developing coastal states would have, in varying degrees, greater fish resources at their disposal and, consequently, greater responsibilities to discharge in order to ensure, or to participate in, the management of these resources. Most of them will require appropriate assistance, at least for an interim period. Therefore I would expect that, in many regions of the world, there would be more increased demands upon FAO and the fishery commissions concerned.

Implications for FAO

Technical assistance.   If then, there is anything at all in the argument I have just made, then it may be expected that FAO will have to strengthen its ability to meet a substantially increased need for technical assistance and transfer of technology to developing countries so as to improve both their management capability and their fishing capacity and fishery industries. This need will be the greater since, as I have indicated, a high proportion of the "conventional" resources that are still underexploited are to be found in areas adjacent to the coasts of developing countries, including some of the countries with the highest populations and the greatest needs for increased food supplies. This is the case, in particular, of the Northwestern Indian Ocean and, at least for pelagic fish, of Southeast Asia.

Assistance to developing countries will have to be tailored to the needs of each individual country. Indeed, some developing coastal states are technically nearly self-sufficient already. But generally, it will be necessary to strengthen national capabilities for research, the collection and analysis of statistics and data, resource assessment and management, use of the most appropriate gear, as well as processing and marketing, to ensure the rational development of national fisheries. As you well know, management of fisheries under the jurisdiction of a single developed coastal state or a couple of them has not always been successful. The lesson of these fisheries is that, even in a country with considerable scientific and economic talent at its disposal, it is not always easy to manage a fishery in a way that gives full biological and economic benefits. Clearly, it will be more difficult to do so in countries where specialized skills are still lacking. A further point is that even if the national expertise required is available and the right solution to management problems is known, some outside independent advice may often exert considerable leverage in overcoming the objections of established short-term interests and in assisting with the implementation of effective management measures.

The assistance required by developing coastal states will, of course, not necessarily come, entirely or even largely, from FAO, but I foresee a special role for FAO in two or three respects. One is that precisely because assistance will have to be sought from a variety of sources, FAO will have to continue to act as a catalyst to tap all sources of bilateral and multilateral assistance. We have already started to do this with a certain degree of success. In fact our Committee on Fisheries has requested that we place on the agenda of its next session, as a major item, the problem of coordination of bilateral and multilateral assistance in fishery development programs.

Secondly, FAO is not only a specialized agency of the United Nations with worldwide responsibilities for the conservation and rational management of the living resources of the sea, but, it has set up within its framework, and is servicing, a number of regional bodies. Six of these bodies serve sea areas where coastal states are predominantly or largely developing, i.e., the Indo-Pacific, the Indian Ocean, the Eastern Central Atlantic, the Western Central Atlantic, the Southwest Atlantic and the Mediterranean. These bodies concern themselves with both management and development and are therefore in a unique position to assist in meeting the needs of their member countries in a balanced development of their fisheries. Over the past few years we have in fact launched, within the framework of some of these bodies and with the help of UNDP and individual donor countries, a series of regional projects to promote fishery development in a coordinated manner in the regions concerned; the first fruits of these efforts are already visible.

We are therefore already in a transitional phase of the expected period of accelerated development and are faced with carrying out a rapidly expanding program of technical assistance. This is in conformity with the policy of our governing bodies. When it last met in November 1973, the Conference of FAO noted that as a result of the Third United Nations Conference on the Law of the Sea, FAO might have to play a more significant role in studying problems of management and assisting countries and regional bodies in their solutions. It added that partial implementation of this role, since it would be technical, need not wait for the conclusions of the Law of the Sea Conference.

Joint ventures. Technical assistance alone, however, cannot always suffice to meet the needs of developing countries for new technology and commercial experience. To a certain extent, capital resources can be provided by global and regional development banks. But there will continue to be a need for some forms of joint venture between developing coastal countries and commercial interests in developed countries, at least for an interim period, to assist in the transfer of technology and experience necessary for the accelerated development and utilization of the expanded coastal resources. Such arrangements are also favored by some developed commercial interests seeking secured access to fishery resources. In this connection, FAO has been responding to an increasing number of requests from developing countries for assistance in the identification of potential joint venture partners and in the handling of joint venture negotiations. A general extension of fishery limits will no doubt add impetus to this trend.

The Conference of FAO also considered this matter at its last session. After stressing that joint venture agreements undoubtedly had benefits for both developing and developed countries, it noted that in some cases, through inexperience, terms were agreed upon which were unfavorable to developing countries. It therefore urged FAO to play a more active role in this field and to assist developing countries in negotiations leading to such agreements.

Implications for regional organizations

What I have said earlier about the need for international collaboration under a régime based on the 200-mile concept, leads, if accepted, to the conclusion that regional bodies, while requiring a good deal of adaptation, would continue to be useful and might, indeed, become more effective. Although I fully realize that the situation may vary considerably from region to region and that it is somewhat perilous to make generalizations, I will look briefly into the possible effects of a 200-mile limit on some of the main features of regional bodies, namely their geographic coverage, their composition, and their functions and powers.

Geographic coverage.   At present, most conventions setting up fishery bodies include in their area of competence not only the high seas but also the waters in which states are entitled under international law to exercise jurisdiction over fisheries. It has generally been considered that the inclusion of these waters is necessary for a rational approach to problems of research and management of migratory resources. This will, of course, be even more valid when, with a considerable extension of national jurisdiction, the bulk of the fishing takes place in these waters.

There is one regional organization whose competence is limited to the waters under the sovereignty or jurisdiction of its member countries. This is the European Economic Community, which is now empowered to decide upon conservation measures in those waters and to prescribe conditions under which fishing activities may be carried out. An extension of national jurisdiction over fisheries to 200 miles would increase considerably the competence of the Community in the North Atlantic, the North Sea, and part of the Mediterranean. It might also require the adaptation of present regional arrangements in these areas.

There are, at present, only three important conventions that specifically exclude certain waters from the area of competence of the fishery bodies they establish; these are the International Commission for the Northwest Atlantic Fisheries, the International North Pacific Fisheries Commission, and the Japanese-Soviet Fisheries Commission for the Northwest Pacific. Since the waters so excluded are referred to as "the territorial waters," this might call for some clarification or readjustment.

      Composition. Although the conditions governing eligibility for membership in existing regional fishery commissions vary greatly, in practice the record of participation is, on the whole, rather good. In most cases, both coastal states and states with a substantial interest in a fishery have chosen, and been able, to become members of the relevant body. An extension of national jurisdiction over areas encompassing the greatest proportion of the stocks of commercial interest, apart from highly migratory species, would clearly make the participation of coastal states of greater and indeed of crucial importance.

      Noncoastal states should also be able to participate in the work of the regional body, especially when they take part in the exploitation of a stock or stocks of fish or other living marine resources that inhabit both the waters under national jurisdiction of coastal states and areas of the adjacent high seas. Their status and the status of noncoastal states fishing in areas under national jurisdiction, pursuant to bilateral agreements or arrangements such as joint ventures, would have to be determined. Several possible solutions could be devised in that respect. This would also apply to landlocked states that would be authorized to fish in the economic zone or patrimonial sea of adjoining coastal states.

      At any rate, it seems obvious that the provisions regarding eligibility for membership and participation in regional commissions would have to be renegotiated.

      Functions and powers. It is not easy to envisage the implications that an extension of national jurisdiction over fisheries would have for the functions and powers of regional bodies. It seems to be expected that they would be substantially affected. It is worth noting in this respect that when the Baltic states adopted, in September 1973, a convention establishing the international Baltic Sea Fishery Commission, they inserted a paragraph in the Final Act of the Plenipotentiary Conference stating that at present none of the participating states claims jurisdiction over more than 12 miles and that the convention would be reviewed in case any of them should claim jurisdiction over a wider area.

      I should perhaps make a distinction here between the regional bodies established within the framework of FAO, on the one hand, and the independent commissions, on the other.

      Since the FAO bodies operate in areas where coastal states are for the most part developing countries, it may be expected that they will broaden and strengthen their activities along the lines I have sketched out a little earlier. I already mentioned that in the view of the FAO Council, they should take a more active role in dealing with the interlinked problems of fishery management and development. When the General Fisheries Council for the Mediterranean decided, in March 1974, to reinforce its role as a management body, it agreed at the same time that it should be better adapted to the new tasks it may be called upon to perform. The Indo-Pacific Fisheries Council also reached the conclusion two months ago that it was necessary to review the whole range of its scientific and technical functions and that particular emphasis should be placed on how it should increase rationally the fishing capability of its member countries and formulate action programs for overall fishery development.

As to the independent commissions, it is more likely that management problems and, in particular, the statistical and scientific bases for management would remain their exclusive or at least principal concern. At the same time, it might well be that their powers could be strengthened. This would of course vary from region to region. A number of delegations at the Sea-Bed Committee and at the Law of the Sea Conference itself have indicated that they would strongly favor such a move and, in my introduction, I gave a few examples of steps that have already been taken in this direction. I could also mention the recent adoption or strengthening of enforcement schemes by some of these commissions.

On the whole, I am inclined to think that an extension of national jurisdiction, coupled with any adjustment that may be required in the composition of regional bodies, would tend to make these bodies more effective. There is no denying the fact that inequality in fishing capability and a certain distrust between coastal states and long-distance fishing countries have been inhibiting factors and have in particular created what I would call a credibility gap regarding the implementation of conservation measures. With the assurance that they would be responsible for and could control the application of these measures, since the waters would be under their jurisdiction, coastal states would perhaps be more willing to accept and abide by even quite far-reaching recommendations made by regional bodies in which they themselves would have a strong voice.

INSTITUTIONAL ARRANGEMENTS ON A WORLDWIDE BASIS

General

I am now turning to the second issue that seems to emerge from the statements and proposals made so far at the Conference on the Law of the Sea and that is of particular relevance to my address: the question of institutional arrangements on a worldwide basis in the field of fisheries.

I should perhaps start by saying that this matter has hardly received the same attention as the question of extension of national jursidiction. However, it gained some importance at the Caracas session of the conference, even though it was considered mostly outside the formal framework for discussions. I am of course aware that consideration of this matter encompassed interests other than fisheries, but I will restrict my comments to fishery aspects alone. Lastly, I should indicate that the subject was taken up mostly in relation to the living resources of the sea beyond a 200-mile economic zone or patrimonial sea. It may therefore be of interest to provide some information on those resources. There are a few important resources presently harvestable, mainly tunas and whales, which occur both within and outside a 200-mile limit. Not more than about 75 percent of whales (by weight) and about 40 percent of tunas are caught outside that limit. There are also unconventional resources which migrate beyond 200 miles, but their harvesting will not be practical for some years or even decades. There are no presently harvestable resources (and possibly no resources) which exist only beyond 200 miles.

Attribution of responsibilities to the proposed seabed authority

At the Caracas session of the conference, several delegations referred to the question of conservation and exploitation of fishery resources in the high seas beyond the proposed area of extended national jurisdiction. These delegations felt that the principle of freedom of fishing, as recognized in the 1958 Convention on Fishing and Conservation of the Living Resources of the High Seas, could not meet the new circumstances created by current technological development, with its threat of exhausting species. They considered that the ocean space beyond national jurisdiction should be treated as a single entity and that there should be no distinction between living and nonliving resources in respect to exploration, conservation, and exploitation. In their view, therefore, the seabed authority to be set up for the seabed and the ocean floor beyond the limits of national jurisdiction should also be made responsible for the water column above, including its living resources. The authority should be vested with a wide and comprehensive mandate and should be empowered to explore and exploit the international area either directly or through other means, and to deal with the question of distributing equitably the benefits to be derived from the exploitation of mineral and living resources.

Although this question had not, or at least not yet, been discussed by the conference, I should like to offer a few comments.

At the outset, I would invite your attention to what I said a little while ago regarding the present status of exploitation of living resources beyond a 200-mile limit. At present, with the exception of the tunas and a few other species, hardly any fish (as distinct from whales) are harvested outside the area proposed to be under national jurisdiction. While a general extension of limits will no doubt encourage some operators to move beyond the 200 miles, the opportunities for this are extremely limited, at least as far as "conventional" species are concerned. Moreover, none of the stocks in question lives entirely or even predominantly outside the 200-mile limit.

I am sure you appreciate, though perhaps some advocates of a comprehensive mandate for the Seabed authority do not, that, unlike minerals, fish are a mobile resource and take no heed of artificial lines drawn for purposes of jurisdiction. Furthermore, unlike minerals, fish are a renewable resource which, if properly managed, can produce a sustained yield. The control of fishing effort with a view to maintaining a stock at its optimum level requires the formulation and implementation of conservation measures that must be applied to the whole stock throughout its range. Having two or more management authorities for the same stocks would not be a workable proposition from the technical, scientific, or economic points of view. I should stress in this respect that the area of competence of existing regional or international organizations concerned with fisheries extends to the high seas and covers nearly all the seas and oceans of the world.

I should add that extending the competence of the seabed authority to living resources in the waters above the international area would also require it to develop a range of expertise and technical services completely different from those relating to mineral resources. This goes not only for what would be the regular program of the authority, but also for the technical assistance operations that it would probably undertake. The cost and trouble involved might well be out of proportion to, if not in excess of, any benefits that could be expected.

Lastly, the attribution to the seabed authority of responsibilities in the field of fisheries would require drastic institutional changes that might prove damaging and are not necessary. At its last session a few months ago, our Committee on Fisheries considered the progress so far achieved by the Conference on the Law of the Sea. On that occasion, several members stressed that there was no need for a new international authority to deal with fisheries. They had in mind the functions and activities not only of existing regional bodies, but also of FAO and the Committee on Fisheries itself.

Attribution of responsibilities to FAO

At the Caracas session of the Conference on the Law of the Sea, a number of delegations from both developing and developed countries made it clear or implied, in their statements or in their formal proposals, that no useful purpose would be served by attributing to the seabed authority responsibilities in the field of fisheries or establishing a new world authority to deal with fisheries. Most of these delegations referred in this respect to the role of regional fishery bodies and of FAO.

In fact, several proposals that were tabled at the conference envisage the discharge by FAO of specific functions. For example, Australia and New

Zealand submitted a draft article on highly migratory species that is of course relevant to areas both within and beyond national jurisdiction. Under this draft article, the director-general of FAO could be asked whether the proper management of these species requires the setting up of an appropriate international or regional organization. If he answered in the affirmative, he would designate the members of the organization and could recommend institutional arrangements.

The draft article for a chapter on the high seas, submitted by the U.S.A., provides that states should cooperate with each other in the exploitation and conservation of living resources in areas beyond the economic zones of coastal states. States exploiting identical resources, or different resources located in the same area, would enter into fishery management agreements, and establish an appropriate multilateral fishery organization to maintain these resources. If such a body could not be constituted among the states concerned, they could ask for the assistance of FAO in establishing an appropriate regional or international regulatory body.

I should also mention the draft articles on fisheries submitted by eight member countries of the European Economic Community. They envisage a significant role for regional or sectoral fishery bodies and provide, in addition, that the activities of these bodies could be supplemented, as necessary, by those of an international fisheries authority, either existing or to be set up. The functions of this authority would be: (1) to promote the establishment of new organizations and, where a competent organization does not exist, to exercise the powers which would normally devolve upon such an organization; (2) to encourage all types of technical assistance to fisheries. It is indicated in the relevant document that the international fisheries authority might be FAO.

These proposed functions would be consonant with the constitutional responsibilities of FAO regarding the proper conservation and management of the living resources of the sea. Indeed, one of the main tasks of our Committee on Fisheries, which is the only worldwide intergovernmental forum dealing with fisheries, is to conduct periodic general reviews of fishery problems of an international character and appraise such problems and their possible solutions with a view to concerted action by nations, by FAO, and by other intergovernmental bodies.

The potential importance of this role was already apparent when the committee was established in 1965, since it was then specifically requested to consider the desirability of preparing and submitting to member nations an international convention under the relevant provision of the FAO Constitution "to ensure effective international cooperation and consultation in fisheries on a world-wide scale." This would in particular allow for the committee to include as members all countries that are members of the United Nations and of any specialized agency (at present it is open to all FAO member nations on a trial basis) and to have wider powers. I mentioned to you earlier that it was agreed that a decision on this matter be postponed until the outcome is known of the Conference on the Law of the Sea. However, the committee has expressed the view, at its last session in October 1974, that FAO and the committee itself would be likely to have a key role in any new régime governing world fisheries.

CONCLUDING REMARKS

Mr. Chairman, I am afraid I have already exceeded the time that you allotted to me and I should now give a chance to the distinguished members of the panel.

By way of conclusion, I wish to stress that I am deeply aware of having barely scratched the surface of my subject. In my defense, may I say that you asked me to describe in thirty minutes what the conference, after four years of effort and negotiations, has not yet agreed upon. This has obliged me to make generalizations, when a detailed region-by-region treatment would have often been more appropriate. I have also tried to look at my subject with the technical and scientific requirements principally in view. I realize, of course, that in the end decisions made at the political level will not necessarily be based on technical considerations alone. But fish have a habit of not always responding fully to political decisions.

Whatever agreement is reached by the conference, complex fishery problems will continue to require, for their solution, close international cooperation. I hope I have convinced you of the increased and crucial role that the regional organizations and FAO will be able to play, and should play, in assisting coastal states in the rational management and development of the living resources of the sea.

Table 6-1. Marine Catches

| | Own Coasts | | | | Other Countries' Coasts | | | | | | | | | | | | Total | | | |
| | | | | | Coasts of Developed Countries | | | | Coasts of Developing Countries | | | | All Other Coasts | | | | | | | |
	a mil-lions of tons	b %	c %	d %	a mil-lions of tons	b %	c %	d %	a mil-lions of tons	b %	c %	d %	a mil-lions of tons	b %	c %	d %	a mil-lions of tons	b %	c %	d %
Developed countries	20.1	50	36	59	10.6	95	19	31	3.6	88	6	10	14.2	93	25	41	34.3	61	61	100
Developing countries	20.4	50	37	95	0.6	5	1	3	0.5	12	1	2	1.1	7	2	5	21.5	39	39	100
World	40.5	100	73	73	11.2	100	20	20	4.1	100	7	7	15.3	100	27	27	55.8	100	100	100

b
→ 100%

c
% of world total
55.8 = 100%

d
% ——→ 100%

Panel Discussion

Gunnar Schram
University of Iceland

Mr. Schram: Thank you. As a matter of fact, I was alloted five minutes by our chairman. Being an Icelander and therefore law-abiding in all matters pertaining to oceans, I will faithfully stick to that five-minutes ruling.

It seems to me that, discussing this subject here this afternoon, we are faced with two issues or two main points. The first is the need for a complete redrafting of the law of the sea with regard to the area beyond national jurisdiction and the living resources that we find there. The second is a complete new organizational setup, a new fisheries organization—new international fisheries commission, if you like—which will be allotted the task of monitoring and conservation of the resources beyond national jurisdiction.

We do not have such an organization today. We have, of course, FAO and its Committee on Fisheries, which we have heard discussed here by our main speaker. This might possibly be built up into an organization like the one I suggested. There is another possibility which many of the developing countries are thinking about. This is an international seabed or ocean agency, which would undertake the responsibility for monitoring and conserving the living resources beyond national jurisdiction.

It does not really matter very much which alternative we choose on this issue. For our main speaker it may though be a matter of some importance, because he has a vested interest in FAO as such and would like to give this new and urgent task to that organization. Undoubtedly FAO could undertake the work of building up an international fisheries agency, which could very creditably do the job. So undoubtedly would the proposed seabed agency.

The main thing is that we have an organizational setup that is capable and willing to undertake the very important work of rational management and conservation of the living resources which will be found beyond national jurisdiction.

This must be done through the Law of the Sea Conference, but,

222

regrettably, the Caracas conference has neglected those two issues. One would hope that, at the Geneva session and at the session which may follow, these issues will receive more attention, resulting in adequate legal rules for high seas fisheries management.

Apart from the great need for an international fisheries organization to undertake these tasks, we have also the question of writing a completely new law on management and conservation of the resources beyond national jurisdiction.

Even if we all go out to 200 miles, and there is hardly any doubt about that, we still have 60 percent of the oceans lying beyond the 200-mile limit, and that is quite a large area of our globe. Our main speaker mentioned, very rightly, that most of the resources are found within that 200-mile limit, but quite a few of them migrate beyond that limit and, to a considerable extent, are caught there.

As the 1958 Geneva Convention is no longer applicable to the situation, we must, at the conference, come up with a new convention which insures that the resources are managed rationally and that conservation is taken care of. This convention must also be accompanied by a scheme of joint enforcement. We can no longer leave this legal issue to every individual state. The task of joint enforcement must be allotted to the international agency concerned, so one has a guarantee of the success of the measures adopted.

These are very briefly the main points I would like to mention here today.

Thank you.

Mr. Christy: Thank you very much, Gunnar, for the importance of your remarks and their succinctness.

Mr. Choon-ho Park, an international scholar of law, who has recently completed a very important study on the fisheries of the East China and the Yellow Seas, will have some brief comments to make about that area. Choon-ho.

Panel Discussion

Choon-ho Park
Harvard Law School

Mr. Park: Thank you, Mr. Chairman.

I wish to say briefly and specifically something about the fisheries problems of a small region, the Yellow Sea and the East China Sea, which involve China, Japan, North Korea, South Korea, and Taiwan.

There are four fisheries agreements, which are intended to regulate fisheries in these two seas. They are the China-Japan Non-Governmental Agreement of 1965, originally entered into in 1955, the Japan-Korea Fisheries Agreement of 1965, the China–North Korea Agreement of 1959, and a multinational agreement among the five socialist countries of Northeast Asia, called the West Pacific Fisheries, Oceanology, and Limnology Research Cooperation Agreement. This last one was signed in 1956 in Peking, but as its name suggests, it is not a regular fisheries agreement, but more a cooperative arrangement. China withdrew from this one in 1967, and very little has been reported on this agreement since 1964. It is not clear whether it is still in existence.

None of the four agreements is binding on all the coastal states of the area, because none of the coastal states is party to all the four agreements. It is something quite unnatural that in a small, semienclosed area of the sea like the Yellow and East China Seas, there is no multinational fisheries agreement. There is a political reason for this.

The relations between the coastal states, including the two Koreas and two Chinas have never been favorable to fostering an atmosphere in which a regional arrangement or any multinational arrangement can be made.

Whether such an arrangement is going to be made in the future depends, in a large measure, on the attitude of China, and China's attitude will, in turn, depend on what the Law of the Sea Conference will produce or fail to produce, especially with respect to the 200-mile economic zone.

At this point, it is interesting to note China's attitude toward the economic zone from a number of points. It seems that China is being dragged into a serious dilemma of its own making. On the one hand, it has been ardently supporting the Third World partition, and on the other hand, however, China's seas, including the South China Sea, are all small and semienclosed waters where the distance from one piece of land to another barely reach 400 nautical miles.

On the hypothesis of an exclusive 200-mile economic zone, therefore, it would not be necessary at all for China to claim 200-mile jurisdiction in order to benefit from whatever its offshore waters have to offer. As a matter of fact, if a 200-mile zone is strictly applied, China would have to abandon its adherence to the natural prolongation of land theory in favor of the median line principle, and this could possibly lead China to have to give up to Japan part of what it has been claiming as its own continental shelf in the East China Sea.

China has been trying to justify this contradiction or dilemma simply by leaving the issues to regional arrangements. For these reasons, China has never been specific on any particular issue of the law of the sea, because the more specific it is, the less support it is bound to get from the Third World countries.

Now how China is going to adjust this situation remains to be seen. Just to quote one example of how China has been nonspecific of the issues, we can take the example of the position of landlocked countries, which I mentioned in the group discussion yesterday.

China has five landlocked countries around its border: Afghanistan, Bhutan, Laos, Outer Mongolia, and Nepal. A careful reading of all the statements China has made since it came into the UN Sea-Bed Committee suggests that there is not any specific support or objection to the position or interest of the landlocked countries. If we take Mongolia, the only way or the nearest way Mongolia can reach the sea would be to go through Chinese territories. In fact, the shortest distance would be through Peking and into the Po Hai Bay. But in the case of the four other countries, they would not have to use Chinese territories. This I just quoted as an example.

Thank you very much, Mr. Chairman.

Mr. Christy: Thank you very much, Choon-ho.

The last panelist is Jim Storer of the Office of Marine Resources of the U.S. National Oceanic and Atmospheric Administration.

Jim.

Panel Discussion

James Storer
Office of Marine Resources, NOAA
U.S. Department of Commerce

Mr. Storer: In the interest of brevity, it might be just as useful if I limit myself to a few comments concerning two or three of the points that Fred Popper has made. He has provided an excellent review of the present status of the regional bodies, of their potential and some of the problems they face.

Some of these problems concern the nature of the relationships of regional commissions to the coastal states in the light of the extended coastal jurisdiction which will come, either through the Law of the Sea Conference or through unilateral action. In this matter there is a real question of how much of a role the coastal states will be willing to give to the regional bodies in terms of actual authority or responsibility since the trend towards complete exclusivity within the zone is so strong.

Also it must be kept in mind that the role of multilateral regional commissions will have to be accommodated in certain cases to that of bilateral arrangements which may be sometimes more suitable for bringing about complementary and effective management programs.

In early discussions of COFI (Committee on Fisheries) of the FAO, when the problems of regional bodies have been considered, one of the aspects frequently discussed has been the financial support. Mr. Popper has indicated clearly the importance of the regional UNDP projects which are associated with some of the regional commissions and which have been an important source of financing stock assessment and other activities essential to the role of management of the regional commissions.

However the complexity and extent of the problems that regional commissions will face in providing the necessary data will be extremely costly and the UNDP is neither able nor the appropriate mechanism to finance these activities on a wide and permanent scale. Other revenue sources will be needed.

There has also been discussion of the financial problems of regional

226

commissions in several sessions of COFI and it is hoped that the Secretariat, i.e., the Department of Fisheries, will address itself to this matter and provide an analysis of the various possibilities that exist for providing greater revenue to the regional commissions.

There has, for instance, been some informal discussion of these matters in the law of the sea forum, most of which was related to the regional commissions concerned with tuna. Among the suggestions has been the idea that a nominal fee, perhaps based upon a percentage of the value of the catch, might be applied to all the fish caught within the area of responsibility of the regional commission. Such a revenue would hopefully provide enough to meet the research and administrative costs of the regional commission and to meet other needs as might be desired.

Many of Mr. Popper's remarks dealt with a relationship of the regional commissions to FAO and the future of FAO and particularly COFI in terms of its role as the only worldwide body concerned with fishery matters. There is much I think to be said for the point that the Committee on Fisheries, as the body of fishery administrators meeting every year to provide advice to the Department of Fisheries, needs strengthening and some revitalization if it is to play a proper role in providing leadership and coordination throughout the world.

In this respect, it is I think a little discouraging to note that COFI, at its last session in November 1974, did not act upon a request made by some delegations that it instruct an appropriate subcommittee to review vital matter of COFI's future role in the light of changing circumstances. Though this proposal was fully discussed at the session, the committee, as Mr. Popper has indicated, finally decided not to take action and to wait until the results of the Geneva meeting were known. This was I think a mistake. There was much a subcommittee could have done in the meantime, especially to be able to provide COFI at its next meeting following Geneva (June of 1975) with a report that would have made COFI more prepared to handle the eventual outcome of LOS. I am a little bothered by this failure as a premonition that the members of COFI themselves are not pushing very far or very fast for a broadening of its role or even for a careful reexamination.

Despite the fact that COFI did not instruct its own subcommittee to carry out this careful review of the interrelationships of COFI, the Department of Fisheries, and the regional commissions, it is encouraging that the department itself will review this matter. Furthermore, it is excellent to note that the Department of Fisheries in carrying out this review is going to go outside of the secretariat and using other experts to get new ideas and viewpoints.

In any event, it is essential that the regional bodies have the necessary capability to perform their management responsibilities and to provide adequate assistance to the member countries in this respect. In part this capability will have to come from their own organizations and activities and the support of their own member countries. In part, however, the capability and efficiency of regional organizations will depend upon the availability of a larger, broader and more worldwide fisheries body which, it is hoped, will be FAO and COFI.

Discussion and Questions

Mr. Christy: Thank you, Jim.
        Could you very briefly describe the relationship of COFI to the Department of Fisheries? I am not sure that—

Mr. Storer: Fred should really do that, although I used to be the secretary of COFI. The Committee on Fisheries is a group of about seventy plus member countries. Anyone in FAO is able to belong to the Committee if he wishes. As I have indicated, that body meets every year and essentially consists of the top fishery administrators of the member countries. In its sessions, it considers the program of the Department of Fisheries and provides advice to that department and to the Council and governing bodies of FAO concerning the activities of the Department of Fisheries. It is also interested in the general state of fisheries development and management throughout the world and receives reports prepared by the Secretariat on these broader matters.

Mr. Christy: Thank you, Jim.
        Some questions or comments from the floor.
        Mr. Edward Miles, I think it is.

Mr. Miles: I'll deal with you later, Chris.

Mr. Christy: Would you identify yourself, please?

Mr. Miles: Ed Miles. I have a number of comments, and I hope my voice holds up to allow me to finish them.
        The first one—I am not often in disagreement with my friend, Gunnar Schram, but I find myself in that situation this afternoon—I do not agree that there are many real alternatives for setting up organizations to deal

with fisheries resources outside of 200-mile economic zones during and after the conference. That is, I don't agree that there are many alternatives to what currently exists in the FAO.

There simply are not sufficient resources outside of 200 miles to allow, to my mind, the cost of setting up an entirely new organization, if it could be done, and I will deal with that in a minute. The duplication would be rather excessive. If you could find the fishery administrators to put in there, I don't know where you would get the money to support that operation, since the value of the task they would be given would not even be equal to the cost of operating that kind of an organization.

I also don't think it is a good idea because the stress that this issue would put on existing difficult negotiations within the law of the sea context would not be justified by the probable outcome. More specifically, since it encompasses a range of other items with respect to control over the water column and the conduct of scientific research therein; this may be an issue on which the conference could founder. It would create a great deal of opposition on the part of a large number of countries.

So I think it is not a real choice to talk about alternatives to the FAO because of the costs, the fact that there are not enough resources outside of 200 miles, and the fact that the additional difficulties which would be created within the Law of the Sea Conference would affect the conference as a whole. So I don't think we have much alternative to the FAO, and within the constraints that that organization has to face, it has done a pretty good job.

One thing worries me, however—Fred Popper referred to the need for continued and increased technical assistance in the event of a 200-mile economic zone—I would like to know where the money is coming from. I don't disagree that there is a need or that the significance of this kind of activity in the FAO will increase. I simply don't see where the money is coming from, unless, say, in the East Central Atlantic the CECAF countries would be willing to reinvest a portion of revenues gained from deals made with distant-water fisheries into stock assessment. But even if this happens I also have doubts about how generalizable the CECAF experience will be for the rest of the world.

Mr. Christy: Thanks very much, Ed.
Gunnar, would you like to respond?

Mr. Schram: Yes, very briefly.
I am sorry if I did not make myself quite clear on this subject, but I was not excluding FAO at all. I simply said that, or meant to say rather, that we have other alternatives, and some of the developing countries have been speaking about other alternatives. FAO does not today, but might of course build the operational capability of discharging these duties which are very

important and must be discharged—a new, if you like, a new commission or a new regulatory body for the area beyond national jurisdiction.

Undoubtedly FAO at present has the most expertise to do this, and possibly the funds. And I would by no means exclude FAO in this respect. On the point of membership, I understand that some very important nations are not members of FAO, but that might be remedied I suppose.

Mr. Christy: Fred.

Mr. Popper: Mr. Chairman, I won't go into the question of whether FAO is a good or a bad organization. Obviously I have a biased view on this. But my real point was that to my mind it makes no sense whatsoever to try and manage the resources beyond 200 miles separately from the resources within 200 miles, because most of the resources outside 200 miles, that are now being caught, or are likely to be caught in the next ten, twenty, or twenty-five years, are the same resources that are also being caught within the 200 miles. So you can't effectively manage them separately.

That was my main point. It does not make much difference who attempts it, nobody will succeed in managing the resources outside 200 miles separately. FAO would fail just as much as the seabed authority.

Mr. Christy: Fred, Professor Miles also raised the question of the finances that would be necessary for this, and I think Jim Storer touched upon this. And I agree with Ed, it's a very critical problem.

Mr. Popper: Yes, well I agree also. I said actually in the paper that I did not envisage that FAO would exclusively or even largely be the vehicle for this. This has to come from other sources, bilateral mainly, either in the form of bilateral technical assistance or through joint ventures, which I think is the more likely way, but there is also for a place FAO in this field, with some kind of a brokerage or coordinating role.

Whether these sources will be sufficient to give money for rapid development of capability where it is needed, I don't know. Dr. Miles referred to the CECAF area, which is by far the most important in this respect, and I think the prospects are not too bad there, but we will have to see what happens. It will depend very much on the general economic situation in which we find ourselves after the Law of the Sea Conference, and according to present indications, perhaps this is not very good.

Mr. Christy: I would like to pursue this a little further, too.

Given a fairly narrow limit of jursidiction, there has been, or one could postulate that there is some rationale for many of the developed countries providing sources of funds for FAO because of the returns they might expect from being able to fish off the coasts of other countries. If the extension is to 200 miles, do you think that this would reduce the incentive on the part of many of the developed countries to continue their support of FAO, the way they have in the past?

Mr. Popper: Well, it's difficult to say. I would not have thought that this was a major consideration in the allocation of funds to FAO. The allocation of funds to FAO is determined on general policy grounds, general policy of developed countries vis à vis developing countries, not in the field of fisheries particularly, but in the general field covered by FAO, food and agriculture.

This may or may not change. Right now, of course, the question of food is very much in people's minds, and perhaps the prospects of having funds allocated for such purposes are not too bad, relatively speaking, but as I said earlier, it will depend on the absolute level, general level of funds that will be made available by developed countries under worsened economic conditions for this kind of purpose, not just in food, but in development work generally.

Mr. Christy: Thank you.
Don McKernan. Briefly, McKernan.

Mr. McKernan: Mr. Chairman, I can't clear my throat briefly. I agree with Dr. Popper's extremely interesting analysis, Mr. Chairman, of the future need for some international cooperation. I would see it just a little differently perhaps than he would, but I would essentially come to the same conclusion.

It seems to me—and I worry about what is going to happen to the production of food from the sea at the present time, in the future, in the near future, and long-range future—it seems to me that we have not done very well in the past in conservation measures, international or national conservation measures, and frankly I don't see much coming out of the Law of the Sea that promises much better rational management of the living resources of the ocean.

And it seems to me that if the direction we are going is going to lead eventually to a more rational use of the ocean, this means then that the two rather fundamental issues, that is, the conservation of the resources, the maintenance of these at a high level of productivity, and the allocation has to be dealt with better than it has in the past.

And here it seems to me then, there perhaps are something like four or five rather fundamental contributions that can be made by some international hands; in other words, by an organization such as FAO or some other one. In the first place, there is going to have to be some strengthening of national institutions. That seems quite obvious if national governments around the world are going to gain better control.

Obviously there is going to be a need for regional cooperation as never before, that is, whether or not we have national control, even in fisheries inhabiting primarily the continental shelf, there will be an absolute necessity for regional arrangements.

And then, as has been mentioned by a number of the panel members, there are some species, and rather important ones at that, who inhabit at some time during their life history, both the inshore waters adjacent to coasts, and also migrate very widely at sea, such as the tunas which are economically at least a very, very important species. And here again, there needs to be some organization, some catalyst, if I might use the term, to bring nations together, and I think FAO has had lots of experience, not all successful, but lots of experience in this area.

Then, of course, their experience in terms of setting up some kind of reasonable statistical areas is another very important area, one that is generally neglected around the world.

Then finally, it seems to me that we have just begun in world fisheries to give much consideration to the question of monitoring and enforcement. And here I don't think FAO has had much experience, but perhaps not as much as some of the nations who are both exploiting resources heavily off their coasts, but in distant waters as well, but it does seem to me that here again if we are going to have any kind of monitoring or enforcement which will provide some rational way of using the resources, either within areas under national jurisdiction, or without, we are going to have to develop a much more highly sophisticated scheme than we have in force at the present time.

So I conclude that there is not any alternative to an FAO or an FAO-type organism if we are successful in providing for more rational use of the resources.

I would like to see that occur sooner, and very soon indeed. In fact, my last remark, Mr. Chairman, is that I tend to share with Dr. Storer some disappointment in the Committee on Fisheries, a committee incidentally that I had a little bit to do with in its beginning, and I think perhaps the nations, like our own, are partly at fault, but at least it doesn't seem to me that it has done all of the things that we had hoped it would do, and particularly now, when I think the need is even greater than ever before, it seems to be lagging in initiative, in taking the rather bold steps that are probably going to be needed in the future.

Thank you, Mr. Chairman.

Mr. Christy: Don, are you suggesting that it would be appropriate and feasible for FAO to assume a considerably stronger role in monitoring and enforcement?

Mr. McKernan: I didn't really deal with the question of whether FAO or some other international organization should assume control, direct control, but I do see the need for some international group, some international body, to at least initiate, bring together, the various schemes that are now in existence, to provide some leadership in this area.

By the way, since you brought me back to the microphone, I might say in terms of the financing problem, this seems to me not an impossible situation if sort of rationally followed, that is, we have not really thought very much about sort of taxing according to use, and I am guessing that a number of coastal states, looking forward to greater control, perhaps renting out the resources in some way within areas which will soon come under national jurisdiction, if not already claimed, it seems to me that one can—without hurting too badly anyway—one can finance on the basis of use, with some schemes of course that would be somewhat different within areas of national jurisdiction and without, nevertheless that might finance on a more stable, lasting basis the kinds of assistance that I think the world needs in the decades to come.

Part IV

Dynamics in Ocean Technology and Projections of Law of the Sea Outcomes

Chairman
H. Gary Knight
Louisiana State University Law Center

Mr. Knight: Ladies and gentlemen, I think we might get started on this morning's program. The theme of today, as indicated in your program, is Dynamics in Ocean Technology and Projections of Law of the Sea Outcomes.

We are going to look at future technologies in four areas today—fishing, shipping and transportation, military use of the sea, and deep seabed mining. For each of these subjects, our speakers are going to give us a glimpse of the future and then discuss with us what some of the implications, if they feel there are any, will be of these future technological developments.

It is commonplace to say that we are in the midst of the Third Law of the Sea Conference because of new political arrangements and perceptions and perhaps even more so because of technological developments. It was, in fact, the developments in offshore oil and gas technology; fisheries, especially with respect to distant-water fishing gear; deep ocean mining; scientific research; and in military hardware that led to the necessity for reviewing and perhaps recreating the law of the sea.

I suggest that unless we are better at anticipating future developments than we were in 1958, we will have the Fourth Law of the Sea Conference sooner than any of us probably want it. Now, before beginning the program, I would like to make an extremely brief contribution in the form of three somewhat unrelated thoughts which you might bear with you as you listen to our futurists discuss what may happen in the next ten to fifteen years.

First, Wib Chapman used to say that nations tend to negotiate their law of the sea positions on the basis of their past interests, not their present interests or their future interests. To what extent is that true in the Third Law of the Sea Conference?

Secondly, we all know that law tends to follow technological development. There was no air law until there were airplanes. There was no need for a deep seabed mining law until we had the technological and economic capability to mine seabed nodules. The question is how far should the law lag behind the technology. If the law comes too soon, and is too highly structured and inflexible, it acts as an inhibition on capital investment and development. If the law comes too late, other public interests are inadequately protected. How do we strike that balance in developing the law to anticipate future technologies?

Third and finally, a personal observation. There are two kinds of prophets—prophets of doom and prophets of progress. It has been my observation that prophets of doom almost always overestimate the calamities they predict, while the prophets of progress almost always underestimate the futures that they envision. If that is an accurate observation, I would suggest that there is no reason for you to be skeptical about anything you may see or hear today. As the British scientist Eddington has said, and I paraphrase him: Future technological developments are not merely strange, they are likely to be stranger than we can possibly imagine. With that, we will turn to the first of the four substantive areas we are going to cover today—fisheries.

We have on our panel today Professor Jon Jacobson, who is immediately to my left, Dr. Joachim Schärfe, to his left, and on the far end of the table, Professor Shigeru Oda.

Dr. Jacobson is going to make a presentation of approximately thirty to thirty-five minutes, and each of the commentators will then address the issues for approximately fifteen to twenty minutes, hopefully, leaving us a good half an hour for your participation.

Jon Jacobson is a professor of law at the University of Oregon School of Law. He is an associate editor of the Ocean Development and International Law Journal, and I mention that only because he has a special assignment, and that is to periodically prepare a section for that journal describing future technological developments that affect the law of the sea. Because of that, I think Jon is particularly well qualified to address us today on the subject of Future Fisheries Technology and Its Impact on the Law of the Sea.

Jon?

Chapter Seven

Future Fishing Technology and Its Impact on the Law of the Sea

Jon L. Jacobson
Director of the Ocean Resources Law Program
University of Oregon Law School

Not long ago, the University of Rhode Island's John Knauss wrote: "Until recently, man's use of the major portion of the earth had undergone such little change that the writings of a seventeenth century Dutchman could continue to serve as the basis for the law of the sea such as it was."[1]

Now, in the latter half of the twentieth century, we are between sessions of a nearly universally attended Law of the Sea Conference, a conference necessitated by the fact that man's use of the wet part of his world has recently undergone such significant changes that the simple rule set down by the seventeenth-century Dutchman no longer suffices. Everyone familiar with the current law of the sea effort realizes that the changes in ocean use which called for the conference are largely traceable to recent technological advances in the methods and devices for exploiting ocean resources. The immediate cause for the United Nations concern that led to the establishment of the Seabed Committee in 1967, and eventually to the present conference, was of course the impending development of deep seabed mining technology for the capture of manganese nodules.

We live in an age of technological innovation, and no human activity is immune to it. Certainly no ocean activity has yet escaped the influence of recent innovation. Ocean transportation and military uses of the sea, as well as seabed mining, have experienced dramatic changes in the past few decades. And, of course, the hunting of wild fishes for food, perhaps the oldest use of the ocean, has been the subject of new and often stressful technological advances, especially in the years since World War II.

Recent times have seen the development and relative proliferation of distant-water fishing fleets, whose vessels are capable of traveling halfway around the planet to exploit high seas grounds traditionally fished by fishermen from nearby coastal areas. Technology has in general increased the efficiency—at least potentially—of each fisherman and vessel. Under these strains, "freedom of fishing" on the high seas, a legal principle that generally sufficed for more than 400 years, began to collapse. It will soon be replaced, either by a new law of the sea treaty or by customary-law evolution from unilateral claims by coastal nations.

The new law of the sea for fisheries management, whatever its source or shape (and last year's Caracas LOS session has revealed the basic outline), will need to cope with ongoing technological innovation or it too will soon need to change. It is therefore not enough that the new ocean regime be designed to cope with ocean activities as practiced in the mid-1970s; it must also be adequate for future ocean practices, if possible. Otherwise, the ink will hardly be dry on the LOS treaty, and the ratification process will have only started, before new innovations call for yet another international LOS conference.

This morning, I will focus on predicted technological advances in one field of ocean activity—commercial fishing—and attempt to assess some of the implications of those advances in terms of the scheme of ocean-fisheries management likely to emerge from (or in spite of) the present Law of the Sea Conference. I will first summarize very briefly the history of fishing methods, with emphasis on innovations brought about as part of the post–World War II technological explosion. Then, future fishing-technology trends, as indicated by fisheries experts, will be examined in light of the fisheries-management regime likely to result from current LOS efforts. Finally, a general conclusion and recommendation on monitoring future developments will be submitted.

SUMMARY OF FISHING METHODS[2]

Capture Techniques

The methods and devices of fish capture in use today are essentially those that have been employed for centuries: nets, traps, hooks and lines, spears and harpoons. Almost all modern innovation in capture techniques has resulted from improvement of these basic devices or their methods of use. The development of long-range sailing vessels and better charts and navigation techniques led fishermen onto the open sea. "Fish-chasing" became a predominant fishing practice, a practice that expanded considerably with the introduction of mechanically powered vessels shortly before the turn of the century; vessel operation became safer and larger gear could be used.

Recent times have witnessed greatly accelerated technological advances in fisheries gear and methods, at least as practiced by the most advanced fishermen. Capture devices have been vastly improved in design and materials; larger, more powerful vessels of advanced design have been produced; powered deck machinery has taken over or greatly assisted such former "muscle and sweat" operations as net- and pot-retrieval.

Today's principal capture methods still depend heavily on nets (though nets are now much more frequently constructed of rot-resistant, man-made materials). The types of nets now in use are essentially the otter trawl, the seine, and the gill net.

Otter trawls are cone-shaped nets towed behind vessels and are so named because of the kitelike "otter boards" (possibly derived from "outer boards") which plane through the water to hold the mouth of the trawl open. Until fairly recently, the otter trawl was almost solely a bottom-fishing device that passed along the seabed on rollers. New designs have increased the efficiency of the bottom trawl and, in addition, have led to the development of the midwater trawl.

The otter trawl is designed to "scoop" fish into the cod end, or tip of the trawl cone; seines, in contrast, are flat nets, with floats on top and weights at the bottom, which are designed to encircle fish. Traditionally, seines were set near beaches by small boats or by hand. More recently, the purse seine, so named because of the purse line that draws the net bottom closed after the fish are encircled, has been widely employed, with great success, by vessels at sea. Large purse seines are a principal, and very effective, method of capturing such pelagic schooling fish as tuna and anchovy.

Gill nets entangle fish rather than enclose them. Otherwise, they are somewhat like seines, being floated at the top and weighted at the bottom.

Another ancient fishing device, hook and line, is also in wide use today. These can be trolled behind a vessel through fish schools. Hooks are most productive, however, when baited and hung on short "dropper lines" from a long, horizontal line strung between anchors or floats. Hooks are often used in this long-line manner for catching large nonschooling fish, such as large tunas, marlins, and sharks.

Traps are stationary devices that attract fish into small openings from which escape is difficult or impossible. Traps range from small and simple shellfish pots—baited to attract crabs, lobsters, and shrimp—to giant 1000-meter-long ocean fish traps.

Location Techniques

Perhaps an even more dramatic innovation-acceleration has lately occurred in the techniques and devices for fish location (as contrasted with fish capture). This progress is both a consequence of new research and development directed at fish detection and a result of spin-offs of technologies created outside of fisheries. For example, echo sounders and sonar are now in common use by fishermen, as a means of navigating (finding a fishing ground) and in locating the fish and, to some extent, in counting the fish located. A type of echo sounder, called a "netzsonde" telemeter, is often attached to a trawl net itself to assist the skipper not only in locating the fish in fairly precise relation to the net, but also to help him determine the net's shape and its proximity to the sea bottom. This sort of device has been especially significant in the fairly recent successful development of midwater (as opposed to bottom) trawls. Some trawlers now also employ a temperature sensor, called "thermosande," which is attached to the netzsonde equipment and monitors water temperatures at trawl depth.

Airplanes and helicopters have been put into wide use as fish spotters in recent years. However, visual observation from aircraft can so far detect only those fish stocks that swim near the surface.

Vessels

The postwar decades have also seen significant advances in fishing vessels, including new on-deck equipment and navigation and communication devices. The development of the stern-trawler—onto which the trawl and its captured fish are hauled over the stern rather than the side—opened the way for the larger factory vessels now operating in fleets around the world. Vessel-propulsion systems have also changed over recent years. New, more compact and effective diesel engines are now made for smaller fishing boats. Many of the former "muscle and sweat" deck operations on fishing vessels are now accomplished or assisted by power blocks, hydraulic winches, and fish pumps. As a consequence, fewer men are needed to operate a fishing boat, and this seems especially true for operations involving pot and trap retrieval.

Modern electronics—loran, radar, depth recorders, radio-telephones—has accounted for many of the newer navigation and communications techniques currently in use on most ocean fishing vessels.

Finally, computer-assisted fleet dispatch and vessel automation seem to be on the way. Making use of a "systems approach," naval architects and engineers are combining electronics, on-deck power, satellite navigation, computers, and new vessel-construction principles to turn out large "superboats" capable of fishing efficiently with half the number of crew members required for conventional boats.

SOME FISHERIES-TECHNOLOGY FORECASTS
AND THEIR LOS IMPLICATIONS

Coming Developments in Gear and Techniques

Published predictions of future fishing technologies and techniques are scarce. Lee Alverson[3] seems to be the resident "seer," in this country at least, and many of the predictions I refer to here are his.

Location of fish will continue to be assisted in some fisheries by aircraft, whose surveys will be enhanced by infrared and advanced photographic techniques to determine temperature differentiations and fish school turbulence. Aircraft, and vessels as well, may also make use of lasers for minimizing back-scatter in underwater searches and for greater depth penetration—perhaps up to 200 meters. Satellite detection of fish schools and water properties will be useful to fishermen, especially for location of the commercially important species that swim near the surface. Acoustic techniques, such as echo sounding and sonar, will continue to be important aids in locating fish, though the maximum range of sonar is expected to be fifteen nautical miles. Passive listening devices, designed to identify species and numbers by sound characteristics, may be increasingly employed. Similarly, fish could theoretically be traced and identified by characteristic odors, by use of gaseous spectrophotometers.

Many such devices—acoustic and nonacoustic—will probably be employed more often in the future on unmanned ocean platforms, such as buoys or artificial logs—the logs both to detect and aggregate for capture.

There are some present indications that fish-finding services, or "fish forecasting," may be more important and widespread in the future. These services will combine information on weather, water temperature and chemical makeup, visual reports, satellite observation, etc., and disseminate advice to fishermen on the "wheres" and "whens" of good fishing.

Capture of fish, once located, will be enhanced through improvement of the conventional gear and techniques summarized earlier. Trawls will continue to improve—midwater trawls will see more use and may be combined with electricity for attracting and stunning the fish. Otter boards will probably be replaced by maneuverable motorized units. We should see remote-controlled trawls, and perhaps even submersibles, manned or remote, to chase and capture fish. Purse seines and gill nets may be set and closed with help from remote-controlled submersibles.

Pots and traps will see proportionally increased use because of new high-speed hydraulic winches and over-the-side handling techniques; the result will be to allow fewer crew members to set a large number of units and to retrieve, rebait and reset in a much shorter time. Moreover, pots and traps will be set in deeper waters farther from shore. And even migratory swimming species might be captured by huge ocean traps, constructed of nets or, eventually, of electricity.

Most nets and traps will continue to be constructed from the newer, nondestructible materials.

In addition to improved conventional gear, future fisheries will experience the addition of some newer, unconventional devices. These will include air-bubble and chemical "fences" to corral the fish or limit their migratory pattern to make capture easier. Lights and electricity are already used for fish capture. Future fishermen may make similar use of odor-producing chemicals, introduced by aircraft or vessel, to attract or repel fish. Recorded sounds duplicating the noises of prey or predators might also be introduced for the same purposes.

Vessels will improve in design and construction. Navigation and safety at sea will be assisted by networks of weather-predicting satellites and buoys. Satellites and other sophisticated positioning devices will allow more accurate navigation. Computer-assisted automation of fishing vessels will be more available.

Farther into the future, automatic fishing platforms will make use of several aggregation and capture devices. Combined with other passive-gear developments this will tend to decrease the importance and use of vessels in fishing.

LOS Implications of Future Technology

When combined with recent developments, these predicted technological developments, and others not mentioned or forseen, indicate some trends important to the law of the sea. These trends include the following: (1) Fishing will become potentially more efficient in general. That is, fewer people and vessels will be needed to capture more fish, at least to biological limits. (2) Passive gear and stationary devices—pots, traps, buoys, automated platforms, etc.—will become proportionally more prevalent relative to vessels and active gear. (3) "Fish forecasting" services, combining several location techniques, will become more important. (4) New technologies and the new legal constraints will combine to force distant-water fleets into some new directions.

The legal climate within which these trends will develop, if they do materialize, will undoubtedly have as its most prominent feature a world-oceanwide system of coastal-nation economic zones at least 200 miles wide. The Caracas session of the Law of the Sea Conference made clear to practically all observers that the 200-mile zone is an inevitable feature of any LOS treaty of fisheries management.[4] Even if the conference fails to reach agreement on the economic-zone concept, subsequent unilateral claims to 200-mile zones will undoubtedly create new customary law favorable to such zones within a few years.[5] In the new economic zones, where most fishing will occur, fishing activities will be managed principally by the nearest coastal nation; it will promulgate and enforce fishing regulations within its zone, but to some extent will cooperate with neighboring countries and with international bodies in certain aspects of fisheries management. The extent to which this cooperation will occur depends on political as well as practical considerations, and, as will be pointed out, the practical considerations will include the influence of technological developments.

Increased Efficiency. Almost all the research and development work in fisheries today is aimed at increasing the efficiency of the fishing operation. The basic question is: How can we make it possible for fewer men and fewer boats to expend less energy and less time (i.e., lower the cost of) capturing more fish?

On the surface of the matter, fishing efficiency does not seem such a bad thing. Economists have persuasively argued that we would all be better off, in terms of maximizing society's production, if there were fewer men and less capital tied up in producing the ocean's food resources.[6] Technological advances in fishing can help make this possible, but not without a new legal framework.

"Freedom of fishing," still the rule on most of the ocean (though now challenged by unilateral claims in many of the best fishing grounds), is concededly an unworkable legal base in this day of limited fish resources. Efforts aimed at controlling overfishing, both within national zones and by treaty on the high seas, have too often manifested themselves in gear restrictions, season restrictions, and area restrictions; in other words, efficiency and new technology are discouraged. A better management approach would allow technology and its consequent efficiency to take their course and would limit the fish harvest by directly regulating the total (but more efficient) fishing effort. Such a control mechanism is of course incapable of being implemented under a "freedom of fishing" or open-entry rule. A complex and effective management scheme is needed.

It is theoretically possible that all coastal states, under a new expanded-zone regime collectively covering almost all of the world's best fisheries, will institute economically rational limited-entry programs, but it is hardly likely. Nothing in the history of fisheries management justifies a prophecy that rational management will be the uniform response to a grant to coastal states of absolute or nearly exclusive management authority. It is much more probable that some states will adopt limited-entry programs, each with different specifics, and that others will attack their overfishing problems by the more conventional means of limiting efficiency. (Others, if the new LOS rules allow exclusion of foreign fishermen, will combine the two approaches by excluding foreign fishing and restricting the efficiency of their own fishermen.) The resulting patchwork of management programs is undesirable from many respects, and at least the following technology-related problems could arise. (1) Total investment in ocean fisheries may actually increase because of the combination of continued necessity for less efficient gear in some zones and the encouragement of new, more efficient techniques in other zones. For example, one state might prohibit use of motorized otter boards, while a neighboring state would not. A vessel fishing both zones might need two sets of boards, if not two different trawls. (2) This situation will, in turn, promote further overfishing stress in some areas, possibly causing animosity between those nations who are unable or unwilling to control fishing effort and those who limit entry and thereby "export" more fishing effort to the stress areas. As new technology enables the limited-entry areas to harvest with fewer and fewer units of effort, more and more effort might be expected to move to unlimited-effort grounds, either to international waters or to those economic zones where foreign fishing is allowed by the coastal states.

It is to be hoped that these pressures, and others, will induce at least regional cooperation in coordinating national responses to new technologies.

Passive Gear Trend.   The location and capture of the great majority of wild ocean fishes will undoubtedly be carried out for many years to come by people in boats. Nevertheless, there seems to be some basis for believing that passive systems—for both capture and location—will become increasingly important over the next twenty to thirty years. This will apparently be part of the overall trend toward greater efficiency and energy conservation, since passive or stationary systems, in general, tend to encourage the fish to use their own energies in coming to capture. Most fishing operations currently involve the use of active gear, meaning that power is applied to take the gear to the fish. In the future, however, important quantities of fish may be located and captured through techniques that depend little or not at all on vessels. Yet it is clear from a reading of several proposals for ocean fisheries management submitted to the Sea-Bed Committee[7] and at least one at Caracas[8] that these proposals seem to contemplate that the living resources of the sea will continue indefinitely to be "fished" from "vessels." While it is perhaps only a small drafting point, some future controversies over the application of a fisheries regime resulting from LOS III might well be avoided if it is clear in the language of the treaty that the rules apply to all forms and methods of exploiting the ocean's living resources, and not just to "fishing" from "vessels."

Another problem associated with passive gear and ocean data acquisition systems (ODAS) will be one of reconciling their use with other uses of the seas, particularly general navigation by vessels. Careful control of the positioning and markings of buoys and fishing platforms will be required. Because rules governing the deployment of these devices might affect general shipping, it is clearly desirable that a uniform worldwide set of rules be developed. Zoning or fairway systems may be needed in some areas; restrictions on the use of certain types of passive gear may be necessary for the protection of general navigation; liability for damage to, or by, passive systems would need definition.[9]

At a minimum, any LOS treaty should include a provision directing fisheries management authorities (whether coastal states or regional or international bodies) to cooperate with the appropriate international agencies (e.g., IMCO, IOC, UNESCO) in establishing passive-gear rules and in resolving gear/navigation conflicts.

"Fish Forecasting" Services.   Although many current and coming sophisticated technological devices (e.g., sonar and radar) are and will be designed essentially for use on individual vessels, certain of the predicted devices and techniques will, by their nature, be useful only if shared by large numbers of fishermen. These would include: obtaining and interpreting infrared and laser surveys by air; satellite detection of fish schools, water characteristics, and weather; any wide network of buoys or submerged instrument platforms designed to assess weather and water characteristics, such as temperature, chemistry, organic content, etc., or to listen passively for "fish noises." The information obtained through these future devices and techniques could undoubtedly be put to its best use by more or less centralized "fish forecasting" services. These services could receive by radio the raw data observed by the various remote sensors, feed it into a computer and then radio broadcast to fishermen the ultimate product—"forecasts" or educated predictions on the times and places of the best fishing.[10]

Fish-forecasting services, while presenting a potential for more efficient and safer fishing, create some of their own problems. Broadcasting fishing information indiscriminately to all fishermen could conceivably cause conflicts and overconcentration of effort in the predicted "best" areas. Therefore, some sort of scheme for allocating the dissemination of information might be necessary. This, though, would in turn raise enforcement problems: How is the information to be kept from nonsubscribers or those fishermen to whom the information is otherwise not to be allocated? The controls would probably be necessarily quite complex.

Nevertheless, fish-forecasting services could assist considerably the efficient production of ocean protein resources, especially if combined with limited-entry programs. But the main point here is that these are techniques that can be implemented effectively only in a cooperative context, where many fishermen subscribe to make use of centrally disseminated information. The techniques would be too expensive—in both the monetary and technical-expertise senses—to be put to good use on a small scale.

Therefore, the expected 200-mile-zone system for ocean management is not, of itself, particularly well suited to manage forecasting services. Each coastal nation might, it is true, operate its own service on a scale adjusted to the size of its own zone and especially designed for the zone's resources and waters; however, this would involve some duplication of effort and expense. It would be preferable, at least for forecasting purposes, to have an international organization—such as the FAO or perhaps one to be established by LOS III—establish and operate a worldwide fish-forecasting service, with advice available to all management entities.

New Directions for Distant-Water Fleets. The 200-mile-zone regime is expected to seriously restrict foreign fishing in the new zones all over the planet. Distant-water fleets will therefore tend to adopt one or more of several approaches: (1) attempt to negotiate entry into coastal areas, perhaps in exchange for transfer of technology and expertise to the coastal countries; (2) adapt to fishing within their own nations' zones; (3) concentrate on those species in international waters. "International waters" would include, of course, the seas beyond 200 miles and Antarctic waters, where there will presumably be no 200-mile zone.[11] One problem is that not many traditionally fished species inhabit international waters, so defined, in any great numbers. Therefore, we can expect the development of technology designed to aggregate and capture such species as krill (found in Antarctic waters), lantern fish, and squid to accelerate in the near future. Pressure on these species will, it is hoped, instigate international cooperation on management rules.

A WORD ON OPEN-SEA MARICULTURE

Some day, man will no longer hunt wild fishes at sea, except perhaps for sport. Commercial production of living marine resources will be carried out almost exclusively by "fish farmers" or "ocean ranchers." In the long run, ocean hunters will be able to withstand the now-rising tide of mariculture no more successfully than the early tribal hunters survived the influence of agriculture.

Certainly LOS III should do nothing to discourage this trend: Mariculture may well prove to be the cornerstone of future food production for the world's billions. The question now is whether LOS III ought affirmatively to anticipate the trend. If our focus is the next two to three decades, then the answer to this question appears to be no. True, mariculture is a growing reality in inland and coastal waters, and is presently of concern to domestic legal systems, but it seems to be the consensus of the experts that the international community has no pressing need to provide especially for ocean farming at this time. Open-ocean mariculture is not likely to develop until well into the next century.

Even though open-sea mariculture is probably not of present LOS concern, there are serious plans afoot for its eventual implementation. At some point in the future, there will be manmade mariculture installations at sea, in midocean as well as in coastal waters. Their success will spell the demise of commercial fishing as we now know it. This, coupled with the very presence of still more artificial islands in the ocean, will require new ocean-use rules and regulations. A future generation will have to supply them.

Fortunately, a head start on the problem is underway. A newly published book entitled *Open Sea Mariculture: Perspectives, Problems and Prospects,* the result of a study undertaken by a group of experts at the Oceanic Institute in Hawaii, is "a systems analysis of open sea mariculture." It examines and correlates such topics as biology, economics, oceanography, sociology, marketing, technology, and law and politics. The book includes a chapter on "Legal and Political Perspectives," and is thorough, well documented, and imaginative. *Open Sea Mariculture* should provide a sound basis for planning the international response to mariculture's impact on future oceanic activities.

A WORD ON POLLUTION

As noted earlier, nets and traps (as well as other gear) will continue to be constructed, where possible, of newer nondestructible materials. While the new materials are of obvious immediate benefit to fishermen, they may have undesirable, longer-range side effects: lost gear made from the new plastics and other "nonrot" materials can have an adverse effect on fish stocks and the ocean ecology in general. For example, an unrecoverable plastic crab pot continues to catch crabs and other species virtually forever, the prior catches providing the "bait" for those animals that follow; a lost, drifting monofilament gill net can also continue to entangle and kill fish.

In short, new gear materials are presenting, and will continue to present, a serious pollution problem. Jurisdiction over stationary material that is lost and remains in place (such as shellfish pots) might well be given to coastal states within their 200-mile zones, especially if the living resources affected primarily inhabit only that zone. However, in the case of lost and drifting materials, rules on their use should perhaps be formulated by a regional or international authority, if the material is likely to drift beyond the coastal state zone in which it is lost.

The same sort of comment is, I think, appropriate to the potential introduction of chemicals for aggregation and capture purposes.

CONCLUSION

It is clear that the interaction of the future and the new fisheries-management regime will be determined by developments in many fields besides fisheries technology. Closely related will be progress in the technologies of marine biological assessment, fish processing, and fisheries-law enforcement methods. Not quite so apparent, but just as important, will be shifts in the tides of international power and politics, global economic redistributions, trends in nationalism, as well as the response to such questions as: Will Americans eat squid?

Mankind's institutions have not yet matured to the point where they can effectively manage the future. We can, and certainly do, affect the future, but it is the interplay of multitudes of crossing events originating from separate points in the system that escapes our control. This seems especially true in the case of international institutions, weak and largely formless as they are.

Whether we like it or not, though, the Third Law of the Sea Conference, one of those international institutions, will have serious and longterm effects for the future, in fisheries management and for all the other oceanic activities. It should be recognized now that changes in those activities will occur in the next decades; some changes we can foresee and others will be a surprise to every one of us. Not all of the fisheries-technology predictions in this paper will come true, but many of them and perhaps many more changes than we can now anticipate will come to pass.

What should LOS III do in view of these rather obvious truths?

The key, it is suggested, is flexibility. Under the 200-mile zone regime, each coastal state will be a rule-making body usually capable of responding to new technologies in its own way and for its own purposes. In a few years, however, unless the coastal states quickly establish broad regional management mechanisms, the varied responses to new technologies could create conflicts and inefficiencies. At some point, probably not too many years from now, someone will suggest a new LOS conference to straighten out the mess. Perhaps, then, LOS III ought to anticipate this problem (and, incidentally, many other similar or analogous problems) by itself scheduling an LOS IV for a definite date, say, fifteen years hence. Under such a provision, at least plans and preparations could get underway well in advance of LOS IV. The current conference could even go so far as to recognize that a new LOS conference will be required every few years to make the adjustments and changes made necessary by the passage of time. For example, LOS III might create a permanent organization or secretariat whose purpose would be to arrange for an LOS conference every fifteen years or so.

At the very least, LOS III should establish, or designate within FAO, an advisory body to monitor technological (and economic and, perhaps, political) developments and make recommendations to coastal states and to the appropriate post–LOS III organization on the advisability of new management rules or new international conferences. The work of the advisory body might be financed by a tax on the total fisheries catch.

If LOS III can successfully devise a method for the international community to respond in a timely fashion to new developments in fisheries technology, it will not only help to assure the proper management of the ocean's fisheries but will also, by example, contribute to the development of effective international institutions.

Mr. Knight: Thank you very much, Jon.

With that stage set, knowing what some of the possible futures are, we are going to turn now to two additional speakers and get, perhaps, some different views on the impacts. The first speaker will be Shigeru Oda, who as I am sure most of you know is professor of law at Tohoku University in Sendai, Japan. He has been, again, as I am sure most of you know, a representative of the government of Japan to the UN Sea-Bed Committee and to the Third Law of the Sea Conference. I am especially grateful to Professor Oda for being here, not only because he is one of the world's foremost law of the sea authorities, but because he interrupted a homeward-bound journey from Calcutta to be with us today and must leave very shortly, as I understand, after this session.

NOTES

1. This paper presents much of the substance of the author's chapter in a forthcoming book entitled *Future International Fisheries Management,* to be published by West Publishing Company for the American Society of International Law. The author is grateful to the Society for its kind permission to present this restatement.
2. John Knauss, "Developing the Freedom of Scientific Research Issue of the Third Law of the Sea Conference," *Ocean Development and International Law Journal,* vol. 1, no. 1 (Spring 1973).
3. The major sources for the information presented in this section of the paper are: J. Bardach, *Harvest of the Sea* (Harper and Row, 1968); C. Blair and W. Ansel, *A Guide to Fishing Boats and Their Gear* (Cambridge, Maryland: Cornell Maritime, 1968): FAO, *Fishing Boats of the World* (New York: Unipub, 1967); FAO, *Catalogue of Fishing Gear Designs* (1972); FAO World Fishing Gear Congress, *Modern Fishing Gear of the World,* vol. 3 (London: Fishing News [Books], Ltd., 1971); *Modern Fishing Gear of the World,* vol. 2 (1963); J. Garner, *Modern Deep-Sea Trawling Gear* (London: Fishing News [Books], Ltd., 1967); R. Haines, *Echo Fishing* (Levittown, N.Y.: Transatlantic Arts, Inc., 1969); P. Hjul, ed., *The Stern Trawler* (Surrey, England: Fishing News [Books], Ltd.: 1972); Royce, *Introduction to the Fishery Sciences* (New York: Academic Press, 1972); J. Sainsbury, *Commercial Fishing Methods* (London: Fishing News [Books], Ltd., 1971); S. Shapiro, ed., *Our Changing Fisheries* (Washington: U.S. Government Publication, 1971); A. von Brandt, *Fish Catching Methods of the World,* rev. ed. (New York: Heinman, 1972).
4. Dr. Dayton L. Alverson is currently Director of the Northwest Fisheries Center, National Marine Fisheries Service. His published work on future fishing technology includes: Wilimovsky & Alverson, "The Future of Fisheries, etc.", *Modern Fishing Gear of the World* (1971), and Alverson & Wilimovsky, "Prospective Developments in the Harvesting of Marine Fishes," *Modern Fishing Gear of the World* (1963).
5. *See generally* United Nations Source Documents on the Third UN Law of the Sea Conference: Caracas '74 [LOS-3] (Nautilus Press 1974).
6. By a surprisingly wide margin (68 to 27), the U.S. Senate of the 93d Congress recently passed S. 1988, a Magnuson-sponsored bill to establish a U.S. 200-mile fishing zone. In the opinion of many observers, the new Congress, both Senate and House, would be inclined to pass a similar measure if the Geneva LOS III session fails to reach agreement on the economic zone issue.

7. *See,* for example, F. Christy and A. Scott, *The Commonwealth in Ocean Fisheries* (Baltimore: Johns Hopkins, 1965).

8. Draft articles or working papers presented to the July–August 1972, Seabed Committee meeting by the United States, Japan, the Soviet Union, and Australia/New Zealand were all guilty of this failure to draft prospectively.

9. Draft Articles on Fisheries, presented by Belgium, Denmark, Federal Republic of Germany, France, Iceland, Italy, Luxembourg, Netherlands. A/CONF.62/C.2/L.40 (1974).

10. *See* UNESCO, Intergovernmental Oceanographic Commission Technical Series: *Legal Problems Associated with Ocean Data Acquisition Systems* (ODAS 1969).

11. *See,* for example, S. Shapiro, *op. cit.,* note 2, P 428; Wilimovsky & Alverson, *op. cit.,* note 3; Alverson & Wilimovsky, *op. cit.,* note 3.

12. The 1959 Antarctic Treaty, T.I.A.S. No. 4780; 402 U.N.T.S. 71; American Journal of International Law, vol. 54, no. 476 (1960), set aside Antarctica for peaceful scientific research and is thought to establish a moratorium on national claims to the continent. *See especially* Article IV (2).

Chapter Eight

Impact of the Fishery Technology on International Law

Shigeru Oda
Tôhoku University School of Law
Japan

It is my pleasure to participate in this ninth annual meeting of the Institute. I attended the inaugural session in 1966 and the second session in 1967 and also a few workshops organized by the Institute. However, I could not participate in the annual meetings during the recent years in spite of several invitations. Today, I am speaking as a private scholar, and whatever I am going to say does not necessarily reflect the views of my government.

My good friend Gary Knight kindly invited me to this meeting when I was at Caracas, and suggested this subject of discussion. Although I made some extensive studies on the legal aspects of international fisheries many years ago, I was at first hesitant to accept this kind invitation because the subject was far beyond my outdated knowledge, and if English is a difficult foreign language for me, my English vocabulary on fishery science and technology is much poorer. Although I postponed further my commitment, I received by mail only a few weeks ago the announcement of this session, in which I found my name already printed as one of the participants. I felt that I should honor the friendship shown by Gary Knight. Meanwhile, I have been thinking of this assignment, and have talked with my colleagues in the Japanese Fisheries Agency, who, however, could not encourage me to take a positive position to this assigned problem.

I have flown here to Miami without any specific knowledge of fishery technology, except that given by my colleagues in the Fisheries Agency. Certainly, Gary Knight did not expect me to be an expert on the technological aspects of fisheries, but he wanted me to talk about the legal implications of fishery technology. I regret being a lawyer, because a lawyer is always expected to comment on any subject, even when he does not know anything about it. I asked myself if the development of fishery technology will have any specific impact on international law and if so, how much and what kind will it be. In fact, the application of technology to this industry is not new, and, for many years, new techniques have been introduced into the fishing industry, and thus the contemporary international law of fisheries has been formulated. Is any breakthrough of fishing techniques expected to take a place in the next few decades? Will there be any radical change in international law in the light of possible technical innovations in the fishing industry? These problems were not taken up at Caracas, and I cannot foresee any change at the forthcoming meeting in Geneva. Fishing is an old industry inherited from past generations and thus it surely will be improved gradually but yet will not be changed drastically. In this respect, it seems to me that fishing is different from other types of uses of the sea, such as deep-sea drilling, dredging for mineral resources, and military use of the ocean, all of which have experienced significant breakthroughs in technology, or which were even not known at all until quite recently.

To put my conclusion first, what we really need to discuss is not the impact of fishery technology on international law, but probably the opposite, namely, the impact on the future development of international fisheries of the new regime, particularly of the 200-mile economic zone concept which is about to be institutionalized. I believe that it is not international law which should adjust itself to the new technological development. To the contrary, the future fisheries management will have to adjust itself to the framework of a new regime of the sea. However, I would like to say a few words on the subject assigned to me.

The first problem I will refer to concerns technological improvements in the construction of fishing vessels as well as in fish storage and processing. Since vessels will remain important ocean-fishing instruments, great progress has been made in the construction of fishing vessels and in their long-range navigation, which, naturally, parallels the general technological improvement in shipbuilding and ship operation. Today, world-traversing fishing vessels operate far away from their home ports, searching for productive fishing areas. New storage and processing techniques, which considerably extend the storage life of the fish catch, have also enabled fishing vessels to remain far from their land ports for a long period of time, particularly if accompanied by large factory vessels. Thus, technological development has been transforming the fisheries from offshore to distant-water operations.

Even in my country, which is considered one of the most highly developed fishing nations, distant-water fishing has come to play an important role in the fishing industry only during the past decade. The statistics for Japan indicate that in 1972 the production of distant-water fishing was more than one-third of the nation's total ocean catch. Only in the 1960s did the Japanese fishing industry appear on a large scale in the Indian Ocean as well as in the Atlantic. Still another example is that of the Republic of Korea. Korea joined the ranks of the developing nations shortly after the Second World War, and, by claiming an exclusive jurisdictional zone, tried to exclude the operation of Japanese fisheries around her territory. Some years later, the Republic of Korea became one of the leading fishing nations and now, fully benefiting from the development of her fishery technology, engages in fishing far from her own coast in the Indian Ocean and the Atlantic.

The technological development of fishing vessels, and fish storage and processing, which has enabled such nations as mine and the Republic of Korea to engage in distant-water fishing, does not require any great capital or ultramodern techniques. It represents a technology that can be rather easily employed by any developing nation. On the other hand, the most industrialized nations are about to lose interests in this relatively primitive industry. Is it likely that these developments will have some impact on future international law? I hope they will. But the reality is different.

Distant-water fishing effort in most cases seeks coastal species in areas adjacent to foreign countries. This distant-water fishing inevitably competes with the coastal fishing of the coastal state. The conflicts, either actual or potential, of fishing interests in any offshore areas between the coastal state and other distant nations are and undoubtedly have been a cause of tensions with regard to fishing among nations. Such conflicts are not limited to those between developed distant nations like my country and developing coastal nations in Asia, Africa, and Latin America or between developed distant nations and developed coastal nations. My previous argument would indicate that there would be a conflict in which a developing distant-water fishing nation might be involved, if there were no legal barrier. As I said previously, it is more than a simple probability that developing nations will get interested in distant-water fishing.

A new regime should have been suggested, which, either on a worldwide scale or on a regional basis, would adjust the seemingly conflicting interests of the coastal nations and the distant nations, because, as I repeat, any nation, either developing or developed (except landlocked ones) could have interests, both as a coastal nation and as a distant-water fishing nation at the same time. But very few drafts were introduced at the Sea-Bed Committee meetings up to 1973 or at the Caracas Conference to give proper accommodation to these contradictory interests. The outcome of the Caracas Conference was, as John Moore said the other day, that the economic-zone concept almost secured a consensus among the participants, and that, in principle, the opportunity for distant-water fishing in the vicinity of foreign coasts will be lost. I am skeptical if this course of action will really benefit the developing nations, which, being potential fishing nations themselves, would otherwise be able to benefit from the development of fishery technology.

Now, I shall turn to the second problem, that is, improvements or innovations in fishing gear and techniques. Research will continue to increase the efficiency of conventional gear, such as hook and line, harpoons or spears, traps and nets, and otter trawls. New, unconventional devices have also been developed. It is said that it may be feasible in the not-too-distant future to construct "fences," or fish barriers, using air bubbles introduced from devices installed on the sea bottom and that the fence could limit the migratory pattern of fish so as to make capture easier. Also, odors, light, electricity, and sound are now being introduced to increase the catch. Furthermore, techniques for detecting the location of fish have been improved with the possibility of using lasers, which will have a depth penetration, or by use of sonar, which can give the direction and speed of the fish.

The progress of these fisheries technologies—the improvement of conventional fishing gears, the employment of new unconventional methods particularly for luring fish, and the new methods for detection of fish—may raise three different legal problems.

First, there may arise a general problem of overfishing as a result of the employment of such modern technologies as I just have described. However, conservation of fish resources is not at all a new problem for international law. No one seems to have ever objected to the necessity of preserving fishery resources from extinction. The methods suggested for implementing the conservation of fish stocks may vary, depending on the judgment of a particular fishery scientist. Yet conservation—in other words, the maintenance of the maximum sustainable yield, or perhaps even the full utilization of resources—is not a problem of policy preference, but an objective goal based upon the scientific studies of the resources to be pursued by natural scientists. We have had many international fisheries treaties, indicating various types of conservation measures applicable to different stocks of fish and to different areas. Such efforts will certainly have to be more effective in the future in view of the improvement in fishery technology, which will make it easier to exhaust the fishery resources of the ocean, unless proper conservation measures are implemented.

Second, competition exists among different gear used to capture either the same species, like trawling and hook, or to capture different species in the same area by sedentary fishing and ordinary fishing. This problem does not seem to have much impact on international law, because competition among parties of the same nation within an economic zone does not raise problems of international law, while competition over fishing between different nations in midocean areas is already the subject of international treaties, which may well settle this type of questions. The 1882 Convention on Regulating the Police of the North Sea Fisheries is often mentioned as a good example of a solution to the conflict over gears.

Third, conflicts have arisen and will arise over the employment of conventional or unconventional devices for fishing and other methods of utilizing ocean space, such as shipping and navigation, harbors, pipelines and cables, and scientific research. Such possible conflicts over the uses of the ocean are most extensively analyzed in UN Doc. E/5120 (28 April 1972): *Uses of the Sea,* although this factual study does not cover any legal aspect of the problem. The problem of how to accommodate the different uses of the ocean in the international legal order is also not a new one for us. Compatibility of different uses has always been averred. While referring to four different types of uses of the high seas as falling under the freedom of the high seas, the 1958 Convention on the High Seas did not forget to say that "These freedoms, and others which are recognized by the general principles of international law, shall be exercised by all States with reasonable regard to the interests of other States in their exercise of the freedom of the high seas." The test of reasonableness should always apply in the case of different categories of uses of the ocean. However, if we look at the problem more closely, and, as the UN document as I have mentioned properly indicates, fishing interferes with other uses of the sea. It is sometimes reported that the trawling causes some damage to submarine cables or pipelines. Yet, introduction of any new techniques of fishing may seldom cause damage to other uses of the sea and at any rate the general rules and procedures of liability must be obeyed in such instances. In the case of actual damage, there is no doubt that those who have caused damage to others are obliged to pay compensation for such damage according to international law.

In most cases, however, fishing is a type of use of the ocean, which is interfered with or affected by other uses of the ocean, such as dredging and drilling of the seabed, explosions in the water column, construction of storage tanks, harbors, superports and submersive habitats, or the use of sea energy, but none of these operations is affected by fishing. We can scarcely predict any impact from the development of fishery technology upon international law in this respect.

I should point out one further problem, which may deserve some consideration. That is the improvement of techniques for luring fish by odor, light, electricity, and sound. If this technique is developed on a large scale, so that the migratory stock changes its migratory range and so that the anadromous stock never comes back to its own mother river, some international regulations may have to be required.

Let me turn now to another important issue which may have some relevance to the development of fishery technology. It is the question of whether or not this development will have any adverse effect on the ecology of the ocean or on the marine environment as a whole and, in case the answer is affirmative, how the marine environment can properly be preserved. The problem of the possible overfishing of certain species has already been discussed. I am talking here about the pollution of the seawater as a possible result of the introduction of some new fishery technology. Nobody thought that fishing in its primitive stage would have any harmful effect on the marine environment, but intensive fishing, in parallel with the development of fishery technology, will inevitably present more occasions for polluting the sea waters. This is, however, nothing but the general problem of vessel-source pollution as a result of intensive uses of the sea, and I do not find any particular problems in fishery technology. Prevention of pollution was one of the main subjects discussed at the Sea-Bed Committee meetings and at Caracas. What I can add at this juncture is that, at the IMCO Conference in 1973, there were some discussions concerning the necessity of regulating the disposal of fish heads into the sea during the course of processing the fish catch aboard. Certainly, this is a very particular problem relevant to fishery technology.

Generally speaking, however, and apart from the operation of seagoing vessels, fishing itself does not have much adverse effect on the marine environment. Instead, fishing is an industry which has to be protected from the pollution of sea waters as a result of other uses of the ocean as well as from land-based pollution.

Finally, I would like to refer briefly to a new type of fishing—aquaculture. True, aquaculture is a growing reality and if I take the example of my own country, the production from ocean aquaculture has increased remarkably in recent years. For 1972 it reached 650,000 tons, which was over 6 percent of the total production figure for the nation. In the government's budget for ocean development allocated to the Fisheries Agency for the fiscal year of 1974, nearly one-half, or roughly $6,000,000, was for the development of aquaculture. The principal products of ocean aquaculture are green lever, oysters, yellowtail, wakame, and scallops. Aquaculture will still remain mainly in inland and coastal waters very close to the coast. The question whether any stock cultivated should be open to all or whether it belongs only to those who have invested in it and have contributed to its cultivation is already of concern to domestic legal systems. Sometimes it is dreamed that dolphin or porpoises will be trained to chase fish stock into traps. I cannot see, however, that this will be likely to develop for a few decades to come. Perhaps in this respect, however, mention should be made of the case of anadromous stocks, which breed and are cultivated in rivers and migrate long range in the ocean. However, I should not discuss this question in detail, since it was the object of talks between my country, Canada, and the United States, the member states of the 1952 North Pacific High Seas Convention.

In conclusion, it seems to be difficult to find any direct or drastic impact on international law as the result of the development of fishery technology. To the contrary, I can talk more about the drastic impact of the new regime of the sea upon the fishing industry. It is important to note that, as I said at the outset, fishing, unlike any other new uses of the sea, is an industry as old as the history of mankind.

I have been suggesting for nearly the past twenty years that the problem of international fisheries is twofold: (1) the conservation of fishery

resources; and (2) the allocation of fishery resources (limited in terms of
conservation), among those nations that are trying to maximize their own share,
if I may add, even at the sacrifice of the interests of other nations. I believe
that this will not change even in the era of new technological developments,
unless and until the time comes when community interests will supersede
national interests. Without having this in mind, any discussion of technological
development of fisheries, etc., will be superfluous, and sometimes, the discussion on fisheries management will be misleading. When we talk about future
types of fisheries management, we must be very careful whether we are talking
of the management of the conservation of fishery resources, or of the management of their allocation among the nations.

It is certainly true that these two aspects are very closely interrelated. But we can never forget that conservation efforts will inevitably require
restraint of fishing. How this restraint should be imposed on different nations
is more important. While we can talk of conservation in a highly abstract
manner and also in very idealistic terms, it would be extremely difficult to
suggest any means of allocation without considering the national interests of
the different nations. For conservation—or in other words, the maintenance
of the maximum sustainable yield and full utilization of the fishery resources—
scientific knowledge based on intensive studies of the ocean will play the most
important role. For this purpose, international cooperation, with the assistance
of the FAO, its regional commissions, or any other regional organizations, will
be required, and this will not be objected to by anyone really concerned with
conservation. In fact, through a network of international fisheries treaties,
many important species of fish are now placed under proper control. It will be
easy for natural scientists to suggest conservation management, but it will be
difficult for lawyers to implement conservation management into allocation
management which inevitably involves national interests.

The contemporary problem facing us is far different from simple
concern for the conservation of fishery resources. Who believes that the 200-mile
economic zone would be the best for the conservation of fishery resources as
the common heritage for the benefit of mankind? In fact, these resources are
claimed as the national resources of the coastal state. On the other hand, who
believes that the freedom of fishing has been advocated by developed nations
out of concern for the proper allocation of this common heritage of mankind?

As I said earlier, the 200-mile economic zone will cut off the
growing interests of any nation in distant-water fishing. The areas which today
are still left to the free access of any nation—in other words, the ocean beyond
the 200-mile economic zone—I understand will eventually be turned into the
"international common heritage of mankind." The famous notion of "water
column" expounded at Caracas was well explained by Mr. Popper yesterday.
The dualism of the narrow territorial sea and the wider high seas will be replaced
by the dualism of the 200-mile exclusive jurisdiction zone and the international

sea areas, where the international regime through international machinery will apply. What then does "international" mean? Up to the present, legal issues of international concern have been properly solved by negotiation and cooperation among the nations. Thus, many international treaties have been ratified. However, this course of action now is challenged in two aspects. One is the problem of the newcomer states, that is to say, the problem of how to accommodate the interests of the newcomer state within the existing framework of international treaties, particularly if these treaties are designed to deal with resource allocation. The other challenge will be made by some developing nations, which, being encouraged by the concept of the common heritage of mankind for the seabed resources, will seek some share of profits from the fish resources in the midocean.

Returning to my original assignment, I would like to say that the progress of fishery technology may be great but its impact on the law of the sea will be minimal, and will only be given a place within the legal or managerial framework which is evolved in the dimension beyond technological progress, that is, in the forum of politics and philosophy. What we really need to do is not to talk so much about the technological impact, but rather to formulate in the international community a philosophy of fishery resources in this period of transition so that we will have an overall picture of the resource management under which fishery technology shall be adjusted.

Mr. Knight: Thank you very much, Professor Oda.

The final speaker on this morning's program is Dr. Joachim Schärfe, who is a marine biologist and fisheries scientist. He is presently senior fishery industry officer of fishing operations with FAO.

Dr. Schärfe expressed some amusement at being the only scientist on the podium with three lawyers, and I suggested to him that that probably reflected the relative merits of the disciplines. One fisheries scientist equals or is worth three lawyers any day.

Chapter Nine

Interrelations between Fishing Technology and the Coming International Fishery Regime

J. Schärfe
Department of Fisheries
FAO

By definition, fishing technology is concerned with fish production through fishing. This excludes aquaculture and it also excludes fish processing, which is often called fish, fishery, or fisheries technology. On the other hand fishing technology is not restricted to fishing gear and methods, but incorporates relevant aspects of design and operation of vessels, auxiliary machinery and electronics applied for efficiently finding, hunting, guiding, attracting or concentrating, and catching the fish. The term "fish" stands for all aquatic organisms which are subject to exploitation, except mammals. The following remarks are essentially limited to technological aspects of fishing.

Marine fishing from inshore to the high seas shares the use of the oceans with other interests, of which shipping is the oldest and still the most important. Other interests, such as submarine cables and the exploitation of minerals and oil on and under the seabed, have developed more recently, but, at least in certain areas, are gaining rapidly in importance. Compatability naturally is required for smooth operation on the national and international levels, even within the same trade, and this requires mutual agreement on codes of behavior and modes of operation which should duly take into account the essential interests of all parties concerned. Since fishing is usually the weakest partner economically, there is a risk of its being neglected, particularly when the basic issues of a worldwide law of the sea are under consideration. Whether such neglect leads to significant disadvantages or, on the contrary, to favorable side effects depends on the particular situation and on the point of view from which the evaluation is being made.

The central issue of the 3rd UN Law of the Sea Conference is the conversion of the customary legal order, which is based on the principle of the freedom of the high seas outside the traditional territorial waters of coastal states, so as to conform to the present concept of international social justice and equity. Although not yet definite, the outcome of the meeting in Caracas shows

259

a strong tendency toward the establishment of exclusive economic zones of 200 miles from the same base lines as the territorial waters in which the coastal state has the exclusive right of exploitation of all resources.[1] This will bring the vast majority of traditional fishing grounds and fish resources under national jurisdiction.

The drastic impact this will have on the world fisheries regime is obvious. Coastal nations will naturally want to harvest their own resources, and this applies in particular to the developing countries which have food, employment, and currency problems. They will therefore make every effort to develop an adequate fishing capacity of their own, although partly assisted by advanced foreign fisheries in exchange for temporary fishing rights through concessions, joint ventures, or similar arrangements and although temporary historical rights will be granted, after an intermediate period most of those traditional resources that were the domain of long-distance foreign fisheries will be incorporated in national-coastal to medium-distance fisheries.

Through this development the new law of the sea will have a significant impact on fishing technology in both advanced and developing fisheries. In advanced fisheries there will be a change of emphasis from large long-distance and fleet operation to medium-distance and coastal fishing, while developing fisheries will have to establish the technical competence to expand their fishing capacity to the new and wider limits. Because of the different conditions and development targets, the technical requirements will differ significantly.

In advanced free-economy fisheries, competition and manpower problems will continue and even further enforce the demand for achieving the highest possible economic efficiency with minimum crews through improved fishing gear and tactics, further mechanization and automation of operations, and better working and living conditions on board. Conventional artisanal and passive fishing methods such as pot fishing, gillnetting, and longlining will be revived and updated. The envisaged smaller size of the future fishing units will probably impose a physical and economic limit on certain types of technical sophistication, such as computer-automated integrated trawling systems and related specific instrumentation.

The developing fisheries, many of which are the beneficiaries of the new fisheries regime, require, for the intensified promotion of their fishing capacity, fishing units that, in addition to satisfactory catching efficiency, are simple, rugged, reliable, and demand modest facilities and skills for their operation, maintenance, and repair. Savings in manpower are not essential, but often rather undesirable. Costs, particularly in foreign exchange, are a major restriction. Increased fuel prices do not favor the high power demands of high speed or towing performance (trawling), and suggest instead passive fishing techniques and even a reconsideration of traditional propulsion (mechanization) concepts. Because of this change in conditions, targets and subsequent requirements of fishing technology cannot be transferred intact from advanced fisheries, but careful evaluation, selection, and adaptation are needed in order to avoid inefficiency and losses of time and money.

While advanced fisheries have the skills and facilities for technical progress, it will be the task of the multi- and bilateral aid organizations, together with private enterprise, to assist developing fisheries in achieving their development targets in a realistic and systematic way. FAO will have an important role in this process by providing direct technical assistance through field projects, including relevant training, as well as through dissemination of knowledge, promotion and coordination of efforts, technical advice and guidance, and acting as an "honest broker" between governments and alien industry.

Apart from reorienting the exploitation pattern of conventional resources, the new world fisheries regime will, it is hoped, promote attempts to develop the exploitation of unconventional or underutilized resources such as antarctic krill, squid, and lantern fish. For advanced fisheries the short-term incentive would be compensation for the loss of traditional fishing grounds to national jurisdiction through the development of alternate employment for existing long-distance fishing capacities. In the long term the potential size of these resources, which is estimated to be several times larger than the reasonably well-known potential of conventional fish resources, will meet the foreseeable increased demand for an important source of animal protein. The task of harvesting alone is of such an order of magnitude that only large-scale operations with comparable economic impact will be able to cope. In view of the considerable development work required, of which fishing technology is an important component, it is certainly not too early to start now. The U.S.S.R. and recently also Japan are already active on krill, and others—such as the Federal Republic of Germany, France, and Norway—are to join soon. FAO's role is that of promoter and eventually also of international coordinator. Related activities include an Informal Consultation on Antarctic Krill, held in October 1974 at headquarters in Rome, and an Expert Consultation on Fishing for Squid and other Cephalopods, planned for autumn 1975 in Japan. The international law of the sea must certainly be tailored to the development of unconventional fish resources from the high seas, encouraging and promoting their exploitation to best advantage if and when the need arises.

These are probably the main effects of the new world fisheries regime on fishing technology. On the other hand, effects of future fishing technology on the new law of the sea will depend on developments in this field. These again will depend on a complex of interrelated factors from different areas, among them: international and national laws and regulations, concerning conservation of resources and protection of the environment; requirements for food and employment and subsequent development targets; technical, economic, and social considerations; and finally, the availability, distribution, and behavior of the natural resources. The accuracy of predictions naturally decreases the further one tries to look into the future, and this is a strong argument for not tightening too strictly the forthcoming international law of the sea, but providing instead for sufficient flexibility to accommodate unforeseen new requirements.

There are a number of educated forecasts of fishing technological developments,[2] which more or less agree that technological progress will be step by step and that no basically new harvesting concepts are in sight for conventional resources. There will, however, be significant improvements in performance and eventually also increases in size of gear and scale of operation. Of these likely developments only those are of interest for this meeting which may interfere with similar or other activities in the same environment, i.e., shipping, fishing, and some types of other uses of the seabed. The following comments refer to J.L. Jacobson's review submitted to this meeting.

The problem of compatibility of communication and navaids as well as of utilizing or participating in the use of sophisticated telemetry, such as satellites, aircraft, and buoys for fish location is actually not limited to fisheries alone and is probably well under the control of the appropriate established international bodies. Care must naturally be taken that the interests of fisheries are safeguarded. Because of physical laws governing certain frequency ranges for certain purposes of navigation, fish detection etc., several vessels operating on the same ground will have to accept some interference with acoustical equipment (e.g., echosounder, sonar, netsonde). With present technology this is not a serious handicap, particularly since the operational range is rather limited. The application of sonar buoys or floating logs will obviously have to comply with existing shipping rules and this may be a serious limitation for such devices. Their usefulness is still open for discussion and will probably be restricted to specific areas and fishing conditions. The expected new fisheries regime will probably not encourage large-scale fish finding and forecasting surveys.

The shift in emphasis envisaged by Alverson,[3] from active to passive fishing techniques, is eventually relevant to this meeting. There are precedents for large marine trap nets, namely, the Japanese set nets, the Mediterranean tonnaras, and the northern European Bundgarne. All these reach the surface and may extend 1000 m or more from the shore. Their installation naturally has to comply with shipping rules and the allocation of sites, which is of great importance for fishing success is usually governed by local or national regulations. These as well as the submerged traps envisaged, for example, for hake, or the barriers for menhaden or other coastal pelagic fish, are well within even present fisheries limits and would therefore fall largely under national jurisdiction. Submerged traps would be susceptible to damage by trawling and would need protection similar to pots placed in deeper water.

The endangered object, in this case passive fishing gear, is always in a weak position, and it would, therefore, be well not to rely completely on protective legislation, which often is difficult to enforce, but to do everything possible to reduce or avoid danger. For submerged gear, the marker buoys serve, on the one hand, for protection against bottom trawls. On the other hand they are a hazard to shipping and midwater trawling. Protective action would be to place such gear on grounds where bottom trawling is not possible and use a submerged marker buoy device with a time release or a mechanism which is triggered, for example, by acoustical signals. The latter would have the additional advantage of reducing the risk of poaching. This is only one illustration of the recommended concept of self-protection.

Although technically not impossible, for operational and economic reasons the commercial adoption of remote motor-controlled otter boards of submarine-towed trawl gear or of the "mammal type" submarine fishing system is considered unlikely, at least for the foreseeable future. There is therefore no need for legal provisions at this stage.

The potential for marine aquaculture on the high seas is still open for discussion. In view of obvious technical, economic, and logistical problems, high-sea enclosures will probably be given lower priority than similar coastal installations, which would come mainly under national jurisdiction. The legal status of open-sea aquaculture installations should probably be analogous to drilling platforms and proper provisions in the new law would clearly be indicated.

The highly undesirable capacity of lost "ghost" pots or nets for continued fishing is a well-and long-known problem that was considerably aggravated by the introduction of stainless steel wire netting for pots and, in particular, of synthetics for both pots and nets. The problem continues to receive considerable attention and some effective countermeasures, such as the use of rapidly decaying material for escape hatches (pots) and hanging twine (gill and trammelnets) have been designed. In some fisheries such features have been made obligatory under national jurisdiction. A comprehensive systematic study on an international scale to first assess the actual magnitude of the problem and then to identify priority areas and to design remedial measures acceptable to the fisheries and suitable for legal enforcement would be highly desirable. FAO could assist in promoting and coordinating such efforts.

The hazard to shipping of floating ropes and nets was created mainly by the introduction into fishing and shipping of the buoyant synthetics polypropylene and polyethlene. They are used mainly because they are cheaper and more easily produced than other synthetics. The buoyancy which could otherwise be overcome by adding heavy material is, however, a distinct advantage for many purposes. There is, therefore, no generally acceptable technical solution for this problem and respective legal provisions are indicated, probably under the general heading "pollution."

The feasibility of using fish sound and odors for detection will always be strictly limited to very few species and conditions, as will be the use of air bubbles, chemicals, or electric fences for guiding and concentrating fish. Therefore, no need for specific legal provisions is envisaged.

One can hardly foresee whether, and, if so, when and to what extent automated fishing systems (platforms) will develop. Apart from economic and technical considerations this will depend largely on the characteristics of the resources to be exploited. For the sufficiently known conventional resources and in view of recent socioeconomic developments, no significant developments of this kind are foreseen, at least for quite some time to come. They may, however, at the same time as or subsequent to sizeable fleet operations, develop in offshore waters and on the high seas for the exploitation of the unconventional and so far unutilized resources of, for example, krill, lantern fish, and plankton, mentioned earlier. Since related technological developments in fishing are in an early state or have not been started yet, no predictions of any accuracy can be made yet. The estimated magnitude of these resources is enormous as is also the sustained fishing potential of hundreds of millions of tons of live weight of animal protein per year. Assuming an increasing pressure for the production of large additional amounts of protein food for an extended period of time and possibly to some extent irrespective of conventional cost/earnings relations, the harvest would require fishing operations of thousands of catcher, processing, support, and transport vessels eventually including an equal number of more or less passive and automated fishing systems which may be stationary or drifting. Pending reasonable and realistic specifications, which are not expected in the near future, legal provisions for the protection of such gear would be premature, but scope should be provided for later introduction when the need arises.

NOTES

1. S.H. Amerasinghe, "Fisheries and the New International Legal Order," Address of the President of the Third World Conference on the Law of the Sea to the FAO Committee on Fisheries (October, 1974), COFI/74/Inf.9.
2. *See*, for example, D.L. Alverson and N.J. Wilimovsky, "Prospective Developments in the Harvesting of Marine Fishes," in *Modern Fishing Gear of the World*, vol. 2, FAO World Fishing Gear Congress (London: Fishing News [Books] Ltd., 1964), pp. 583–589; N.J. Wilimovsky and D.L. Alverson, "The Future of Fisheries and Rapporteur's Summary on Fishing in the Future," in *Modern Fishing Gear of the World*, vol. 3, FAO World Fishing Gear Congress (London: Fishing News [Books] Ltd., 1971), pp. 509–515; and A. von Brandt, "Entwicklungstendenzen der Fischereilichen Fang-und Ernetetchnik" [Development Tendencies in Fish Catching and Harvesting Techniques] in *Interocean 70*, vol. 1 (Dusseldorf: Internazional Kongress mit Ausstellung f. Meeresforschung u. Meeresnutzung, 1972).
3. *Modern Fishing Gear of the World*, vols. 2 and 3.

Discussion and Questions

Mr. Knight: We are a little pressed for time. So, I would like to go ahead with the interrogation that you may have for our panelists. Unfortunately, Professor Oda, who made some most interesting remarks, particularly concerning the position of Japan, I imagine, had to depart because he does have to catch a plane to Tokyo at noon today and will not be here to respond to your questions. However, Dr. Schärfe and Professor Jacobson would be happy, for a few moments, at any rate, to respond to or discuss or hear any comments you might have.

Mr. Knauss: My name is John Knauss and I have a comment rather than a question. I agree with the speakers that we will have a 200-mile economic zone, and I, also, agree with them that technology is not likely to have much affect on the law of the sea, but rather vice versa. I would like to bring up one additional aspect of this problem which they did not address.

One thing that has happened in the past thirty years is that technology has made it possible for us to catch all of the fish that can be caught in the ocean. We have essentially reached (or are about to reach) the maximum sustainable yield on a worldwide basis. In some sense, one might consider the 200-mile economic zone as a reasonable response to this aspect of our increasing technology.

In my opinion, within twenty-five years, say by the end of the century, we will reach the maximum sustainable yield within the economic zones of all nations; that is, each state will be catching all of the fish it can catch in its local area, or leasing those rights to such countries as the U.S.S.R. or Japan or other distant-water fishing nations. Once we reach the maximum sustainable yield, I think the emphasis will be on capturing those fish at the minimum cost. To me that suggests the fishing industry will become more capital intensive, because the greatest cost in catching fish is still the cost of hunting for the fish, i.e., the labor costs of going out and looking for them.

If you accept my premise of a capital-intensive, maximum sustainable yield fishery, I think we can foresee some major problems in fisheries management. One thing that has often been overlooked in fisheries discussions is that we have very large fluctuations in wild stocks. The kind of fluctuation one sees in the anchoveta fishery off Peru, for example, is one of the most dramatic of the kinds of fluctuations that occur regularly in natural populations. The job for fisheries managers is to predict what the future catch will be, what next year's catch will be, or the year's catch beyond that. If you have a capital intensive fishery, there is going to be intense political and economic pressure to maximize those predictions. For example, if one year the fisheries manager decides that next year's catch can only be 50 percent of what would be normal, there will be a large amount of pressure from the fishing industry to revise that prediction upward to at least 60 percent or 70 percent of the normal catch. Since fisheries predictions are not all that precise, it will be possible to build a certain amount of credibility to the fishermen's argument that the predicted catch should be revised upwards.

Now, I think it is fairly easy to show in any kind of a fisheries model that if you have a fluctuating stock and if you occasionally overestimate how much fish you can catch, you will eventually drive that fishery down. Thus the long-range effect of occasionally overestimating the maximum sustainable yield will be to exacerbate the management problem. It seems to me a primary concern of the next twenty-five years will be this problem of how to manage maximum sustainable yield fisheries.

It is going to be difficult enough to do this on a country-by-country basis; an even more difficult problem, as I see it, relates to the fact that many, if not most, fisheries are "regional," such as the Georges Bank fishery which is shared by Canada and the United States. What happens if one year the Canadian managers say that we can catch 80 percent of the haddock and the U.S. says only 70 percent of the normal haddock catch? It is going to be hard enough to tell U.S. boats their quota has been reduced to 70 percent of normal; it will be almost impossible if the Canadian managers are estimating 80 percent. These are the kinds of pressures and difficult management problems that one must face, and the regional nature of many fisheries is going to make the problem even more difficult. For example, I think there are something like fifteen nations along about 2000 miles of West Africa coastline which border a very major fishing area.

One thing you might hope to do in the present law of the sea negotiations—and I emphasize "hope," because I do not think there is much chance of success—is to mandate regional fisheries management programs as part of the economic zone. I think the chances of mandating such programs into the law are rather unlikely, but perhaps one could at least "encourage" such regional efforts in the treaty.

Mr. Knight: Would either of our speakers like to comment? Dr. Schärfe?

Mr. Schärfe: Without being really competent in fisheries management, I would like to say that I fully agree with what the speaker said about the importance and necessity of proper fisheries management, but I would, also, like to point out that this is not a technological problem and, therefore, not strictly within the scope of this session.

It was mentioned that fishing technology if it becomes too efficient may become a threat to the stocks. I tried to refer to that in the last part of my remarks by saying that, in principle, fisheries management and fisheries technology are complementary. It, of course, depends on what you make of it. It would, for my feeling, be completely wrong to curtail fishing technological development to protect the stock. This is basically wrong, because this would stop all development. This is being done, but as I say, in my opinion, this is wrong. What you have to do is to adjust both points of view and accommodate the improved fishing technology to respective management action. And one possibility would, for instance, be to establish quotas rather than to ban too efficient fishing gear, because if you have quotas, you can, within a fishing technique, catch your quota in the shortest possible time, in the most economic way and then either go to the pool and sit in the sun or do something else or go somewhere else and fish something else.

You mentioned yourself that there is a labor problem, and this alone is strong reason for continuing development in fishing technology because you may be faced with a situation where you either cannot pay for the labor anymore, and the operation becomes uneconomic or people do not care to go to sea anymore. Both these situations have occurred.

Thank you.

Mr. Jacobson: Let me just make a short comment, Gary. I agree with, I think, everything that John said, and it provides a good addendum to what went on this morning. Essentially it underscores, I think, one of the points I tried to make, and that was that lack of uniformity of response to technological developments, as well as to other types of developments, has shown a need for regional bodies, international cooperation. I also agree that that sort of thing is not a likely result of the Third Law of the Sea Conference, but at some point it will be seen as necessary, at which point we will have to do something about it, and I think that John underscored that.

Mr. Kolodkin: Thank you, Mr. Chairman. Very briefly, Mr. Chairman, allow me to stress that I am in favor that we must speak not so much about the impact of technology on the law of the sea but also about the interrelations between the law of the sea and technology. That is why I draw your attention to some questions which arose at Caracas.

First of all, I fully support the provision which was expressed by Professor Oda as to maintaining the freedom of the fisheries in the high seas and the implications of this provision. Then I should like to stress that as to the economic zone we can take into account this factor the issue of technology and support the proposal as to the provision that if a coastal state does not take 100 percent of the allowable annual catch of any stocks of fish or other living resources in the economic zone, fishermen of other states shall be granted licenses to fish for the unused part of such catch.

Permission for foreign fishermen to fish in the economic zone of a developed coastal state shall be granted on an equitable basis. Foreign fishermen may be allowed to fish in the economic zone of a developing coastal state by the grant of special license. Then I should like to emphasize that I am in favor of the doctrine as to the preferential rights of coastal states over anadromous species outside the economic zone.

Thank you, Mr. Chairman.

Mr. Knight: Thank you very much. I think we can have time for one more question or comment at least. Dr. Nweihed?

Mr. Nweihed: Thank you, Mr. Chairman. I am Kaldone Nweihed from Universidad, Simon Bolivar, Caracas. Actually I want to make clear that although I was in my country's delegation to the Caracas conference last summer, this question is only of personal concern, and it was intended to be addressed to Professor Oda who now has to leave, but since we have two distinguished jurists on the panel, including the moderator, the question goes as well.

Dr. Oda mentioned that among the side effects of the development of techniques to improve fishing, there would be inevitably a negative one, as pollution in adjacent waters is produced, within the respective economic zones of states concerned. That pollution would be partially the result of the development and sophistication of gear on the one hand, but mainly it would come out of the intensification of shipping and navigation activities, as more boats would be fishing around. So, my question to our distinguished lawyers would be: Won't that be, in the long run, another argument sufficient to enhance and strengthen the already valid argument of developing coastal nations having to exercise full control over pollution, or antipollution measures in the economic zone, and participate fully as well in scientific research in that zone?

Thank you very much.

Mr. Knight: Would the distinguished jurist, Dr. Jacobson, like to respond to that?

Mr. Jacobson: Yes, I made a passing comment about pollution finding its source in fishing gear, mainly in talking about the gear made of the new nondestructible materials, crab pots, shellfish pots that fish forever, gill nets that drift around and kill fish for some time.

Perhaps, if chemicals are used to aggregate fish, they may cause a pollution problem. Dr. Oda amplified that by suggesting that nondestructible lines and ropes may be getting in the way of general navigation, and my comment, although I made it briefly, was that perhaps I would see no objection to having coastal-state economic zone control over the sorts of polluting devices, in the sense that I have used the term "pollution," that affect only activities within that zone; for example, a stationary shellfish pot that affects only a species that inhabits that zone and has no effect on the general ecology or on other species outside of the coastal state zone may be appropriately regulated by the coastal nation.

On the other hand, if we are talking about the types of pollution—again, as defined—that may have an effect on adjacent zones, on international waters, it would be, I think, more appropriate to have some international rules for regulation of those sorts of things.

Mr. Knight: Thank you. Dr. Schärfe, did you have any comment on this?

Mr. Schärfe: No. I am not a lawyer.

Mr. Knight: I want to thank our two remaining speakers, both of whom, like Dr. Oda, came quite long distances, even though Professor Jacobson is a United States citizen, coming from Oregon to Miami is about as far as you can go in this country.

Thank you very much, gentlemen. We appreciated your contribution.

We are now going to shift in midstream to the problem of maritime shipping and transportation, its developments in technology, anticipated developments and their impacts on the law of the sea. Perhaps we will find that the law of the sea is going to have more impact on the technology than vice versa, as we did with fish.

The paper that is being delivered today is a joint paper prepared by Professors E.D. Brown and Alistair Cooper, both of whom are from the University of Wales Institute of Science and Technology.

Professor Cooper is being represented at the podium today by Dr. Peter Fricke, who is a lecturer in shipping management and marine sociology at the University of Wales Institute of Science and Technology. Many of you, I am sure, know Professor Brown. He has appeared at the Law of the Sea Institute before. He is the author of innumerable articles and two very fine books on law of the sea issues. Today's paper which he will be presenting is entitled Future Shipping and Transport Technology and its Impact on the Law of the Sea. Professor Brown?

Mr. Brown: Thank you very much, Mr. Chairman. I would like to begin, ladies and gentlemen, by stressing what Professor Knight has just said. This is very much a joint effort by Professor Cooper and myself, and the technological input is very much Professor Cooper's.

So, like some of my predecessors, lawyers, this morning, let me disclaim very much knowledge in the realm of technology and express my gratitude to Dr. Fricke who is with us on the platform and has agreed to handle any questions which might arise on the hardware side of my subject.

One final remark by way of preface: I have discovered in the course of preparing this paper that many of the legal implications of developments in marine technology are of a maritime law nature rather than a public international law nature, and I would like to say that I do not hold myself out as an expert in this area either, but I think it is worth drawing attention to some of these problems in passing because their resolution will, in fact, require international collaboration.

Chapter Ten

Future Shipping and Transport Technology and Its Impact on the Law of the Sea

E.D. Brown and **A.D. Couper**
University of Wales Institute of Science
and Technology

INTRODUCTION

Decisions to initiate or adopt technological advances are made, largely, because of the productive function of technology. By improving technology a greater output can be obtained for the same, or less, input of capital or labor. In the case of sea transport, output can be measured in several ways, including changes in costs per ton-mile of cargo carried or by the ratio of deadweight tonnage to tons-miles performance over time. The changes in maritime technology have been prompted primarily by the wish to increase ship productivity in these respects.

Some technological changes in shipping have also been brought about in response to legislation aimed at reducing the costs, and other effects, which shipping may impose on society through collision, pollution, and other hazards.

The principal forces behind technological changes in sea transport are, therefore, commercial and legal. The purpose of this paper is to consider their interplay in an attempt to predict likely developments. Consideration is given first to the decision parameters in adopting technical changes, then to the projection of likely changes with their legal implications, and finally, the discussion focuses on the routing and control of highly advanced and environmentally and socially dangerous vessels.

DECISION PARAMETERS AFFECTING
TECHNOLOGICAL CHANGE IN SHIPPING

The variables which will most likely exert an influence on decisions are:
Existing financial commitments. Most shipowners would expect a life of about fifteen years from their vessels, so that many of the ships now sail-

271

272 E.D. Brown and A.D. Couper

ing will still be operating in the 1980s and many of those currently on order (see Appendix 1) will be sailing in 1990. Given the present high level of cost inflation and the likelihood of overtonnaging in the near future (see below, *Route Parameters*), this factor must be expected to have an inhibiting effect on technological change.

Trade forecasts. It is anticipated that world tonnage of seaborne trade will increase at a rate of about 5 to 8 percent per annum, but the trade in specific commodities will change in form and direction of flow. Oil-producing countries in the Arab world will enter more strongly into refining and petrochemical production and will export *refined* products. Moreover, there are clear indications that they will wish to use their own shipping for this purpose. As was reported in the London *Times* on 28 December 1974, "Leading oil producing countries in the Middle East are showing increasing interest in acquiring both tanker and dry cargo tonnage." According to the same report, Kuwait Shipping Company has placed orders with a South Korean firm for five general cargo ships each of 23,200 tons d.w., for delivery in 1977 at a cost of $80 million. The same two companies signed ten contracts worth $156 million in November 1974. In addition, the Arab Maritime Petroleum Transportation Company (representing seven Arab oil-producing states) has asked the Oslo-based ship-brokerage firm of R.S. Platou to arrange the purchase of seven supertankers for Arab oil-producing countries.

At the other end of the trade, a recent report on trends in tanker supply in Japan indicates that Japan may be expected to make increasing use of host government oil tankers—including possibly some very large crude carriers which have yet to be built—to cover her oil import requirements in the second half of this decade.[1]

We might also note that further changes in trade patterns may be expected to result from continental shelf oil exploitation. The United Kingdom and Norway, for example, will become net exporters of crude oil.

So far as the law is concerned, one of the main implications of these projected changes is that within the next decade or so the Arab countries may be expected to be major shipping states, and they and other developing states lacking an established maritime tradition will, inter alia, have to set about preparing sophisticated maritime codes. The need for expert advice and for the harmonization of these new codes is of course obvious. The opportunities which the fulfillment of this need offers to the international community is perhaps less obvious.

As will be seen, the lack of standardization in navigational equipment and in crew training is a major impediment to progress in marine navigation control and, therefore, in maritime safety and environmental protection. Much work has already been done to improve the position. Thus, the carriage of modern electronic navigational equipment which, for the most part, was previously voluntary, will become mandatory for parties to the recently amended International Convention for the Safety of Life at Sea, 1960. IMCO has supplemented these requirements by developing performance standards for each item of equipment.

Less progress has been made on the question of crew-training requirements and qualifications for certification of masters and officers but work is proceeding in IMCO on this matter also.[2] The Assembly has adopted two recommendations dealing with basic principles and guidelines on ship-handling during watchkeeping and with the training and qualifications of officers and crew of ships carrying hazardous or noxious chemicals in bulk. The ultimate intention (hopefully to be realized in treaty form at a conference planned for 1977) is to specify minimum qualifications for training and certification for all grades of officers and crew on board merchant ships, with priority for those immediately responsible for the safe navigation and handling of the ship.[3]

When it is realized that the masters' training and certification requirements are quite different under the British and French systems, for example, it will be appreciated that there are certain advantages to be gained by starting from scratch and designing internationally harmonized codes for emerging shipping states.

Fortunately, IMCO is seized of the problem and is well placed to provide assistance. The present position is succinctly stated in a recent Secretariat report, as follows:

> 114. The International Development Strategy has as one of its main objectives the development by the developing countries of their own national shipping lines as a means, *inter alia*, of improving their balance of payments position in world trade. One of the principal problems faced by developing countries, in the development as well as the operation of national shipping lines, is the non-availability or inadequate supply of the technical expertise required for the administration, manning and servicing of shipping concerns. By virtue of its activities in respect of technical and specialized fields of shipping and related matters, IMCO is particularly equipped to provide assistance in this field. A programme of technical assistance to developing countries is in operation and expert assistance has been provided to the developing countries in diverse fields such as:
>
> (1) Safety of navigation and maritime training
> (2) Administration of ship safety
> (3) Design of ships and technical aspects of ship construction
> (4) Carriage of goods by sea
> (5) Prevention and control of pollution of the sea by ships
> (6) Transport of containers
> (7) Special ships and off-shore craft
> (8) Facilitation of maritime traffic
> (9) Ports operations
> (10) Law and regulations applicable to ships and shipping
> (11) Maritime law.[4]

It seems unlikely that the difficulties that are presently being experienced in some countries in recruiting suitable crew will be significantly affected by changes in trade patterns or improvements in equipment and training. If this is so, then an intensification of the trend towards ever-greater automation must be expected.

Route Parameters. Some owners will design ships for specific routes or in relation to major route characteristics. It is likely that draught limitations in straits will remain, limiting the upper size of ships on some trades, and the dimensions of the Panama Canal will impose a constraint on others. On the other hand, the opening of the Suez Canal to deep draught ships (ultimately to above 200,000 tons), a greater use of pipelines and land-bridge transfers and, in the long term, a new, enlarged sealevel canal across the Isthmus of Panama will have the effects of allowing increased vessel size and reducing the rate of growth in tons-miles requirements in seaborne-trade and hence the demand for shipping.

The end-result may well be overtonnaging and fierce competition. If so, this will be another reason for reviewing codes of conduct. Such a review has already taken place in relation to liner conferences. At the UNCTAD Conference in Geneva, in April 1974, a Convention on a Code of Conduct for Liner Conferences was opened for signature.[5] It will be recalled that the new code rules, if and when they come into force, will guarantee membership in the conference (basically a rate-fixing carrier cartel) to flag lines of the states at either end of the trade served, reserve a share of the trade to these lines, permit third-flag carrier membership in limited circumstances, subject rates to certain broad standards and control increases, and provide an elaborate mechanism for international settlement of disputes. The code is, in essence, an attempt by the developing states to achieve a measure of control over costs and service by the promotion of the national flag carriers. It thus has a strong protectionist element, emphasizing market allocation and related economic controls and thus reducing the role of competition and commercial judgement. For this reason, the code failed to attract the support of many of the major maritime states. Nevertheless, it was adopted by 72 votes to 7, with 5 abstentions, the negative votes including those of Norway, the United Kingdom, and the United States.

The same split between the developed and developing shipping states which was apparent in the UNCTAD proceedings will undoubtedly mold national attitudes if, as envisaged above, present trends culminate in overtonnaging. Increased competition will not necessarily result in the withdrawal of the less efficient operators.

Systems parameters. With the further growth of multinational companies, industrialists are tending to take advantage of factor-cost differentials on a world scale, by moving chemicals, steel, ores, and other raw materials and semi-finished and finished products between production areas in different countries by special vessels and by combined carriers. Many of these require expensively designed berths and backup facilities at ports.

The use of unitized systems (container ships, pallet-system ships, barge-carrying vessels) are also specialized and make for the concentration of shipping into fewer focal ports. This is so because, of course, the ship's time is a major element of cost and it is thus more economical to provide for a fast turn-around by the large trunk-line vessel at a single port, supplemented by local distribution by smaller vessels and other transport systems. The adoption of specialized and unitized systems thus not only gives rise to a need for feeder ships but also for control over the movement of materials and units in wide national and supranational hinterlands by land and waterway transport.

The new problems which unitization in particular presents may be illustrated by the case of the international transport of dangerous chemicals in containers. Does the acceptance of the cargo by the container company in through transport constitute acceptance by the carrier? There have been disturbing instances of dangerous goods being loaded in containers and passed from one mode of transport to another without the carriers being fully aware of the contents. Current carriage of goods statutes also assume a railroad-sea transport network in which the carrier is easily identified and insurance and documentation will be under local control in each phase of the carriage. In the case of the through-transport of containerized cargoes, however, there is no way of determining in which leg of a railroad-sea voyage damage has been sustained. There is thus a need for an agreed form of combined transport document and for clear treaty rules by which to determine questions of liability in relation to the carriage of goods in containers through various countries by various modes of transport.

The negotiation of a convention intended to deal with this problem (the Convention on the International Combined Transport of Goods—the "TCM Convention")[6] has once again revealed a developed- versus developing-states split, with the developing states apparently feeling that recognition of a through-carrier (the combined transport operator) would simply harden the monopoly of the developed maritime states, deprive the transit states of full control over internal transport policies and possibly raise freight rates.

Port and industrial parameters. Ships have to fit with port characteristics. Ports with high labor costs and slow handling induce shipboard and portside changes in the direction of more mechanization; conversely, ports with low labor costs and a good handling ratio may not require a technological input. The problem which has still to be resolved is in ship design, where ports with these different characteristics lie at either end of a trade route.

Once again, the interests of the developing state will frequently conflict with those of the developed state. The ports and shippers in the developing states have now learned that there is strength in numbers and in coordination. Thus liner conferences, in considering technology and carriage procedures, have now to deal not simply with a number of separate shippers, but with shippers' councils, set up as a countervailing power to the conferences and backed by national laws.[7]

Problems raised by dangerous and noxious industries in port areas may be expected to lead to long-term shifts in industrial location, including the establishment of such industries on offshore artificial islands. The jurisdictional questions raised by the construction and regulation of activities on such man-made structures are not of course new, but it seems likely that there will be an increasing need for their reconsideration if such industrial relocation takes place.[8]

It is hardly necessary to remind this audience that the need to import crude oil into the United States may give rise to similar problems. In May 1973, Professor Knight presented to the Law of the Sea Workshop in Nassau, the Bahamas, a thorough study of the "International Legal Problems in the Construction and Operation of Offshore Deep Draft Port Facilities". In the course of his paper, Professor Knight expressed the view that it was "still appropriate to question some of the assumptions which have led to the conclusion that such port facilities are a necessary and unique solution to the existing energy supply problems".[9] Another approach would be to make provision for more transshipment terminals for deep-draft tankers outside the United States. A £12 million terminal in the Bahamas was scheduled to begin operations in January 1975. Middle East crude will be transshipped there for delivery to Shell refineries on the Gulf and Atlantic coasts.[10] This approach does of course raise different problems in relation to the crewing and flag of the ship to be used for the transshipment of United States–purchased oil to United States ports—not to mention the question of environmental acceptability to the terminal host state.

Ship operational parameters. The economies of size of vessel may continue to be obtained, but requirements for canal transit, increased movement of refined oils, and high insurance premiums will influence decisions. The increased price of fuel will give rise to considerations of lower-speed engines and alternative sources of power.

The rising costs of manning and shortage of recruits in some countries will lead to more automation and demands for a reduction in manning requirements. There are, too, complementary reasons for the increased use of automation of essential functions. As Professor Frankel has recently noted, "nearly 50 percent of all ship losses and a larger percentage of spills are the result of human error". He goes on to report that "particular emphasis is given now to the introduction of shipboard devices which eliminate routine tasks such as data logging, routine inspections, check out, look-out, inventory, and various communication functions. A number of ships are now equipped with one or more computers which perform the above functions and are, in addition, programmed to accomplish effective start-up, cargo-pumping (loading or unloading), sequencing, ballasting or deballasting, cargo planning and so forth."

In the light of such developments, it is necessary to ask whether current manning scales are now outdated. Are there in fact any reasons other than psychological blockages for requiring, for example, more than the nine-man crew recently proposed by the Japanese as adequate for a 200,000 ton tanker?[12]

Safety parameters. The requirements of the 1973 International Convention for Prevention of Pollution from Ships on subdivision and damage stability for oil tankers and for side and double-bottom protection on chemical carriers[13] increase the weight of steel per deadweight ton. This may also influence decisions on size of vessels.

PROJECTION OF SHIP TYPES
FOR THE FUTURE

In the short and medium term (five to ten years), Tables 10-1 and 10-2 indicate the vessel types and flags which will be operational. There may, of course, be some developments that would render many of these ships obsolete over a relatively short period, but the decision-makers in shipping would tend to avoid this.

Table 10-1 contains lists of the numbers and tonnage of vessels on order as of 30 April 1974, classified by type of vessel and flag state. One of the most striking features of these lists is the position of the leading flag-of-convenience state, Liberia. Liberian ships on order, on 30 April 1974, were as follows:

Type	Number	Tonnage
Dry cargo ships	69	708,373
Container ships	7	148,360
Tankers of 150,000 tons d.w. & above	179	52,077,314
Tankers below " " "	181	13,842,895
Ore/oil and ore/bulk/oil carriers	9	1,062,350
Bulk carriers	142	5,363,829
Totals	587	73,203,121

The Liberian total orders of 587 ships of a tonnage of over 73 million tons compares with world total orders of 3,570 ships of a tonnage of over 273 million tons.

There seem to be good grounds for the view that flag-of-convenience vessels have a worse safety and pollution record than ships under conventional flags[14] and that, at least, much of the fault lies with deficiencies in officer certification and crew training. The need for further progress on the question of crew-training requirements and qualifications for certification of masters and officers referred to earlier is thus all the more pressing in relation to flag-of-convenience tonnage.

The lists in Table 10-2 give some idea of the range of specialized vessels which are now in service. In particular, there are eighteen different types of vessel listed under Liquid Gas and Chemical Carriers. The significance of these vessels for changes in the law will be commented on below.

In the medium and long term (10 to 20 years), the changing parameters outlined above will exert an influence on decision-makers. Consequently,

Table 10-1.   Vessels on Order 30 April 1974

	Number	Tonnage
Total	3,570	273,037,858
Dry Cargo Ship		
U.S.S.R.	214	1,205,779
Liberia	69	708,373
Greece	49	567,600
Great Britain	58	520,760
Panama	56	465,620
Japan	56	454,680
China	43	382,460
Argentina	29	360,000
Containers		
Greece	28	565,140
U.S.S.R.	31	445,500
Denmark	14	262,300
France	13	210,000
Argentina	10	210,000
Japan	7	179,580
Liberia	7	148,360
United States	7	144,560
Tankers of 150,000 tons d.w. and above		
Liberia	179	52,077,314
Norway	59	19,117,150
Japan	64	16,507,173
Great Britain	43	12,559,430
France	26	7,917,400
Spain	22	5,794,800
Panama	20	5,434,200
Greece	18	5,017,881
Tankers below 150,000 tons d.w.		
Liberia	181	13,842,895
Norway	113	7,861,704
Japan	105	5,367,920
Greece	56	4,444,234
Great Britain	88	4,319,042
Singapore	43	3,722,700
United States	61	3,543,530
U.S.S.R.	94	2,069,140
Ore/Oil and Ore/Bulk/Oil Carriers		
Italy	16	1,548,900
Norway	13	1,514,700
Brazil	8	1,483,000
Liberia	9	1,062,350
Japan	7	968,400
Great Britain	6	838,850
France	4	708,550
India	5	583,500

Table 10-1 continued

Bulk Carriers		
Liberia	142	5,363,829
Norway	53	3,816,769
Japan	60	3,202,830
Great Britain	45	2,247,720
India	44	1,626,710
Greece	37	1,302,310
Panama	37	999,850
Germany (W)	13	757,500
Passenger and Ferries		
U.S.S.R.	40	229,400
Japan	20	128,000
Great Britain	13	95,527
Sweden	14	90,532
Spain	10	68,800
Greece	16	62,500
Denmark	9	49,990
Finland	4	46,500

Source: "World Ships on Order," *Fairplay*, Supplement No. 39, 23 May 1974.

Table 10-2. Types of Commercial Vessels Above 1000 GRT, as of 30 April 1974 (excluding Fishing Vessels)

(1) *Conventional Vessels*
Cargo liners
Tramp ships (SD14 type)

(2) *Ferry & Passenger Vessels*
Container ferry
Ferry/cargo vessel
Car (passenger/trailer/container) ferry
Train/vehicle ferry
Ferry
Ferry/pallet carrier
Train ferry
Vehicle ferry
Excursion ferry
Truck ferry
Passenger/container vessel
Passenger/cargo vessel
Passenger liner
Passenger/train/vehicle vessel
Passenger vessel
Passenger/pallet carrier
Passenger/part refrigerated vessel
Cruise liner
Passenger/car carrier

(continued)

Table 10-2 continued

(3) *Bulk Carriers and Combined Carriers*
Bulk coal carrier
Bulk salt carrier
Bulk fishmeal carrier
Bulk sugar carrier
Bulk woodchip carrier
Bulk cement carrier
Bulk carrier
Bulk carrier, ore-strengthened
Bulk timber carrier
Bulk carrier, self-unloading
Bulk vehicle carrier
Bulk wood-pulp carrier
Bulk bauxite carrier
Bulk slurry carrier
Bulk wood pulp/sulphuric acid carrier
Timber carrier
Vehicle carrier
Ore carrier (under 12,000 tons d.w.)
Ore/oil carrier
Ore/oil/bulk
Tanker/heavy-lift vessel
Ore/oil/slurry
Bulk/oil carrier
Ore/oil carrier
Ore/coal carrier
Ore carrier
Pallet carrier
Ore carrier, self-unloading
Ore/vehicle carrier

Refrigerated Vessels
Refrigerated container vessel
Fruit ship
Fish carrier
Refrigerated liner
Refrigerated meat carrier
Refrigerated vessel
Refrigerated pallet carrier
Refrigerated/trailer vessel

Tankers
Bunkering tanker
Molasses tanker
Crude oil carrier (VLCC)
Crude oil carrier (medium)
Parcels carrier
Products carrier
Water carrier
Vegetable oil carrier
Wine tanker
Sludge carrier
Mud carrier

(4) *Unitized Vessels*
Container/barge carrier

Table 10-2 continued

Container liner
Container ship
Container/pallet ship
Container/part refrigerated
Container/ore carrier
Container/trailer ship
Container/rail-car carrier
Pallet ship
LASH ship
BACAT ship

(5) *Liquid Gas and Chemical Carriers*
Bulk sulphur carrier
Bulk phosphate carrier
Bulk wood pulp/sulphuric acid carrier
Phosphates carrier
Chemical carrier
Acid carrier
Ammonia carrier
Sulphuric acid carrier
L.P.G. carrier
L.N.G. carrier
L.P.G./ammonia carrier
Solvents carrier
Chrome tanker
Chemical/oil tanker
Sulphur tanker
Phosphorus carrier
L.P.G./chemical tanker
Ethylene tanker

(6) *Special Craft*
Pipelaying barge
Oil storage vessel
Accomodation barge
Bucket dredger
Cutter suction dredger
Dragger dredger
Gravel dredger
Grab dredger
Cutter dredger
Sand-loading dredger
Tin dredger
Dredger
Rock-breaking dredger
Suction dredger
Trailing suction dredger
Suction dredger/waste disposal
Icebreaker/bouy tender
Icebreaker/lighthouse tender
Icebreaker
Icebreaker/research vessel
Salvage vessel
Search & rescue vessel

(continued)

Table 10-2 continued

Training vessel
Cable ship/icebreaker
Cable ship
Cable repair ship
Air pollution vessel
Bouy tender
Supply/anchor landing vessel
Oil-rig supply vessel
Supply/tug anchor-handling vessel
Lighthouse tender
Oil-drilling rig
Semisubmersible oil rig
Drilling vessel
Pilot tender
Tank-cleaning vessel
Offshore supply/tug
Seismic research
Fisheries research
Research vessel
Polar research vessel
Rescue & submarine rescue vessel
Oceanographic vessel
Satellite tracking ship
Research/supply ship
Survey ship
Weather ship
Exhibition ship
Survey/research vessel
Icebreaking supply ship
Supply ship
Replenishment tanker
Support ship
Shore ship
Logistics vessel
Berthing tug
Tug
Salvage tug
Tractor tug
Waste disposal vessel (liquids)
Deepsea mining vessel
University ship
Diving support ship
Workship
Self-elevating oil rig
Drilling rig

(7) *Barges*
Bulk cement barge
Barge
Self-unloading barge
Articulated barge
Cargo barge
Barge carrier
Tank barge

Source: "World Ships on Order," *Fairplay*, Supplement No. 39, 23 May 1974.

it is likely that we shall see more specialization in ships for the haulage of semi-processed and liquified chemicals and gases and an increase in the movement of chemicals by containers and barges to inland areas. The demand for low-pollutant fuels will give rise to more and bigger liquid natural gas (LNG) carriers of 200,000 cubic meters and more. Figure 10-1 illustrates the nature and scale of the hazard which a casualty involving such a vessel would present.

The integration of sea and land transport modes and the concentration of line hauls into fewer ports, which we have already noted, will require the construction of more feeder-type ships—the roll-on/roll-off (RO/RO) and barge-aboard-catamaran (BACAT) vessels in particular—especially on a multinational, regional basis in archipelago areas such as the Pacific and the Caribbean.

Ships may also become more finely adjusted in design to specific regional economic and physical conditions. The extension of marine transport inland is an example. The Seabee system (the largest of the barge carriers) the medium-sized lighter-aboard-ship (LASH) system and the smaller barge-aboard-catamaran (BACAT) system will expand. These systems, all of which involve the carriage of barges for use in inland waterways, meet a number of changing parameters. They require few port installations, they combine the high speed or

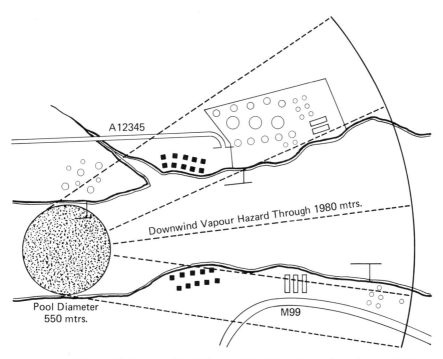

Figure 10-1. Possible Effects of Collision Involving a Large LNG Carrier in an Industrial Estuary (Spillage of 24,000 Cubic Metres)

turnaround of the expensive mother ships with slower, more labor-intensive barges (giving compatability to labor-intensive and capital-intensive port require-ments in developing and developed trading areas), and they make possible long ingress into a continental area without break of bulk. The opening of connec-tions such as the Rhine-Main-Danube waterway will reinforce the trend to this technology.

The likely expansion of such integrated systems also once again underlines the need for some form of combined transport document and clear and harmonized carriage-of-goods rules.

Another likely trend is an increase in the use of seagoing "pusher barges" which are already in use on the United States coast and to a more lim-ited extent in the North Sea. The expensive propulsion unit in this system is detachable and, being classed as tug and barges, such a system of 30,000 tons or so needs only a small crew. This poses the question as to when a barge becomes a ship? The fact that the propulsion unit can be disconnected appears to justify a barge designation. Clearly, however, such a barge designation may be used to circumvent manning scales for ships.

The extent to which tankers will increase in size in the medium term is problematic for reasons already given above. The million-ton tanker should not, however, be ruled out in the long term. Such a vessel, highly automated, steaming at an economic speed (using crude oil for fuel) and refining oil on board en route, could provide delivery, storage, and industrial processes at sea.

In the event of such mammoths materializing, the question would have to be asked whether, given the change of function of the ship to a slow-moving oil storage-tank and refinery, it was necessary to specify a maximum allowable size for tanks and whether other safeguards were necessary to mini-mize the catastrophic environmental threat which a casualty involving such a tanker would pose.

The combination of ever-increasing manning costs and rising fuel costs will give rise to more decisions to adopt automation and nuclear power in the medium term. The latter requires bigger ships to be economic. The countries most likely to adopt nuclear propulsion on an increasing scale are the United States, the Soviet Union, Japan, the Federal Republic of Germany, and the United Kingdom. New shipbuilding and ship-repairing capacity will develop in the next ten years specifically for nuclear-powered ships. It has been estimated that by the end of the century, the United States should have in excess of 200 nuclear-powered ships.

As the use of nuclear-powered vessels becomes more common, it will clearly be necessary to develop further and, in particular, to harmonize port regulations, rules for the entry into ports of nuclear-powered ships and the law relating to liability for nuclear accidents.

Little progress has so far been made on the international law level as regards the liability of operators of nuclear ships. It will be recalled that the

Brussels Convention on the Liability of Operators of Nuclear Ships, 1962,[15] has not entered into force and that visits of nuclear-powered vessels to foreign ports are usually made subject to bilateral conventions regulating the question of liability. An early example was the Exchange of Notes between the United Kingdom and the United States in anticipation of visits of N.S. *Savannah* to ports in United Kingdom territory.[16] The similar agreement between the United States and Norway of 1 March 1963[17] goes further than the United Kingdom-United States agreement by requiring the prior approval of the Norwegian government for the entry of the *Savannah* not only into Norwegian ports but also into Norwegian territorial waters. It is unlikely that anything other than general rules for the passage of such vessels through the territorial sea and straits will emerge from the Third United Nations Conference on the Law of the Sea. As will be suggested below, more detailed provisions will certainly be required later as nuclear propulsion becomes more widely used.

Flying freighters. There will, in the long term, be attempts to close the gap between the high speeds and low loadings of aircraft and the low speeds and high loadings of seagoing vessels. The beginnings of this can be observed in the experimental work being carried out on surface skimmers or air-cushion vessels. The biggest vessel so far is believed to be a 500-ton Russian craft—the "ekronoplan experimental"—capable of operating at heights of ten to twenty-five meters above sea level and presently undergoing tests in the Caspian Sea. Similar research is being undertaken in the Federal Republic of Germany, France, Japan, and the United States, with projects ranging from small utility machines to 1400-ton cargo machines capable of carrying up to 860 tons at a speed of 250 knots. It is, moreover, considered possible that the future may see such craft of up to 5000 tons traveling at 200 knots. Needless to say, a very considerable revision of the Rules of the Road for Preventing Collision at Sea will be required to accommodate such developments.[18]

Subsurface merchant vessels with nuclear propulsion will also be used in the future. These may prove particularly valuable for the transportation of oil. This technology is seen by some as an economic solution for the haulage of crude oil from Alaska. The 100,000 ton and upwards submarines will load at undersea oil terminals beneath the ice and will follow a transpolar route under the ice to Europe or the United States. The navigational problems may be overcome by the placing of acoustic transponders along the seabottom over this route.[19]

Given the suspicious attitude of a great many continental shelf states towards the emplacement of devices on the seabed, it may be found necessary in the future to regulate the emplacement and maintenance of such navigational aids. A more pressing need, however, will be to provide for the adoption of the International Convention for the Prevention of Pollution from Ships, 1973, which will be necessary to provide for the risks presented by submarine tankers.

SHIPS ROUTING, TRAFFIC SEPARATION
SCHEMES, AND PRIORITY LANES

Perhaps one of the most striking facts that emerges from the above review is that future developments in marine technology will certainly bring with them increased navigational risks and pose a considerable threat to the port and coastal environments. A diversity of specialized vessels designed to carry chemical, nuclear, and other hazardous materials, nuclear-propelled surface and subsurface craft, and the emergence of the new breed of high-speed surface skimmers will considerably aggravate the existing navigational hazards in busy straits and congested port approaches. There seems little doubt, therefore, that the international community will not only have to press ahead with the current plans to introduce compulsory routes and traffic separation schemes but will also have to think seriously about the introduction of priority lanes for vessels carrying dangerous cargoes and shore traffic control at port approaches.

The questions of ship-routing and traffic-separation schemes are of course being considered by LOS III in relation to the various draft articles submitted on passage through the territorial sea. Attention will be focused in this paper on two of the more important of these drafts, namely (1) the Draft Articles on Navigation through the Territorial Sea including Straits Used for International Navigation, sponsored by Cyprus, Greece, Indonesia, Malaysia, Morocco, Philippines, Spain, and Yemen (hereafter the Eight Power Draft and (2) the Draft Articles Relating to Passage through the Territorial Sea, sponsored by Fiji (hereafter Fiji Draft).[20]

Article 8 of the Eight Power Draft, which is "applicable to all ships"[21] simply provides that:

> The coastal State may designate in its territorial sea lanes and traffic separation schemes, taking into account those recommended by competent international organizations, and prescribe the use of such sea lanes and traffic separation schemes as compulsory for passing ships.

In two supplementary provisions, even the reference to the need to take account of the recommendations of competent international organizations disappears. Thus, Article 16(c) asserts the right of the coastal state to prescribe, as a condition of passage for ships carrying nuclear substances or other hazardous materials, the "use of designated sea lanes." Similarly, under Article 22(3), foreign warships "may be required to pass through certain sea lanes as may be designated *for this purpose* by the coastal state" (emphasis added).

Not surprisingly, a number of states expressed disquiet over the degree of discretion allowed the coastal state in designating sealanes and traffic-separation schemes and it is clear that these provisions of the Eight Power Draft cannot be regarded as providing a very promising basis for negotiation.

The provisions of the Fiji Draft are much more tightly drawn. Under Article 6, sealanes and traffic-separation schemes—both horizontal and vertical—may be designated in the territorial sea *for ships having special characteristics.* In exercising their discretion to designate such lanes and prescribe such schemes, however, coastal states must take into account not only "(a) The recommendations of competent international organisations," but also "(b) Any channels customarily used for international navigation; (c) The special characteristics of particular channels; and (d) The special characteristics of particular ships."[22]

The coastal state is further required to demarcate all such sealanes designated by it and to indicate them on charts to which due publicity must be given.[23]

Finally, under Article 4(2), "Except to the extent authorised under the provisions of these articles, there shall be no suspension of the innocent passage of foreign ships . . . through sealanes designated under the provisions of these articles." This provision is complemented by the provisions of Article 6(7):

> A coastal State may from time to time, after giving due publicity thereto, substitute other sealanes for any sealanes previously designated by it under the provisions of this article.

Although, from the point of view of the international community, these limitations on coastal state discretion are a step in the right direction, they are unlikely to be considered to have gone far enough by the major maritime powers. There is a very clear conflict of views between the two sides on this issue. On the one hand, the "coastal states" regard the prescription of sealanes as an exercise of sovereignty and are prepared merely to "take into account" the recommendations of competent international organizations. On the other hand, the "maritime states" emphasize that the regulation of a right recognized by international law—the right of innocent passage—must be in accordance with internationally prescribed standards. The United States has emphasized, for example, that there should be a treaty obligation to respect international traffic separation schemes in accordance with the Rules and Procedures established by IMCO and in the International Regulations for Preventing Collisions at Sea. Although this proposal was made specifically in relation to straits, the argument is basically the same in relation to the territorial sea generally.[24]

It is important, if agreement is to be reached on new rules, that this conflict between the two interest groups should be resolved and it is the writer's view that it can be satisfactorily resolved on the basis of an IMCO/collisions-regulation regime if two points are stressed. First, it must be appreciated that the initiative in proposing sealanes or separation schemes in these waters would lie with the coastal state. Secondly, it should be more widely realized that the intention is that these schemes would be internationally binding and not merely IMCO recommendations. In the hope that it may contribute to such an understanding, IMCO's role is considered in some detail below.

The role of IMCO. IMCO's policy on ship routing and traffic-separation schemes has developed over the years since the question was first dealt with in detail at the Fourth Extraordinary Session of the IMCO Assembly, which met in November 1968 in the aftermath of the *Torrey Canyon* affair.[25] The Assembly adopted a Recommendation on Establishing Traffic Separation Schemes and Areas to be Avoided by Ships of Certain Classes.[26] A number of points in the resolution are relevant in the present context.

The Assembly confirmed the view that "IMCO is the only international body responsible for establishing and recommending measures on an international level concerning the separation of traffic in congested areas and related questions."[27] That this matter falls within IMCO's jurisdiction is clear from Article 1(a) of the IMCO Convention which provides that:

> The purposes of the Organization are:
> (a) To provide machinery for co-operation among Governments in the field of governmental regulation and practices relating to technical matters of all kinds affecting shipping engaged in international trade, and to encourage the general adoption of the highest practicable standards in matters concerning maritime safety and efficiency of navigation

That IMCO is empowered only to *recommend* measures in this field is equally clear from Article 2 of the IMCO Convention, under which "the functions of the Organization shall be consultative and advisory," and from Article 3, which empowers IMCO to make recommendations to member states or to recommend instruments to them.[28]

In 1970, IMCO published *Ships' Routeing and Traffic Separation Schemes,* describing the general principles of routing, the methods used, and the areas on which traffic-separation schemes had been agreed. In an Introduction, it was again stressed that "The use of traffic separation schemes is not compulsory; it is for ships' masters to decide, after assessing the situation and circumstances, whether or not to follow the recommended routes."[29]

Accordingly, in Resolution A.161(ES.IV), adopted in November 1968, the Assembly, having adopted a number of traffic separation schemes and areas to be avoided, merely

> *Invites* the governments concerned to advise ships under their flags to follow the recommended schemes and avoid navigating within the areas which are "areas to be avoided by ships of certain classes."[30]

A second lot of schemes was adopted by the Assembly in October 1969.[31]

The original Resolution, A.161(ES.IV), also adopted in its Annex II terms, definitions, and general principles covering traffic separation and routing. Inter alia, it is provided that

> A government proposing a routeing system or an area to be avoided, any part of which lies within international waters, should consult with IMCO so that such system or area may be adopted or recommended by IMCO for international use.

The purely functional nature of IMCO's concern is further underlined by the provision that:

> Nothing in this Annex shall be deemed to affect the rights, claims or views of any government in regard to the limits of territorial waters.[32]

The same formula of *inviting* governments to *advise* ships under their flags to follow the *recommended* routes was used in the two later Assembly Resolutions whereby further schemes were adopted in October 1971.[33]

Also in October 1971, however, a further Resolution, A.228 (VII), was adopted, marking a departure from the permissive policy followed previously. On the basis of a study of experience in the operation of the Dover Strait traffic-separation scheme, the Assembly recommended:

> . . . that Member Governments of the Organization should make it an offence for ships of their flag which use any traffic separation scheme adopted by the Organization to proceed against the established direction of traffic flow.[34]

A number of governments have now done so, including the United Kingdom under the Collision Regulations (Traffic Separation Schemes) Order 1972,[35] which came into force on 1 September 1972 and was first used as the basis of a prosecution in July 1973.[36]

Nonetheless, on the international plane, the IMCO recommendations remained recommendations. As an IMCO officer informed Sub-Committee III of the United Nations Sea-Bed Committee, in July 1972,

> There has been no question of IMCO deciding unilaterally or otherwise, to promulgate schemes which are automatically binding on States. The schemes adopted by IMCO bodies derive their legal effect and mandatory character - when they do - solely from their

having been accepted by individual States and incorporated in national legislation. What IMCO does is offer its forum for the consideration and elaboration of the most practical and feasible schemes; and then pass them on to governments for their adoption and implementation. The fact that many governments adopt and implement these schemes, wholly or in substantial part, is due mainly to the respect which these schemes command by virtue of their origins and the manner of their adoption.

The reproduction of two other passages in this statement may serve to underline the technical nature of IMCO's role and the organization's sensitivity to the need not to interfere in the domestic affairs of coastal states. First, on the method of adoption, it was stressed that:

> . . . these schemes are proposed and adopted in close co-operation not only with private commercial and industrial concerns interested in the subject. In adopting, reviewing or amending any of these schemes due account is taken of the views and wishes of all States and other bodies interested in or affected by the proposed schemes. The result of this method of work is that when the schemes are finally adopted, they generally command universal or near-universal acceptance and support.

On the question of noninterference in domestic affairs, it was emphasized that:

> . . . the establishment of traffic separation schemes in designated areas does not have any bearing whatsoever on questions relating to sovereignty or jurisdiction in respect of the areas concerned. The objective of the schemes is purely technical, in the sense that they are aimed at preventing collisions and other maritime accidents and thus avoid loss of life and property and impairment of the marine environment.[37]

On the other hand, it had become clear, on the basis of experience in the operation of schemes, that some means would have to be found of making these schemes more effective. The ways in which this is now being done are described in an IMCO document submitted to Sub-Committee III of the Sea-Bed Committee in March 1973.

First, it was reported that

> A number of major maritime countries have introduced, or are in the process of introducing, national legislation making it mandatory for ships under their flag to follow the general direction of traffic whenever they navigate within traffic separation schemes adopted by the Organisation.[38]

Secondly, a new convention on the International Regulations for Preventing Collisions at Sea, 1972, was signed in October 1972, revising the existing regulations to take account of current technical developments.[39] Under Article I of the convention, parties undertake to give effect to the rules annexed to the convention. Rule 10 consists of a list of rules to be observed by ships navigating in or through traffic separation schemes adopted by the organizations,[40] and it is provided in Rule 1(a) that "These Rules shall apply to all vessels upon the high seas and in all waters connected therewith navigable by seagoing vessels." Accordingly, once the convention enters into force,[41] states parties will be legally bound to adopt legislation making it compulsory for ships under their flag to comply with the rules enumerated in Rule 10 when navigating in or through traffic separation schemes adopted by IMCO.

If the history of this question has been rehearsed at apparently inordinate length, it is because a proper understanding of it suggests that there is no real conflict of interest between the major maritime powers, anxious to safeguard the rights of passage of their vessels, and those of other coastal states, which tend to view IMCO as the guardian of the interests of the ship-owning states and are concerned with asserting their sovereign rights to regulate passage through their offshore waters. The adoption of schemes in the way described above would seem to offer both sides the guarantee they are demanding, especially if it is recalled that the initiative in proposing the adoption of a scheme may be taken by the coastal state concerned. Finally, IMCO has helped to make the system more acceptable by carrying out a review of all the schemes so far adopted, for the purpose of ensuring that adequate aids to navigation are provided in each particular case to enable an accurate position determination to be made by the mariner. The principles of navigation within the schemes have also been revised to accord with those in the new collisions regulations.[42]

Suggested final formulation. The above consideration of the provisions of the Fiji Draft on sealanes and traffic-separation schemes has largely ignored the fact that these provisions relate only to "ships having special characteristics." It is the writers' view that, while the desire to confine to the minimum regulations on innocent passage is admirable, it is also misguided in this context. As IMCO has pointed out,

> It has been the view of governments in IMCO that measures of accident-prevention, including the 'Maritime Rules of the Road'— of which the Traffic Separation and Routeing constitute an important part—should apply to *all* ships. For, in a collision between a super-tanker and a small dry-cargo ship it would not be of any significance which was to blame, if the result of the collision is widespread oil pollution.[43]

The text of a provision on sea-lanes and traffic-separation schemes, which is suggested in the following two paragraphs, reflects this point of view.

Para. X

The coastal State may require the use by foreign ships exercising the right of innocent passage of such sealanes and traffic separation schemes as have been adopted by the Intergovernmental Maritime Consultative Organization. Such sealanes and traffic separation schemes shall be indicated on charts to which due publicity shall be given by the coastal state.

Para. Y

Parties to the present Convention undertake to adopt the necessary legislation to ensure that ships flying their flag, when passing through sealanes and traffic separation schemes established in accordance with paragraph X, shall comply with Rule 10 of the International Regulations for Preventing Collisions at Sea, 1972, including such amendments of the said Rules as may be adopted under Article VI of the Convention on the International Regulations for Preventing Collisions at Sea, 1972.

Under Article IV of the 1972 Convention, the new collisions regulations cannot enter into force *as such* before 1 January 1976 and may be delayed further if the provisions of Article IV are not satisfied before that time. If there is undue delay, some such formula as that suggested in Paragraph Y above would allow the substance of Rule 10 to enter into force earlier.

The question still remains whether additional special provisions are required for ships having special characteristics. In the writer's view the time is rapidly approaching when it will be necessary to establish priority lanes for certain classes of vessel such as oil tankers, chemical tankers, nuclear-powered ships, and vessels carrying nuclear materials or other hazardous materials. It may well be prudent therefore to facilitate the orderly allocation of priorities and the expeditious passage of ships through congested areas by adopting some such rules as those proposed in Article 6 of the Fiji Draft.

Article 6 identifies three classes of "ships having special characteristics" and these are commented on in turn below.

Submarines and other underwater vehicles. As the Explanatory Note puts it, "greater flexibility is sought in relation to the passage of submarines." Both they and "other underwater vehicles" are given a choice under Article 6(1). They may either navigate on the surface and show their flag or, if they wish to make an underwater passage,

(a) have given prior notification of their passage to the coastal State: and
(b) if so required by the coastal State, confine their passage to such sealanes as may be designated for that purpose by the coastal State.

Since this proposal gives a more favorable position to the submarine than under the present law, it will no doubt have the support of the major maritime powers in relation to the submarine vessels considered in this paper, that is, merchant vessels.

Tankers and ships carrying nuclear or other inherently dangerous or noxious substances or materials. Under Article 6(2), such vessels may be required to give prior notification of passage and to confine their passage to such sealanes as may have been designated for that purpose by the coastal state.

Marine research and hydrographic survey ships. Under Article 6(5), research or survey activities by such ships require the prior authorization of the coastal state. This is in line with the present law.

Article 6(4) of the Fiji Draft goes on to provide that the coastal state may require such ships to give prior notification of their passage and follow designated sealanes.

If such proposals are ultimately adopted it may be of some value to incorporate also the provisions of Article 6(10) of the Fiji Draft

> In order to expedite the passage of ships through the territorial sea the coastal State shall ensure that the procedures for notification under the provisions of this article shall be such as not to cause any undue delay.

TRAFFIC CONTROL AT PORT APPROACHES

Finally, brief reference must be made to the question of shore-based marine traffic control (MTC) at port approaches. In a recent study, two of our colleagues in the University of Wales have found that ". . . the introduction of radio equipment for detection, positioning and communication, and the development of computers have revolutionised the situation in the last decade and have made total shore-based control feasible. It is only the question of cost in all its forms—economic, environmental and social—which will dictate how much shore-based control of vessels is adopted."[44]

So far as the law is concerned there would appear to be three gaps which will need to be plugged if MTC is to make an important contribution to safety of navigation. First, as in the field of air traffic control (ATC), provision must be made for the training and licensing of marine traffic controllers and they must be subject to the same penalties as their ATC counterparts in the event of incompetence. Secondly, provision must be made for the adequate training of the masters and pilots who will be required to cooperate with traffic controllers. Finally, "an internationally agreed set of general procedures for identification, reporting, etc. is urgently needed and will need enforcing in order to clear up the chaos and confusion which can occur on the VHF radio telephony channels at present."[45]

NOTES

1. H.P. Drewry (Shipping Consultants), *Japan: Trends in Crude Products and Tanker Supply,* 1974, reported in the *Times* (London), 22 October 1974.
2. Secretariat of IMCO, *The Activities of IMCO in Relation to Shipping and Related Maritime Matters* (UN Doc. A/CONF.62/27), 13 June 1974, p. 13, para. 50.; *Ibid.,* para. 51.
3. A joint IMCO/ILO Committee on Training is constantly reviewing training requirements for masters, officers, and seamen, for the *guidance* of governments. *Ibid.,* p. 14, para. 52.
4. *Ibid.,* p. 31, para. 114.
5. For Final Act of Geneva Conference, including text of the Convention, and Introductory Note, see XIII *International Legal Materials* (1974), p. 910. For a very useful introduction to the problems raised by the liner conference system, see UNCTAD, *The Regulation of Liner Conferences (a Code of Conduct for the Liner Conference System),* report by the UNCTAD Secretariat (TD/104/Rev.1), 1972.
6. TCM stands for *transport combine merchandise.*
7. But the economic strength of shippers in developing countries is much less than that of their Western European counterparts and their shippers' councils are correspondingly less able to redress the balance of power between the shipper and the shipowner. See further UNCTAD, *Shipping in the Seventies,* report by the UNCTAD Secretariat (TD/177), 1972, pp. 3–5.
8. *See,* e.g., N. Papadakis, *Legal Aspects of Artificial Islands* (London: David Davies Memorial Institute of International Studies, 1974); H.F. van Panhuys and M.J. van Emde Boas, "Legal Aspects of Pirate Broadcasting," A.J.I.L. 60 (1966), p. 303, and United States v. Ray, 423 F. 2d 16 (5 Cir. 1970), A.J.I.L. 64 (1970), p. 954; lower court opinion - 294 F. Supp. 532 (S.D. Fla 1969), A.J.I.L. 63 (1969), p. 642.
9. G. Knight, in T.A. Clingan and L.M. Alexander eds. *Hazards of Maritime Transit* (1973), pp. 91–136; *Ibid.,* p. 91.
10. P. Hill, "Tanker Fleet Likely to Get New Look," the *Times* (London), 3 January, 1975, commenting on the part played by Burmah Oil's shipping operations in bringing about its serious cash crisis at the end of 1974.
11. E. Frankel, "Present and Future Approaches to the Creation of Systems for Reducing Risks through Improvements in Technology and Regulation," in Clingan and Alexander, *op. cit.,* note 9, pp. 49–65, at p. 58.
12. On the international law requirements, *see* the following ILO Conventions and Recommendations: Convention No. 57 Concerning Hours of Work on Board Ship and Manning, 1936, Part III: "Manning," which lays down both general guidelines and specific required numbers of officers and deck ratings for ships of specified tonnages; Convention No. 76 Concerning Wages, Hours of Work on Board Ship and Man-

ning, 1946, Part IV: Convention No. 93 Concerning Wages, Hours of
Work on Board Ship and Manning (Revised 1949), 1949, Part IV; and
Convention No. 109 Concerning Wages, Hours of Work on Board
Ship and Manning (Revised 1958), 1958, Part IV and ILO Recom-
mendation 109 of 1958.

13. *See,* as regards oil tankers, Annex I, Regulations 13, 14, and 25 and, as
    regards chemical carriers, Annex II, Regulation 13 and Code for
    the Construction and Equipment of Ships carrying Dangerous
    Chemicals in Bulk, adopted by the IMCO Assembly in Resolution
    A. 212 (VII).
14. See "OECD Study on Flags of Convenience," *Journal of Maritime Law and
    Commerce* 4 (1973), pp. 231–254.
15. A.J.I.L. 57 (1963), p. 268.
16. U.K.T.S. No. 37 (1964), Cmnd. 2411.
17. 524 UNTS 185.
18. See further R. McLeavy (ed.), *Jane's Surface Skimmers,* 1974.
19. See further J.A. Cestone and E. St. George, "Underwater Arctic Navigation,"
    Journal of Navigation 27 (1974), pp. 342–361.
20. A/AC.138/SC.II/L.18, 27 March 1973, *Report of the Committee on the
    Peaceful Uses of the Sea-Bed and the Ocean Floor beyond the
    Limits of National Jurisdiction,* General Assembly Official Records:
    28th Session, Supplement No. 21, (A/9021), 1973, Vol. III, pp. 3–
    10; A/AC.138/SC.II/L.42 and Corr.1, 19 July 1973 (*op. cit* pp.
    91–98).
21. It falls under *Section 1. Rules applicable to all ships.*
22. Article 6 (8).
23. Article 6 (9).
24. See Mr. Stevenson's speech in Sub-Committee II of the Sea-Bed Committee
    on 28 July 1972, A/AC.138/SC.II/SR.37, at p. 3.
25. See further E.D. Brown, *The Legal Regime of Hydrospace,* 1971, at p. 139
    et seq.
26. Res. A.161 (ES.IV) *IMCO Assembly, 4th Extraordinary Session and 6th
    Session. Resolutions and Other Decisions,* 1969, p. 11.
27. Preambular para. 5.
28. N. Singh, *International Conventions of Merchant Shipping,* 2nd ed. (London:
    Stevens, 1973), p. 1591.
29. At p. 5.
30. *Loc. cit.* in note 26.
31. Res. A.186 (VI), *loc. cit.* in note 26, at p. 168.
32. *Loc. cit.* in note 26, at p. 29; *Ibid.,* p. 30, para. 6.
33. Res. A. 226 (VII) and A. 227 (VII) *IMCO Assembly. Seventh Session Reso-
    lutions and Other Decisions,* 1971, pp. 114 and 129.
34. *Ibid.,* at p. 133.
35. S.I. 1972: 809.
36. The *Times* (London), 28 July 1973.
37. A/AC.138/SC.III/L.21, p. 3.
38. A/AC.138/SC.III/L.30, pp. 5–6.

39. IMCO, *International Conference on Revision of the International Regulations for Preventing Collisions at Sea, 1972. Final Act.* 1973.
40. Rule 1(d) provides that: "Traffic separation schemes may be adopted by the Organisation for the purposes of these Rules."
41. See Article IV.
42. *Loc. cit.* in note 38, p. 6.
43. *Loc. cit.* in note 37, at p. 2.
44. W. Burger and A.G. Corbet, *Training for Marine Traffic Control* (presented at a national meeting in Brennen of Deutsche Gesellschaft für Ortung und Navigation E.V., 15–17 April, 1975); typescript, p. 1. See also K.H. Best, "Through the Proper Channels," *Journal of Navigation* 27 (1974), p. 383.
45. See further *ibid.*

Discussion and Questions

Mr. Knight: Thank you very much. I think that there has been plenty of material put forth here for discussion, and in anticipating, perhaps, a 1:15 afternoon start, rather than a 1 o'clock, let us take time now, a few moments and have your questions and comments.

Ed Miles, identify yourself, please?

Mr. Miles: Yes, I figured you would say that. Ed Miles. I am sympathetic to the difficulty in which Professors Brown and Fricke are finding themselves, and what I have to say makes the difficulty even greater, but I think the paper is a very important one, and the implications are very important.

If one talks about technology *in abstracto*, one tends to treat the developments in terms of their own dynamics only, as if they do not respond to external constraints, including the regime within which they are developed. Therefore, one tends to make projections on the assumption that the regulatory future will look more like the past than anything else. On the other hand, if Professors Brown and Fricke had attempted to control the thresholds, i.e., step level changes in the way in which these problems are conceived and dealt with, then that paper would have been a book, and the outer edge of the projections concerning technological developments would have been changed somewhat.

I do think that now we are at a threshold in which the world is beginning to think about the regulatory problems of ocean transport in very different ways. As more information is released, the issue becomes more salient to governments. Priorities are increased. More attention is paid, and governments begin to respond in different ways which at some point will affect the development of the technology and will force those who build larger and larger ships to weigh considerations other than the economies of scale to be derived from increasing size and to weigh the increased vulnerability which arises from the rigidity of routes. This will lead to different kinds of regulatory regimes than

297

those envisaged by Professor Brown or the United States government or the U.K. government or the Soviet Union in the Law of the Sea Conference.

I think that even if in law of the sea negotiations we were to get a situation in which IMCO were to decide on standards and in which coastal-state regulation were to be confined to traffic-separation schemes, this would not be stable and would not last very long because as more information is injected into the system the process that I just described will come into play, and more and more governments will attempt to respond by introducing different kinds of restrictive legislation to control not only traffic or passage but design, and then the question will be at what point do the builders decide to deal with this by looking for flexibility instead of economies of scale?

Mr. Brown: I would simply like to say that I agree very much with everything which Professor Miles has said. It underlines what I was trying to say—that there is a clear need, highlighted by the developments I have tried to outline, for giving the coastal state considerably more control over the passage of vessels through congested areas. Obviously, we must have harmony; we must have internationally agreed rules on this, and I think Professor Miles' remarks might also suggest that we need a continuing review of these rules. We do not want this kind of thing to be handled by mammoth conferences like Caracas and Geneva.

Mr. Fricke: I would like to add a little bit to that. I think one of the problems here is that we have had to condense a rather long paper which would have addressed many of the issues that you raised into just a few minutes. There are many solutions proposed, ranging from licensing solutions through an international agency to quite a number of regulatory systems through IMCO.

I think the important thing, really, is to say that this is where things stand now. Where are we going to go? And it is this question of what is going to become international law that I think is the important thing, and this is the threshold step that you pointed out as being the next stage.

Mr. Stockman: I am Robert Stockman from the University of Washington. I have a question for Professor Brown. You referred to a lifetime of vessels being something on the order of 15 years. In his popular book, Noël Mostert in *Supership*, that is, estimated the design life for VLCC's was something on the order of ten years. I would like to ask you what this, in practical terms, means, in terms of what happens when the design life is met or the lifetime is met? Presumably vessels are used for periods of time after that. What does that mean in terms of safety of operation, accident rates, maintenance costs, things of that sort?

Mr. Brown: I think this is a question for Dr. Fricke. Would you like to respond, please?

Mr. Fricke: I was highly intrigued by *Supership*, a rather nice approach, I think, in terms of popular ideas. The design life obtaining is the design life that the shipping organization goes and waves at a bank in order to get the mortgage to build a ship. In other words, they will recoup their investment after ten years or so.

Fifteen years is the average working life of a tanker or bulk carrier. After that time it becomes prohibitively expensive to continue repairing it and maintaining it to the already existing international standards, and so after about fifteen years a vessel reaches the end of its working life. This is the accepted criteria for this type of operation.

Mr. Knight: I think we can take, perhaps, one more short question. Yes?

Mr. Patermann: My name is Chris Patermann. I am Science Attaché and First Secretary of the Washington Embassy of the Federal Republic of Germany. I would only like to say that I completely agree with the conclusion of the speaker that as a consequence of developing future shipping and transport technologies there will be an increase of hazardous risks for navigation in shipping all over the world, and this increase of risk will lead to a need for an improvement in communication, not only for safety in distress but also for general communications; and I would like only to draw your attention to the fact that to remedy this situation there are quite a few developments of modern technology underway to replace the conventional communication system where there is already a considerable congestion in shortwave and midwave, by means of satellite. For example, in the United States there is ComSat and RCA, who are heavily involved in developing MARSAT, and the European Space Research Organization is just developing the so-called "MAROTS" satellite. Just to show you how completely independent from Geneva and Caracas, there will be developed a totally new international framework for maritime communications. There will be under the auspices of IMCO, in April of this year, a plenipotentiary conference for establishing a worldwide maritime satellite communications system, the so-called "MARSAT." I think that is an excellent example to show that apart from the conference of the law of the sea which is really a mammoth conference, there is quite silently going on very good work in this important area. I missed a little bit in your lecture that you did not stress more the question of nuclear-propellant ships, because I think if you really deal with new sophisticated technologies of shipping, you should not leave that out. For example, the United States has the *Savannah.* In Germany, we have the *Otto Hahn,* and now there are just plans underway in the United States to have quite a few tankers with nuclear propellant, and here you have, for example, very, very interesting and very important legal problems for safety, for insurance risks, in ports and on the high seas, where you already have some legal instruments existing, the Brussels Convention and some which are just now being reviewed. So, this is also developing totally apart from Caracas and Geneva and just to give you one more example that you should not put everything that would have something to do with the law of the sea into this big mammoth conference.

Thank you.

Mr. Brown: May I just say that in the fuller version of our paper, we have, in fact, dealt with the question of nuclear propulsion and the questions of liability and insurance to which it gives rise in rather more detail.

Mr. Knight: Professor Fricke, did you want to comment?

Mr. Fricke: I was just going to comment, if I might, on the satellite navigation system. There are two areas in which the satellite system is most important in terms of shipping, and again, possibly I did not touch on these adequately. First of all, of course, is the simple relaying of routine instructions, ordinary messages that presently clutter the airways. The second one is pinpointing navigation positions. On board ship computers in quite a number of British ships at present are using satellite navigation systems to provide extremely accurate navigational aides, and this means that for much larger ships the navigation risk has been reduced quite considerably.

Mr. Knight: I would like to thank both Dr. Fricke and Professor Brown for coming so far and presenting these papers and for being so generaous in compressing their presentations because of our time problem.

Mr. Knight: We have two more substantive topics this afternoon on the general theme of dynamics and ocean technology and projections of law of the sea outcomes. The first deals with military technology and the second with deep seabed mining.

We are very fortunate on the subject of future military technology and its impact on the law of the sea to have Dr. Jozef Goldblat, who is the senior member of the research staff of the Stockholm International Peace Research Institute. Dr. Goldblat has been involved during his career in questions of military technology in his capacity as a political officer of the Disarmament Division of the UN Secretariat, as an adviser on disarmament matters to the Foreign Minister of Poland and as an adviser and delegate to the Conference of the United Nations Committee on Disarmament.

This afternoon he will apply his expertise to the law of the sea in his paper entitled "Law of the Sea and the Security of Coastal States."

Chapter Eleven

Law of the Sea and the Security of Coastal States

Jozef Goldblat
Stockholm International Peace
Research Institute

INTRODUCTION

There seems to be a consensus that the present legal system concerning the oceans is inadequate and does not reflect the realities of the contemporary world. The main question facing the international community now is not how to preserve the traditional freedom of the seas, but how to restrict it to the advantage of all, so that a new body of law might be more complete and more effective. Consequently, the controversies in the ongoing debate on the law of the sea are about the scope of future restrictions rather than about the need to bring them about. Because of diminishing food supplies, the growing shortage of raw materials and the spread of pollution, attention has been focused on the economic exploitation and distribution of sea resources, both renewable and nonrenewable, marine environmental protection and related scientific research. Security considerations, playing an important role in the shaping of individual states' positions on practically all the issues involved, have been discussed in detail only in connection with the status of international straits and, even then, principally in the context of great-power interests. In other cases they have been referred to tangentially. And yet, competition among maritime powers may lead to conflicts; nations may resort to arms in order to assert various kinds of authority in the seas.

  The purpose of this paper is to examine how, in the light of inevitable further limitations on the freedom of the seas, some minimum security requirements of states could be incorporated in a comprehensive treaty. Measures calling for restraint in military activities do not figure explicitly on the agenda of the Law of the Sea Conference, but they are inherent in the main theme of the conference—the peaceful use of ocean space. The recommendations which will be formulated here concern such measures of restraint in the high seas, on the continental shelf, and in international straits, taking into account the present

301

and future developments in the military uses of the sea. They should not be confused with arms-control agreements, as they cannot, by themselves, significantly circumscribe the arms race. Some of them may, perhaps, in a specialized forum or fora, be expanded and developed into full-fledged international agreements, on a global or regional scale, with provisions for verification and enforcement. This would be particularly applicable to measures concerning the seabed, as under the Sea-Bed Treaty the parties have undertaken to continue negotiations for the prevention of an arms race in that environment, and the treaty is coming up for review already in 1977.

HIGH SEAS

The reason usually given for the steady shrinkage of the area normally considered as high seas, open to all nations, is that modern technology has been continually providing more effective means to explore and exploit the resources of the oceans. Since the U.S. proclamation in 1945 of a claim to broad jurisdiction over continental-shelf resources beyond the territorial sea, an increasing number of coastal states, notably small- and medium-size states, have been asserting sovereignty or special rights over large portions of the adjacent waters. This development has been of crucial consequence. But it should be borne in mind that military uses of the oceans have also contributed to restricting the openness of the high seas. In particular, the great powers have been using parts of the high seas for large-scale military maneuvers, for nuclear weapon tests and long-range missile re-entry tests, as well as for the emplacement of military installations and devices for tactical and strategic purposes. The air space over the high seas, outside the testing and military exercise zones, has not been entirely free, either. In 1950 and 1951, the U.S.A. and Canada established Air Defense Identification Zones (ADIZ), extending in several areas to a few hundred miles from the shore, where observance of certain procedures by the pilots over the high seas is required as a condition for foreign planes to obtain permission for entering the air space; violations of ADIZ regulations may subject the offending aircraft to interception. In the early 1960s, France set up a similar zone, called a "zone of special responsibility," extending some 80 miles off the coast of Algeria. Apart from unilateral actions by smaller and larger countries, some areas and certain types of military use of the seas have been restricted by multilateral arms-control agreements.

Military maneuvers
It is generally considered lawful, in peacetime, for certain portions of the high seas to be declared temporarily dangerous for navigation on account of explosions connected with conventional naval target practice. The question is more complicated when it comes to large-scale naval maneuvers and the testing of nuclear weapons or target accuracy of ballistic missiles. While most maritime nations engage in military maneuvers at sea on the basis of reciprocity, only

a few have been conducting nuclear and ballistic missile tests. In the latter case, dangerous zones are established for a longer time and are much larger than the zones set up for conventional exercises. A conventional exercise can be stopped immediately to avoid damage to an airplane or a ship entering the area by mistake or for other reasons. This may not prove feasible in the case of nuclear and ballistic-missile testing. In a few instances action was taken to inhibit and interfere with the presence of foreign vessels in the designated danger zones.

In the case of nuclear weapon explosions, there is an additional problem, that of environmental contamination by radioactive products. The 1958 Convention on the High Seas provides that measures should be taken to prevent such pollution of the seas (Article 25). Also the UN Declaration of 1970 requested states to prevent pollution and contamination of the marine environment, and the UN Conference on the Human Environment of 1972 declared that states have the responsibility to ensure that their activities do not cause damage to the environment of other states or of areas beyond the limits of national jurisdiction. Besides, a treaty prohibiting nuclear-weapon tests in the atmosphere, outer space, and under water, has been in force since 1963.

From the point of view of the law of the sea, the important fact is that some large-scale naval maneuvers, as well as tests of nuclear weapons and ballistic missiles, impede free access to very large areas for fishing and maritime navigation and amount to a claim to appropriate parts of the high seas for exclusive use, albeit on a temporary basis. Whether or not military activities in the oceans meet the requirement of reasonable regard to the interests of other states in the exercise of the freedom of the high seas, as stipulated in Article 2 of the Convention on the High Seas, is a question which should not be decided exclusively by states engaging in these operations. It is primarily up to states subject to restrictions to judge the reasonableness of deprivations imposed upon them. Certainly not all the exercises mentioned above can be deemed to belong to the category of activities carried out in the seas for traditional purposes.

It is likely that under the pressure of world public opinion, and as a result of progress in underground testing technology, nuclear tests in the atmosphere (including those conducted over the high seas) will be brought to a halt. It would be less realistic to expect cessation of military maneuvers and ballistic missile tests on the high seas. If anything, their frequency will probably increase in view of the increasing emphasis being placed on naval strategies, and because of the continuous development of missile guidance systems. Usually, the dangerous zones for testing exercises on the high seas are activated and deactivated by notifications, issued on a voluntary basis. In addition, the U.S.A. and the U.S.S.R. have established a common code of conduct for the commanding officers of their respective ships and aircraft engaged in naval operations, under a bilateral agreement on the prevention of incidents on and over the high seas of 25 May 1972, and a protocol to this agreement of 22 May 1973. The two powers have also undertaken to notify of actions on the high seas which represent a danger to navigation or to aircraft in flight, and to exchange information between themselves concerning incidents between their ships and aircraft. But military exercises at sea can jeopardize the safety of navigation of ships and aircraft of other states, as well. Some exercises can also pose, or be perceived as, a threat to national security, interfere with the economic exploitation of the sea, or even cause damage, They should be subject, therefore, to strict, generally applicable international rules, binding for all.

A formula might be considered under which major military maneuvers (the term "major" must be defined) and ballistic-missile target practice, as well as any other military exercise presenting a danger to navigation or to aircraft in flight, should not be conducted in an area of international waters and international air space closer than, say, 200 miles from the coast of other states without their express authorization, and also outside this area where there is heavy international traffic. The state or states engaged in these exercises would be under an obligation to issue advance notification *ad omnes,* indicating the nature of the exercise, its estimated duration, including the estimated time of its beginning and end, and the geographical area involved. They would also be required to take all the necessary precautionary measures to avoid damage being caused to other states, or to their physical and juridical persons. If, notwithstanding the precautions, damage were caused, the state or states responsible for it should be liable to pay equitable compensation, according to procedures to be agreed upon separately.

Antisubmarine detection systems

Surveillance of foreign fleets has become a customary activity at sea and is limited only by international rules of the road under the 1960 Regulations for Preventing Collisions at Sea, annexed to the Final Act of the International Conference on Safety of Life at Sea. The U.S.-Soviet agreement of 1972, on the prevention of incidents on and over the high seas, has reinforced the legitimacy of surveillance by including a provision aimed at avoiding risks of collision between ships of the two powers engaged in this activity. But the most disturbing development in surveillance operations is in the field of antisubmarine warfare (ASW).

The characteristic feature of ASW lies in continuous dissemination in the ocean environment of systems of detection, the first necessary step towards identification, localization, and eventual destruction of enemy submarines. The detection is carried out mainly by acoustic means and can be active or passive. Passive techniques rely on the detection of sound waves emitted by moving submarines. Active techniques (sonar) rely on reflection from the hull of the submarine of sound waves generated by a controlled source. The systems of detection may be mobile or fixed. In mobile systems, aircraft and helicopters as well as surface ships and submarines are used.

Aircraft, land-based or carrier-based, drop so-called sonobuoys into the water to trace sounds of moving submarines; the latter can then be localized by magnetic anomaly detectors. Sonobuoys are sonars attached to floating buoys which are fitted with a radio transmitter to relay the data back to the aircraft; they can be submerged to preset depths. Magnetic anomaly detectors are instruments capable of revealing changes in the geomagnetic field produced by the hulls of submerged submarines. Helicopters can, in addition to dropping sonobuoys, also lower sonar sets into the water by cable, while hovering above. Surface ships have sonars mounted on the hull or towed at some distance and at various depths. Sonars mounted on or towed by attack submarines, called "hunter-killer" submarines, preferably nuclear-powered, are considered to be most effective. The faster, the quieter, and the deeper-diving the "hunter-killer" submarine, the better are its chances of detecting another submarine.

Fixed antisubmarine detection systems consist of arrays of hydrophones deployed in an ocean basin, which are in communication with a shore-based computer, and can locate the submarine and track it. Such systems can detect the presence of a submarine at a distance of hundreds of kilometers. Arrays of bottom-mounted, upward-listening, interconnected sonars are emplaced along the coastlines of several nations. Other surveillance systems consist of sonars mounted on submerged towers. Thus, for example, a system set up north of the Azores Islands consists of sonars mounted on three or more 130-meter high submerged towers.[1] Yet another system now being developed consists of long-life sonobuoys, dropped from the air, which would moor to the bottom of the ocean and transmit information to receivers installed on satellites or aircraft.

Two types of mission are assigned to ASW forces. One mission consists of detecting adversary submarines entering certain large areas of the ocean with a view to tracking and keeping them under constant surveillance. Another mission consists of detecting adversary submarines in an area surrounding ships, both merchant and naval, with a view to protecting these ships and securing their safe passage. Both are probably unavoidable during war, especially all-out war, when the aim is to destroy any enemy craft, and when, in addition to the use of antisubmarine missiles, acoustic or magnetic mines[2] could be quickly laid at certain "choke points" in the oceans to destroy enemy submarines. But in peacetime, the first type of mission does not seem to be essential or even desirable. In addition to ASW aircraft, helicopters and surface vessels, as well as "hunter-killer" submarines, normally used for sea-lane defense, it requires fixed long-range ocean-surveillance systems. To keep pace with the development of countermeasures, including technological improvements of submarines which are becoming faster and quieter and can remain submerged for long periods of time, even more sophisticated acoustic detection underwater installations may be emplanted on the ocean floor and impede peaceful activities in the high seas. From the military point of view, the installations in question may be helpful in any ASW operations, but for the second type of mission they do not seem indispensable. Moreover, inasmuch as it is also directed against ballistic-missile-carrying submarines, large area ASW detection combined with tracking activities can be extremely destabilizing for the strategic balance. It could be seen as an attempt to undermine the survivability of submarine forces, a keystone in the global strategy of the big powers, even though the likelihood of destroying all, or nearly all of these forces, simultaneously, and by a sudden attack, is remote.

A new important factor is that the range of submarine-launched ballistic missiles is constantly increasing. The present U.S. Poseidon missiles have a range of 2500 miles, the Soviet missiles on "Yankee" class submarines— 1500 miles, and those on one or two new "Delta" class submarines—4200 miles. The future U.S. Trident submarines will carry missiles initially with a range of 4000 miles (C-4) and, subsequently, probably 6000 miles (D-5), while the recently test-fired Soviet missile, the SS-N-8, has already achieved about 4900 miles.[3] Once submarine-launched ballistic missiles with a range exceeding 4000 miles are deployed in sufficient numbers by both sides, to the extent allowed by the SALT agreement (and this is expected to happen within the next four years), the area from which missiles can reach their vital targets will increase enormously. This will provide the strategic submarines with operational flexibility to select patrol areas susceptible to blunt attempts of acoustic ASW sensors to detect them, such as areas of prevailing seasonal storms, high biological noise or other phenomena. Submarines are becoming ever more versatile and elusive to ASW methods of warfare, but soon they may not even need to leave their closely guarded territorial or adjacent or internal waters to strike the enemy. The U.S.A. and the U.S.S.R. will, in practice, have their own coastal ASW-free sanctuaries. Long-range surveillance systems in the oceans may then become dispensable. The feasibility of trailing nuclear-missile-carrying submarines will be considerably reduced and the invulnerability of the sea-based deterrent will, thereby, further increase.

As long as no specific restraints concerning submarine and anti-submarine warfare have been agreed upon, a rule could perhaps be established proscribing the deployment of large, fixed AWS surveillance arrays in the high seas, so as to remove undesirable obstacles to navigation and the economic exploitation of the oceans, and also to curb the development of ASW strategic capabilities. From the point of view of security, excessive transparency of the oceans may prove harmful. From the point of view of the law of the sea, national appropriations of the deep seabed as well as the resulting military control by maritime powers of the areas appropriated, are not compatible with the UN resolution declaring the ocean bottom to be the common heritage of mankind.

Regional restrictions on military uses of the sea

Four international treaties have been concluded in the post–World War II period, restricting the military uses of the seas.

The Antarctic Treaty, effective since 23 June 1961, declared the Antarctic as an area to be used for peaceful purposes only. This declaration was reinforced by the prohibition of any measures of a military nature, such as the establishment of military bases and fortifications, the carrying out of military maneuvers and the testing of any kind of weapons. Nuclear explosions of any kind and the disposal of radioactive waste material have also been prohibited in Antarctica. The provisions of the treaty apply south of the 60° south latitude. The relevant point is that not only the Antarctic continent but also the ice shelves which surround the continent and occupy an area estimated at 800,000 square miles, have been put under a demilitarized régime.

Next came the treaty banning nuclear-weapon tests in three environments, called the Partial Test Ban Treaty (PTBT), which entered into force on 10 October 1963. One of the environments prohibited for testing is the underwater environment, and to stress the comprehensiveness of the prohibition, the text of the treaty enumerates, for illustrative purposes, territorial waters and high seas. High seas have been singled out to remove the possibility of an argument being put forward that these parts of the seas were not covered by the prohibition because they are not under the "jurisdiction or control" of any party, as stipulated elsewhere in the treaty. And once the high seas had been mentioned, it was found expedient to denote them, at least by implication, as a direct extension of the territorial waters, irrespective of the breadth of the latter, and not to leave any gaps in the banned environment.

The treaty prohibiting nuclear weapons in Latin America (Treaty of Tlatelolco) was signed in Mexico City on 14 February 1967, and has been in force since then for each state which has ratified it and waived the requirements specified in one of its articles. The zone of application of the Treaty of Tlatelolco is the whole of the territories for which the treaty is in force, but the term "territory" is defined as including the territorial sea, air space, and any other space over which the state exercises sovereignty "in accordance with its own legislation." Considering the existing legislation in Latin American countries, the zone may encompass large portions of the Atlantic and Pacific Oceans, which are considered by most other states as high seas. Indeed, the treaty provides that the zone will eventually cover an area between 150° west longitude and 20° west longitude, and will thus extend hundreds of kilometers off the coast of the states party to the treaty. The U.S.A. which is party to Additional Protocol II of the Treaty of Tlatelolco, and has undertaken to respect the statute of military denuclearization of Latin America, stated that its ratification could not be regarded as implying recognition of any legislation which did not, in its view, comply with the relevant rules of international law. A statement in similar terms was made by the U.K. and France. These three powers are, therefore, not bound by the treaty stipulations extending beyond the limits which they consider as defining the territorial sea "under international law." But China made no reservation on the extent of the zone; it has, thereby, accepted limitations on its military activities in the same broad area of the high seas that the Latin American countries designated as free of nuclear weapons.

The Sea-Bed Treaty, which is in force since 18 May 1972, prohibits emplanting or emplacement on the seabed and the ocean floor and in the subsoil thereof beyond the outer limit of a seabed zone (coterminous with the 12-mile outer limit of the zone referred to in the 1958 Geneva Convention on the Territorial Sea and the Contiguous Zone) of any nuclear weapons or any other type of weapons of mass destruction as well as structures, launching installations, or any other facilities specifically designed for storing, testing, or using such weapons. However, the language of the treaty implies the possibility of the nuclear powers establishing submarine nuclear installations within a 12-mile seabed zone of another state, with the consent and authorization of the latter.

With the exception, perhaps, of the Antarctic Treaty, the arms-control value of the international agreements enumerated above is questionable. But from the point of view of the law of the sea, they all reflect an important trend towards submitting large portions of the oceans to a restrictive régime by prohibiting or foreclosing certain military activities there.[4]

This trend continues, as exemplified by proposals put forward in recent years for the setting up of so-called peace zones, or zones free of nuclear weapons, in different parts of the globe. Thus, for example, the 26th UN General Assembly in 1971 declared that the Indian Ocean was designated as a zone of peace. It called upon the great powers to enter into consultations with the littoral states of the Indian Ocean with a view to halting the escalation and expansion of their military presence in the ocean, and eliminating bases, military installations, logistical supply facilities, nuclear weapons, and other weapons of mass destruction and any manifestation of great-power military presence "conceived in the context of great power rivalry." It also called upon the littoral and hinterland states of the Indian Ocean, the permanent members of the Security Council, and other major maritime states using that ocean, to enter into consultations with a view to ensuring that warships and military aircraft do not make use of the Indian Ocean for any threat or use of force against the sovereignty, territorial integrity, and independence of any littoral or hinterland state of the ocean. Subject to these restrictions, the right to free and unimpeded use of the zone by the vessels of all nations would not be affected. In the debate on this issue, it was pointed out by several states that the principle of the freedom of the high seas had been abused as a cover-up for unrestrained military activity and for intervention and domination by powerful maritime nations.

In October 1974, the U.S.S.R. reiterated its suggestion that Soviet and U.S. ships and submarines carrying nuclear weapons on board should be withdrawn from the Mediterranean.

Other plans, such as those concerning the establishment of nuclear-free zones in South Asia, the Middle East or Africa, have not been spelled out in detail, but it may be assumed that the prohibitions are intended to cover also the seas in the respective regions in addition to national territories.

It is difficult to see how in the present situation all these proposals could materialize. But the situation may change, if international détente persists and if it contributes to restraints on military activities. The law of the sea must not stand in the way when measures for the control of armaments in new areas become politically acceptable to states directly concerned. Universal acceptance of such measures, though desirable, is not absolutely necessary. None of the arms-control treaties hitherto concluded has been adhered to by all states. Neither is it expected that a new law of the sea convention will be ratified by everybody. But in the event of arrangements imposing regional restrictions on military uses of the high seas, the consent of littoral states and other users of the waters in the region would be indispensable. It seems, therefore, advisable to include in the law of the sea convention a proviso to the effect that nothing in the convention affects the right of littoral states to conclude treaties limiting or prohibiting certain types of military activities in the high seas in their region, in agreement with other maritime states using the sea in that region. (A precedent can be found in the Treaty on the Non-Proliferation of Nuclear Weapons, which, in Article VII provides that nothing in this treaty affects the right of any group of states to conclude regional treaties in order to assure the total absence of nuclear weapons in their respective territories.)

CONTINENTAL SHELF

The legal status of the continental shelf, as determined in the Geneva Convention of 1958, is unclear. Article 2 of this Convention states that the "coastal state exercises over the continental shelf sovereign rights for the purpose of exploring it and exploiting its natural resources." The emplacement of military devices on the shelf by the coastal state is neither expressly allowed nor expressly forbidden. One interpretation is that the coastal state does not have the right to use its shelf for military purposes or for purposes other than exploration and exploitation. Others claim that the coastal states are entitled to use the shelf for any purpose, as long as there is no impediment to navigation and fishing. One can, of course, argue that the right to explore and exploit implies the right to use means for the defense of these activities. It will be recalled that under Article 5 of the said Convention the coastal state is entitled to establish safety zones around the installations and other devices necessary for the exploration and the exploitation of its natural resources, and to take measures necessary for their protection, without causing interference to the use of recognized sea lanes essential to international navigation. This right is likely to be maintained and perhaps even reinforced in a new law of the sea convention, in view of the proliferation of bottom installations for oil extraction in different parts of the world.

Another point at issue is whether states have the right to install devices unrelated to the exploration and exploitation of natural resources, and especially military devices, on the continental shelf of other states, contrary to the wishes of the latter. Some countries, for instance Mexico, which regard the continental shelf as part of the national territory, consider that any emplacement of weapons thereon by any other state is already prohibited by their own legislation. Canada holds the view that a coastal state has the right to verify, inspect, or effect the removal of any weapon, structure, installation, facility, or device implanted or emplaced on the continental shelf, or the subsoil thereof, appertaining to that coastal state. A similar right was claimed by India at the time of its accession to the Sea-Bed Treaty, even though the treaty deals only with the prohibition of emplacement of weapons of mass destruction. The U.S.A. responded by insisting that the rights of coastal states over their continental shelves are limited by the Convention on the Continental Shelf and "other principles of international law."

In 1969, Canada advanced the concept of a 200-mile zone extending from the outer limits of a 12-mile coastal band, in which only the coastal state, or another state acting with its explicit consent, would be able to perform the defensive activities not prohibited under the Sea-Bed Treaty. Nigeria suggested a 50-mile zone for a similar purpose. In the UN Sea-Bed Committee in 1973, a few Latin American states suggested that the emplacement of any kind of facilities on the seabed of the "adjacent sea" should be subject to authorization and regulation by the coastal state, and at the 1974 Caracas Law of the Sea Conference, Kenya and Mexico, supported by some other states, formally proposed that no state should be entitled to construct, maintain, deploy, or operate on or over the continental shelf of another state any military installations or devices or any other installations for whatever purposes without the consent of the coastal state.

Considering the recent ban on the emplacement of nuclear weapons and other weapons of mass destruction beyond a 12-mile seabed zone, and the much older restrictions on laying mines in peacetime outside territorial waters, it is difficult to see what kind of conventional weapons could be safely emplanted on the continental shelf of other states. Shore bombardment weapons and installations from which manned incursions could be mounted against a coastal state, were mentioned in the debate on the Sea-Bed Treaty a few years ago. But the military value of such costly offensive systems would be doubtful, given their detectability and the need to protect them. More useful would appear to be devices monitoring communications of the coastal state and/or capable of disrupting them, submarine navigation systems, devices monitoring the entrance or exit of submarines to and from harbors, as well as instruments designed to render ineffective the surveillance and defenses of another state. These devices and instruments would be more autonomous than weapon systems, but still pose problems of information transmission and supply of power. They would also be sensitive to possible countermeasures. But technical difficulties can be overcome and the risks inherent in operations conducted far from the shores of the emplanting state might, perhaps, be found worthwhile taking under certain circumstances.

It will be noted that the trend towards a coastal state's wider jurisdiction over the marine resources, including protection of the marine environment, as expressed in the concept of a 200-mile economic zone or "patrimonial" sea, may imply the right for the coastal state to impose certain regulations and, in particular, to restrict certain military activities as well as research for military purposes (insofar as the nature of research can be unambiguously determined), in an area often even wider than its continental shelf. Coastal states may assert that the installation of military devices by another state in a zone of their economic activities would interfere with such activities. Indeed, exclusive or preferential economic rights could not be effectively exercised without the right to prevent emplantation of undesirable objects on the seabed, or the use of peaceful facilities for nonpeaceful aims. In possible competing uses peaceful applications must have priority over military applications. What matters most is the status of the shelf because this is a more convenient place to emplant the devices in question than the outlying areas.

Whatever the situation *de lege lata,* the fact is that only a few states have the capability of carrying out, with required sophistication, significant submerged operations of military importance. This is what they actually do on their own continental shelf. But it would be unjust to give them the right to use for military purposes the continental shelf of others, a right which in most cases could not be reciprocated. Military installations in the proximity of other states cannot be justified on the grounds that they serve the defense interests of the state emplacing them, even if the installations are not of a patently offensive nature. Moreover, the question of neutral rights and duties under the law of war could arise, if these activities were directed aagint a third state. It would seem useful, therefore, to establish a seabed security zone adjacent to the coast, in which the coastal state would have the exclusive right to mount military equipment or other devices for military purposes (without obstructing international navigation) as well as to conduct research for such purposes. The zone would have to be sufficiently large to promote a sense of security among the smaller nations; preferably, it should cover the whole continental shelf. (The legal status of the superjacent waters must not be affected by the rules governing the seabed.)

Under the existing rules, consent of the coastal state is necessary even for peaceful ventures on the continental shelf, namely for research concerning the shelf and undertaken there. A consent régime for military ventures would certainly also be in order. In principle, the coastal state must have the right to allow another state to use its continental shelf for military purposes in the exercise of collective self-defense. In practice, however, certain countries would probably never use this right.[5]

INTERNATIONAL STRAITS

A different situation prevails in international straits. There, the problems are closely connected with the width of the territorial sea: a general extension of territorial waters to 12 miles, as has been proposed, would bring more than 100 important straits, which have hitherto contained a band of high seas, completely under the sovereignty of the coastal states. In the existing conventions there is little to provide guidance for the solution of the arising difficulties. The rules relating to international straits are included in the 1958 Convention on the Territorial Sea and the Contiguous Zone in conjunction with rules governing the so-called innocent passage through territorial waters in general. While in territorial waters innocent passage of foreign ships can be temporarily suspended, if this is essential for the protection of the security of the coastal state, such suspension is not allowed through straits that are used for international navigation between one part of the high seas and another part of the high seas or the territorial sea of a foreign state. Innocent passage has been qualified as not prejudicial to the peace, good order, and security of the coastal state; submarines are required to navigate on the surface and to show their flags.

For most nations the right of passage through international straits is important from the point of view of merchant navigation. For major naval powers it is also important for military purposes. The U.S.S.R. contends that its security depends on communications through international straits, and has indicated that it expected concessions on this issue in return for its agreement to a 200-mile economic zone. The U.S.A. has taken a similar line, insisting on air and sea mobility, and warning that it would not recognize a 12-mile limit as the breadth of the territorial sea, unless its postulates concerning straits were satisfield. In view of their global political and strategic aspirations these powers want to have complete freedom of transit through and over international straits, between one part of the high seas and another part of the high seas, including the right for submarines to transit submerged, instead of on the surface.

Another extreme position is represented by China, among others, which considers a strait lying within the limits of the territorial sea to be an inseparable part of the territorial sea of the coastal state, and suggests that passage of foreign military ships be conditional on prior notification to or authorization by the authorities of that state.

A remarkable feature of the dispute over straits is that it is conducted more in legalistic than in practical terms. Not all international straits are of equal importance. Except when no other course is physically possible, as in Gibraltar or the Bosphorus and the Dardanelles, a strait may be a convenient but not an indispensable route for ocean transport. There may be a case for concentrating on those straits that are deemed to be vital for international navigation, instead of establishing a general principle. Specific agreements concerning transit through such straits could perhaps be concluded with due regard to the peculiarities of the region and the interests of the riparian countries, while in other straits an innocent passage rule, as appropriately defined, would be applicable. There are already straits subject to special régimes under international treaties, and there is no noticeable tendency to sacrifice them in favor of some new uniform regulations.

Many nations consider the right of innocent passage as good enough. But the problem with innocent passage through territorial waters is that it has been very poorly defined in the Convention on the Territorial Sea and the Contiguous Zone and, for some states, straits used for international navigation, which are a part of the territorial sea of one or more states, fall under the same legal régime as that of any other portion of the territorial sea. A broad formula just requiring observance of good order and security of the coastal state is subject to subjective interpretations, and may be taken advantage of by the littoral states to the detriment of others. Attempts to work out a more precise definition seem to have been partly successful insofar as merchant shipping is concerned, but serious divergencies remain with regard to the passage of warships.[6] Some states contend that passage of warships cannot be innocent (even though the 1958 Convention appears to have assumed that there is a right of innocent passage for all ships) and do not allow entry of foreign navy vessels into territorial waters without their consent. If such interpretation persisted, the coastal state would be in a position to block passage of warships of some or all states, also in the strait under its control.

In the present situation no compromise seems conceivable, unless it is accepted that less strict rules should apply in straits lying in the territorial waters of one or more states than in territorial waters outside straits, at least with regard to the passage of warships. In practice, this could mean that all passage in international straits would be considered innocent, unless it fell within some clearly defined categories of activities, such as acts of war.

On the other hand, an unqualified right to free transit could be used abusively, either to exert political pressure on littoral or hinterland states by demonstrations of naval force, or even for surprise intervention from a convenient vantage point. But on this issue the major users of straits are willing to give a number of assurances. The United Kingdom, for example, has suggested that ships would not engage in any activities other than those incident to their normal modes of transit, and that they would refrain from any threat or use of force against the territorial integrity or political independence of states adjacent to straits. The U.S.S.R. is prepared to provide that warships in transit through straits should not engage in any exercises or gunfire, use weapons of any kind, launch or land their aircraft, undertake hydrographical work, or engage in other similar acts unrelated to the transit.

To minimize further the apprehensions of the coastal states, it might be useful to consider the introduction of an obligation to notify coastal states of forthcoming movements of major military vessels through international straits (the term "major" remaining to be defined). This would add to the quid pro quo concessions on the part of the users of the straits. And while in principle there should be no right to suspend passage through international straits, coastal states must be entitled to take measures with regard to foreign ships that refuse to comply with generally accepted regulations.

The problem of the submerged passage of submarines through international straits has assumed excessive importance. For tactical submarines such passage in peacetime is not crucial. For strategic submarines with nuclear ballistic missiles on board, transit through straits in general, whether on or under the surface, is gradually becoming less essential in view of the increasing range of missiles. Besides, not all important international straits may be deep enough to allow submerged passage of modern strategic submarines. There may soon be no need for ballistic missile–carrying submarines to cross any international strait, whatsoever, in order to cover significant targets on the territory of the other side. This will probably happen sooner than any new law of the sea treaty would enter into force.

The improvement in monitoring technologies is making it increasingly possible for coastal states to detect submarines. Nevertheless, passage of a submerged submarine close to the shore may be regarded as ominous in view of its clandestine nature. It would appear, therefore, advisable to maintain in straits the same requirement for submarines as in the territorial waters outside straits, namely, to navigate on the surface and to show the flag, even though in certain instances submerged passage might be safer from the navigation point of view. Nothing could prevent a coastal state or states from allowing transit of submerged submarines, either generally, or in individual cases upon prior notification, notwithstanding the acceptance of the above principle.

Traffic safety regulations in the straits, especially with regard to nuclear-powered ships, tankers and ships with dangerous cargoes, are generally deemed indispensable to minimize incidents and risks of collision. Damage caused by violation of these regulations to states bordering the straits should entail international responsibility, irrespective of the type of vessel involved. Coastal states acting contrary to the existing regulations would have to be liable for damage caused to foreign ships.

As it is universally recognized that there is no right of innocent passage through the airspace over the territorial sea, detailed rules concerning aircraft would have to be worked out separately. The right of free overflight by military aircraft would have to be subject, *mutatis mutandis,* to similar restrictions aimed at ensuring the security of the coastal states as those regulating the passage of ships through straits.

SUMMARY AND CONCLUSIONS

All activities in the seas are interrelated, and economic, military, technical, and scientific problems form one complex. A legal régime ignoring this interrelationship would be incomplete. In the last analysis, it may even prove unstable.

A new system of rights and responsibilities in the oceans must, therefore, take account not only of the aspiration of the international community to achieve a just distribution of marine resources but also the states' natural right to security and self-preservation. With this in view, it is recommended that the future convention on the Law of the Sea should include provisions which would:

1. prohibit major military maneuvers and ballistic-missile target practice, as well as any other military exercise presenting a danger to navigation or to aircraft in flight, in certain specified areas of the high seas; require timely notification in the case of such exercises being conducted in other portions of the high seas, as well as equitable compensation for possible damage;

2. proscribe the emplacement of large ASW surveillance arrays on the ocean floor;

3. provide for the right of littoral states to conclude regional treaties limiting or prohibiting certain types of military activities in the high seas, in agreement with other maritime states using the sea in the region;

4. allow the establishment of a seabed security zone adjacent to the coast, in which the coastal state would have the exclusive right to install devices for military purposes and to conduct research for such purposes;

5. allow unimpeded passage of warships and military aircraft through international straits, subject to restrictions aimed at ensuring the security of the riparian states, including notification of movements of major military vessels; prohibit unauthorized submerged transit of submarines through international straits;

6. grant the coastal states the right to take measures with regard to all ships and aircraft refusing to comply with generally accepted regulations concerning passage through international straits.

Assuming that other contentious matters of importance will be successfully solved by the Law of the Sea Conference, it is thought that a few rules dealing with security matters, as suggested above, might help to meet the growing need for orderly development in the oceans.

NOTES

1. A plan for another bottom-anchored array, of gigantic dimensions, is described in a SIPRI publication on anti-submarine warfare as follows: "The 'Suspended Array System' (known as SAS) involves a high tripod tower resting at 3000 fathoms which will be so large that each leg of the tripod will be 10 kilometres away from the other two legs. Acoustic transducers mounted on this tripod will be of such size and power that just one such installation will be capable of surveying an entire ocean." Whether or not the project is realistic, it illustrates the line of thinking within certain military establishments.
2. The use of automatic submarine contact mines is restricted under the Hague Convention of 1907.
3. For the U.S.S.R., long-range submarine-launched ballistic missiles are especially important for geographical reasons: to reach the North Atlantic,

Soviet submarines coming from the bases on the Kola peninsula have
to cross the Greenland-Iceland-United Kingdom "barrier" which is
under constant surveillance by U.S. air and naval patrols and can be
mined during wartime.
4. It is worthwhile noting that, by 31 December 1973, as many as 106 states had
been party to the PTBT, and 52 to the Sea-Bed Treaty.
5. Thus, for example, Norway is unlikely to agree in peacetime to the military
use by another NATO power of its continental shelf in the Barents
Sea north of the North Cape, as the U.S.S.R. would regard this as a
threat to its northern fleet.
6. The term "warship" has been defined in some international documents, including the 1972 U.S.-Soviet agreement on the prevention of incidents on and over the high seas, as meaning a ship belonging to the
armed forces of a state bearing the external marks distinguishing
such ship of its nationality, under the command of an officer duly
commissioned by the government of that state and whose name appears in the appropriate service list, and manned by a crew who are
under regular armed forces discipline.

BIBLIOGRAPHY

Brown, E.D. *Arms Control in Hydrospace: Legal Aspects.* Oceans Series 301.
Washington: Woodrow Wilson International Center for Scholars,
June 1971.
Department of Defense Appropriations for 1975. Hearings before a Subcommittee
House Committee on Appropriations, 1974, Part 2.
*Fiscal Year 1975: Authorization for Military Procurement, Research and Develop-
ment, and Active Duty, Selected Reserve and Civilian Personnel
Strengths.* Hearings before the U.S. Senate Committee on Armed
Services, 1974, Parts 4, 7.
The Future of the Law of the Sea. Proceedings of the Symposium on the Future
of the Sea Organized at Den Helder by the Royal Netherlands Naval
College and the International Law Institute of Utrecht State Uni-
versity, 26 and 27 June 1972, ed. by L.J. Bouchez and L. Kaijen.
The Hague: 1973.
Tsipis, K., A.H. Cahn, and B.T. Feld, eds. *The Future of the Sea-based Deterrent.*
Cambridge, Mass.: 1973.
Gehring, R.W. "Legal Rules Affecting Military Uses of the Seabed." Military Law
Review 54 (1971): Fall.
Hussain, F. "No Place to Hide." New Scientist 63 (1974).
Janis, M.W. and D.C.F. Daniel, *The USSR: Ocean Use and Ocean Law,* Occa-
sional Paper No. 21, Law of the Sea Institute, University of Rhode
Island. May 1974.
Moore, J.E., ed. *Jane's Fighting Ships.* London: 1974.
Myrdal, A. "The Military Threat to the Ocean." Paper presented at the Pacem in
Maribus conference. Malta, 1974.
Sollie Finn. "Norway's Continental Shelf and the Boundary Question on the

Sea-Bed." *Cooperation and Conflict: Nordic Journal of International Politics.* 1974: 2/3.

Vår marina miljö 1971. (Studie utarbetad av arbetsgruppen "AG havsbotten" inom marinstaben.)

SIPRI PUBLICATIONS

The Militarization of the Deep Ocean: The Sea-Bed Treaty. World Armaments and Disarmament, SIPRI Yearbook, 1969/70. Stockholm: 1970.

Preventing an Arms Race on the Sea-Bed. World Armaments and Disarmament, SIPRI Yearbook, 1972. Stockholm: 1972.

Towards a Better Use of the Ocean. SIPRI. Stockholm: 1969.

Prospects for Arms Control in the Ocean. SIRPI. Stockholm: 1972.

French Nuclear Tests in the Atmosphere: The Question of Legality. SIPRI. Stockholm: 1974.

Tactical and Strategic Antisubmarine Warfare. SIPRI. Stockholm: 1974.

United Nations. Third Conference on the Law of the Sea:

A/CONF. 62/C.2/L.3
A/CONF. 62/C.2/L.6/Corr.1
A/CONF. 62/C.2/L.11
A/CONF. 62/C.2/L.16
A/CONF. 62/C.2/L.19
A/CONF. 62/C.2/L.20
A/CONF. 62/C.2/L.42/Rev. 1
A/CONF. 62/C.2/L.47
A/CONF. 62/C.3/L.17

Discussion and Questions

Mr. Knight: Thank you very much for delivering a very stimulating, and I think, in fairness, controversial paper. The floor is now open for discussion.

Mr. Alexander: I am Lew Alexander from Rhode Island. You mentioned the possibility of a security zone being established next to the coastal states where presumably emplacements might be limited. Might this not very likely move into the 200-mile economic zone? In other words, if the concept were accepted, this might include the whole 200-mile zone and the sea floor associated with this, which as Dr. Hodgson pointed out, takes care of 36 percent of the world's ocean.

Mr. Goldblat: I have not actually specified the extent of the zone. I have mentioned as an example 200 miles, which would, indeed, coincide with the breadth of the economic zone. But even if the ban on the emplacement of military devices off the coast of states extended to 200 miles, what would be wrong about it?

Mr. Alexander: The implication of my question is that a great deal of the outer continental margin of the world, beyond the continental shelf, would thus be closed off to foreign military activity.

   I question whether the larger military states would go along with this type of an interpretation. This adds still another restriction in the 200-mile economic zone beyond the limits of the continental shelf.

Mr. Goldblat: Restrictions concerning the emplacement of military devices on the seabed were already discussed during the Seabed Treaty negotiations in Geneva, where a similar proposal was submitted.

318

Mr. Lapointe: Paul Lapointe, Canada. Sir, I found your exposé most interesting, but perhaps, if I may be permitted to say so, a bit unrealistic to the extent that we are now engaged in a negotiating process which we hope to terminate in the very near future, and I wonder if it is truly realistic to talk of banning naval maneuvers, of restricting the use and deployment of naval forces over a very large portion of the oceans. Furthermore, I wonder if we should not really, realistically limit ourselves to certain controls, in particularly dangerous areas, such as certain international straits. I would tend to agree with you that perhaps we have been trying to take too big a bite of the cake by talking of all of the 100 and more international straits covered by 12-mile territorial sea. But I do not see, no more than I could see it for the merchant navies of the world, I do not see how it would be feasible in the present state of development within the international community, to say that coastal states will have complete and sole say in the matter of controlling the deployment of the navies of the world.

Would it not be possible to agree—at least for the time being until more progress has been made in the field of disarmament—to agree that all ships have a right of passage in international straits, but go on—and in light of the particular circumstances of the most important straits—go on to say that in certain cases there should be certain regulations and that perhaps, in the case of submarines, one could envisage transit on the surface? As you have said, and I agree with you, there are certain straits that are too shallow to permit submerged transit. So it is a bit unnecessary to me to spend so much time arguing that submarines should go in a submerged mode when they cannot, in practice, do so.

It seems that if we could divorce ourselves from what I considered a rather simplistic theory today of something that is called "innocent passage" or something that is called "free and unimpeded passage" and look instead at passage and try to regulate it where necessary. To go much beyond that and imply that the major powers or the big naval powers will agree to extensive controls all over the place, to suggest that they will be obliged to notify everyone whenever they want to deploy their forces, would not, in my opinion, be feasible in practice.

If you were to limit the deployment of naval forces within 200 miles, think of the situation in the Mediterranean, where are they going to pass? I do not see any of the major naval powers ever agreeing to limiting their deployment capabilities in such areas which are sensitive for many reasons.

Thank you, sir.

Mr. Goldblat: I am optimistic. This is in the very nature of my work. I have been engaged in disarmament matters for the last 20 years, and I would have changed my profession a long time ago had I lost my optimism. But I am afraid that this time I have simply been misunderstood. I am not going so far as to propose severe limits on the deployment of the navies. What I actually suggest is to introduce some order in the seas. Since there are military maneuvers and naval exercises, there should at least be an obligation to notify about their nature. I also think that they must be prohibited in certain areas, especially in areas of heavy traffic. There should also be a responsibility for possible damages. Law should replace the anarchy. This is the essence of my recommendations.

As regards the proposal for a seabed security zone, may I remind you that Canada and also India and some other countries have already stated that they would use force to remove any military devices placed on their shelf. A number of states consider the shelf as an extension of their national territory and, therefore, claim the right to remove foreign installations emplanted there without their consent.

I would not consider my suggestions as very far-reaching. I recognize that there are many other urgent problems to be solved by the Law of the Sea Conference. But from the arms control point of view my suggestions are rather modest.

Mr. Wolf: My name is Atwood Wolf, and I am here from New York City. I am a lawyer, not a military or a naval man. I have read Mr. Goldblat's paper and listened with a great deal of interest to his presentation this afternoon from the point of view of a lawyer who has observed the developments in law of the sea since the item first appeared on the agenda of the General Assembly in 1967. While I appreciate his point, that he is not interested in piling on problems to be disposed of at the Law of the Sea Conference itself, I take the liberty of suggesting that his paper, together with his recommendations, does seem to serve that purpose rather more forcefully than one would have appreciated before listening to the discussion this afternoon.

I do not believe it a coincidence that one of the first steps taken by the Sea-Bed Committee of the United Nations when the item was first considered was a general, if informal agreement that all references to arms control, to disarmament or, if you will, the peaceful uses of the seabed should be referred to the eighteen-nation Committee on Disarmament, which was then stiting in Geneva, and I would remind you that the Seabed Treaty barring the emplacement of nuclear weapons and other weapons of mass destruction was, in fact, not the product of the Sea-Bed Committee or the Law of the Sea Conference, but of an agreement reached, I believe, under the aegis of the eighteen-nation committee, the Disarmament Committee, and was, in any event, the result of direct negotiations between the United States and the Soviet Union along with other interested and, shall we say, active parties.

I think this accounts for the fact, which Mr. Goldblat noted at the very beginning of his presentation, that the subject of the uses of armed force on the sea, under the sea and over it, has been comparatively neglected in the

course of the discussions both in the Sea-Bed Committee and in the Law of the
Sea Conference.

I do believe, and I am reverting to my role as a lawyer, that to raise
the problems, the existence of which I do not deny, which were discussed by
Mr. Goldblat today, would probably serve, at best, to delay the completion of
the work of the conference, and that should the proposals, or any variations,
made by Mr. Goldblat in his paper be adopted by the conference, the result
would be a treaty which I would assume would be unacceptable to at least two,
if not all of the major maritime states. I am not privy to the negotiating position
of my own government, even less so, quite obviously, to that of the Soviet
Union, but I do find it quite difficult to believe that either of those two governments could accede to a law of the sea treaty reached by an agreement amongst
150 or a two-thirds majority of 150 nations which would effectively restrict
their exercise of the freedom of the seas, or more specifically, their freedom to
make use of the seas for the protection of what they might consider their
vital interests.

From that point, I would also suggest, if I may, that the recommendations which Mr. Goldblat so interestingly advances, are, I think, perhaps
not truly appreciative of some basic concepts of modern naval strategy. The
introductory portions of his paper and those sections dealing with the high seas
in particular seem to emphasize the use of submarines by a major maritime power
as a means of delivering nuclear-armed ballistic missiles presumably against
whatever portion of the earth might be at any given time considered hostile.
The restrictions which would be imposed on the freedom of the major powers
to use the seas for military purposes if the Goldblat recommendations were to
be adopted all seem to be grounded in that perhaps very realistic fear.

However, I would respectfully suggest that the mission of a navy, be
it the United States', the Soviet Union's, or any other navy of a substantial size,
extends far, far beyond maintaining the power to destroy the territory, the
state, and the people of a hostile nation. The mission of a navy and the mission
of its submarines, in particular, extends far, far beyond that, and I would suggest
that very careful consideration should be given in this discussion, to the fact that
by attempting to restrict the use of submarines to the delivery of nuclear-armed
ICBMs, we very well may be creating a situation, assuming that the major
powers were to respect such restrictions, that when a major power finds its vital
interests threatened to the point at which it must consider the use or a show of
force, and that possibility has been brought home within the United States by
Mr. Kissinger quite recently, the only force which the United States or any other
capable nation could use would be that of the intercontinental ballistic missiles.

Going on to the potential strategic use of submarines as a further
example, and I create an imaginary scenario, it would seem to me, looking, say,
to the Eastern Mediterranean, that the deployment of submarines in the Eastern
Mediterranean under circumstances when the United States might feel that its

vital interests are threatened, would, in fact, be less a threat of the use of ballistic missiles against one of the smaller nations in that area than a reminder to them that were they to attempt to maneuver a more powerful ally into participation in the confrontation, they are then asking their more powerful ally to face a very real risk of very serious difficulties with the United States.

Lest I be accused of being chauvinistic, I would suggest that the same scenario could be applied to policy decisions on the part of the Soviet Union with respect to its deployment of submarines in the same area.

In short, if we are going to use missiles in the Eastern Mediterranean, I would think that the principal reason for that is to display the fact to the smaller states that we are, in a given set of circumstances, prepared to use them. If, on the other hand, we are not permitted convenient access to that area, we would not be able to make that sort of an exhibition, and thus could not provide a reminder that the world is perhaps somewhat more complicated than the small states in the area sometimes care to think about. The same thing, of course, would be true for the Soviet side or for any other country so armed and knowing the same international responsibilities.

I noticed that in the first of the recommendations which Mr. Goldblat made, he suggested that a proviso be included in the treaty that nothing therein served to prevent the reaching of subsequent agreements. Speaking as a lawyer, I would suggest to him that such a provision is unnecessary, because quite obviously, no agreement can possibly be construed as preventing the making of another agreement. It hardly appears necessary to say that you do have such a right. Furthermore, lawyers and diplomats, for that matter, I would point out, have a habit of feeling that no words are used in an agreement that do not have some meaning, and I would, therefore, suggest that such a proviso might subsequently be construed as to impose an obligation on the states to reach these agreements, and I think that, too, would be embarrassing.

In conclusion, I would suggest that this is not a really appropriate topic to be seriously considered in the Law of the Sea Conference but should be left to rather more delicate and sensitive negotiations which are presently being conducted in the context of the SALT talks and in the context of the mutual force reduction talks in Europe. There is far more involved here than questions of the law of the sea, at least in the context that those questions have been discussed in the conference and the preparatory committee.

Mr. Goldblat: I appreciate your point of view, but I beg to differ. I have not been convinced, for instance, by the argument that it is necessary to keep submarines, with nuclear missiles on board, close to the shores of other states in order to assure the allies that assistance would be coming, if needed.

On the other hand I understand that at this stage it would be difficult to add new problems to the Law of the Sea Conference. This is a question of procedure and tactics, rather than of substance. To my mind the recommendations which I have outlined are related to the general problem of the orderly development in the oceans.

Mr. Knight: We do have another topic of great public interest on the program and the major presentation before the coffee break. So, I think at this point I would like to thank Dr. Goldblat for his presentation. It was a very stimulating, and as I say, a controversial one. I am sure he would be happy to discuss these issues with you privately after the meeting or at the attitude adjustment hour or at dinner.

Thank you very much, Jozef.

The next topic, as you all know is deep seabed mining. This issue has been discussed before in this Institute at this meeting. However, we today have John E. Flipse, who is the president of Deepsea Ventures, to discuss with us in the vein of the theme for today, the technology involved. I think there has been a great deal of misunderstanding about this among other issues involved in the negotiations, and I hope that Mr. Flipse's contribution and a description of the technology and its possible impacts on the law of the sea will serve to remove some of the confusion and doubt.

Jack Flipse is, as you all know, President of Deepsea Ventures, Incorporated, a rather notorious, famous company these days. What you may not know is that Jack has engaged in many other activities in his career, all related to the sea.

He is a sort of renaissance man. He has been a teacher on the faculty of the U.S. Merchant Marines Academy. He has been an inventor, and still is, I presume. He has been a consultant on naval and commercial ship design, and he has been a corporate manager.

Today, he brings the expertise he has developed with respect to seabed mining to us and will talk to us about the technology of seabed mining and its impact on the law of the sea.

Chapter Twelve

Deep Ocean Mining Technology and Its Impact on the Law of the Sea

John E. Flipse
President
Deepsea Ventures, Inc.

It is a pleasure to be here with you, and I appreciate Gary's "apologetic" introduction. We will see if we can live up to the billing.

First, the objective of my being with you is to bring you a case history. Let us look at an ongoing business and relate it to some of the theoretical discussions that we have enjoyed in the last couple of days.

I would like to describe briefly Deepsea Ventures itself before we talk about its program. The company was founded in 1968 as a spin-off from the Newport News Shipbuilding and Dry Dock Company when that organization was acquired, through merger, by Tenneco. We were offered the opportunity to take a six-year research program and continue it as a separate business. We were assured funding for a number of years, and we were given a set of objectives to accomplish within a time period and a budget.

Until uncertainty intervened, regarding the law of the sea, we conducted the program and met our objectives within our budgets. We give thanks to the other divisions of Tenneco for their financial support.

Second, our friends the Arabs taught the United States an interesting lesson regarding mineral resource availability. This awareness led to increased developmental activity on the part of American and foreign companies which were impressed by the extent of control of world petroleum resources. This led to an added emphasis on the availability of *hard minerals* and the ocean floor as a source.

The result was the formation of several international groups. Deepsea Ventures is involved with a joint venture known as Ocean Mining Associates, composed of a subsidiary, in each case, of Tenneco, United States Steel, Union Miniere of Belgium, and a Japanese group led by Nichimen, C. Itoh, and Kanematsu-Gosho, Ltd. These four organizations have formed a joint venture and Deepsea is under a service contract to the joint venture.

Later in the presentation I will describe the program and the work involved. Assuming that the work is successfully completed, and the risks are reasonable for the returns expected, the three parties will buy from Tenneco equal shares in Deepsea Ventures, and the final ownership of Deepsea Ventures will be with these four companies, with a minor interest in the hands of the management group.

Figure 12-1 depicts very broadly the activities of our company since its founding, and the activities projected in the years ahead. We have been concentrating on the research and development phase which was completed at the end of 1974. The research was started in 1962 under Newport News Ship-building. The tasks included locating several potential mine sites, testing components, testing a mining system, running a pilot plant of the process, identifying the products, and making preliminary economic estimates that indicated ocean mining could be a worthwhile business.

The next phase of the program, scheduled for the next three years, is described as the development and evaluation phase. We have filed a claim to a deposit of nodules, as discussed yesterday. We have the considerable task of describing the mine in mine-engineering terms and determining that there is a mineable resource that will serve as a source of metals over a reasonable length of time.

This work is at sea, highly visible, and hence the need for the claim. The R/V *Prospector* sailed yesterday. We are also going to dredge some tons of nodules from the mine site, using a prototype mining system. This will test the equipment in the deep water and will also supply us with nodules for additional work in processing.

The nodules that are recovered will be used to further test the process. We are now running a one-ton-a-day feed pilot plant. We expect to run a

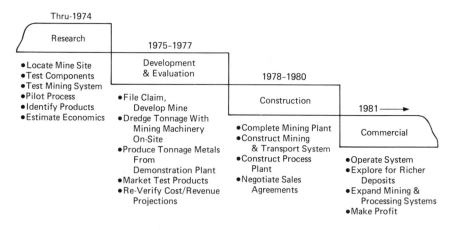

Figure 12-1. Activities of Deepsea Ventures

thirty- to forty-ton-a-day plant on a continuous basis which will demonstrate the technology of the process and also help us to estimate its costs.

The result of that operation will be metal for market testing, again, considered essential to demonstrate the technical feasibility of the program. A parallel activity will be preparation of contract plans, specifications, cost and revenue projections to determine the economic feasibility of the ongoing program.

Assuming we are successful in development and evaluation, we will enter a construction phase which we estimate will take three years. Preparation of the mining plan and evaluation of the resource at sea will continue. We will build a full mining and transport system. The processing plant will be constructed, and we will, it is hoped, negotiate favorable contracts for the disposal of the metals gained. Commercial ocean mining will then be a reality.

Figure 12-2 presents order of magnitude estimates for the Deepsea program. The "total system" that we are developing includes a sea floor deposit of a mineral resource, a dredging device to remove that material from the sea floor and bring it to the surface, a pump and duct to transfer nodules from the mining ship in a slurry to the transport vessels, and the ore carriers to transport the nodules to the beach where they will be processed in a shoreside plant.

The first step is exploration. The Research Vessel *Prospector,* which is going to be a museum piece when we are finished, is 150 feet long and 30 feet wide and was an outstanding bargain. We paid $50,000 for it and put $900,000 into its refurbishing and outfitting.

The ship has a tremendous area in which it can function. And the resource is also tremendous. I contend that the argument that nodules on the sea floor are a limited resource is nonsense. It is an issue that is introduced for an argument's sake.

We are now using "horse and buggy" equipment in our exploration program. Real-time television in the sea has been used for more than 15 years. The camera hangs on the end of a 5/8-inch cable that is 30,000 feet long. With it you can peer at the ocean bottom and observe the deposit. The results are

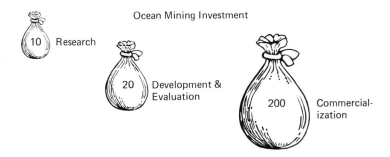

Figure 12-2. Ocean Mining Investment (in millions)

very affirmative, can be taped, and the corresponding legend serves as a record of the trip.

It is also highly desirable to take samples of the bottom so that soil-mechanics analyses can be done. Many rugged and useful coring devices exist. They take a core a couple of feet deep, giving you an undisturbed sample. You can count and weigh nodules, apply penetrometers and sheer vane measurers, and so on. Again, a very old-fashioned gadget.

We also use the same primitive dredge baskets as used on H.M.S. *Challenger.* Our more successful dredge baskets are proprietary.

May I suggest that this kind of equipment must be improved upon to enhance the economics of ocean mining. Several organizations, including the University of Georgia and AMR (the German group), have worked very hard on an in-situ analysis machine to fly over the deposit while doing analysis of the key metals, nodule concentration measurements, and mapping, all at once. Integrated navigation systems to do the navigation-mapping work will soon be available, but the assay work is likely to be done on deck for a number of years.

The Deepsea Ventures approach to the recovery of nodules from the ocean floor is a hydraulic system. We believe a hydraulic system is the most effective and have operated such a system on the Blake Plateau off the coast of Georgia and South Carolina in 3000 foot depths. We are confident that this equpiment will also work in 18,000 feet. The equipment includes a dredge head which moves along the floor of the ocean, pushing away obstructions and gathering up nodules to a suction inlet where the moving water carries them up the pipe. In the Pacific Ocean, the dredge head will be considerably more sophisticated, although the fundamental task is the same.

In handling the dredge pipe, we borrowed heavily from the offshore oil industry. In fact, we employed an outstanding service company, SEDCO. The pipe handling for the shallow test was very straightforward and simple. Handling the pipe string for a 15,000- to 16,000-foot operation is more complex, but it is not impossible. When we first proposed this technique in 1962, they laughed at us. Since then the *Glomar Challenger* not only lowered pipe to greater depths, they also twisted it and drilled into the sea floor. In ocean mining, the pipe moves with the ship, dragging the dredge head along the bottom to do its work.

Dr. Mero, who follows me on this program, will describe the continuous line bucket system. There are many other systems being proposed, but let me suggest that you keep two things in mind in evaluating them. First, whatever system is used, it must be a *continuous* system. If you look at the patent art, you will see hundreds of examples of batch systems, in which you fill a barge and it floats to the surface, and so on. These systems are fundamentally unsound, because if you are working in an area where there is a reasonable nodule deposit, the cycle time is much too long, due to the water depth. The other essential of an ocean mining system is that it be *economic.* We are convinced that ocean mining must be competitive in the open marketplace, and the economics of moving material are very, very critical.

The traditional technique for winning metals from ore is a pyrometallurgical process. It has several problems. One is that it is not too efficient. It often adversely affects the environment, but it is wonderful because it uses existing plant which may be fully depreciated. The efficiency question, I think, is open to considerable argument and improvement. Organizations that find economic ways of doing pyrometallurgy and do not have to meet the environmental requirements of the United States will probably be very competitive.

Our approach has been to use a hydrometallurgical system, one of many. The chloride system is the one we prefer, in which you change the metal oxides that are found on the sea floor into soluble chlorides; the chlorides are then pumped through ion exchange units, yielding very pure streams where the metals can be electroplated. This technology is sophisticated. It is expensive, but it is excellent from the point of view of the environment and efficiency. The overall economics will have to be determined during the development and evaluation phase of our program.

Let me suggest at this point that you now know enough to understand why a mining operation must have exclusive use of a deposit. Our approach is sufficiently sophisticated, although much less so than that of some of our competition, that if we had to go from one deposit of nodules to another deposit, it would cost us anywhere from 30 to 75 percent of our capital investment. Some of our competition contends otherwise, but I believe that when they get to the point of making technical/economic decisions, the "nature of the beast" will lead them to the same conclusion. The idea that all nodules are the same is simply not true. You must design both your mining system and your processing system to suit the deposit, and to be a continuing economic operation you must have continuing access to one deposit, hence the claim.

The output of Deepsea's plan is metallurgical grade manganese, and cathode grade nickel, copper, and cobalt. We are now happy to report that molybdenum and vanadium are also likely to be recovered and zinc is a possibility. The nodules contain about fifteen other metals which offer future potential for recovery as the technology advances.

The economics of this operation are illustrated in Table 12-1. The three mines—A, B, and C—are the last three 100- to 300-million-dollar mining investments made on the North American continent. That is the *quality* of the material that is being mined by a conservative mining industry supported by its ultraconservative banks, faced with threats of law suits by the environmentalists. On the left is the assay of the ocean ore.

Figure 12-3 gives an indication of the United States' net import level and dependency on foreign sources for these metals. I think it is more than coincidental that the government of Canada should challenge our claim. The nations of the other members of our joint venture have even more severe re-

Table 12-1. Comparative Assay (%)

	Deepsea Nodule Mine	Recent U.S.-Canada Mines		
		A	B	C
Mn	29.00	–	–	–
Ni	1.28	–	0.43	–
Cu	1.07	0.29	0.25	0.56
Co	0.25	–	–	–
Mo	0.13	0.0005	–	–
V	0.06	–	–	–
Zn	0.15	–	–	9.90

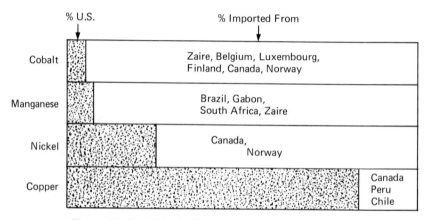

Figure 12-3. Major U.S. Sources

quirements than the U.S. It is a fact that the ocean-mining nations are on one side of the equator. I contend that there is a good deal more economics than ideology in why we should, or should not, be ocean mining.

Now let us address the politics of ocean mining. The credibility of the other party is of prime importance during a negotiation. Our problem with the Law of the Sea Conference and any optimism regarding the expected treaty has been severely affected by the credibility of the United Nations as an organization. The seating of the PLO, the treatment of South Africa, the muzzling of Israel through limitation of discussion, and similar acts by the supposedly responsible body of that organization raises serious doubts as to the validity of any long-range agreements or contracts with them.

I recently took part in a program entitled "The United Nations Comes to Texas." The meeting was held in Houston, Texas, where Mr. Waldheim, the Secretary-General of the United Nations, was greeted by a large sign as he drove from the airport to the hotel that said, "Get the U.S. out of the UN, get the UN out of the U.S." It was not a joke, and is not atypical of the feeling toward the UN in that part of the country.

The Law of the Sea Conference discussion of ocean mining is not encouraging. To illustrate how far the thinking has changed, let me quote a report prepared by SIPRI in 1968, the year of Deepsea's organization. Many of the people concerned with this report are still very much involved in law of the sea deliberations. "The Symposium makes the following recommendations, that without prejudice," et cetera, "a system of registration of claims to quiet possession ad interim be established. The object of the system would be to eliminate uncertainty as to priority of use, and subsidiary objectives would be to reduce the tension caused by unpublicized activity and a reduction and elimination of hazards to other users."

The report also suggests that we should give warnings to shipping and use reasonable standards of precision in describing the claim. It states that applications for registration of claims would be made on behalf of persons and public corporations by their governments. Please note the similarity of the above to the recently filed Deepsea Ventures claim.

Cartel fever, mob rule, and the extension of the Law of the Sea Conference into 1976 do not encourage us to seek a solution through the UN effort. The ocean-mining bills will be reintroduced in the U.S. Congress. There should be a sense in the Congress that we are not going to place ourselves at the mercy of others in regard to essential metals for U.S. industrial production. The same principles govern our partners. The fundamental trade-off will be this: A good law on the books of the United States under which a joint venture such as ours can operate, with enough protection and enough incentives to offset the taxes and the restrictions, including environmental restrictions, found in the United States, or foreign domestication.

Otherwise, we *will* go foreign. If there is any message I can bring you, it is that there are foreign nations that will welcome this kind of business activity. Will their incentives be any better than those in the United States? We have not yet seen *any,* in the United States.

Existing international law is, we feel, a good starting point. Before criticizing our claim, please read the opinion. It is worth perusing before you decide that it is not an alternative that the United States should keep open in its negotiations, an alternative that all governments may need. It may well be the only law for many, many years.

What is next? Well, we have a lot of work to do in the technical and economic areas. We have a feasibility report to prepare. It will be a masterpiece and will *not* be made public. We are very optimistic at Deepsea about the technology. Our employees are a devoted group of very competent people, and we think we know enough now to decide that the technology will work.

The economics? They are going to be good. We have been conservative. Fortunately, the people who are sponsoring our work have petroleum, steel, additional technology, and real motivation—the need for metals.

The decisions we are going to be making during the next couple of years (do not look to 1977 or 1978 for a law of the sea conference that will serve the emerging mining industry) include: Where will we domesticate this operation? Where will we put the process plant? One million tons a year or three or four times that? And, what will be the market strategy?

I sincerely believe that through the involvement of some excellent companies, not only in our joint venture, but also in the Kennecott, and the soon to be announced INCO venture, and the cooperation of many nations, solutions to the problems will be found for the ultimate good of mankind, of which, I insist, we are a part!

Discussion and Questions

Mr. de Soto: Alvaro de Soto of Peru. Thank you, Mr. Flipse, for your fascinating statement, especially the first part—including the projection, of course. I almost felt inclined at one point to apologize for the rude interruption by the law of the sea of your activities, but then after your comments on the UN, I wonder who interrupted whom. In any case, with regard to the law of the sea, there is a view very widely held by a large segment of the international community that any activities without a regime, any activities before a regime of exploitation for the seabed area beyond national jurisdiction are not legal, and even under the High Seas Doctrine, it can be argued that an exclusive claim is not tenable.

Also, without referring to the Moratorium Resolution, Principles 4 and 14 of the Declaration commit states to guarantee that their nationals will not carry out activities except under the regime—which is not yet established. So, whether or not this is a legal instrument of international law, whether or not this is binding upon states, in any case, there seems to be a political commitment on their part to prevent their nationals from carrying out such activities, and I am glad that most governments so far, at least, are not in any case encouraging such activities.

Now, if you can perhaps depart for a moment from the fundamentals of your activities and, since your address is referred to the impact on the law of the sea of deep seabed mining, I wonder whether you can tell us whether you are aware of the potential conflicts that might arise from deep seabed commercial-mining activities without a regime, and whether this has weighed at all in the plans that you have made—I believe you have set as a target date, 1981, for commercial activities—whether this is a factor that you are weighing in your plans in any way?

Thank you.

333

Mr. Flipse: It is a pleasure to respond. We are weighing the political/economic risk. In any business assessment you must come out with a "bottom line," in other words, a profit or return on investment, in order to justify the investment of some 200 million dollars.

If you cannot complete the bottom line because the political risk is overriding, then you cannot go ahead. I think that it is obvious that the strategy of the lesser developed countries, by means of moratorium resolutions, et cetera, is to make it appear that there is a very high risk. Our evaluation now, after the experience of petroleum control and the OPEC cartel, is that ocean mining may entail less risk than being subject to control by others for essential mineral resources.

The State Department has confirmed that the freedom of the seas *does* permit ocean mining, today. The U.S. voted against the several resolutions that you mentioned, and they have no legal effect. We are not breaking the law.

We certainly share your wish for a long-term solution. We would like to have a stable, workable, international treaty. We recognize that any domestic legislation will be superseded by an international treaty. We want some insurance that if the treaty makes it uneconomic for us to operate, the investment is not lost but rather is the responsibility of the U.S. government. We are sincere in wanting a stable and a predictable international regime under which to mine so that we can complete the "bottom line."

I would suggest that if there is a workable regime that permits the United States to move its technology ahead, it will be not only for its advantage but for the advantage of everyone. We should look at law of the sea as a dynamic problem, and what we need is a short interim solution. Operating under existing international law, which does permit ocean mining, then under national legislative programs until there is a treaty seems a logical course.

Mr. Knight: Are there additional questions?

Mr. Hosni: My name is Hosni from Woods Hole Oceanographic Institution, a visiting scholar there. My dear friend and colleague Alvaro, I am sure has saved me a lot of what I wanted to say, but there is something very significant in what the speaker on the seabed has just said, and that reminded me, really, of one or two things that we have been confronted with during the whole time that the Seabed Committee or the Caracas Conference was meeting, really.

He just said that the benefits that might accrue from any deep-sea mining might be substantial and all that has been said that there was little there to be concerned with is just talk for some reasons. Well, some of us have always thought this a matter of suspicion, and maybe that was one good reason why we said that some of the studies which have been produced in a hurry, including, if I may say, with all respect, one from the United Nations itself, have not generated a feeling of confidence that we could know exactly what is being said, and maybe that is a good reason to say to the speaker and others that there is good reason in waiting for more studies and not hurrying to a decision that might institutionalize principles that we do not know for how long they are going to continue.

I felt that this was one main point that the speaker had made and that it was really very important and surprising to me. The other point, I believe that the speaker said, and I do not know whether he had been advised by the State Department, but he repeated many times that it is the status of the existing rule of international law which supports their operations now and maybe for a long time that they would prevent an interference on the part of the law of the sea or any other member of the international community.

I am not sure if he is talking about an exclusive right to mine or a concurrent right to mine. If it is a concurrent right to mine, of course, we are all aware that the general notion of the freedom of the seas might support this, and it might not be a good chance for me to advance so many other legal concepts and norms that would show how weak this, even the concurrent right to mine in these areas in the present even existing circumstances of international law statutes, but I hope he can give me one good legal principle to justify his claim that an existing rule of international law supports an exclusive right to mine, and this would really go very close to what my dear friend Alvaro has just said. Is he aware of the potential conflict that might arise because of such activities within the present status of international law, even existing rules or not.

The last thing which I might like to comment on is I am not sure if now—regardless of whatever the United Nations has said or whatever resolutions have been passed—if the speaker has considered that if similar companies have been formed and wanted to undertake the same sort of activity and had resorted for protection, also, to their own governments, what security would his operations have, and in this framework, I do not know that magnificent and very promising program that he has, how far could we believe that it would be secure for him, and why has it been said for a long time that deep-sea mining is very risky, and therefore not very attractive to any one particular company, and unless there is a regime of security and very important stability in the area, no one company could risk such big capital? I wonder if his capital has not been risked, and I hope I can hear from him something about this.

Thank you.

Mr. Flipse: First, we believe that all companies entering ocean mining need reasonably competitive prices for the metals in order to justify their operations. Our estimated mining and transportation costs are $26 a ton for the nodules, compared to a couple of dollars for some low grade ores. This answer overlooks the effects on cost of transportation and infrastructure for the land mine. The basic approach, in our business as well as all free-market businesses, is that there must be profit to justify investment. There will be no opportunity for us to operate if the prices of key metals are seriously reduced over a prolonged period.

The rates of production that we foresee are amply provided for in the expected increased use of these metals. No single country should have to close down a single mine that is basically competitive. We have never contended that land mines will close, nor have the other companies that I consider our competitors. We all realize that it will be a highly competitive business, with reasonable metal prices, if we are to continue in business. The expected growth in the markets for these metals will take care of the production of one, three, or five ocean-mining undertakings before the end of the century.

Your second point, as I understand your question, addresses the consequences of going out there now and mining. The reason we feel confident is that reasonable people, be they governments, an authority, or a competitive company, have the same basic need that we do for a continued supply of nodules to feed a very expensive system. They are not going to come over and fight with us about our nodules—the deposit that we claim. They will much prefer to select another deposit, and, I assure you, there are many. Except for our investment in the claimed area, we could have claimed any one of three other areas, with almost as good a total economic forecast. We believe that anyone who goes into mining will definitely want his own deposit, a deposit he can count on to be available to him for the life of the project so that he can write off his investment. Unlike the fishing industry, the investment is so significant that you must be assured of a continued supply of ore.

Regarding exclusive rights, let me cite one example. The pearl beds off Ceylon, now Sri Lanka, run out for 20 to 30 miles beyond the coastline. The continental sea was three miles when these claims were made. So, there is a 40- to 60-year history of pearl beds on the ocean floor, beyond the territorial seas, that have been claimed for exclusive use.

Regarding the risk of investment and the physical security of the operation, we have served on the Law-of-the-Sea Advisory Committee, and we have argued this point as eloquently as we could at Geneva and at Caracas. If the UN comes up with a treaty that has a sea-floor resource authority under which the costs are predictable and the continuation of the operation is forecastable, in other words, a treaty that the ocean mining industry can live with, it would be by far the most desirable arrangement. We believe that without that the United States government is in a position in which it must pass interim legislation that will say, in effect: In the event there is a treaty, you must obey the treaty, but if it costs you money, we will make up the difference or we will pay you off and close you out. If ocean mining must be a "trading good" and be traded off, so be it. Let them pay the price. I believe that this issue probably will be in debate for a prolonged period. It is not in the United States' interests to delay further the development of this technology. The incentives are very high now because of our awareness of the petroleum situation. I sincerely thank the Arabs regularly, for if they had not shaken our management, and the management of other companies worldwide, the joint venture might have been further delayed.

Mr. Knight: I think we have time for a question or two before coffee. Sam Levering?

Mr. Levering: I think that perhaps another voice from the United States is in order at this point. I am Mr. Flipse's very friendly opponent in the Congress and have led vigorous opposition to unilateral action by our Congress, and you would know, of course, that this opposition is rather wide also, so that I am not speaking for myself only. I think though that we ought to be realistic about this situation, those of us from all over the world. These nodules are going to be mined not too many years in the future. There is not much doubt of that. Nothing that I can do in Washington and nothing that anyone else can do is going to prevent this.

The only issue is on what basis they are going to be mined and what goals you have in mind in the development of this potentially large resource. I think that for me, anyway, the goals are something like this. I think the needs of man will be best met if there is orderly mining and at a considerable rate.

In other words, I do not think simply limited or periodic mining is for the benefit of a world that needs these metals. Second, I think that they should be mined on a basis with participation across the broad area of humanity, with sharing of benefits and participation in the process, and I think this certainly is the object of the law of the sea.

They should be mined in a way that develops international law and minimizes conflict, rather than stirs up and intensifies conflict. It should be a way that is equitable and recognized generally as equitable. And from my standpoint there is another opportunity, a tremendous one here, a really unique, viable international organization can be established for the deep seabed, at least, one which has its own revenue, which has its own peaceful means of enforcement rather than war, and which has balanced and equitable means of control. This could be a precedent for arms control and disarmament that would not have the handicaps which damage present international organizations. It could be an equitable and workable and effective one.

This could be a step to prevent ultimate disaster for mankind. I think that this is a time when rhetoric and extreme positions are not in order, and a time of honest searching for what makes these objectives possible. Our organization, headed by Ambassador Goldberg, has worked out some prospective middle-ground positions on Committee I which we would be glad to share with you. It is not that we have the answers, but at least we would like to raise some questions and seek any answers you may have. I think this is tremendously important, and I hope we do not get lost in rhetoric or extreme positions.

Mr. Knight: Thank you, Dr. Levering. Before we break for coffee, as I indicated, I had promised Dr. Niemotko the opportunity to make a statement.

Commentary

H. Waldemar Nietmotko
Woods Hole Oceanographic Institution

Mr. Niemotko:　I came from Poland. I am associated at present with the Woods Hole Oceanographic Institution. My comments are intended to propose a compromise. On Monday, when this discussion had its start, the point was emphasized that progress at the Geneva conference as regards the ocean floor mining could be successfully accelerated by focusing on the managerial implementation of the common heritage issue rather than on the political one, and also that the mixed system in dealing with the ocean floor commercial development is likely to prevail.

I am concerned with reducing substantially the fears and objections of the many nations who at present suffer from a lack of technical capabilities, in case the highly industrialized negotiators elaborate a model for a constructive managerial pattern which would meet the crucial technological, financial, and environmental standards and all the risks concerned, thus preventing the international community from using any irresponsible exploitation methods in terms of marine environment protection, which model would be flexible enough to be applicable in different areas of the world, even on a regional basis.

One of the terms which was frequently in use during yesterday's and today's discussion was "risk." In Figure 12-4 you have a diagrammatic presentation of one possible approach to simplifying the complicated problem of a comprehensive and adequate allocation of the risks and liabilities concerned. This approach could also be used by a potential entrepreneur, whether a middle-sized one from an industrialized country or any entrepreneur from a developing country, as a vehicle for starting his commercial operations on the ocean floor.

The central factor in the profile is management, accompanied by financial and technological capabilities, requiring highly trained personnel. These activities are to be based on legal grounds granted by the appropriate authority, whether national or international.

The burden of risks and liabilities is still quite an unknown area,

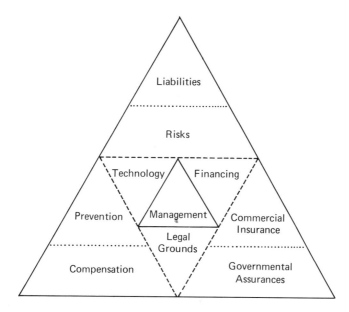

Figure 12-4. Interactions in Managing the Risks and Liabilities of Ocean Floor Exploitation

which could easily cause the inner triangle to collapse, unless it is supported both by governmental assurances and commercial insurance, and also by effective compensation and prevention systems. All the factors inscribed in the outer triangles can be characterized as a feedback type of interaction.

One of the traditionally recognized devices for coping with maritime risks is insurance. This word was merely used in the working paper A/CONF.62/C.1/L.9 submitted by Japan during the Caracas proceedings. Again a managerial approach is required to cope with the risks involved, since a significant difference is to be observed in offshore-drilling operations in comparison with the expected manganese-nodules mining, in which the raw material is itself less dangerous, but the operation as a whole can cause undetermined adverse effects on the marine environment and, the developer, as well, is subject to substantial losses through the difficult adaptation of his shoreside process plant to an alternative land-based source of the raw material.

I would appreciate Director Flipse's comments on the question, what would be the response to this international issue of Deepsea Ventures, the nation's most advanced corporation in dealing with the matters involved.

Mr. Knight: Thank you for your statement. Jack, would you like to respond to that?

Mr. Flipse: I would like to place the question in square brackets. I do not mean to be facetious. I do not really know how to respond to the question. I am sympathetic to the notion of insurance. You can be self-insured in certain areas and not in others. There is conventional insurance available, and we would never look to a government or other agency where conventional insurance was available.

On the other hand, where the risks are unique, there are many cases in all governments where the government will stand, for instance, in the development of atomic energy in the United States, in war-risk insurance and so on, where the risks are not under the control of the operators. That is the logical place for the government to assume insurance responsibilities, but I would appreciate a copy of the question, and I will try to answer it for the record.

I do not think that long a question can be satisfactorily answered off the cuff.

Mr. Knight: If I can induce you to find your seats, we will begin the last portion of today's program. Our final speaker, but still on the subject of deep-ocean mining technology, law, policy is John Mero. John is the President, as the program indicates, of Ocean Resources, Inc., of La Jolla, California. Some of you may not know, although I imagine most of you do that he wrote a book entitled *The Mineral Resources of the Sea* which was the first analysis of the technological and economic feasibility of mining manganese nodules. It is not an exaggeration, therefore, to say that John Mero is a pioneer in the field of deep seabed mining.

Mr. Mero: I would like to make some comments, first on points that were raised yesterday, one of which concerned freedom of research in the sea. I would say that it is absolutely necessary that as much freedom of scientific investigation be preserved as possible. Practically all of the mineral resources of the sea that we are aware of at the present time came about as a result of scientific work, and it was during the International Geophysical Year that a haul of nodules that happened to be rich in cobalt was discovered in relatively shallow water that led to the project that discovered that manganese nodules would be economic to mine and process. So, if scientific research is sequestered, I am afraid the world is going to be deprived of a lot of resources for a much longer period of time than it would be otherwise.

Concerning the Canadian suggestion for an extension of the 200-mile limit, if that happens, it may, unfortunately, put some of the deep-sea manganese nodule deposits within the jurisdiction of the Latin American nations, and if they considered those deposits a structure and therefore have the right to extend their borders out around that structure, their borders will extend a good share of the way across the Pacific Ocean. Once the Peruvians and the

Chileans discover that, I am sure their opposition to the mining of manganese nodules will evaporate in a very short period of time.

Concerning Deepsea's claim on the basis of discovery, several people have said that I should make a protest because, of course, Deepsea did not discover that deposit. Their right to claim it is probably better based on the fact that they have done a tremendous amount of work in the deposit, but the deposit, in fact, was discovered by an expedition of the Scripps, again, scientific research expedition in 1958 and a certain graduate student at Berkeley ran the assays in 1960 and published them in a book in 1963.

There really is a great need for developing the nodules of the deep sea, although the world is not really aware of it, and it is environmental needs that bring this about. The capital of the world, in the form of its atmosphere, is rapidly being used up by all of the crap that we have been dumping into it all these years, and some of the crappier of the substances are the sulfur dioxide gases and fumes that come about from the smelting of sulfite ores around the world. It does not make any difference where these ores are mined and processed, those fumes and that sulfur dioxide go into the atmosphere and are spread all over the earth.

The manganese nodules offer us an opportunity to cut all of that air pollution down, also to eliminate a lot of the land pollution, and because it will be a new type of technology, we can design it from the beginning to be almost totally nonpolluting and to have almost no impact, whatsoever, on the environment.

On the other side of the coin, I believe that we will be able to obtain metals like nickel, and cobalt, copper, from manganese nodules at substantially lower cost than getting them from land, and since there is an essentially unlimited amount of these things available, we will be able to start using the stainless steels which require large amounts of cobalt and nickel in building our cars and our bridges and our buildings.

We get a fantastic increase in conservation of other resources because these stainless steels are probably three times as strong and very noncorrosive. So, any kind of blockages that are put on the development of the manganese nodules are just simply stalling the day when we will be able to clean up the environment and have a better world for everybody.

Chapter Thirteen

The Great Nodule Controversy

John L. Mero
Ocean Resources, Inc.
La Jolla, California

It was almost exactly one hundred years ago that some strange, stone-like objects were found to be widely distributed throughout the three major oceans of the world. But they did not sparkle and they did not have a public relations agent so they were soon relegated to shelves either in the basement of the British Museum or, paradoxically, in the attic of the Natural History Museum in Washington. Some eighty years later an obscure graduate student at the University of California at Berkeley was asked to examine some of these stones or nodules (as they are called for they are thought to form by the agglomeration of small colloidal precipitates of manganese and iron oxides within the ocean rather than by the disintegration of larger rocks) to determine if they had any economic potential. After a year or so of study, this student came to the exciting conclusion that not only were the deep-sea nodules an apparently less expensive source of various industrially useful metals such as nickel, copper, cobalt, etc., but that, because of the nature of the deposits, it would be highly advantageous from a number of standpoints—not the least of which would be a tremendous net gain in the quality of the environment by forcing the closure of pollution-prone, land-based, sulphide mines—to obtain these metals from the deep-sea deposits. That elated and excited student could not wait to tell the mining industry of his assumed, momentous discovery. His great news was greeted by the mining industry with a monumental and almost total lack of interest. Using a few deleted expletives to purge his frustration, the student would have abandoned his work on the nodules but for two reasons: by this time he did not know what else to do for a living (a common problem with people who are frequently called pioneers in their fields); and a wise old professor took him aside and explained that any new idea so totally ignored by the mining industry must be of great value.

So it is with no little surprise that I now find the deep-sea nodules to be the center of a "great controversy." For the past few months I have been attending various conferences and listening to a mind-numbing amount of cogent, rational, and smooth talk on the law of the sea—so much so that I wonder where the controversy lies. But everyone seems to agree that one is there. I must admit that I am at a total loss to understand how the nodules could possibly be the center of anything, especially controversies such as using the nodules as a basis for an effective world government, funds for which the nodules are magically supposed to supply; or as a source of development capital or just plain spending money for the poor people of the world. Most of these "get-rich-quick" schemes are, of course, avidly supported by the potential get-rich-quickees who, in general, appear to know little or nothing about the deep-sea deposits—which, I suppose is a logical extension of one or the other of Parkinson's Laws. It would appear that the "great controversy" is an artificial one manufactured to suit the ends of those who enjoy negotiating at law of the sea conferences in the pleasant places of the earth with lots of good food and drink. Or I suppose some politician someplace, who first made the generous gift of the deep-sea nodules to the poor people of the world, was under the impression that 1.5 trillion tons of nodules times $100 per ton worth of metal equalled $150 trillion just waiting to be gathered up and distributed. This arithmetic trick can, of course, be played with almost any ton of rock on earth. It is an illusion, unfortunately, for while we may indeed be able to extract $100 worth of metals from a ton of the nodules, it will probably cost at least $30 per ton to do it and require a capital investment of up to $200 per ton of annual capacity to provide the means with which it can be done. But while the deep-sea nodules may, among rational persons around the world, have been re-relegated to the status of simply being a large, stable, potentially pollution-free, and, possibly, less expensive source of some industrially important metals, many politicians appear to have failed to be so re-relegated.

The hooker appears to be the possibility that the nodules will prove to be a less expensive source of certain metals than are the present land sources, which, if true, would pose a potential threat to the economies of some nations as they are now structured—Zaire in the case of cobalt, Cuba in the case of cobalt and nickel, Zambia and Chile in the case of copper in the long run—which nations are presently dependent on those metals for much of their foreign exchange. So these nations are doing what they can to discourage the development of those deep-sea resources. Astonishingly, they have managed to enlist the aid of many of the developing nations in their efforts. As consumers of these metals, the developing nations have the most to gain from having freely available, stable, and inexpensive sources of important industrial metals which they can produce with their own labor for use in their own markets. While the technology, as described by other speakers here today, to mine and process the nodules can, indeed, be very complicated and expensive, I believe we can do it in another way, one which is relatively simple and inexpensive and which would involve about $10 million of capital investment in a system to mine and process the nodules at a level of about 300,000 tons per year. Surely any nation that can afford to buy jet airplanes either for its military or national airlines can afford such a capital investment to mine and process the nodules. Even if it cannot develop or build the necessary equipment, many companies in the industrialized nations would be delighted to do so.

Since the day in 1957 when I initiated the research into the technical and economic factors involved in developing the deep-sea nodule deposits, I have constantly searched for the least expensive methods by which to mine and process them. I was aware of the fact that if these deposits were to serve as a source of metals for all people of the world, the poor as well as the rich, the methods of mining and processing must be kept as simple and inexpensive as possible. Even though I invented the deep-sea hydraulic dredge—the technique by which many of the companies presently involved in the development of the deep-sea deposits plan to mine the nodules—I abandoned my work with this system when it became apparent to me that the mechanical continuous line bucket (CLB) offered a much less expensive and much more simple and flexible way to mine the nodule deposits. The same can be said for the differential leaching technique versus the more expensive and complicated, albeit more efficient, differential precipitation processing technique. Thus, the system I am proposing for use by the developing nations to mine and process the nodules would involve the CLB system, a relatively simple nodule-mining method consisting of a loop of cable to which are attached, at 25- to 50-meter intervals, nodule-gathering buckets. The loop of cable is driven by a traction machine on board a surface vessel, so that the buckets descend along one side of the loop, skim over the nodule deposits on the sea floor, filling with nodules, while disturbing the sea-floor sediments as little as possible, and are hoisted to the surface on the third side of the loop. Full-scale tests of this system have already been conducted in over 4700 meters of water and additional tests are planned to prove the system on a production basis. Since the cable loop consists of plastic cables, which are naturally buoyant in seawater, the overall weight of the installed system is quite low and, thus, the system can be operated from small, highly maneuverable and inexpensive vessels. The estimated capital investment in such a system designed to produce about 1000 tons of the nodules per day is $3 million, excluding the cost of the surface vessel which is assumed to be chartered for the operation. The total operating cost of the system, assuming labor costs prevailing in the developing nations and including the cost of the chartered vessels, would be about $3000 per day; the nodule mining cost would thus be about $3 per ton. The CLB system can be scaled up to units with productive capacities as large as 15,000 tons per day with attendant lowering of the operating costs, but, of course, increasing the capital investment. A 1000-ton-per-day CLB system is not necessarily the smallest economic production unit possible with this approach; however, it is one which does produce a satisfactory quantity of metals at economic price levels.

Since the mining vessels are rather small, the nodules, as they are mined, must be transferred to ore carriers, assumed to be barges or small, 10,000-ton or so vessels. The cost of transporting the nodules to a process center would be about $0.001 per ton-mile or about $4 per ton for a 4000-mile round trip. With shoreside handling, etc., it would appear that the nodules would involve a total cost of about $8 per ton to get them from the ocean floor to a shore-based process plant.

At the process plant, the nodules would be crushed to about minus 20 mesh in a single pass through a roll-crusher and the crushed material conveyed to a leaching pond or tank in which the crushed nodule material would be mixed with sulphuric acid at proper pH and temperature levels. After a rather short leach period of ten minutes or less, the solution, containing the bulk of the copper in the nodules but relatively little of the other metals, would be drawn off. This solution would be purified by solvent-extraction removal of unwanted impurities and the resulting purified solution could be concentrated and subjected to electrolysis for precipitation of electrolytic grade copper. The copper could also be directly precipitated from solution as it is drawn from the leach pond as cement copper on scrap iron, or as copper sulphide using hydrogen sulphide, and then refined to metallic copper by standard smelting techniques. In either case the sulphur would be captured and recycled in the leaching solution.

Subjection of the nodule material in the leaching pond to sulphuric acid for longer periods of time will put the bulk of the nickel into solution and the nickel could be recovered in a manner similar to that of the copper. The estimated costs of operating such a plant are about $8 per ton of nodules handled. The estimated capital cost of the process facilities would be about $4 million assuming power for the operation can be purchased from existing power-generation facilities.

Such a system should be able to recover a minimum of 70 percent of the copper and nickel in the nodules. Assuming the grade of the nodules is 1.5 percent nickel and 1 percent copper, a conservative estimate, the value of the products recovered in this operation would be about $50 per ton of nodules processed, assuming a nickel product value of $2 per pound and a copper product value of $0.60 per pound. Assuming that additional costs of $4 per ton of nodules handled are incurred in overhead expenses, etc., the total cost of handling a ton of the nodules would be about $20 and the indicated gross net profit before taxes would be $30 per ton of nodules handled.

In addition to the $3 million capital investment in the mining system and the $4 million investment in the process system, $2 million of operating capital would be included in the total capital investment as well as a $1 million allowance for preliminary feasibility studies and the design of the mining and process systems.

The gross return on a 300,000-ton-per-year operation thus would be about $9 million or about 90 percent per year on the investment. If taxes are assumed to be 50 percent of the net, the return to the investor would be at a rate of 45 percent per year on equity. The indicated cost of the nickel and copper produced would be about $0.57 per pound of metal. This production cost figure can be reduced substantially, of course, by mining a higher grade of nodules (thus far the highest grade of nodules found in the ocean is 35 percent manganese, 1.9 percent nickel, 2.3 percent copper, and 0.2 percent cobalt) at substantially no increase in capital or operating costs, or by recovering a greater percentage of the available metals in the mined nodules, which procedure would require an upgrading in the process technology, which would, in turn, involve an additional capital investment. The ability to start with a rather low capital investment and then upgrade the facility as it generates income in excess of expenditures would seem to be a major advantage of the system herein proposed.

With respect to the location of the nodule deposits for mining, sufficient information is now available in the published literature, or is available at nominal cost from Ocean Resources, Inc., to indicate those general areas of greatest economic promise. Prior to a mining operation, of course, a rather detailed survey of the minesite would be required. It is estimated that the cost of conducting such a survey would be about $250,000, which cost is included in the mining-system capital cost. With this exploration expenditure, a reserve of five to ten million tons of mineable nodules could be blocked out covering an area of about 2000 square kilometers of sea floor. At the present time the total reserve of nodules in the high-grade zone of the Pacific Ocean is estimated at between 200 and 500 billion tons of mineable nodules.

The deposits of the nodules themselves are huge and they would accommodate as many miners as wish to mine them for hundreds of years into the future. In the light of this knowledge, it is simply not in the interests of the developing nations to oppose deep-sea mining. Of course, this observation is being made by one who has a tendency to look for rational reasons for human actions which, may be a Diogenes-type of search in the arena of international politics where emotion appears to play at least as great a motivating role as reason—if reason plays any role at all.

At any rate, by Ambassador Pardo's selfless gift of the nodules to the poor of the world in his definition of the nodules as "the common heritage of all mankind"—a relatively banal use for a poetic and rather stirring slogan which might more eloquently and rationally be used to describe man's right to a reasonable degree of freedom in his pursuit of knowledge or happiness, or of man's right to breathe unpolluted air, drink unpolluted water, and nourish himself with unpolluted and unartificial food, or, indeed, even to all resources of the earth, but not to the deep-sea nodules—we are faced with the political leaders of the bulk of the poor nations of the world, which, incidentally, include such poverty-stricken nations as Kuwait, actually believing that they own the resources of the deep sea and that they should have absolute control over the deposits. I will never understand, as long as ownership to resources is so easy to come by, why they do not announce that they own Kuwait's oil or Saudi Arabia's oil—

those resources, discovered, developed, produced, transported, processed, marketed, and used by almost everyone except the Kuwaitese and the Saudis (although they seem to derive the bulk of the benefits), in many cases squandering precious development capital. Such a resource really represents substantial wealth which can be realized in a rather short time span for the poor nations of the world. Even if we could magically produce a $100 billion plant to produce a $10 billion profit by stuffing 10 times the copper, nickel, cobalt, etc., down the world consumer's throat that he is now swallowing, there still would not be sufficient funds in that $10 billion profit to carry the bureaucracy, which would surely spring up to administer the deep-sea mining operations if the world enterprise concept is used to produce metals therefrom. I, for one, being one of the poorer people of the world, would certainly be willing to agree to give up my Pardo-given right to the nodules, if Kuwait would agree to give up its Churchill-given right to the oil which Kuwait did not discover, does not produce, does not transport, does not refine, does not distribute, and does not use.

Thus, the so-called controversy which is said to enmesh the deep-sea mineral deposits appears to me to be of the nature of an issue in a play in the theater of the absurd, with actors who are either devilishly clever and who are using the deep-sea deposits as bargaining chips in some global poker game, or are simply misinformed or misguided. As a result, the real world will go on, vaguely aware of the spectacle being played out in the law of the sea conferences, and the deep-sea deposits will be developed, first for the benefit of those who need them most, that is, the industrialized nations, not only as a stable, secure, and, one would hope, less expensive source of vital metals, but as a counter to the atmosphere- and land-polluting sulphide mines on land, which are presently the major source of these metals. But eventually, and most importantly, the deep-sea deposits will benefit the developing and poor nations who need these metals to industrialize in an environmentally sound way and who, presently, are factored out of the market due to the high cost of these metals.

Thus, I feel that there would be no better way for the developing nations to participate in the great benefits to be generated for humanity in the mining of the deep-sea nodules than for those nations to actually mine and process the nodules with their own equipment and facilities and with their own labor. Such a procedure would, of course, in the long run be advantageous not only to the developing nations, but to the industrialized nations as well, for once a competitive position is established in the deep-sea mining business, metals produced at less cost by the developing nations could be merchandised in the industrialized nations at even lower cost than those nations could produce them for themselves.

Much of the misunderstanding concerning the deep sea deposits is, like most misunderstandings among humans, based on a lack of knowledge about the subject under dispute. There is little excuse in the case of the deep-sea nodule deposits for such misunderstandings because adequate knowledge is available to all who might choose to avail themselves of it. If more effort were devoted to such education by the diplomats who argue these matters, and less effort to blind discussions at international conferences, the vision of the deep-sea mineral deposits as bringing great benefits to all people on earth could be realized without the rancor which presently appears to be developing over this subject.

Always, when any new development appears on the industrial or political scene there will be vested interests who oppose it as a threat to their position in the established system. The deep-sea deposits are no different in this regard. But with the efforts of those who are actually doing the work in developing these deposits, common sense and the common good should prevail, not always, but, certainly, I hope, it will in the case of the deep-sea mineral deposits.

Discussion and Questions

Mr. Knight: John, thank you.

I used the chair's prerogative only one time today. I would like to ask a lead-off question if you are willing to answer it, and that is, Jack Flipse alluded in his speech to the fact that there were different technologies being utilized, developed and utilized for the mining of deep seabed nodules, one of which was the CLB system. Would you be willing to describe that briefly for the audience, so that they are aware of the alternative technology?

Mr. Mero: Incidentally, I hold the patents on the first of the deep-sea hydraulic dredges, and for many years, in fact, worked with Jack Flipse, in the years 1962, and 1963, and 1964, to further develop that system for mining, and of course, I was emotionally wedded to it.

When I was approached by a Japanese around 1967, with an idea for a simple mechanical cable bucket system, I discounted it for some time until one day I received a report that he had managed to test this thing in 5000 feet of water, and his cables did not entangle, and the machine seemed to work. I took an interest in it and have since discovered that it looks like it is a very simple machine. Its estimated capital investment per unit of productive capacity looks like it should be less than one-half of the hydraulic system, and I think its operating cost will be less than one-half. So, I have since put my efforts behind promoting the development of that and organized the first of the international consortiums in 1972, which group consists of twenty major natural resource firms from all over the world, from six different nations, from Australia, Japan, France, Germany, the United States, and Canada, and such companies as International Nickel and Phelps, Dodge, and Lay Nickel and Atlantic Richfield Oil Company, all sustantial companies that are working to develop that system for mining the nodules.

In the end I do not know what system is going to win out. The one that produces a ton of nodules at the cheapest cost of course, will win out. In a start-up system, I feel the CLB system, as it has come to be known, has greater flexibility in working in changing depths of water and working over hills and around obstructions and so forth, and it is attractive for that reason.

Once you have a deposit and you get it all blocked out, and you understand it, and you understand the topography and you plan to use the same dredge in that deposit for the next twenty years, possibly a hydraulic system would be somewhat more efficient.

Mr. Knight: We are now open for questions from the floor or discussion. Yes, sir?

Mr. Hosni: I, first, certainly want to apologize for taking the floor so often, but maybe I should give more than just apologies. I happen to come from one of these Arab countries who have been described as sitting on their ass and collecting or ripping off all those revenues. I might, by way of a little, I would say correction, suggest to the speaker that his figures are absolutely wrong, and I hope that he can check on them, and if he wanted some better authority figures, I can give him how much any of these Arab countries, one by one, is taking out of any barrel of oil. This is not the subject of the debate, and I am sure I do not want to go into it.

The main thing that really concerns me now here is the very fact that if any of these countries which had that natural resource would be allowed or would be willing to trade off any of its wealth or resources in consideration of internationalizing resources of the deep sea or otherwise, this seems to me as the impression I got from the speaker. If I am wrong, I hope I will be corrected. If this is a true understanding of what I got, I really wanted to see where is the point of analogy or at least comparison.

I wish to mention that not only these resources are either in the onland territory of these countries, but so far all that has been discovered, and they are taking it is on their continental shelf, and I am sure the continental shelf doctrine has not been generated or discovered by any of these countries. As we all know, it is an American doctrine.

More than this, I really have been fascinated by the comparison, only because it reminds me of a system of law within which such rights and obligations could be traded off. If we really would like to carry this system of comparison, I am wondering if all the system of law that we are applying now would be the proper framework of our—not only negotiations and understanding—but all of our system of rights and obligations and therefore law in general.

Definitely, in the present community of nations where every country is not only sovereign over its territory but holds, also, international obligations towards others, I am not sure if this method of comparison is a proper one. However, I happen to have come across another, across the same, really, con-

352 Discussion and Questions

cept of comparison but within a different system of law, and since I am so close
to that system of law, I may be allowed to quote it. It is a concept of the Islamic law, which perceives of the whole world community as one community
owning everything, whether on land or offshore, in domestic jurisdiction as we
know it now, or international jurisdiction. With it, I have come across one very
interesting publication which states that within such framework of system of
law, you can really make a trade-off of the resources, whether they are on land
or in an international jurisdiction area. The whole concept is based on one actual
basic principle in Islamic law which I may be allowed to quote, translated from
the Arabic it says, "people of the whole world are partners in three basic things:
water, that means water resources in general; grass, or food, really, in general;
and the third is fire." By the way that signifies energy only. At that time, I do
not know if these Arabs did not know anything about energy, but, however,
they came as close as this, and this concept which is deeprooted in the whole
system of Islamic law, that perceives of world community as one. I think the
system of trade-offs like the ones that just now might be a proper one, and I
submit in our present system of law it might not.

Thank you.

Mr. Knight: Thank you. I regret that the Law of the Sea Institute, unlike the
United Nations now, in its recent decision, does not have Arabic translation
facilities. John, did you want to respond to that?

Mr. Mero: In response, of course, I have to backtrack and qualify my statement about the Arabs. Of course, the vast, vast majority of the Arabs are hard-
working people and poor people. I should have said that a small, few Arabs, and
probably few in terms of hundreds of persons, sitting around on their asses and
collecting hundreds of billions of dollars. As far as this business of internationalizing all resources of the world, I am in favor. I do not know whether the resources of the deep sea would serve as a nucleus to expand that to the rest of
the world or not, but if there were a chance that that could happen, I would be
perfectly willing to give up any of my right. I cannot give up Jack Flipse's rights
or Kennicott's rights to go out there and mine the nodules, but I would be perfectly willing to give up my right to go out and do that in hopes that the Soviet
Union and the Arab countries and Latin America and the United States and
Canada and Australia and China and everybody else would open their resources
to competitive bidding for production of any group around the world that
wanted to do it. The royalties thus generated would be distributed to every
individual on earth, not the governments but the individuals, and if the individuals within those governments thought enough about their governments, they
might share some of their money with them.

It does no good to give money to governments because they just piss
it away on useless things like airplanes and bombers and things like that.

Mr. Knight: John Knauss?

Mr. Knauss: John, I think further discussion of the political nature of these problems may be somewhat sterile in this particular setting, and I would like to return to the problem of technology.

You are one of the world's experts in the matter of technology of deep-sea mining, and you made two points which I would like you to elaborate on. I think they are particularly significant in the light of the fact that there seems to be increasing pessimism with respect to the development of a law of the sea treaty in the next few years. The first point relates to your thought there might be a minimum of fifty mine sites in the Pacific that would be available, in the sense that each mining company could have its separate mine site. Second, you made some remarks that led me to believe that perhaps the capital investment to put together a mining operation is considerably less than what we have been led to believe on the basis of the work of Kennicott, Jack Flipse's group, the Hughes' organization and so forth.

I think these have rather interesting implications; namely, what is going to be the cost to put together a mining operation? How much capital investment is going to be necessary, and how many real honest-to-goodness mine sites are there out there?

Mr. Mero: It depends on how you want to define mine site. As Jack said, they had three of them that they could have chosen, and they picked the one that they decided to file a claim on. Maybe they had some engineering basis, and maybe had a small edge over the others in depth of water or evenness of topography or continuity of deposits, but even the most conservative of the estimates of the reserve that is available in the high-grade zone of the central Pacific Ocean is somewhere in the neighborhood of 100 billion tons of ore, and if a company needs, let us say, 20 million tons to constitute a mine, that gives us enough room for 1000 different operators, each having at least twenty or thirty years in which to operate.

So, we ought to be able to carve out of that area fifty mines that do not overlap. As far as the cheaper ways of doing these things, there are lots of ways of traveling between here and New York, some of which require capital investment of $20 million, and some of which do not require any capital investment at all, except possibly $5 to buy some food while you are hitchhiking on up there.

Now, the systems that Jack was talking about, including the systems under development for Summa Corporation, or Hughes' group, Kennicott group, in general a hydraulic-mining system in differential-precipitation processes, these are processes—the processing process by which you put practically everything into solution and then differentially precipitate the metals from these solutions or separate them in some way. These things that are advocated by most companies that have studied the manganese nodules tend to be very complicated.

They are highly engineered, and thus expensive. I may have indicated some pique at the bureaucrats who do things in complicated and conservative ways to really prevent anything from happening because as long as nothing happens at all, the bureaucrat's job is secure. Engineers are, also, guilty of playing con games on the public. An engineer likes to do things that challenge his ability and therefore, very complicated and very expensive systems come out. I am sure that this is why the missiles and the rockets to the moon and everything else are done. It is because the engineers appreciate it and have more fun with those toys than they do with electric trains, and that is what is going to happen with some of this ocean-mining stuff. The systems are going to be highly engineered and complicated and thus expensive, because any engineer who is worthy of the name is going to do it that way.

While it is true that such systems, if they work properly, will produce a high recovery efficiency of the metals in the nodules recovered, although not necessarily a high recovery efficiency of the nodules in the deposits themselves—that is, Mr. Flipse will be getting 90 to 100 percent of the metals out of the nodules that he mines—it is incumbent upon these companies to do so, for the mining systems that they plan to use involve high operating costs per ton of nodules mined, and so having a considerable investment in the nodules, it is necessary for them to get as much revenue as possible from them.

Now, these high-technology, high-cost systems naturally scare the developing nations from the idea that they will be able to go out and mine and process the nodules, even though those nations probably will be able to buy that technology, at all costs, certainly less than they spend on armaments, but the way I am proposing is a simpler way and a cheaper way and one that I think that any nation that has any kind of industrial base at all can operate. I think that this can be done at a level of a few hundred thousand tons per year at a capital investment of about $10 million.

If you want me to go into the details of the breakdown of that investment and exactly how it is going to be done with the mathematics involved, I will be teaching a course at UCLA next summer, and in the two days' time that I will be teaching, may partially get into that, but I think it would simply take too much time to do that here.

Anyway, that is the outline, John, $10 million for a few hundred thousand ton per year system from which you may get 60 percent of the nickel and 60 percent of the copper, but since you do not have much of an investment in the nodules, by the time you get them ashore, you are not required to get a high-recovery efficiency, and since the deposits are relatively unlimited, it is not necessary to have a high recovery efficiency.

Part V

Obstacles to the Negotiations
and Proposals for Their Removal

Chairman
Edward Miles
Institute for Marine Studies
University of Washington

Mr. Miles: Shall we begin?

All the panelists are not up here yet, but I am told they are in the vicinity and should arrive shortly.

Since we are not home in Rhode Island this time, I might mention, for the benefit of any members of the press in the audience, that the panelists come here and participate purely in their individual capacities and should not be taken to be representatives of their governments. Unless this condition is observed, the exchanges the Institute fosters would obviously lose whatever utility they might have. That is especially the case this morning, since we have a rather provocative paper from Doug Johnston. Doug, would you proceed, please?

Chapter Fourteen

The Options for LOS III: Appraisal and Proposal

Douglas M. Johnston
Faculty of Law, Dalhousie University
Halifax, Nova Scotia

THE PARAMETERS OF CONFERENCE SUCCESS AND FAILURE

It is in the nature of things that conferences end, even lawmaking conferences as contentious as the Third UN Conference on the Law of the Sea (LOS III). Moreover, they are usually judged to have ended either in success or in failure. Usually the judgment is made solely by reference to the official objective set for the conference.

By the criterion of official objective, the First UN Conference on the Law of the Sea (LOS I), held at Geneva in 1958, was judged at that time to have been partly (or even mostly) successful, except for the failure to resolve two major issues: the maximum breadth of the territorial sea and the maximum extent of exclusive fishing rights. By the same token, its successor (LOS II), held at Geneva two years later, was judged at that time to have been a complete failure, *because it failed to resolve these two outstanding issues.* Yet by applying other criteria retrospectively, reflecting a new philosophy of lawmaking for the 1970s, LOS I is now regarded by many as more of a failure than it seemed at the time; and the alleged failure of LOS II might now be judged to have been a blessing in disguise.[1]

Not everyone accepts these judgments, but it may be conceded at least that the results of LOS III will be judged by criteria more complex than those inherent in the official objective of the conference. A failure to attain the present official objective of LOS III will not necessarily be judged in the future as a *total* failure. Indeed, even if there is no treaty outcome at all, the conference may not be judged to have been a total failure, except in the narrow, and ephemeral, official sense. LOS III is surely a lawmaking exercise which has

The author is grateful to Dr. Nicholas Poulantzas for his most helpful comments on the first draft of this paper.

acquired the urgency and impetus of a law-reform movement, shaped by sharply perceived moral imperatives and guided mainly towards the securing of equitable redress. Even without any treaty outcome the conference would still stand as the clearest reflection of important changes in the contemporary authoritative conception of world community interest in the use of the ocean. Even in this rather negative eventuality the evolution of the conference debate would have the effect of accelerating the emergence of new norms and institutions, region by region, through lawmaking processes other than the conventional device of a grand conference of plenipotentiaries culminating in a formal signing ceremony.[2]

On the other hand, it now seems very improbable that LOS III can result in an absolute success, judged by the single criterion of official objective. Diplomatic impossibility is the function of time and the issues involved. The importance and complexity of LOS III issues, the diversity of national interests, and the comprehensiveness of the agenda all conspire against the official conference objective: namely, the conclusion of a single all-encompassing convention supported by universal (or near-universal) consent. The prospects of reaching this objective are further reduced by the reluctance of many states to permit the conference to run beyond 1975, or even beyond one further protracted session of negotiations on the substantive issues. Given these attitudes, it seems impossible that all issues on the agenda can be resolved in treaty form within the projected time frame in a manner acceptable to almost all of the participants.[3]

If the official objective seems impossible, it is not very helpful simply to review the factors that make it so. It would be better to urge an extension of time for completion of this crucial lawmaking exercise. After all, the official objective of LOS III is certainly optimal: if the law of the sea is to be reformulated in treaty form, it should be done thoroughly and systematically in a manner that is acceptable to all. This is surely the ideal. But if the ideal is apparently not attainable, then attention should focus on the alternatives, the *limited treaty outcomes:* outcomes which are regarded as admittedly *suboptimal,* but attainable within the time frame of the conference in its present form. From the operational standpoint of participating delegations, then, the real prospects of conference success should be regarded as dependent on the prospects of overcoming the obstacles to negotiation directed at these limited but attainable objectives.

Even if some of the suboptimal treaty alternatives for LOS III seem to fall far short of the ideal, they cannot be discarded out of hand. In the first place, most states cannot afford the cost of indefinitely prolonged legal confusion at sea. There is too much at stake in the ocean. The weak, as usual, will go to the wall, if license prevails over regulation in the use of the marine environment and its resources. Second, and perhaps even more seriously, international law and United Nations organization cannot afford another humiliation. Dozens of UN delegations have expended a vast amount of energy and initiative in preparations for the conference. The fact, or even the appearance, of another major failure in lawmaking diplomacy would seriously demoralize those on whom we all depend to advance this important aspect of civilization.

What, then, are the alternative, more limited treaty objectives for LOS III, and how should we evaluate them?

THE LIMITED OBJECTIVES FOR LOS III

The Orthodox Alternatives

A Single Comprehensive Treaty Based on Majority Consent.   There are two fatal objections to this limited objective. First, the lack of universal or near-universal consent for such a fundamental treaty would have the political-legal effect of polarizing the world community, generating conflicts which the treaty system is designed to avert or minimize and putting intolerable strains on the law of treaties and the existing inadequate mechanisms for dispute settlement.[4] Second, the comprehensiveness of such a treaty, with a direct bearing on resource allocation issues, would serve to aggravate the gathering crisis in lawmaking which is evident in most areas of international economic law.

A Single Limited Treaty Based on Universal Consent.   This suboptimal objective might become acceptable when it had become evident that certain major issues could not be resolved by the consent of a sufficiently large majority but that universal consent had emerged, on the other hand, in support of important new principles, criteria, institutions, and procedures to the point that a regime could be elaborated in treaty form. There are, however, reasonable doubts about the feasibility and utility of such an objective. Given the interdependent nature of so many items on the conference agenda, it would be difficult to secure unanimity on the principle of severance, and even more so on the mode. There is overlapping between all three of the main committees, especially between the second and the third, and in any event there is no immediate prospect of unanimity in any of them. However, one can imagine, if not predict, the emergence of near unanimity on a declaratory type of treaty articulating several carefully worded, general principles: for example, the special interest of the coastal state, its right to exclusive resource authority in near-coastal areas, qualified rights of transit in designated areas, state responsibility to avoid unnecessary forms of pollution, and of course the common heritage of mankind. Certain criteria might also be agreed to unanimously as guidelines for applying these principles; and an international seabed authority might be established, albeit with an ambiguously worded mandate and an uncertain prospect of operational effectiveness.

In all probability, however, the unanimity of support for such a convention would be illusory, if the instrument stood alone as the sole outcome of the conference. The generality of the treaty language would invite diverse interpretations, leading to disputes which would not be easily resolved in the absence of universal consent on dispute settlement procedures. The lack of precision would give rise to numerous reservations to the instruments of ratification and accession after the signing of a limited treaty of this kind. At best it would serve as a leaky umbrella affording inadequate protection for the development of more specific rules and institutions at the regional level.

A Single Limited Treaty Based on Majority Consent.   This objective, based only on majority consent, is subject to the first of the objections against a single comprehensive treaty. Moreover, although such a treaty, being limited in scope, would not have the same degree of lawmaking significance as an all-encompassing instrument, it would presumably purport to establish new principles and procedures, and therefore be subject also to most of the criticisms against a single limited treaty based on universal consent. If the dissenting minority included countries with substantial maritime interests, as we might suppose, the effectiveness and validity of the treaty would be limited, at best, to certain regions. In short, this global outcome would be no better than the functional equivalent of a regional agreement establishing a special regime for the region.

Multiple Limited Treaties of Equal Ranking Based on Majority Consent.   This objective would presumably be considered only in circumstances where it proved impossible to secure a sufficient majority in support of any single "package" for incorporation in a single comprehensive instrument, in which case at least one of the multiple treaties would also be weakly supported. If all such limited treaties were of equal juridical ranking, the outcome would have the same flaws under the law of treaties as the four Geneva conventions concluded at LOS I in 1958, though not necessarily to the same degree of debilitation. It would have to be assumed, however, that the lack of ratifications or accessions and the proliferation of various reservations associated with this scenario would create confusion and uncertainty, endangering the interests of resource management, navigation, and environmental protection in certain regions of the world.

The Unorthodox Alternatives
Because of the objections which can and would be raised against all the above alternative limited objectives for LOS III it may be necessary to consider other possibilities. Two come to mind and each of these might be characterized as unorthodox as well as suboptimal.

A Parent Convention and Several Derivative Treaties.   The advantage of this objective is that it might be negotiated in such a way as to combine the best of a single, limited universal-consent treaty and multiple, limited majority-consent treaties, described above. The parent convention might be limited to the affirmation of general principles and criteria and the establishment of institutions and procedures, as in the former, so as to attract nearly universal support; and for those wishing to go further in the assertion of rights within specifically defined areas and in the acceptance of responsibilities, as provided for in the latter, it would be possible to do so by adopting the derivative treaties, which might be designed along functional lines to elaborate special regimes within mining, fishing, resource management, and environmental protection zones. In this way certain more specific matters that cannot be resolved by unanimous consent within the ambit of the parent convention can be removed to these functional areas of the agenda where negotiations would then proceed with the more limited and more realistic objective of attaining only substantial majority consent. By the same token, the removal of many of the most contentious issues from the ambit of the parent convention would improve the prospect of securing nearly unanimous support for that instrument.

Those states that were parties only to the overarching parent convention would have the solace of knowing that the derivative treaties, which they were unwilling to adopt, were juridically subordinate to the parent convention that all states had accepted, and would have to be interpreted and applied in a manner that was consistent with it. Likewise, national legislation adopted unilaterally by all states would be required to conform with the parent convention, whether or not they had accepted any of the derivative treaties, and this in turn would facilitate regional, subregional and bilateral treaty making between parties and nonparties to the globally negotiated derivative treaties. At one or both of these two different levels of specificity there would be linkages among all states in the form of treaty commitments designed to facilitate the harmonization of national legislation affecting the use and management of the ocean.[5]

Another benefit that might be derived from this hybrid or eclectic approach at LOS III would be that the law of the sea in the more specific subject areas could be developed more easily along the lines of functionalist logic suggested within the ambit of each derivative treaty, limited as each would be to a single set of activities and related concerns. In this way it might be possible, for example, to secure majority agreement on more precisely delineated lines of functional jurisdiction than in the case of an all-purpose or multi-purpose zone. For one thing, separate uni-functional zones established in separate treaty instruments need not be of a uniform breadth, since they would be defined in accordance with the diplomatic dynamics and the rationale operating in each context.

A Non-Treaty Instrument. It may, however, prove to be impossible to negotiate any of these limited, suboptimal treaty outcomes, or not worth the diplomatic energy that would have to be expended on them—for there may be an energy crisis in the final stages of the conference! In this sad event, the final fall-back objective would be the approval of an instrument lacking "treaty character" (say, a Caracas declaration), preferably so worded that it attracts nearly unanimous support. In short, we might be brought by events to the realization that the law of the sea cannot be reformulated within the treaty-making system operating at this stage in the development of international law.[6] A Caracas declaration lacking treaty character would, though not legally binding on the adopting states, be regarded as important evidence of emerging norms contained or reflected in the declaration, reinforcing trends in various forms of state practice such as national legislation and treaties concluded at regional levels. The principle of the economic zone, for example, may become established in the new law of the sea without any global treaty foundation or, for that matter, any nontreaty outcome of the conference, but presumably a declaration containing the principle of the economic zone would facilitate and accelerate its incorporation in customary international law.

The potential juridical significance of a nonbinding declaration is enhanced by the rules of procedure adopted for LOS III. The safeguards provided for procedure by consensus are so intricate that they would be used to obstruct a call for resort to voting procedure over a period of several weeks, perhaps as long as the remainder of the conference session.[6] The irony in this would be that procedural obstruction justified by reference to the "gentlemen's agreement" on consensus[7] could, in frustrating treaty making by voting, lead to more expeditious lawmaking on certain issues by consensus-type processes that are invoked only in the aftermath of a stalemated treaty-making conference!

An Evaluation of Conference Objectives

In summary, then, the official objective of the conference—a comprehensive convention based on universal or near-universal consent—is the most desirable but the least feasible of the objectives discussed. The diplomatic obstacles, taken in combination, are insuperable, and no realistic proposal for their removal can be entertained, given the restricted time frame of the conference. To make the problems soluble at the global treaty-making level it would be necessary to drop preconceived time limits, reorganize the agenda, and change the format of the conference. The heroic approach has failed.

The four "orthodox" limited alternatives are all at least a degree less infeasible than the official objective, but none is immune from fundamental objections. In short, none of them seems to be worth the effort that would be involved in realization. Too many problems would remain unsolved.

This brings us, by default, to the two other limited alternatives characterized as "unorthodox." Of these, the second seems to me less desirable than the first, representing a course to be counseled only in final despair. It is, of course, the less complicated and, therefore, more attainable of the two. Most states may prove to be willing *in extremis* to trust in nontreaty lawmaking processes despite the dark uncertainties associated with them. We might now be at a stage in the history of the law of the sea when basic lawmaking has to go through a declaratory phase, in which the primary purpose is to clarify community intentions or aspirations rather than to secure individual commitments of a strictly binding "contractual" character.[8] To attempt to secure innumerable binding pledges of this kind in the new charter law of the sea may be to overburden the treaty mechanism now operating in the world community.[9] In this case, of course, the lawmaking processes of the United Nations have been subjected to unfair abuse in the last seven years.

I am reduced, then, by my own premises and logic to the conclusion that a parent convention and several derivative treaties represent the least objectionable blend of feasibility and desirability, and the only option for Caracas that deserves a close examination from the point of view of obstacles to negotiation. Before this, however, the proposal should be developed.

THE PROPOSAL

At the Geneva session of LOS III in Spring 1975 it will become apparent to all that the official objective of the conference cannot be attained within the projected time frame. There are only two alternative courses of action to save the conference from absolute failure, in the official diplomatic sense: either extend the time available for reaching the desired kind of treaty outcome, or reduce expectations to one of several alternative, suboptimal objectives. Of those reviewed, the best (or the least objectionable) is universal (or near-universal) consent to a parent convention, and the largest possible majority consent to a number of more specific, functionally defined treaties which would be derived from the parent and juridically subordinate to it.

The balance of the Geneva session and the months following should be spent in attempts to agree on the language to be incorporated in the parent convention. The conference would come out of committee during this period but stay in plenary until the delegations had agreed to send an approved text of draft articles for the parent convention to the drafting committee. The latter would endeavor to complete its work on this text by the end of the 1975 session of the UN General Assembly, so that a signing ceremony at Caracas could be held early in 1976.[10]

It is also proposed that the conference should be reconvened later in 1976 to continue the work of the committees in light of the Caracas Convention just signed, so that more specific issues can be further negotiated. The committees should be rearranged at that stage so as to reflect different functional areas: say, marine resources, navigation, and environmental management.

It is crucial to the attempt at drafting a parent convention of the kind proposed that it is generally understood that the purpose of such a convention is to strike a balance between competing but legitimate interests. It is vital in particular that the new charter should be drafted in such a way that it can be trusted by everyone as a reasonable and rational accommodation of inclusive and exclusive uses of the ocean. The most striking feature should be the *complementarity* of elements in the new regime. An imbalance *either* on the exclusive side *or* on the inclusive side should be avoided as destructive of the overall principle that the ocean *as a whole* belongs to the common heritage of mankind.

   With this in mind, it is suggested that the drafting might proceed by including at least the following nine principles:

1. *The ocean as a whole, both within and beyond limits of national jurisdiction, belongs to the common heritage of mankind.* (The ocean is the most critical natural component of the life-supporting environment. Accordingly, even within the territorial sea, the coastal state's right of use, though sovereign, is held in trust for all succeeding generations and is subject to the coastal state's responsibilities to the rest of the world community.)
2. *All states have both the obligation and the right to participate in global, regional, and other international organizations designed to protect the marine environment and its resources.* (Landlocked states should be encouraged to participate in such organizations, especially where it can be shown that their interests are affected by the misuse or overuse of marine resources).
3. *All coastal states have a special interest in the resources of the coastal sea and adjacent marine areas, which entitles them to establish extraterritorial zones of special interest which may not exceed 200 miles in breadth.* (Within these zones coastal states may enjoy exclusive rights to nonliving resources and exclusive or prior rights to living resources.)
4. *The baselines for these zones of special coastal interest should be drawn in accordance with the criteria prescribed in the parent convention, including especially the primary consideration of maintaining a reasonable balance between inclusive and exclusive authority in the law of the sea and the duty to avoid unreasonable entrenchment upon the domain assigned to the International Seabed Authority.* (These criteria might otherwise be similar to those prescribed in the 1958 Geneva Convention on the Territorial Sea and Contiguous Zone and subsequent rulings of the International Court of Justice, but an adjudicative procedure of some kind would have to be provided to deal with the problem of "special circumstances" in individual cases.)
5. *All coastal states have a special interest in the maintenance of the productivity of the living resources out to the margin of the continental shelf.* (In areas where the shelf exceeds 200 miles in breadth the coastal state has not only *sole* managerial responsibility within 200 mile limits but also *primary* managerial responsibility beyond these limits out to the margin. In discharging the latter responsibility the coastal state is under a duty to consult with neighboring and adjacent states, as well as international

organizations accepting a managerial role in these marginal shelf areas.)

6. *The coastal state has a prior right to exploit the nonliving resources of the continental shelf beyond 200 mile limits, where geography permits, provided it is willing to participate in revenue-sharing arrangements with the International Seabed Authority.* (Criteria for helping the authority to devise reasonable *formulae* for revenue-sharing purposes would, preferably, be included in the parent convention.)

7. *Subject to other principles prescribed in the parent convention, the International Seabed Authority has sole authority over the uses of the seabed and the deep ocean floor beyond the seaward limits of extra-territorial zones of special coastal interest.* (The authority would be responsible for entering into negotiations with enterprises and the states with which they are linked, so that the appropriate forms of technology can be brought to bear on the resources of the seabed and the deep ocean floor within the authority's domain.)

8. *None of the principles prescribed in the parent convention shall be construed as entitling the Authority or any state or organization to interfere unnecessarily or unreasonably with the normal flow of international navigation, especially in areas recognized to be established sea lanes, nor with the laying of cables and pipelines; nor shall they be construed so as to impair the freedom of overflight outside territorial limits.* (Ideally, a procedure should be set out, whereby complaints of violation of this principle can be heard, prior to legal proceedings in national or international courts.)

9. *Coastal states which are especially vulnerable to the threat of catastrophic spillages near their coast or directly exposed to the effects of frequent incidental discharges of polluting wastes are entitled, subject to their treaty obligations, to take exceptional preventive measures, commensurate with the actual risks and injuries involved, in appropriate areas of the marine environment.* (The parent convention should include criteria to help determine a priori what might be deemed to be an "especially vulnerable" coastal state: by reference, for example, to the volume of shipping, the types of cargo carried, the concentration of natural hazards, the hydrographic characteristics of the environment, and the technical difficulty of rehabilitating the area after the fact of pollution. The convention should also include criteria for determining, in a given set of circumstances, what are "appropriate areas of the marine environment".)[11]

The proposed parent convention should also provide for the establishment of the international seabed authority, and preferably for resort to one of several alternative schemes for dispute avoidance *and* dispute settlement. The language chosen to define the powers of the authority and the applicability of the dispute treatment provisions must not be so specific as to prevent the convention from becoming a near-universal instrument.

Because of the importance attached to securing universal consent, or the closest possible approximation, it is strongly recommended that the proposed parent convention should be subject to signature only, so that it comes into force immediately after the signing ceremony at Caracas.[12] Ideally, also, the convention should expressly provide that a signature is invalid if it is accompanied by a reservation with respect to any of the general principles, since this would have the effect of destroying the balance inherent in the text.

OBSTACLES TO THE NEGOTIATION OF A PARENT CONVENTION

The obstacles to negotiating a parent convention, as described above, are much the same as those that would have to be overcome in negotiating a limited treaty or a nontreaty declaration that could secure virtually unanimous support. Success would depend, first, on the possibility of persuading everyone that it is desirable and worthwhile to articulate in a declaratory type of instrument a number of general principles, criteria, and institutional procedures that are central to the "new law of the sea"; and second, on the possibility of reaching general agreement on the selection and characterization of principles, criteria, and institutional procedures that deserve to be so affirmed. On the first of these problems, the chief difficulty lies in diversity of historical perspective; on the second, in diversity of national interest.

Historical Perspective
The purpose of the parent convention would be to provide a new legal foundation for emerging maritime regimes, not to create the regimes themselves in specific detail. A government's attitude to this kind of undertaking will be strongly colored by its approach to the interpretation of history in general and by its "legal philosophy" in particular. An attachment to exploitative theories of history, however simplistic or sophisticated, is conducive to trust in the general contemporary judgment that the classical doctrine of the freedom of the high seas was exploitative in purpose and effect. From this perspective, the major purpose of the declaratory instrument might be variously described: to reduce the dominance of the current maritime powers; to check abuses by shipping and distant fishing states; to provide for benign discrimination in favor of developing states in the use of marine resources; or to protect the threatened interests of coastal states, especially those in the developing world.

A parent convention reflecting this attitude is not likely to be acceptable to the "target states" if it seems unreasonably restrictive in intent. They will certainly not lend their signatures to a new law which is designed to be used as an instrument of revenge against themselves. The instrument will have to reflect the need to maintain a juridical balance—albeit a new balance—

between inclusive interest and exclusive interest, even in the knowledge that developed nations, by definition, are able to participate more fully than developing nations in the benefits of inclusive interest.

On the other hand, the developed states should be persuaded that we are all passing through a constitutive, or reconstitutive, phase of lawmaking, not least in the law of the sea, and that declaratory instruments such as the proposed parent convention are an important and necessary feature of legal development at this point in history. Skepticism regarding the utility of such instruments should be tempered by the realization that they need to be accompanied or followed by more specific, rule-making treaties designed to reduce uncertainty about interpretation and application of a parent convention.[13] In envisaging the future development of the law of the sea along these lines it is not too helpful to resort to analogy with national experience in constitutional development. The Austinian model and other "vertical" models of lawmaking are very clearly inapplicable to the world community, in which power and other values are too diffuse to sustain a single, centralized, and sufficient system of judicial and other rule-making tribunals of the kind that assist in constitutional development in the national community. Some degree—it is to be hoped, a tolerable degree—of regional diversification may be expected in the interpretation and application of a parent convention in the law of the sea. The potential damages inherent in this prospect should, of course, be fully weighed during negotiations prior to adoption of the parent convention at the global level. Specifically, it is important that this proposed instrument should contain guiding criteria and procedures for the purposes of interpretation and application, even though it proves impossible to get universal agreement on an actual mechanism for the settlement of disputes.

On suspects that successful compromise diplomacy directed at the kind of parent convention I am proposing would result in something less than wholly satisfactory treaty language. One also hopes, however, that relative dissatisfaction with the outcome would not be so strong that it prevents any state from adopting it. Dissatisfaction with the parent convention should instead be regarded as a legitimate concern and motivating factor in the negotiation of the derivative, and more specific, rule-making treaties which should begin immediately after the conclusion of the parent convention.

Perhaps the strongest objections to the above proposal will come from conservative lawyers who are disturbed by the present trend towards lawmaking through the medium of declaratory resolutions introduced and voted on in the UN General Assembly. To avoid unnecessary and sterile debate on the "binding" juridical character of such instruments, it is suggested that use be made *both* of the "consensus" mechanism available in the Assembly *and* of the "consent" mechanism of a treaty-signing ceremony attended by the plenipotentiaries of all states. This might be done through the following sequence of objectives:

1. *Geneva, Spring 1975:* agreement by the conference in plenary session on draft text of the kind suggested to be submitted to drafting committee
2. *Geneva, Summer 1975:* refinement of the draft text, under the terms of Rule 53, in the form of a draft resolution prepared for presentation to the UN General Assembly
3. *New York, September 1975:* meeting of the main committee of the conference for the sole purpose of agreeing to submit the draft resolution to the UN General Assembly
4. *New York, November 1975:* debate in the UN General Assembly on the substance of the resolution, resulting in a vote of approval and the decision to reconvene the conference
5. *Caracas, May 1976:* the drafting committee reconvenes in order to put the approved resolution in the form of a formal treaty (the draft Caracas Convention), and to make it ready for signature in the official languages of the conference (Chinese, English, French, Russian, and Spanish)
6. *Caracas, June 1976:* the conference reconvenes in plenary: first, to sign the Caracas Convention; second, to rearrange the agenda and committee structure in such a way as to facilitate the negotiation of the proposed derivative treaties; and third, to resume discussion in these new committees of the items outstanding and any new items introduced in plenary.[14]

National Interest

It may be objected, on the other hand, that the diversity of national interest reflected at LOS III precludes the possibility of gaining nearly unanimous consent to the inclusion of general principles, criteria, and procedures of the kind suggested for the proposed parent convention. It should be emphasized once again, however, that the proposal is admittedly born out of frustration and is not intended to represent an optimal outcome. It rests on the optimistic assumption that most extremist states will be willing in the final resort to concede a little in order to establish a universal treaty foundation for the new law of the sea, which will accommodate and balance competing considerations in the interest of the world community as a whole. Naturally I am reluctant to believe, before the effort is made, that our statesmen are not equal to the task.

The credibility of the proposed convention depends finally, therefore, on the possibility of common agreement on how to describe the new balance in general terms without violence to sharply perceived interpretations of national interest. The formulations suggested above will be difficult for some states to accept, even on the all-important assumption that they are willing in the first place to enter into negotiations for an outcome consisting both of a parent convention and several derivative treaties. But the mix of principles suggested, appropriately amplified and refined in treaty language, may represent roughly the range of norms necessary to hold the parent convention together as a sufficiently comprehensive declaration of general principles. The drafting of these principles would be directed at the aim of reflecting and accommodating in general terminology all legitimate forms of national interest in the ocean: the interest of the disadvantaged, in principles 1 and 7; that of the landlocked, in principle 2; that of the coastal state, in principles 3, 5, and 6; that of the "special case," in principle 4; that of shipping and aviation states, in principle 8; and that of the environmentally vulnerable, in principle 9.

Some of the states in these categories will no doubt find a parent convention of the kind proposed inadequate for the advancement and protection of its most vital interests, even on the assumption that the conference might be able to agree on somewhat more specific language than that suggested in this paper. Ideally, no state should be entirely satisfied with the final draft of that instrument, so that each state is sufficiently, though variously, motivated to enter into the second stage of negotiations directed at the proposed derivative treaties dealing with specific issues along functional, or other mutually acceptable, lines.

CONCLUSION

The comprehensive approach to LOS III has proved to be overwhelming. The lawmaking circuit has been overloaded and we are all heading for a "blackout" when the fuse blows. The ideal solution lies in extending the time limit for the conference, but as this is likely to be regarded as politically unacceptable by many states it is necessary to consider various suboptimal alternatives to the present, official optimal objective of LOS III. The objective proposed here is obviously far from ideal, but it seems to me the best, or the least objectionable, method of saving the United Nations from what most of the world is likely to regard as a major failure in lawmaking, and the second successive failure of this kind in the law of the sea.

It is possible that some states would prefer one of the other suggested suboptimal outcomes, other than the one proposed here. If so, one hopes that their preferences are based on a generous perception of world community interest that allows for an accommodation of diverging national interests, and not on a narrow and short-range conception of their own national interests. Above all, one hopes most earnestly that the unattainable official objective of LOS III is not allowed to induce a stalemate, which is still avoidable. In the final analysis, there is no kind of immediate national gain that ranks with the national interest in the peaceful and progressive development of the legal community of nations.

NOTES

1. These "revisionist" sentiments are associated chiefly with developing coastal states, by whom the proposed economic zone or patrimonial sea is envisaged as an extension of their economic base which would

give them a protected opportunity to close the gap between themselves and the resource-rich countries. The same sentiments are
also reflected in the claims now made by states in three other
categories: first, the disadvantaged states which see in the International Seabed Authority a new and potentially promising source
of badly needed revenues; second, those states which are claiming
special consideration by virtue of "special circumstances" of one
kind or another; and third, the environmentalist states, which are
pressing for a bolder and more comprehensive approach to the
problems of marine pollution prevention and control. For all four
categories, their present claims would be more difficult to advance
in the teeth of a "successful" LOS II which had, for example,
limited the territorial sea to six miles and exclusive fishing rights
to twelve.

2. This view, that the "process" is more important than the "product," rests
on the premise that the *primary* purpose of an international lawmaking conference today is to elicit the *consensus* of the world
community, and that the soliciting of *consent* from each of the
states is only the secondary purpose. This premise is not so radical
today, in 1975, as it was several years ago when the UN Seabed
Committee began its preparatory work for LOS III.

3. This does not necessarily mean that failure to achieve the official objective
of LOS III was inevitable, and that it was a mistake to adopt the
comprehensive approach in the first place. The reasons for this
approach were fairly compelling. *See* Riyadh al-Qaysi, "The Prospects for Agreement," in *The Law of the Sea: A New Geneva
Conference,* ed. Lewis A. Alexander (Proceedings of the Sixth
Annual Conference of the Law of the Sea Institute, June 1971),
p. 173, note 10. Possibly the time devoted to conference preparations was not put to the best use. See J.L. Hargrove, "A Third Law
of the Sea Conference: Machinery and Strategies for Reaching
Agreement," *Ibid.,* pp. 147-52.

4. *See* Douglas M. Johnston, "Some Treaty Law Aspects of a Future International Fishing Convention," prepared for the Working Group on
Living Marine Resources, Panel on the Law of the Sea, The American Society of International Law [publication pending].

5. The parent convention envisaged here, in the form of a (nearly) universally
signed treaty, would have a more evidently "binding" character
than the UN "charters" adopted by resolution of the General
Assembly, such as the recently adopted Charter on the Economic
Rights and Duties of States. The relationship between the proposed
convention and the derivative treaties at the global level would be
similar to that proposed between a *traité cadre* and a *traité loi*
within the European Community at the regional level, designed to
harmonize future treaty-making within the community as well as
future statute-making by the component states. *See* Dionyssios M.
Poulantzas, *Aspects juridiques de l'association prevue par l'article*

238 du traité de la Communauté Economique Européenne (1959), p. 9. It has been argued that the 1958 Geneva Convention on Fishing and Conservation of the Living Resources of the High Seas was intended to have the character of a *traité cadre* providing only a general scheme of conservation principles, the implementation and enforcement of which would be left to the parties. For this view, *see* Nicholas M. Poulantzas, *The Right of Hot Pursuit in International Law* (1969), p. 181. The failure of the 1958 Convention can be attributed to a number of defects, not the least of which may be, in retrospect, the lack of a more specific, "derivative" fishing treaty which would have provided the linkage between a potentially global *traité cadre* and divergent national measures for implementation and enforcement.

6. See Chapter VI of the Rules of Procedure adopted at the twentieth meeting of the Third UN Conference on the Law of the Sea on 27 June, 1974, and amended at its fortieth meeting on 12 July, 1974 (UN Doc. A/CONF. 62/30/Rev. 1). Various kinds of "obstructions" are provided for, especially, in Rules 37, 39, 42, 43, 44, and 45.

7. See Declaration incorporating the "Gentleman's Agreement" made by the president and endorsed by the conference at its nineteenth meeting on 27 June, 1974 (*ibid.,* Appendix).

8. In the language of policy science, it might be that the constitutive process today in the world community is characterized by common agreement that the primary need is to reformulate the basic public order goals at relatively high levels of abstraction through a variety of modalities, including quasi-legislative global charters. "The basic goal values postulated for preferred public order cannot of course be representative only of the exclusive, parochial values of some particular segment of the larger community of mankind, but such values can admit a very great diversity in the institutional practices by which they are sought and secured. In different particular communities and cultures very different institutional practices may contribute equally to overriding goals for the increased production and sharing of values. When overriding goals are accepted, experiment and creativity may be encouraged by the honoring of a wide-range of functional equivalents in the institutional practices by which they are sought." Harold D. Laswell and Myres S. McDougal, "Criteria for a Theory about Law," 44 *So. Calif. L. Rev.* 362 (1970–71), p. 394.

9. Johnston, *supra,* note 5. *See also* Douglas M. Johnston, "The Regional Consequences of a Global Fisheries Convention," in *Fisheries Conflicts in the North Atlantic: Problems of Jurisdiction and Enforcement,* ed. Giulio Pontecorvo (1974), pp. 35–51.

10. For a suggested timetable, *see* page 20, *infra.*

11. Preferably, these general principles would be elaborated in such a way as to acknowledge a normative evolution through other forums like the UN Conference on the Human Environment, held at Stockholm

in 1972, where principles of state responsibility related to the
preservation of the marine environment were approved.
12. *See* page 20, *infra.*
13. What is suggested here is not entirely novel. An analogy might be drawn,
for example, with the 1967 Treaty on Principles Governing the
Activities of States in the Exploration and Use of Outer Space,
Including the Moon and Other Celestial Bodies. Article 5 of this
instrument, which is a kind of "parent convention," was later
developed in more specific detail in a kind of "derivative" treaty:
namely, the 1968 Agreement on the Rescue of Astronauts, the
Return of Astronauts and the Return of Objects Launched into
Outer Space. Similarly, Article 6 and other parts of the 1967 Treaty
were implemented more specifically through the 1971 Convention
on International Liability for Damage Caused by Space Objects.
14. It is possible, of course, that the drafting committee may be able to work
more quickly than assumed here towards a final text in treaty form,
so that it could be attached as appendix to a UN General Assembly
in the fall of 1975 and voted on at that time. In this case there would
be little, if anything, for the drafting committee to do between
the Assembly session and the Caracas meeting of plenipotentiaries
in the following spring. This would bring the lawmaking procedure
closer to that which has been adopted in recent years in the fields
of outer space, arms control, and economic and resource issues.
On the other hand, the timetable suggested would have the advantage
of rendering largely irrelevant the potentially divisive issue between
lawmaking by consensus and lawmaking by consent.

Mr. Miles: Thank you very much, Doug.
We had hoped to have with us today Dr. Djalal of Indonesia, but
he at the last moment was not able to attend and Dr. Kusumaatmadja also was
not able to stay on, so the first panelist will be Dr. Leonore B. Emich of the
Austrian Mission to the United Nations.

Panel Discussion

Leonore B. Emich
Austrian Mission to the United Nations

Ms. Emich: Before making some comments on the paper presented by Professor Johnston, I would like to thank him for having worked on a topic which will be of paramount importance to all of us very soon, but which so far has hardly been discussed openly. Each of us has certain preferences for the outcome of LOS III and these preferences may differ according to the special interest in the subject matter. I find it very useful to discuss already at this stage various alternatives for a "successful" (in the broadest sense of the word) conclusion of the conference and I am very grateful to Professor Johnston that his paper gives us an impetus in this direction. The comments I will make are my own views and do not necessarily reflect the views of the Austrian government.

I will not review the orthodox alternatives proposed by Professor Johnston and I will refrain from commenting on the legal implications of his unorthodox alternative, the "parent convention," on which the author expanded so elaborately this morning. In my view suboptimal solutions need not necessarily be considered at this moment, which might in itself be an unorthodox approach. However, I would like to make a short comment on the analogy the author draws between his idea of a "parent convention" for LOS III and the questions of outer space as dealt with by the United Nations. In fact there is a certain similarity between "our" Declaration of Principles (Resolution 2749 [XXV]) and the Declaration of Legal Principles Governing the Activities of States in the Exploration and Use of Outer Space, adopted by the General Assembly on 13 December 1963. The provisions of this Declaration were later embodied in the Treaty on Principles governing the Activities of States in the Exploration and Use of Outer Space, Including the Moon and other Celestial Bodies, which was approved by the General Assembly on 19 December 1966 and came into force on 10 October 1967. The similarities of the two declarations are striking; both contain for example the following principles: the principle that the exploration and use of the areas concerned shall be carried out for the benefit of all mankind (paragraph 7 of Sea-Bed Declaration and paragraph 1 of Outer Space Declaration); the principle that the areas concerned are open to use by all states (paragraph 5 of Sea-Bed Declaration and paragraph 2 of Outer Space Declaration); the principle that the areas concerned are not subject to national appropriation by any means including claim of sovereignty (paragraph 2 of Sea-Bed Declaration and paragraph 3 of Outer Space Declaration); the principle that activities in the areas concerned shall be conducted in accordance with international law, including the Charter of the United Nations, in the interest of maintaining international peace and security and promoting international cooperation and mutual understanding (paragraph 6 of Sea-Bed Declaration and paragraph 4 of Outer Space Declaration); the principle that in their activities in the areas concerned states shall pay due regard to the corresponding interests of other states (paragraph 12 of Sea-Bed Declaration and paragraph 6 of Outer Space Declaration); and the principle that states shall bear responsibility for national activities in the areas concerned, whether undertaken by governmental agencies or nongovernmental entities and that the same responsibility applies to international organizations and their members for activities undertaken by them in those areas (paragraph 14 of Sea-Bed Declaration and paragraph 5 of Outer Space Declaration). Another principle in this category which did not appear in the 1963 Declaration but was included in the Outer Space Treaty is that states shall encourage (or promote) international cooperation in scientific investigation (or research) in the areas concerned (paragraph 10 of Sea-Bed Declaration and Article I of the Outer Space Treaty).

Apart from these similarities of the general principles covering both the regime of the seabed and the regime of outer space, there are, however, also some basic differences. One major difference derives from the fact that while little is yet known about the resources of the moon and other celestial bodies, we know that the seabed and the ocean floor are rich in minerals and other resources and some have, as we heard yesterday, the technological know-how to exploit them. I hardly need to mention that the interests of states in law of the sea questions differ depending on their geographical location (coastal states, landlocked states, states with broad shelves, archipelago states, etc.), while in the regime of outer space there does not exist a separate category of states that might be called space-locked states—which might make the task easier for outer space!

Having made these brief remarks I would like to concentrate on two items:

1. The necessity of concluding LOS III with a *viable* convention, whatever form this convention might have

2. Some essential elements which a convention as well as a "parent convention"—if this course of action is followed—should, in my view, comprise.

As regards the first point, I did not have the opportunity to follow the work of the Seabed Committee from its very beginning as did some of the distinguished participants in this conference. But reading the committee papers and reports and listening to the discussions in the various subcommittees of the Seabed Committee in the last years gave me some idea of how substantially the subject changed since it was first suggested by Ambassador Pardo in 1967. During the following years, states participating in the work of the Seabed Committee became more and more aware of the difficult technical and some-times entirely new subjects, for example, the concept of the economic zone, with which they had to deal and formulate their opinion. The Sea-Bed Committee had only 91 members as compared to more than 140 states which participate in LOS III. Thus more than 50 states had the difficult task of getting acquainted with the various subjects dealt with in the Sea-Bed Committee before or while participating in the conference. Taking this into account I cannot share the pessimistic views about the outcome of the second session of the conference in Caracas. It is in my view simply not possible to deal with such a complex subject of importance to all states around the globe without giving all of them enough time to get thoroughly acquainted with the various facets of the problem. This simply takes time. I understand that it creates difficulties for some countries that have actively participated in the work of the Sea-Bed Committee and have discussed several questions over and over again. I under-stand that they favor the end of the long discussions as quickly as possible, first because we might be overtaken by events and furthermore because it becomes increasingly difficult for small countries—and among them certainly also my country—to send delegations for eight and ten weeks to a conference without any substantial progress being made. But despite these difficulties I would prefer an optimal solution to a suboptimal, even if it takes more time, not an unlimited amount of time, but some more time. So far we have not agreed on a specific time frame, but my assumption is that we would like to finish our work as soon as possible, preferably in Geneva. But even sticking to a time frame is not as important in my view as the need to achieve a *viable* treaty. The general theme of this conference is "Caracas and *beyond*" and it should be our task in participating in LOS III to seek to avoid potential sources of future conflicts. This seems only possible if we take into account the interests and the needs of all states and if we strive for a well-balanced treaty. The optimal conclusion of LOS III for me would be a single comprehensive convention based on universal or near universal support. This is admittedly not easy to attain, but given the difficult interdependence between the various subjects, I have serious doubts whether the suboptimal conclusion of a "parent conven-tion" is much easier to work out and whether we could not, within the timetable suggested by Professor Johnston up to June 1976, be able to reach the optimal conclusion.

In reference to the second item, I would, nevertheless, like to make some comments on the essential elements which a "parent convention" should contain. Any treaty has, as Professor Johnston rightly points out, to strike a balance between competing but legitimate interests. One task of the conference has certainly to be the harmonization of two opposing tendencies, one being the extension of national jurisdiction by a number of coastal states and the other being the emergence of the new juridical notion of "common heritage of mankind." This concept represents a new stage in the development of the law of the sea, supplementing the old notion of *res communis* and thereby transforming the principle of "free use for all" into the principle of "use for the benefit of all." This very positive development of modern international law should not be offset by creating at the same time vast exclusive zones destined for the sole use of a limited number of states. My friend and colleague from Peru, Alvaro de Soto, referred the day before yesterday to the importance to developing countries of both notions, national sovereignty and the "common heritage" principle. I share his views about the content of the common heritage principle (nonappropriation, no claims of sovereignty, equitable sharing, joint participation, etc.), but I cannot agree that the extent of the international area is less important in this context than the principle itself. If we do not want the common heritage principle to remain a dead letter, we have to implement the spirit of this concept, which would not only have to be mentioned, but be reflected throughout a treaty so as to provide for the creation of an economically meaningful international area with enough significant resources left to be shared among all states in the near future. Obviously the question of limits is very important in this connection.

One important principle, which would also have to be reflected in any form of convention, would be the principle of equitable sharing in the living and nonliving resources in the area adjacent to the territorial waters of a coastal state and outside the international area. In the course of the second session of LOS III, the participation of landlocked States in the exploration and exploitation of the living resources in fishing zones of neighboring coastal states on an equal basis as nationals of coastal states has been supported by a large number of countries. I would like to mention particularly Article 9 of the Declaration of the OAU in this context. This certainly represents a major but only a first step towards an equitable distribution of benefits for all members of the international community. A certain category of resources, namely the nonliving resources, cannot be excluded from sharing and Austria has supported a paper to that end in Caracas. I have to stress, however, that in the revenue-sharing no distinction between coastal and landlocked States should be made: any state participating in the exploitation of the nonliving resources should contribute a fair share of its revenues to the international community for the ultimate benefit in particular of the less-developed members of the international community.

There are certainly more comments to be made on the various principles put forward by Professor Johnston. I could probably agree with a new idea in his first principle, that the ocean as a whole, even within the territorial sea of a coastal state belongs to the common heritage of mankind, provided this does not prejudge the possibility of plurality of regimes outside the territorial sea. But specifically I would like to comment on Principles 5 and 6 which imply certain rights of coastal states outside an eventual economic zone of 200 miles up to the continental margin.

We all endeavor to create a new law of the sea because we feel that the rights and interests of all states are no longer adequately dealt with in the existing legal framework. The rules relating to the continental shelf as embodied in the 1958 Convention do not adequately take into account the interests of certain countries, but they altogether ignore the interests of landlocked states. This is somehow understandable: the famous proclamation of September 1945 emanated from a country which did not have to take into account the interests of any landlocked state in its geographical area and due to the general political situation any misgivings against the principle as such were not likely to be voiced. Furthermore, at the 1958 Geneva Conference, of 86 participating states, only 10 were landlocked, while 149 States are invited to LOS III of which 29 are landlocked. I might just add that two thirds participating in LOS III did not become a party to the Geneva Convention on the Continental Shelf. Considering the geophysical notion of the "Continental Shelf" I think it has been amply clarified that the shelf is not only the extension of the landmass of the coastal nation but that shelf, slope, and rise are of the same nature as the continents themselves. Thus all states of a "continent" should have the right to explore and exploit the natural resources of the continental shelf. Concerning the delimitation of the continental shelf I think that any reconfirmation of the exploitability criterion in a new convention would be unacceptable because it would contradict the Declaration of Principles in Resolution 2749 (XXV) in having the effect of voiding the area. The establishment of an economic zone as proposed at the conference should also provide for the exploration and exploitation of the nonrenewable natural resources and if such a zone is created I can see no necessity for maintaining the juridical concept of the continental shelf; on the contrary, the legal content of the term "continental shelf" should be absorbed by the new juridical notion of economic zone, which would bring the necessary clarification of the legal framework.

I apologize for having elaborated that long on what I consider important criteria for any treaty of LOS III. In the proposals of Professor Johnston I can find the interests of landlocked countries only mentioned in Principle 2 with regard to the regional and international cooperation concerning the protection of the marine environment and this is in my view not enough for a well balanced treaty which has to take into account the interests of all groups of states. I know that my comments will be considered controversial by some participants and I am looking forward to an interesting debate.

Panel Discussion

Donald L. McKernan
Institute for Marine Studies
University of Washington

Mr. McKernan: Mr. Chairman, in order to conserve time and to attempt to the best of my ability not to repeat what has been said, I think I would like to go right to what I consider to be the heart of the problem or heart of the suggestion that has been made by Professor Johnston.

First, it seems to me that he has done us a great favor. He has produced a very thoughtful and scholarly paper, and one that I believe will be of use to all people interested in this subject, both those who have some responsibility in negotiating this difficult problem, as well as people in the public with special interests.

Having said that, then I want to go right to his suggestion of a suboptimal solution and criticize it.

It seems to me there are some fundamental problems with this suggestion. Some of them have been raised already by Dr. Emich and I do not want to dwell on those, but it certainly does show—her comments do indicate—the complexity of attempting to renegotiate on a different basis this very complicated convention and subject.

It seems to me that at this point in the history of the law of the sea negotiations to introduce what appears to me to be a new concept in negotiation would be virtually impossible, and to expect within the time frame outlined by Professor Johnston to reach agreement on new formulations of somewhat different nature, with somewhat different concepts involved, would be in my opinion, anyway, out of the question.

Many of the suggested principles include very controversial issues. For example, the extent of authority of the seabed authority itself. This is one of the issues, of course, that has held up agreement, and yet Professor Johnston, if I may be permitted to say so, sort of summarily includes this as one of the principles that could rather easily, or he indicates perhaps even universally be

378

agreed upon, and yet in my view this is still a very difficult subject and one which will yet require a great deal of negotiation.

In opening up the question of new principles, it seems to me that it reopens a number of issues that, to some degree at least, have been almost or literally closed by the discussions that have taken place over the past six years, and having been a party to this for most of that period, I find it, frankly, difficult to believe that this could be done in any reasonable time frame available to us.

Returning for just a moment to the question of timing, I would like to agree with Professor Johnston in believing that we do have a limited time to resolve these issues, or at least to show very substantial progress in the resolution of these issues.

He judges that it will be necessary virtually to reach agreement by the spring of 1976, and, from my observations, I would not argue with that. I believe in my own country and in other countries of the world, having talked to a number of people, that the world community, the public, is not only anxious but frustrated by our lack of progress, and I do see, as he obviously has, that it is necessary for us to move forward and to move forward rather rapidly, so that while I would agree that with the complexity of this subject it would be highly desirable to have good deal more time, I believe that the opportunity for broad agreement will be foreclosed if very substantial and significant progress is not reached at the Geneva meeting.

Dr. Johnston, it seems to me, begs some very important questions in considering his principles. Now, it is true, as he has mentioned this morning, that he has not intended to provide an overall list of such principles that might be included, but I would submit that every time he adds one, he of course increases the difficulty of reaching virtually universal approval.

As Dr. Emich mentioned, there is very little stated about geographically disadvantaged states. There is virtually nothing said about archipelago states. Little is stated about the question, very important to my country, of the navigation through straits, where jurisdiction, of course, will be altered significantly with an extension of the territorial sea. The boundary questions themselves, both the territorial sea and the boundaries of national jursidiction of the seabed, are other issues that are not treated in these principles.

Now, it might be said that one must stay away, in the broad treaty, from such principles, but once again I would submit that on some issues, particularly on certain issues of jurisdiction, even jurisdiction over nonliving resources, Professor Johnston has treated those issues in his principles.

So my primary objection is that while his suggestion for suboptimization is itself a good suggestion, and it is, in my judgment, a valid approach to this question, and as he has stated, I think very well indeed, or better than I can, this particular approach may well be an approach for the future—that is to say, essentially a broad, umbrellalike convention encompassing either regions or functional uses on the earth's surface. Nevertheless, it seems to me that the approach we have taken, looking behind us now, does not seem to have been the best approach: to take a very comprehensive look at all issues, to draft an agenda which is quite politically inspired and not too logical in some instances.

Nevertheless, it is the approach we have taken now for a long period of time. It is the approach that nations understand, I believe, at the present time. It is an approach that is the basis for national positions of a very large number of nations, keep in mind, and to attempt to reverse the trend of their thought seems to me to be unwise and impractical.

It seems to me it also introduces some other complexities and some other problems which are quite serious. For example, a number of nations, including my own, have indicated the desirability of a very broad convention, one that would take into account all of the issues that we see as important for our future use and for the future use of the community of nations in the ocean, and to attempt to shortcut this, to come up with an alternative which does not, in fact, look at all of these issues, seems to me brings up another seriously controversial issue, and one that cannot easily be resolved in a short time.

I do not share the view of Professors Johnston and Miles that the game is over and that defeat is at hand and that, in fact, we must run for cover at this particular point. I think, in this regard, I see things more as Dr. Emich does.

It seems to me that, for a number of very complicated reasons which may or may not be justified, we didn't do a very good job in our pre-paratory meetings. But at least in my view, in Caracas, the issues were made clear and many nations were not only made aware of these issues but had an opportunity to express themselves for the first time, as has been pointed out.

It seems to me on most issues, on most important issues before the Law of the Sea Conference, the alternatives have been narrowed, have been sharpened, and are now before nations in such a way, and understood by nations, so that they can be negotiated if nations want to negotiate them.

So I believe it is too early, it is premature, to predict failure for the Law of the Sea Conference. My own limited experience in very small nego-tiations leads me to believe that, at this stage in the negotiations of issues as complicated as the law of the sea, it is too much to expect nations to have revealed the extent of their willingness to find common ground on important issues vital to their development and security and, as they see it, to the general welfare of their people and of mankind as a whole.

So I, myself, have a rather simple formula which seems to me ought to be given an opportunity, and that is, I would like to see emerge in the very early days of Geneva an anonymous draft treaty text, a comprehensive one, one that attempts at least to take into account the various alternatives that are before the conference, one that does not necessarily reflect my country's point of view, but would give my country a basis for negotiating from the middle or some median position.

I expect that nations, including our own nation—and here, again, as all speakers have mentioned, I am speaking personally and not for my government, with no authority to speak for it, of course—but I expect all nations are going to try very hard, and are going to try and look at moderate positions, positions which take into account the view of the other fellow at Geneva.

In conjunction with this, I would remind the audience of the rather interesting remarks made by Mr. Paul Lapointe concerning the question of navigation. By the way, they were not remarks I want to associate myself with, but the point was that people are searching for a common ground, and I think that is simply an example of what I would expect to be prevalent at Geneva.

Next I would like to see a greater exercise of leadership by the officials of the conference itself; that is to say, if the leadership can push, cajole, lead, stay ahead of, incur the displeasure, perhaps, of a number of nations, I think this itself would help us.

I think that taking what appears to me to be the obvious interest of all countries to reach an agreement, and not looking at the alternatives before us if we fail, that we can , in fact, reach agreement in principle at least in the spring, and then possibly following the general, bold timetable that Professor Johnston has suggested in his paper, one could see a completion of a successful conference in 1976. Thank you very much.

Panel Discussion

Frank Njenga
Mission of Kenya to the United Nations

Mr. Njenga: First of all, I must apologize for the fact that I will not be able to speak as much as I would have wished, not only to give other members who are participating the opportunity to speak, but mainly because inexplicably I came from New York to Florida to catch a cold. So my voice is not as good as it should be and consequently I cannot speak at length.

I would like first of all to thank Professor Johnston for his very interesting analysis of the present situation of the law of the sea and of a possible way to overcome what he sees as a possible failure of the conference.

I think it is a challenging analysis which is also very thought provoking, and which requires very careful consideration.

As for myself, and like the other participants, I must point out that I can only at this stage speak for myself and not for my government. I start by asking, what is the purpose of the whole exercise? I do not think that the purpose of the exercise, the conference which is now in progress, or the whole effort since 1967—the Sea-Bed Committee, the Preparatory Committee, and the conference—is merely to conclude a new treaty on the law of the sea.

The desirable aim, I would agree, is to produce a comprehensive convention on the various issues on the law of the sea, but the purpose, I believe, is deeper than this. The purpose is to effect what many states consider to be necessary changes in the exploitation and the uses of the seas for the benefit of all mankind.

To that extent, therefore, we have to judge success or failure of the conference not purely on whether we have obtained a convention, but on whether we have obtained a convention which brings about the changes necessary to create new equities in the uses of the sea for the benefit of mankind as a whole.

So even if the conference failed to produce a generally unanimous

382

convention, which is quite likely, this would not necessarily mean that the efforts since 1967 have been in vain. I do not believe that things will ever be the same again in the oceans as they were in the good old days before 1967, when the benefits of the sea were mostly appropriated by those in a position to do so.

I think you will all agree with me that the main reason that Ambassador Pardo raised the issue of the seabed and the concept of the common heritage of mankind is due to the challenge that has been created by the emergence of technology to the present point at which a few states or, rather— and this is important—the corporations in those few industrialized states, are in a position to go out there and rake up the wealth of the oceans in proportions unimaginable when we were just dealing with fishing.

That is why it was considered necessary to have rational management of these resources of the seas, not only because they belong to the international community as a whole, but also because the new technology brings with it very considerable risks which cannot be restricted to the users of the oceans, those with the technological know-how, but which, in fact, might affect not only the whole of the international community, but might also tend to work irreversible and harmful changes ot the marine ecology, to the catastrophe of the users as well as everybody else.

And so began the concept of the common heritage of mankind, which I do not believe is a meaningless concept. Yesterday when some representatives of the industry and the corporations were speaking, I got the impression that for them the common heritage of mankind means, in effect, the common heritage of multinational corporations.

A friend of mine who was sitting next to me observed the graph being introduced by the speaker, and the final result was, in capital letters, MAKE PROFIT! For whom? For these companies. There was no PAY TAXES. So it would appear that this message that the oceans or the seabed beyond national jurisdiction is a common heritage of mankind has not sunk in. I believe, however, that this is a view not shared by the governments of these corporations, so there is still hope for the conference in this area.

Secondly, as negotiations continued in the Sea-Bed Committee, the developing countries realized—what many of them had realized before but which was now in an organized form—that the seas, as such, under the guise of the so-called "freedoms of the high seas," had been used purely for the benefit of a few countries who used this freedom of the seas as a license to benefit their own economies without consideration for the ecology, or the rights of other states, particularly the developing states. The whole subject of protecting the seabed broadened to one of looking at the sea as a comprehensive whole, wherein all states have rights and obligations, and where all states are entitled to share meaningfully in an equitable manner.

This was what caused the emergence of the concept of the exclusive economic zone. It was a defensive mechanism, defensive for those developing countries not in a position to protect themselves; to have an area where they could obtain protection from exploitation by fishermen from distant developed countries and at the same time guarantee the legitimate interests of all the states in the international community.

This is how one has to look at this concept of the exclusive economic zone if we want to develop it in a meaningful fashion, and I still believe that without this concept, a successful convention on the law of the sea is going to be something unobtainable.

It incorporates a number of elements. The first main element is that within this area of a maximum of 200 nautical miles the coastal state will have exclusive jurisdiction to determine who is going to exploit the resources in that area. Second, it will also have exclusive sovereignty over the resources in that particular area. In other words, it will have sovereignty and it can decide to exploit the resources itself or it can allow others to exploit under such arrangements as it may lay down.

Third, the coastal state will exercise jurisdiction for the protection of the resources and for conservation purposes, so as to ensure that no damage is done to itself, or to its resources.

These elements, I believe, are very important if we are going to talk meaningfully about this subject.

Then, finally, the other states would be entitled to other legitimate uses of the area, like navigation and overflight. That is the package. If it is accepted by everybody who has come into the negotiations, that gives hope for the conference to succeed. If it is not accepted, I believe that the changes will still come, but they will not come through agreement, but through other means. We have a choice either to work our changes through agreement or to work out changes through unilateral action and regional arrangements, regional agreements, and so on, which could lead to chaos and perhaps which will lead to a lot of conflict in the future.

I believe that at present the interests to be protected in the sea, the interests which are going to be the business of agreement, are fairly broadly well known. It is, therefore, not necessary perhaps at this stage to talk about a fallback position. I think what is necessary is for those who are going to negotiate at the conference to decide that we are going to work changes and that, in the process, sacrifices will have to be made. They then should go to the conference determined to negotiate on these changes, rather than to try to hide behind a convention which is maybe so vague as to be meaningless, or alternatively, to work out a declaration which in the end would just end up postponing the problems for a later date.

We definitely face a lot of difficulties at present, including first and foremost, the rules of procedure, which are so complex as to insure by themselves that a conference cannot be finished in one session, as we have proposed in the Geneva session. These rules of procedure are not the desire of developing countries. They are a result of the insistence of the developed countries on consensus; in other words, an effort to block changes which will, in the end, perhaps help the developed countries more than the developing countries. In the process of change, it is only rational to expect that those who are overprivileged at the present should be the ones to sacrifice something.

Second, it has been argued that the number of participants is too large. I, however, think the fact that we are having, for the first time, a conference with participants from all over the world, bringing their diverse interests, is perhaps the strongest hope that if we arrive at an agreement, it will be long-lasting. I do not think that the size is necessarily a weakness. It only means that we have to go to the conference prepared not necessarily to protect our own interests, but to work out changes in such a way that we do not sacrifice what we consider to be the legitimate interests; that we effect sacrifices so as to create equities.

As for the proposals that have been made by Professor Johnston, I do not think that I need criticize them point by point, because by and large I agree with the criticisms made by the two other panelists, that while his proposals for a general convention and a parent convention leave out quite a lot of what are considered to be vital interests, when you come to what Professor Johnston has laid out as the basic interests, they are also loaded interests.

Let us, for instance, examine some of them. The first one, common heritage, making the ocean as a whole a common heritage, would completely negate what we have been trying to do. I think you cannot reconcile the economic zone with the notion of a common heritage of mankind. Common heritage would be confused if it is meant to apply to the ocean as a whole.

The area within national sovereignty, or the national zone, as it is called sometimes, cannot be considered to belong to the international community. This would just lead to confusion. It is the area beyond that which should be considered as the common heritage of mankind.

We had a very pertinent criticism from Dr. Emich of the almost total omission of interests of the landlocked countries. I am glad she quoted the OAU declaration, because in this process of making concessions to the landlocked countries, I think the African countries have gone the farthest. These are not really concessions, because we feel that we are giving to the landlocked something to which we feel they are entitled. We have gone the farthest, in that we have given them full participation in the exploitation of living resources of the economic zone and on an equal basis with the nationalists.

Dr. Emich also made a very useful criticism of the principles dealing with the continental margin, both for the living and nonliving resources. I do not think that we can, merely by silence, extend the rights of the coastal states with broad shelves, and these are mainly developed countries again, so as to allow them to, in effect, appropriate unto themselves the greater part, the more useful part of what should be considered to be the common heritage of mankind. You cannot have a common heritage of mankind without giving up exploitability criteria. Once you give up exploitability criteria, you have really no leg to stand on when you insist that you are entitled to the margin, because the margin can only be gotten today from the existing definition if you use exploitability as a test.

If you look at the law as it exists at present, as it evolved, it was 200 meters or beyond if it was exploitable. If we have left out exploitable, then we have to work out another test, and I would entirely agree with her that the only fair test would be a uniform distance applicable to everyone, within which you would have both the living and the nonliving resources, plus adequate accommodation for landlocked countries.

If a margin has to be accepted—and here I think Professor Johnston has an element which we should not lose sight of—we have to consider very seriously a regime of revenue sharing. This should not be just a phrase. It must be worked out in such a way that we have a formula which allows the rich states to turn in much more of the revenue from the margin than the poor states for the benefit of those who are most disadvantaged, particularly the landlocked. But it has to be a formula which effects that. It involves sacrifices for those in a position to make sacrifices for the benefit of those who are losing, in effect, part of the common heritage of mankind.

I will leave the matter of freedom of navigation where it was left by Professor McKernan. It is not that it is not important for us, but it is one area on which you cannot find agreement on a general proposition such as we have here, which perhaps does not go into the very complex issues involved, the straits and the general navigation issue within the economic zone.

Part of this general issue involves pollution. I do not think we can be satisfied on the question of pollution with a general statement that there is an obligation not to pollute or that the international agreement at present provides adequate safeguards. If we are going to create an acceptable solution, you must accept, as Professor Johnston has proposed here, that the coastal states will have a primary interest in the prevention of pollution within areas falling under their national jurisdiction. He has referred to especially vulnerable situations, and the volume of shipping, and the possible hazards from topographical factors as some of the factors to be taken into account. But I would go farther and say that each coastal state, because the economic zone is an area within which it has sovereignty over the resources, because it is an area within which the coastal state is threatened, has to be given a primary role in the prevention of pollution therein.

So, in conclusion, I do not think that we would get anywhere if we went to Geneva and expected to try to change the course of the ship, as it were, by trying to work out a general parent convention. I believe that we should go to Geneva believing that changes will have to come and, therefore, to work out the changes, not so as to prevent any harm to our interests—definitely some interests are going to be harmed; definitely the rich will have to give up something; definitely the industrialized countries, and particularly their companies can no longer go on exploiting the sea as if it were theirs—but so as to guarantee and safeguard legitimate interests, and evolve a new, equitable framework for uses of the sea.

I believe that the time has come, if we have such flexible instructions about working changes, when we can aim at finishing the work of the committee. We did not oppose several sessions for the conference because we believe we can finish in one session. We opposed a succession of sessions because the more sessions we have, the more the states are going to refuse to show their hand in the negotiations. If we go there for one session which we all believe is going to be the main session, I believe we can finish the work of the committees, and then we can provide sufficient time in 1976 to put this work in treaty form in the final convention in the plenary. But to negotiate for a parent convention at this stage would amount to merely postponing the issues. What would come out would be so general that no state would be in a position to sign it, and if it was signed, it would be interpreted differently, so that you would find that in the end it would just lead to further frustration and not to the desired goals which caused this subject to be put on the agenda in the first place.

I thank you very much.

Panel Discussion

Jorge Vargas
National Center for Science and Technology
Mexico

Mr. Vargas: As it is customary in this case, I should start by saying that I am speaking in a personal capacity, and not as a member of the Mexican delegation to the Third United Nations Conference on the Law of the Sea, or as an official of the National Council for Science and Technology (CONACYT).

I read with great interest the well-structured and thought-provoking paper written by Dr. Johnston. I think it is a serious academic exercise that analyzes in a systematic and constructive manner the most viable alternatives which the LOS Conference would have before it in the event of failing to reach its "official objective," namely the formulation of a comprehensive and global treaty on a new law of the sea. Or, if you want to put it in a different way, the question could be: Which "suboptimal outcomes"—as Dr. Johnston calls them— should the LOS Conference consider in the event of being unable to produce a global treaty, universally accepted, covering the totality of the 92 items and subitems included in its agenda?

In reviewing each of these possible alternatives, or suboptimal results, Dr. Johnston departs from the premise that the LOS Conference is definitely going to fail if it insists on achieving its official objective, given the numerous and complex issues of its agenda, on the one hand, and the proximity and improrrogable deadline that has been assigned to it for this task, on the other hand, namely May 10, 1975, when the conference is going to finish its third period of sessions at Geneva. In the first place, I would like to mention that I agree with Dr. Johnston—and with many of you here today—that the conference will not be able to conclude a comprehensive and final treaty on the law of the sea at its forthcoming session in Geneva.

In addition to the reasons already mentioned, this is bound to be because the conference's official objective was established in an artificial and precipitate manner. Artificial, because the large majority of states have consistently recognized that they are not yet ready to reach such an objective. I believe this commitment was made more on the basis of intense rhetoric than as an intelligent and realistic decision. And I think it was precipitate because it was within the ambit of the Committee of the Sea-Bed and Ocean Floor—now extinct—that the activities to formulate legal principles, eliminate alternatives, and draft articles of the future convention should have been conducted.

The work of the Sea-Bed Committee was severed and left unconcluded in order to enter, still unprepared, into a more complex and a more difficult new phase. Had the Sea-Bed Committee finished its otherwise normal and necessary task, its results could very well have been compared to the draft articles produced by the International Law Commission for the First United Nations Conference on the Law of the Sea in 1958.

Contrary to the opinion advanced by Dr. Johnston, I believe that it will indeed be possible to extend the time limit of the conference beyond May of this year. This time extension would transform the conference into an open-ended conference, which will conclude at the final period of sessions during which the comprehensive treaty on the law of the sea is signed.

It should be evident that if the Geneva session produces concrete, positive, and substantial results—even if those results are neither all-encompassing nor even complete—there is no reason to impede the continuation of the conference's work in the future. Therefore, the plenary of the LOS Conference, as a sovereign body, has the right to convoke any number of additional sessions it deems necessary in order to ultimately conclude and suscribe the final international instrument.

By adopting this time mechanism, which eliminates the establishment of fixed, artificial deadlines, the conference will be apt to finish its work, since it is impossible to estimate a priori, without any solid basis, the exact number of sessions necessary for the conference to eventually conclude its work. There is still another defect that prevents the conference from achieving its current official objective. That is that we are attempting to move from a traditional or "old law of the sea" (principally embodied in the four 1958 Geneva Conventions) into a more innovative law of the sea (which should ideally come out of the forthcoming session at Geneva), without having previously created a "bridge," or a vincula, a legal structure linking the two systems. This link should consist of a basic and interim regime applicable to the oceans.

A precedent for this type of regime could be found in the Declaration of Principles Governing the Activities in the Sea-bed and Ocean Floor Beyond the Limits of National Jurisdiction, approved in 1970 by the United Nations resolution 2549-C, which established a legal bridge between an existing regime and a new regime about to be established. However, it was unfortunate that when this measure was adopted for such an area, a similar mechanism was not contemplated for the other ocean spaces as well.

What should be, then, the viable alternatives for Geneva? In his paper, Dr. Johnston elaborates on what he calls "suboptimal outcomes of the conference." Changing his terminology a little bit, I would like to submit for consideration a possible "optimal subobjective." This subobjective of the LOS Conference should be composed of the following two capital elements:

1. A Declaration of Basic Principles on the Law of the Sea, accepted by the consensus of the participants to the conference and selected on the basis of the competence assigned to each of the three principal committees
2. A general moratorium.

It should be pointed out that this optimal subobjective is similar, in various respects, to the unorthodox alternative described as "Non-Treaty Instrument," in Dr. Johnston's paper.

With respect to the *First Committee,* the proposed declaration should at least include the fifteen principles contained in the Sea-Bed Declaration, approved by the General Assembly in 1970.

Regarding the *Second Committee,* the following principles could be considered: (1) A territorial sea of 12 nautical miles conditioned upon the existence of an economic zone up to a limit of 200 nautical miles; (2) The recognition of the special interest of the coastal states over the living resources adjacent to its coast; (3) The convenience of having a special regime for certain marine species, such as tunafish and salmon. In relation to (4) the outer limit of the Continental Shelf, (5) transit through and over international straits, (6) the high seas, (7) the situation of landlocked states and geographically disadvantaged states and (8) archipelagoes, the existing status quo should be maintained until the interim regime is superseded by the final treaty.

Finally, regarding the *Third Committee,* I think the formulation of basic principles applicable to the preservation of the marine environment, scientific research, and the development and transfer of technology, should not offer serious difficulties. It should be recalled that among the positive outcomes achieved in Caracas, a series of fundamental principles on marine scientific research were included.

These general principles are offered here as a simple illustration of the type of basic guidelines that could be incorporated into the declaration, and, therefore, they by no means constitute the result of a serious and detailed consideration on the part of this speaker of each one of them. However, this speaker is strongly convinced that the declaration referred to, if and when adopted, should include, in the first place, a set of principles on which there is already common agreement albeit in general terms, such as the breadth of the territorial sea and of the economic zone and, on the other hand, certain provisions destined to maintain the status quo on those issues on which there is still no common agreement, such as the outer limit of the continental shelf and transit through international straits.

In order to insure that no state will depart from the general character of the commonly agreed-on principles, or attempt to disrupt the status quo in those areas where there is no agreement, a general moratorium should be adopted. The best guarantee of the survival of the interim regime for the oceans will be the establishment by this proposed moratorium. Therefore, this moratorium would contribute stability to the interim regime and provide a more formal protection against possible unilateral actions which would result in confusion and anarchy in the oceans. This kind of situation cannot be afforded by the international global community, since even today we have a more or less stable and agreed-upon legal order (composed mainly of the four Geneva Conventions of 1958), despite the alarmist statements made by some that there already is a state of actual conflict, anarchy, and confusion in the oceans. I estimate that such alleged conflicts are today more ideological and potential than real.

What should be emphasized is that in the adoption of the contents of the proposed declaration, special attention should be given to responsibly identifying those areas on which there is an authentic common agreement, and not only an assumed or desired one. In this respect, I suspect that Dr. Johnston's listed principles are offered as mere illustrations, and not as embodying indisputable concepts. This observation is formulated in view of the fact that, in my personal opinion, some of the principles contained in Dr. Johnston's proposal do not reflect an actual common agreement by the international community. For instance, Principle 1 has never been accepted by the international community and is, rather, a simple idealistic expectation on the part of its author.

I am aware that the first valid criticism which could be advanced against the proposed declaration of principles is that such an instrument is not necessarily a binding one. This is a valid point. However, a declaration is a real *optimal subobjective* given the fact that most countries are reluctant to sign any treaty that is not the final comprehensive treaty on the law of the sea. Also, it should be remembered that the reason a subobjective is proposed is simply that the official objective of the conference is just not realistically attainable. Therefore, a mere declaration, despite its lack of legal binding force, is not necessarily worse than its alternative, such alternative being the adoption of no instrument whatsoever, with the consequent result that since no expression of the international community's will on the subject is materialized, the door is left open for unilateral action.

It should be understood, then, that the main distinction between this proposal and that of Dr. Johnston is the inclusion of the moratorium provision in the declaration. We can go even further in this respect: If the conference considers that it would be realistically possible, it could also establish a *second optimal subobjective;* namely, the adoption of a protocol of adherence to the declaration of principles, whereby the provisions of the declaration could be placed into a legal framework. This protocol of adherence would be open to all states participating in the conference. Its objective would be to give a legally binding force to the provisions of the declaration, which would come into force as soon as the first adherence is produced, being applicable only inter-partes.

As can be appreciated, the protocol would be the equivalent of a camouflaged treaty. However, the very fact that this protocol would be an accessory instrument to a mere declaration, and not to a main treaty, as is normally the case with all protocols, might induce states to adhere to it as a way to make the declaration a meaningful instrument from the legal standpoint. This protocol, no matter how unorthodox it would be, could constitute a feasible solution to be contemplated as another optimal subobjective responding to the eventual failure at the Geneva session.

Despite the fact that many would regard a declaration of principles as a meaningless instrument, from this speaker's point of view such a device would open the doors for future negotiations that should lead to the achievement of the original and still untouched official objective of the conference. After all, the formulation of the new law of the sea should be understood as a process in itself, which cannot be suspended with artificially fixed deadlines. The lawmaking process is a constant and uninterrupted process which will go beyond Geneva. From this basic premise arises the necessity that the new law of the sea should include institutional mechanisms which will allow for its periodical updating and reshaping.

I would like to close my remarks by recognizing that mankind is in a hurry to establish a new legal order for the oceans. However, let us be aware of the danger represented by those who claim that if this legal order is not achieved in 1975, then no legal order will ever be achieved. The intention behind such threatening pronouncements is their desire to justify the unilateral measures which, to the detriment of the interests of mankind and for the protection of their own, they are planning to undertake immediately after the Geneva failure.

The world community should certainly be willing to wait, as long as necessary, for the establishment of a sound and equitable new legal order for the oceans, but should not be impatient to fall into an anarchical situation which would do nothing but preserve the fundamental inequities of the old system.

Panel Discussion

Ranjit Sethi
Indian Mission to the United Nations

Mr. Sethi: Ever since this seminar started one could understandably have been asking oneself: Is the conference already a failure? I don't think so. To be sure the paper presented by Mr. Johnston does anything but affirm that the conference is or will be a failure. I agree with a lot that is in the paper and indeed would find it difficult to add anything of substance to it now.

We keep hearing here that the conference will fail. Perhaps it will; since there is no method of procuring a guarantee for success. But it is also said, persistently, that it will fail because there are too many participants in it and the issues are complex: as if the conference is something other than and distinguishable from a UN Conference on the Law of the Sea. It is, after all, not a conference in some sort of abstract or absolute sense; one suddenly swollen to a membership of 150 and peremptorily called upon to deal with the law of the sea. It is not a conference which should be thought of as condemned to failure because it has, somehow unreasonably, been ordered to deal with the law of the sea.

Even if, referring to the proceedings of Monday afternoon, the study of the "Dynamics of Conference Diplomacy" is necessary and desirable I am not sure that in the course of this study we have not, somehow, got lost in a methodology which we do not and, perhaps, cannot know where to apply and how to apply.

It is simply not convincing to say that if the membership were smaller the conference would be more manageable. Shall we then, for convenience, reduce the number? Shall we for instance take away Lesotho and Tanzania from Africa and Laos and India from Asia and, choosing at random, ten more from each of the continents? Perhaps we should remove a total of seventy or—to use a magic number—seventy-seven participants. Will the conference be more manageable then? It is unlikely. I might say, at this point, that a democratic and universal world community is immeasurably more important than a manageable conference—whatever that means. We have a world community which acts democratically and which, with the advance of decolonization, is now nearly universal. It seems irrelevant to think of the manageable dimensions of certain problems which can be both defined and solved by what we have heard described as the "capable nations"—incidentally not a very happy phrase.

Why is it difficult to get a single comprehensive treaty? It is not because there are too many nations in the world but because these nations do not want to vote in a law of the sea convention by a simple majority. If there were fewer nations there is no reason to think that they would be more able or more inclined to vote in a single convention than a larger group. The Rules of Procedure, and particularly Rule 37 which is portrayed as a sort of monster, are not an obstacle but a simple symbol of the will of the conference to produce a widely acceptable law. Given this the innovative rules of procedure are, in a sense, irrelevant as the will to arrive at a conclusion by consensus exists independently of them. However, they are there, they did not take as much time to devise as it was feared they would—the June 27 deadline was met—and the conference will no doubt manage with them as it would indeed have managed without them. It may take time to formulate a full convention or even a partial one as suggested in the several Johnston alternatives but we have certain facts, not the least of which is the short life of the 1958 treaties, which warn us against haste.

One reason for slow progress is, in my personal view, undoubtedly that the logic of starting from general propositions and proceeding to particular cases has too often either been inverted or ignored in LOS negotiations. Too often a participant will wish to negotiate partially on a specific issue which can easily be included in a general provision. This has been true, for instance, of the discussions on archipelagoes, the territorial sea, and the continental shelf. Would I offend the legal experts present among us by saying that this only underlines the existence as distinct disciplines of law and logic?

Another problem in the negotiations has been current vocabulary. The problem is largely that current vocabulary is the same as past vocabulary. The terminology that is used now is basically the same that was used in the past. It does not fit the meanings we are seeking to express. The uses of the seas have evolved, as has technology. The hazards from new uses and technology have also multiplied. The old vocabulary contains an accretion of established meaning which cannot fit the new ideas for which we are using it as a vehicle. For this reason the terms passage, innocent passage, continental shelf, etc., present enormous difficulties. These difficulties are, of course, being overcome. Everyone remembers the debate on "peaceful uses." There persists the deepest confusion about the meaning of the phrase. It has been said, not without reason, that we live in an age in which all acts, including the most violent, are described as peaceful and justified as destined to establish peace. However the phrase "peaceful uses" is, now, accepted because it is widely believed to be invested with a meaning that no one wishes to circumscribe too narrowly, much less to challenge seriously.

I come to another point. On Tuesday we talked about the international area and mining in it. The inspiration for the common heritage principle is both very important and very simple. We look at it historically. The whole point is that we do not wish to extend to the sea, in the twentieth century, a system that we saw on the land in the nineteenth. The parallel may not be exact. But the point of difference is, exclusively, that the land is inhabited and inherited. Legally and historically the comparison is telling. There was in the nineteenth century the same sort of legal vaccum on land that is perceived by some on the sea today. Indeed the empire builders could not wait for the emergence and stabilization of a nation-states system. And no doubt they had technology, accumulated capital, and, indeed, religion on their side. If I may recall what Mr. Greenwald said to us the other day, I would remark that, historically, I assume that the East India Company had boats and machines in the sixteenth century as does Deepsea Ventures today and that, no doubt, its stockholders were in as much of a hurry then as are those of Deepsea Ventures now. We are only just finishing the dismantling of the old system. The entire will of the international community is directed at preventing disorder and the growth of an untidy system which would have to be taken apart or at least altered radically. That is why the UN moratorium resolution and declaration of principles were adopted. Mr. Greenwald said, "The Lord helps those who help themselves." Perhaps. I simply do not know. I would, personally, wish to withhold judgment at least till judgment day.

A few words on the continental shelf. It has been suggested that some kind of numerical criterion should be used for limiting the continental shelf. Paradoxically, it is also admitted that over the continental shelf a coastal state in fact already enjoys sovereign rights and that it constitutes a natural resource for it.

There are two points that should be made. The first is on the quality of a natural resource. The second is that the land mass to the outer edge of the margin is considered submerged land territory with the full attributes of sovereignty. We live in an age of sovereignty over natural resources. Allied with this the legal doctrine of acquired rights makes it difficult to quantify and limit the claim to the continental shelf. (I would here say that difficulties of vocabulary that I have already spoken of exist today with regard to the doctrine of the shelf as indeed the word "shelf" is used commonly to englobe the shelf— properly so-called in a geomorphological sense—the rise and the slope.)

Now if the shelf or margin is indeed a natural resource it should be treated as being equivalent to any other natural resource like a mineral or oil. We are indeed very far from a system whereby we can apportion resources worldwide on the basis of per capita equality. Therefore a numerical limit seems impossible to think of, as we would encounter impossible problems of definition and application. These problems would only be compounded if we seriously considered questioning claims to sovereignty, which is indeed claimed fully under the "legal doctrine on the continental shelf" by a distance criterion irrespective of the geomorphic characteristics of the offshore ocean bed.

A final word for L4. I would say first that L4 seems to me to be wrongly described as a "Canadian" paper. L4 is no more an exclusively Canadian paper for having been presented by the Canadian delegation than was L38 of the Sea-Bed Committee an exclusively Indian paper for having been presented by the Indian delegation. The cosponsors of both these papers should not be ignored. Indeed it would be as unfortunate to limit L4 to its Canadian association as it would be unfair to consider Canada compromised (and particularly Ambassador Beesley's position as the chairman of the Drafting Committee) for having cosponsored the paper.

It has also been said that L4 failed, or at least ran into opposition because it was confused with the convention. In fact no one was looking so far ahead on July 29, in Caracas. But it is to be recalled that it was in the preceding week that we were talking about a conference declaration. Perhaps L4 was confused with that idea. There was, anyway, some confusion and it seems that we had our only (procedural) vote on that occasion.

Discussion and Questions

Ms. Mariani: I would like to make just a few comments.

First, I agree with Ms. Emich and Dr. Vargas that viability of the treaty is much more important than drawing up an artificial deadline, and that should be kept in mind.

Passing in review the different solutions proposed by Dr. Johnston in his paper, I would stress the inconvenience of the suboptimal solution, but first, about the optimal solution, I would say that the notion of majority has to be precise, because it should not be a simple, numerical majority; a treaty which does not take into account vital interests of different groups will not be a viable treaty, so the question of majority really has to be made clear, and it is not a simple question of number. You have to take into account all the interests, especially those of the landlocked countries, developing and developed, and so on, so this is something which is important.

Second, about the suboptimal solution, there is the inconvenience of the parent convention, and the difficulty is to draw a line of distinction between what is very necessary, what is to be put into this convention, and what has to be implemented, because sometimes the questions are so closely linked that it is difficult.

I take the example of Committee I. For some states, it is very important, especially for the developed one who has presented this rule and regulation paper, that the general principle of exploitation should be put in the convention and not left out and not considered as an implementation question. So that is to be considered.

As far as suboptimal solutions are concerned, I think that the declaration of principles, if it is not in binding form, within a treaty, would not bring about anything because it will always be in the same position, so a declaration of principles would not be a solution; only if it is in binding form,

397

such as a treaty or a protocol. But just in the resolution framework, it will reopen the questions posed by the declaration of principles over the seabed.

Another remark is that it is difficult when you have to agree on an organizational provision. You really have to have a convention, and, of course, it is not possible, for instance, to establish an agreement only on general principles. You have to know exactly what you have to agree upon.

As far as the conclusion of this conference is concerned, if it is not possible to agree on all the issues, I think there should be a determination of priority, and the jurisdictional issue especially has to be considered because that is going to determine the solution of other issues.

Finally, I am wondering if even if we consider a declaration of principles in a binding form, for instance, any form of declaration of principles should not be accompanied by a principle paving the way for the settlement of disputes even in the interpretation of these principles, because I think that when you have drawn up the principles, the most important, of course, is to interpret and settle disputes, so I think that any instruments that would be adopted by the conference should cover the settlement of disputes or the interpretation of the principles. This is very important.

I end this intervention by stressing that these views are only my own and not necessarily reflecting the government of France. Thank you.

Mr. Miles: Thank you very much. Professor Kolodkin?

Mr. Kolodkin: Thank you, Mr. Chairman.

First of all, I should like to express my appreciation to Professor Johnston for his fundamental report, which is very comprehensive and very exact. I also should like to make some comments in connection with this report because I am not in agreement with all of these provisions, of course.

On the first, it is very difficult for me to accept the approach as to the nontreaty instruments which may be laid as the basis of the further development of the codification and progressive development of the international law of the sea.

It seems to me that we have only two types of sources of international law—the treaty and customary law—and we could not leave to national legislation and to national practice such serious matters as the interests of all mankind regarding the principles of ocean activity.

On the second, it seems to me that it is very difficult to accept the first principle of Professor Johnston that the ocean as a whole, both within and beyond limits of national jurisdiction, belongs to the common heritage of mankind. I should like to stress that it is not a new principle. We can find also in the literature in the United States in 1971 and 1972 the indication that the ocean as a whole is the common heritage of mankind.

It seems to me that this approach implies a danger to the sovereignty of states. Besides this, I should like to ask Professor Johnston if he would kindly express the legal implications of including this principle.

I am afraid that the inclusion of this principle may lead to the creation of international machinery not only for the seabed but also for the high seas as well as the territorial waters and economic zones which lie, as you know, under national jurisdiction.

I should like not to accept the eighth principle because I see in the eighth principle a lacuna, in my opinion. I do not wish to repeat my approach to scientific research because we discussed this problem at the last meeting, but among the rules which Professor Johnston proposed in this principle we cannot find the freedom of scientific research and the freedom, beyond national jurisdiction, for fishermen which was mentioned yesterday by Professor Oda.

I could not accept your proposal that we can adopt the parent convention in the next session immediately after the signing ceremony; that we must not wait for the process of ratification and for the process of endorsement by the high supreme organs of all institutions of the states in accordance with their legal systems.

In accordance with the internal legal systems, especially the English system, it is not enough that the supreme organ of the state ratify and endorse, but the treaty must also be implemented in the internal legal system by the adoption and elaboration of the new appropriate law.

Finally, it might, in my opinion, be desirable to have among these principles three general principles.

First of all, it will be desirable to find a balance between the interests of coastal states and the international community. That is why I fully support the opinion of the distinguished panelist Mr. Njenga, from Kenya, who stressed that we cannot accept the proposal about the spreading of the concept of the common heritage of mankind on the economic zone. We can find the balance if we recognize this concept and if we wish to establish the international machinery on the seabed we can leave to national jurisdiction the other maritime spaces, for example, the territorial waters.

In this principle, I should also like to stress that we can maintain— and I support the principle which was proposed by Mr. Vargas—the existing rules and principles of international law; for example, the principles of the freedom of navigation and the freedom of transit through the international straits, and that is why I could not accept the approach of Mr. Goldblat in yesterday's report, for all the international straits are an indispensable element of international navigation. If we restrict the freedom of passage through the international straits, we cannot speak about the freedom of navigation.

The second principle, in my opinion, is the maintenance of the existing rules and principles of international law on the sea when we, at the same time, make an attempt to elaborate the new rules. Of course, the impact of technology leads to the need for the elaboration of the new principles to fill the lacuna in the law, to remove the gaps in several cases.

But it seems to me that this new approach, and this is my third principle, ought to be in accordance with the main principles and rules generally accepted in international law. We cannot forget that the law of the sea is only a part of international law. It is not a separate branch of law at all, but an integral part of the contemporary international law.

That is why I fully support the last sentence of your report, Professor Johnston. I shake your hand and I should like to quote: "In the final analysis, there is no kind of immediate national gain that ranks with the national interest in the peaceful and progressive development of the legal community of nations."

Thank you very much.

Mr. Miles: Thank you. Doug, would you like very briefly to reply?

Mr. Johnston: The comments fall into three categories: first of all, expressions of relative optimism on the probable outcome of the conference, as it is presently constructed. Only time will tell whether Professor Miles and I will have to eat our pessimistic words, but I think most of us in the room are more interested now in eating something more nutritious than words, so I pass very quickly to the second category.

Some of the comments questioned the desirability and feasibility of something like the proposed parent convention. This is a difficult question that could be argued out at great length. I would have thought that it is essentially a human energy problem, whether the motivation is high enough on the conference circuit to redirect diplomatic energies at this stage. The question really is whether there are more attractive alternatives, and only time will tell there, too.

The third category of comments raised substantive questions as to what you would put into a parent convention, supposing such a thing were conscionable. As I said during the presentation, the proposed list of principles is intended mainly to describe the order of generality that one would expect to capture in the parent convention, and suggests one way of addressing oneself to the problem of finding a balance. I would be the first to agree that a massive effort would have to be made through negotiation to find the right balance. This is not necessarily the right balance, but it is a balance of a kind.

The only other thing I would mention, since everybody has talked about it, is the proposed "enlargement" of the concept of the common heritage of mankind. Such an "enlargement", as far as I am concerned, should be motivated by the desire to enshrine in a parent convention a conception of universal answerability to succeeding generations for the management of the ocean environment.

Mr. Miles: Thank you very much.

I have been asked to remind the audience that everybody will be welcome again in Caracas for the signing ceremony. As one who enjoyed the rather munificent hospitality of the Venezuelan government, I have no vested interest in failure and I certainly, were we both Doug and I to be proved wrong, would be in Caracas cheering along with everybody else.

I thank you very much for attending and for your patience. I particularly thank Dr. Johnston and our panelists for the very serious consideration of a rather difficult problem and for taking time out from their busy schedules to come and be with us here at the Ninth Annual Meeting of the Law of the Sea Institute.

Part VI

Concluding Thoughts

Chairman
William T. Burke
School of Law
University of Washington

Mr. Burke: May I have your attention, please?

Those of you who have been to these annual meetings before are probably aware that we have a banquet at the end. Today we have substituted a luncheon. We usually have a speaker; this time we have two speakers.

Our first speaker is Michael Hardy, who is legal advisor to the European Economic Community. He is also a member of the Excutive Board of the Law of the Sea Institute.

Remarks

Michael Hardy*
Commission of the European
Economic Community

Mr. Hardy: Ladies and Gentlemen, As I understand it, the task assigned to
Mr. Hawkins and myself is to give you a short, snappy number in which we wrap
up the proceedings of the Law of the Sea Institute Conference, explaining in a
few brief phrases what has gone on and summarizing what appears to be present
state of play.

As regards then the Law of the Sea Conference itself, the general
impression that has emerged from the discussions, formal and informal, can be
summed up in two propositions. First, there is a fairly large degree of consensus
on the content of the emerging law of the sea, but, secondly, there is a lack of
positive, categorical optimism as regards the forthcoming Geneva session. Both
these remarks would need to be qualified—as regards the first proposition I
would refer you to Ed Miles' paper, which explains how difficult it is to find
evidence of substantive agreement once one starts to look into the details.
Nevertheless, if those who have followed the conference closely were asked to
put down on a sheet of paper what they believe the law of the sea will look like
in, say, five years—at any rate at some date after the immediate stage—the results
would, I think, show a high degree of similarity. We might discuss—indeed, that
was the subject of some of the papers—whether the consensus, actual or emerging, is 50 percent, or 70 percent, or 80 percent, but it seems generally conceded
that there is a relatively high level of agreement as to what the future law will
look like. That being so, the fact that optimism over the Geneva session is not
widespread appears paradoxical, and even contradictory. The reaction to this
state of affairs was reflected in this morning's discussion, appraising the options.
There are those who stress that efforts must continue, that the endeavor to
establish the "right" law of the sea must be pursued without diminution or loss
of intent. They are certainly correct, but it is necessary to take account of the

*The remarks made were expressed solely in a personal capacity.

405

change in circumstances which may start to take place as time proceeds; time is likely to become an increasing factor as the conference continues, affecting both the outcome and the means used to find a solution. As John Norton Moore said on the opening day, the main question at the present juncture is: How long can negotiations go on before unilateral pressures build up?

There appear to be two paths opening up before us. If on the one hand, for the sake of argument, one accepts the hypothesis that the Geneva session may not produce the definitive treaty, or something approaching it, well what then? The next session would presumably be in 1976, but in the interim a number of states, including some in the Northern hemisphere, would be likely to have taken unilateral action as regards extension of their national limits. States which have already adopted such measures could hardly object if this was to occur. A point which has become progressively clearer, and which is worth mentioning at this juncture, is that fisheries regimes are going to be significantly different from one another—they will be more regionally diverse than the Law of the Sea Conference has so far really considered. "Fish" and "navigation" interests will, however, have to be separated; in all probability they will be, but it is undeniable that if regulation of the limits problem proceeds by unilateral action, there will be some increase in the risk of interference with navigation. As regards the nodules—well, you heard Mr. Flipse yesterday and the remarks of other speakers. In general then, if the conference is continued in 1976 or later, it will start to change its nature, becoming progressively a ratificatory rather than a lawmaking conference. Nevertheless, there will still be a lot of law writing to do, and it may be pertinent to point out that in a sense the work of the conference will in any case never come to an end. In a decentralized world we are engaged in a steady march towards a qualitative change in the law of the sea which will be both permanent and complicated. It will never again be possible to neglect the law of the sea, or to leave it aside; it is clear that it will continue to require international attention on a regular, organized basis.

The other path consists of presupposing that the Geneva session does prove successful or, to put the point more narrowly, of asking what can best be done to make the session a productive one, and, linked with that, of asking what can realistically be achieved there. Here I would mention that there will be only nine weeks left between next Monday, 13 January, and the start of the conference on 17 March. Most delegations will presumably be obtaining their instructions and clearance from their superiors in January or early February, so that the period is further reduced. The central issues would be, on the one hand, the elements of the limited, nuclear, umbrella package, and, on the other, the question of who would negotiate this, and how. The first issue was dealt with this morning and the second to some extent on the opening day.

The gallant ship on which we embarked in 1968 set sail on a voyage of great promise. The promise remains: the common heritage idea is one of unique potential and we would all be the losers if little or nothing were to come of it. We have made substantial progress. But, as was pointed out on Monday, there are many hands on the tiller, and the course immediately ahead is uncertain. The intensity and complexity of the maneuvers absorbs us all. It is indeed a remarkable spectacle by any standards. We will undoubtedly learn something about the international system that we could not discover by any other means, namely, whether a matter of this magnitude can be negotiated in today's world, as we struggle to find our way, with one coast behind us and one just over the horizon. As regards the immediate question of the Geneva session, there seems to be some sentiment that the ship may be about to drift on to a sandbank, unless very serious efforts are made between now and 17 March and during the session itself. We have in a sense all the time there is—perhaps time is one of those resources for which the distinction between a "resource" and a "reserve" does not apply. But time (which has, of course, other names as well, like "technological change") is short if we are to control (that is to say, keep within an agreed-on international framework, which alone can provide equity and reduce the possibilities of friction) time the new actor in our midst. And that, as I read the entrails, has been the main sense of our meeting here this week.

Mr. Burke: Thank you, Michael.

Our next speaker is Gordon R.S. Hawkins, who is a consultant to the United Nations Institute for Training and Research.

Remarks

Gordon R.S. Hawkins
United Nations Institute for Training
and Research

Mr. Hawkins: Chairperson and people—I hope that is an unexceptionable salutation in a conference that has had one woman participant.

I stand before you as the thirty-forth platform speaker of the seminar, thus outdoing those from the floor by two. I was brought in as a substitute, I am told, for the unavailable Prime Minister Pierre Elliott Trudeau of Canada. This is what in your jargon, I think, is called an unorthodox, suboptimal alternative.

I also recognize that I am in a sense speaking to the loyal and determined members of the seminar, or those with bad plane connections. I am assuming that this residual group is either waiting to move on to another conference or reluctantly having to go back home, known in the jargon respectively as the migratory and anadromous species of conference-goers.

In any case, this is not the moment for new hard truths or startling revelations. To try to set the parameters or the conceptual framework—one falls easily into the jargon—of such an occasion, I decided to put to you the problem that I face as a Director of Training of UNITAR, one of whose tasks is to help train those middle members of middle-sized permanent missions to the United Nations, whom a speaker yesterday rather disdainfully called the tertiary officials—an odd term of abuse from someone who is trying to make a profit out of geology—in what is going on in UN affairs. One of our immediate tasks is to try to convey next month to those members of permanent missions in Geneva, who are going to be drawn into the Geneva sessions of the conference, some sense of what the issues are. They may have been reading some telegrams; they may not. They may have been earlier involved in the Sea-Bed Committee: most likely they have not.

So I came here with a rather specific mission of finding out what kind of program one should put on for a group of this kind.

What should one tell them? Well, on the first day of this seminar it became very plain to me what one should tell them: that if you are very careful in your definition of what was success and what was failure, then you could safely say that Caracas was either a success or a failure; that there was quite general agreement at Caracas that there would be a 200-mile economic zone, except that there was no general agreement as to what should be meant by a 200-mile economic zone; that there could, indeed, be third-party dispute mechanisms, but it wasn't very clear if it was going to be possible to create third-party dispute mechanisms; that in difficult straits you could be controlled without being impeded.

By the end of the second day it became clear to me, in my well developed naiveté, that what one should do for these middle-range, these tertiary-level diplomats in Geneva, is enhance their awareness of the technological base, let them know more about the complexities of the issues upon which their delegations would be flying in to negotiate.

But at the end of the third day, as they say in Genesis, I had something of a different sensation. The complexity of the seabed issues was coming in on me in a way that was giving less illumination and more discomfort. As one listened to a description of the problems of creating seabed machinery; as one listened to some of the fishery technologies and their possible alternative futures, of discussion as to whether these should be in the hands of the seabed authority or the FAO or some other organization; as one listened to the problems of pollution control, the problems of vessel separation, and the simple fact that maritime traffic control training was in its infancy, I began to have a sense that I was in some way being technologically steamrollered—if you can imagine the sensation—and I began to have some sense of sympathy for those of the middle-sized delegations who were going to try to do a job in Geneva, that they too might feel that they were in some way being technologically steamrollered if one put on a program of gee-whizzing technological instruction.

There was built into this seminar, I thought, a superpace, a kind of scientific hustle, which made me resistant to some of the points of view that were being put forward, even though they were based on very sound technology.

Today I looked for salvation (as one does on the fourth day in a short working week) and I thought it was to be there in the paper that said, as I read it, that if we can now move on to agree on the rules of the game, we will all be able better to play the game. But when I heard the first critic say that this was a paper of which everybody should be taking full cognizance in the years to come, I knew, alas, that that proposition was doomed.

I confess, then, that I seek advice—and before we take our planes I would be glad of it—as to what, after this kind of discussion, which may have served your purposes very well and served mine personally very well, I take to the boys in Geneva, the sloggers there in the back rooms who are sharpening

their pencils, trying to organize the Niagara of documents on the law of the sea
that has been pouring in there for years and preparing to take an intelligent
part in what is to happen there in March and April, and thereafter.

One can give them some technology, but technology, however you
put it, has its own bias, even technology with flip charts. There is now even a
new category: technology with Flipse charts.

One can certainly not present in a couple of days and a balanced
way the kind of material of which they should be made aware. So do you say,
"Here is some of the material, but things have become very complicated. You
may think there is the prospect of a new international economic order, you
may think that this is a device for a new income distribution, but I have to tell
you that the word from back there in the research and development base is that
things are not up to Pardo, that it is going to be exceedingly difficult?"

That would be a fair message to convey. Is it the right one to
convey to this kind of group? Or does one say, "The word I get is that, because
of their technology, you have to help these boys out. They are in danger of
unilateralism. Save them from their unilateralism."

Clearly, one cannot do that. A simple, battered, old adult educa-
tionalist, working in the sanitized scene of the United Nations, can do nothing
of the sort. He can display a few facts. He can try and get things in some sort
of proportion. He can persuade them that the issues are going to be resolved
on the basis of this particular input. But that is not going to be enough at this
stage, as I read the intricacy of the argument that has been happening here.

The solution to this problem may still lie with you here. Let me
illustrate. UNITAR has just put on another seminar in Geneva where we asked
forty members of these diplomatic missions to play the role of other countries
within an UNCTAD negotiation—a simulation exercise, in a word—and to
develop the position of another country in negotiating a contentious issue
brought before the Trade and Development Board of UNCTAD. It was gratifying
to a battered educator's heart to watch them go through this process and demand
more at the end of it, because, as part of their professional training, "to see
ourselves as others see us" is not something that is provided for in very large
measure.

Somewhere in institutions like the Law of the Sea Institute, I am
arguing, one may need to develop not only the kind of enlightening and
sometimes confounding expertise that backs alternative opinions, but also a
means by which those who are trying honestly to argue out a position that they
think is in their own national interest can see more clearly than they can by any
other existing available process the background to other people's explicit and
well articulated national positions.

I would submit that if there is to be another Law of the Sea Institute
between Geneva and whatever happens after Geneva, one might well spend a
lot of time thinking out the format of the next conference in order to get into

the picture the perspective of having others see us as we don't quite see ourselves.

It may be that nobody is going to be helped by any more of the facts. Nobody is going to be helped by an appeal to any outside existing authority. Only by introducing each other into a more perceptive awareness of the other's position are we going to move—at least so it seems from an adult education perspective—from Caracas to Geneva to whatever is to come after.

Mr. Burke: If you will bear with me for two or three more minutes, I would like to introduce the rest of the table here. These are the people, other than the two speakers, who were actually responsible for the program: Ed Miles from the University of Washington; Frank Christy, from Resources for the Future; Tom Clingan, who is here as a chairman of a session and not as an official of the Department of State, who was responsible for one of the days; and John Gamble, who oversaw the whole operation.

I would like to acknowledge the financial support we have received for this specific conference from the Ford Foundation, the United States Coast Guard, the Office of Naval Research, the International Research and Exchanges Board, and the Office of Sea Grant in the Department of Commerce.

Finally, I would like to thank all of you for attending and managing, I guess, some of you, to get a word in edgewise.

Thank you very much, ladies and gentlemen. The meeting is adjourned.

Participants List for the Law of the Sea Institute Ninth Annual Conference

Clemens E. Ady
University of Miami
School of Law
Coral Gables, FL

Paul C. Ake, JAGC, USN
International Negotiations—
Joint Chiefs of Staff (J-5)
Washington, DC

Lewis M. Alexander
University of Rhode Island
Department of Geography
Kingston, RI

George W. Alexandrowicz
Queen's University
Faculty of Law
Kingston, Ontario, Canada

Dorothy W. Allan
Washington, DC

Donald M. Allen
National Marine Fisheries Service
Miami, FL

Harry H. Almond, Jr.
Office of the General Counselor, DOD
Washington, DC

Edward A. Ames
The Ford Foundation
New York, NY

Henry S. Andersen
U.S. Dept. of State
Washington, DC

Andrew W. Anderson
University of Miami
Ocean and Coastal Law
Coral Gables, FL

Lee G. Anderson
University of Delaware
College of Marine Studies
Newark, DE

Walter G. Andry
Office of the Oceanographer, USN
Alexandria, VA

Perry J. Anglin
Northern Affairs Program
Ottawa, Canada

Leo D. Barry
Ministry of Mines and Energy
St. John's, Newfoundland, Canada

Gordon L. Becker
Exxon Corporation
New York, NY

Charles Behrens
Falls Church, VA

William W. Behrens, Jr.
Falls Church, VA

Peter Bernhardt
U.S. Department of State
Washington, DC

Michael Betty
University of Rhode Island
Master of Marine Affairs Program
Kingston, RI

Jean-Pierre Beurier
Nantes, France

William K. Bissell
University of Miami
School of Law
Coral Gables, FL

Robert C. Blumberg
United Nations
New York, NY

John R. Botzum
Nautilus Press, Inc.
Washington, DC

Paul G. Bradley
University of British Columbia
Department of Economics
Vancouver, Canada

William C. Brewer
NOAA
Washington, DC

Sid Brodie
University of Miami
School of Law
Coral Gables, FL

E.D. Brown
University of Wales
Institute of Science and Technology
Cardiff, Wales, U.K.

James E. Brown, Jr.
Department of Transportation
U.S. Coast Guard
Washington, DC

George Bulkley
University of California
Institute for International Studies
Berkeley, CA

William T. Burke
University of Washington
School of Law
Seattle, WA

Morris D. Busby
U.S. Dept. of State
Washington, DC

Donald L. Capone
University of Miami
Department of Geography
Coral Gables, FL

Margaret Jane Caskey
Dept. of Environment
International Fisheries & Marine
  Directorate
Ottawa, Ontario, Canada

Francis T. Christy, Jr.
Resources for the Future, Inc.
Washington, DC

Dan Ciobanu
Woods Hole Oceanographic Institution
Woods Hole, MA

Thomas A. Clingan, Jr.
Department of State
Washington, DC

Mark D. Coler
Department of Treasury
Office of Raw Material & Oceans
   Policy
Washington, DC

Freida G. Collins
University of Mississippi
Sea Grant Legal Program
University, MS

Salvatore Comitini
University of Hawaii
Department of Economics
Honolulu, HI

John Cooper
Government of Canada
Department of Environment, Ocean
   & Aquatic Affairs
Ottawa, Canada

Dorian Cowan
University of Miami
Ocean Law Program
Coral Gables, FL

David A. Crowley
University of Miami
School of Law
Coral Gables, FL

Alvaro deSoto
Mission of Peru to the U.N.
New York, NY

K.B. Dickson
University of Ghana
Department of Geography
Legon, Ghana

Alexander Dragovich
Southeast Fisheries Center
Miami, FL

Paul S. Edelman
New York, NY

Gudmundar B. Eiriksson
Associate Law of the Sea Officer
United Nations
New York, NY

Leonore B. Emich
Austrian Mission to the UN
New York, NY

Henry H. Esterly
N.Y.C. Community College
Brooklyn, NY

Frank H. Featherston, USN
Office of Naval Research
Arlington, VA

Willy J. Feuerlein
Florida Atlantic University
Boca Raton, FL

Ivan W. Ficken
University of Miami
Ocean Law Program
Coral Gables, FL

Peter Finkle
Memorial University
Department of Political Science
St. John's, Newfoundland, Canada

Luke W. Finlay
New York, NY

John E. Flipse
Deepsea Ventures, Inc.
Gloucester Point, VA

Gerrish C. Flynn
National Security Council
Washington, DC

Alvaro Freda
Coastal Resources Management
  Council
R.I. Department of Natural Resources
Providence, RI

Peter H. Fricke
Department of Maritime Studies,
  UWIST
Cardiff, Wales, U.K.

Robert L. Friedheim
Center for Naval Analyses
Arlington, VA

Victor A. Gallardo
Woods Hole Oceanographic Institution
Marine Policy & Ocean Management
  Program
Woods Hole, MA

John King Gamble, Jr.
University of Rhode Island
Law of the Sea Institute
Kingston, RI

Joan E. Gill, Editor
Florida International Commentary
Miami, FL

Robert N. Ginsburg
University of Miami
Rosenstiel School of Marine Sciences
Miami Beach, FL

Jozef Goldblat
Stockholm International Peace
  Research Institute
Stockholm, Sweden

Alan J. Goldman
Rhode Island Coastal Resources
  Management Council
Providence, RI

Craig G. Goodman
University of Miami
School of Law
Coral Gables, FL

Richard J. Greenwald
Deepsea Ventures, Inc.
Gloucester Point, VA

George W. Haight
New York, NY

Michael Hardy
Legal Service
Commission of E.E.C.
Brussels, Belgium

Edward A. Hauck
Herndon, VA

Gordon R.S. Hawkins
U.N. Institute for Training and
  Research
New York, NY

Armin Hiller
Embassy of Federal Republic of
  Germany
Washington, DC

Robert D. Hodgson
Department of State
The Geographer
Washington, DC

Sayed M. Hosni
Woods Hole Oceanographic Institution
Woods Hole, MA

John F. Hussey
U.S. Senate Commerce Committee
Washington, DC

Robert C. Huston
McLean, VA

Jon L. Jacobson
University of Oregon
Law School
Eugene, OR

Lawrence Jarett
U.S. Merchant Marine Academy
Kings Point, NY

Jerry E. Jirgl
Bowers Reporting Co.
Falls Church, VA

Douglas M. Johnston
Dalhousie University
Faculty of Law
Halifax, N.S., Canada

Albert C. Jones
National Marine Fisheries Service
Miami, FL

Joseph M. Jones
Ocean Research Project
Miami, FL

Thomas E. Kane
Attorney at Law
New Bern, NC

Reed R. Kathrein
University of Miami
School of Law
Coral Gables, FL

David A. Kay
American Society of International Law
Washington, DC

Rahmatullah Khan
Princeton University
Princeton, NJ

John K. King
Bethesda, MD

John A. Knauss
University of Rhode Island
Provost for Marine Affairs
Kingston, RI

H. Gary Knight
Louisiana State University
Law Center
Baton Rouge, LA

Christopher L. Koch
University of Miami
School of Law
Coral Gables, FL

Dennis P. Koehler
University of Miami
School of Law
Coral Gables, FL

Andrey A. Kokoshin
Academy of Sciences of the USSR
Institute on USA & Canadian Studies
Moscow, USSR

Anatoly L. Kolodkin
States Scientific & Research
Institute of Marine Transport of
   the USSR
Moscow, USSR

Gerald J. Kovach
National Academy of Sciences
Washington, DC

Mochtar Kusumaatmadja
Ministry of Justice of Indonesia

Lucille T. Laliberté
Department of Transportation
U.S. Coast Guard
Washington, DC

Paul A. Lapointe
Government of Canada
Department of External Affairs
Ottawa, Canada

Pierre Lebaube
ERAP
Paris, France

Edward G. Lee
Government of Canada
Department of External Affairs
Ottawa, Canada

Roy S. Lee
UN Secretariat, Deputy Secretary
First Committee of the Third UN
   Conference on Law of the Sea
New York, NY

Shi-tao Lee
University of Miami
School of Law
Coral Gables, FL

Sam Leonardi
Deep Sea Salvage, Inc.
Fort Lauderdale, FL

Charles M. Levy
University of Miami
School of Law
Coral Gables, FL

Joel G. MacDonald
University of Miami
School of Law
Coral Gables, FL

Bernard G. Makowka
Fairfax, VA

Lawrence G. Mallon
Woods Hole Oceanographic Institution
Woods Hole, MA

Gerard J. Mangone
University of Delaware
College of Marine Studies
Newark, DL

Georgette Mariani
Centre Pour L'Exploration Des Oceans
Paris, France

Jonathan Maslow
Juris Doctor Magazine
New York, NY

Michael K. MccGwire
Dalhousie University
Department of Political Science
Halifax, Nova Scotia, Canada

Walter J. McNichols
Heed University
Hollywood, FL

Donald M. McRae
University of British Columbia
Institute of International Relations
Vancouver, Canada

Donald L. McKernan
University of Washington
Institute for Marine Studies
Seattle, WA

Gabriele Menegatti
Permanent Mission of Italy to the UN
New York, NY

Sofian T. Merican
University of Miami
School of Law
Coral Gables, FL

Yaacob H. Merican
University of Miami
School of Law
Coral Gables, FL

John L. Mero
Ocean Resource, Inc.
La Jolla, CA

Kai D. Midboe
Miami, FL

Edward Miles
University of Washington
Institute for Marine Studies
Seattle, WA

Frederick F. Monroe
University of Miami
Coral Gables, FL

George Montgomery
Vanderbilt University
Knoxville, TN

John Norton Moore
Chairman, U.S. Interagency Task
   Force on Law of the Sea
Department of State
Washington, DC

John J. Mullane, Jr.
Nautilus Press, Inc.
Washington, DC

H. Waldemar Niemotko
Woods Hole Oceanographic Institution
Woods Hole, MA

Francis X. Njenga
Permanent Mission of Kenya to the UN
New York, NY

Myron Nordquist
U.S. Department of State
Washington, DC

Kaldone G. Nweihed
Licenciado Estudios International
Universidad-Simon Bolivar
Caracas, Venezuela

Joseph S. Nye, Jr.
Harvard University
Center for International Affairs
Cambridge, MA

Dennis M. O'Connor
University of Miami
Ocean/Coastal Law Program
Coral Gables, FL

William E. O'Connor
Daytona Beach, FL

Shigeru Oda
Tohoku University
Faculty of Law
Sendai, Japan

Choon-ho Park
Harvard Law School
Cambridge, MA

Christian Patermann
Embassy of the Federal Republic
  of Germany
Washington, DC

Susan Peterson
Woods Hole Oceanographic Institution
Woods Hole, MA

Alain Piquemal
University of Nice
Institute of the Law of Peace and
  Development
Nice, France

Vladimir D. Pisarev
Academy of Sciences of the USSR
Institute of U.S. and Canadian Studies
Moscow, USSR

Giulio Pontecorvo
Columbia University
Graduate School of Business
New York, NY

Fred Popper
Assistant Director-General (Fisheries)
FAO of the UN, Rome

John B. Ray
University of Wisconsin
Whitewater, WN

Peter C. Reid
Australian Missions to the UN
New York, NY

Walter C. Retzsch
SUNY
Marine Sciences Research Center
Stony Brook, NY

Frank P. Rossomondo, Jr.
Washington, DC

Brian J. Rothschild
Southwest Fisheries Center
NMFS
La Jolla, CA

Guiseppe Sacco
University of Siena
Instituto di Economia
Siena, Italy

Joachim Schärfe
FAO of the United Nations
Department of Fisheries
Geneva, Switzerland

Leo N. Schowengerdt
U.S. Department of State
Washington, DC

Gunnar G. Schram
University of Iceland
Reykjavik, Iceland

Eleanor R. Schwartz
Department of the Interior
Washington, DC

Earle E. Seaton
Supreme Court
Hamilton, Bermuda

Ranjit Sethi
Permanent Mission of India to the UN
New York, NY

Gary P. Settles
University of Miami
School of Law
Coral Gables, FL

John L. Seymour
Texas A & M University
Department of Management
College Station, TX

Don Sherwin
Government of Canada
Department of Energy, Mines
   & Resources
Ottawa, Canada

David C. Simmons
National Marine Fisheries Service
Miami, FL

Leah J. Smith
Woods Hole Oceanographic Institution
Woods Hole, MA

Alfred H.A. Soons
Cambridge University
Cambridge, U.K.

Romuald Sorokin
Expert on Law of the Sea
U.S.S.R. Navy
Moscow, USSR

Barry B. Stamey, Jr.
College of Charleston
Charleston, SC

Donna E. Steigerwald
Falls Church, VA

Jane Stein
Smithsonian Magazine
Washington, DC

Robert E. Stein
American Society of International Law
Washington, DC

Walter P. Stepien
University of Miami
School of Law
Coral Gables, FL

Robert Stockman
University of Washington
Institute for Marine Studies
Seattle, WA

James Storer
NOAA
Office of Marine Resources
Rockville, MD

William L. Sullivan, Jr.
U.S. Dept. of State
Washington, DC

Bradford V. Swing
University of Miami
School of Law
Coral Gables, FL

John T. Swing
Council on Foreign Relations, Inc.
New York, NY

Alberto Szekely
University College of London
London, England

Viktor F. Tsarev
Central Scientific Institute of Fisheries
    of the USSR
Moscow, USSR

Albert E. Utton
University of New Mexico
School of Law
Albuquerque, NM

Bill N. Utz
National Shrimp Congress
Washington, DC

Jorge Vargas
National Council for Science
    & Technology
Mexico City, Mexico

Bension Varon
World Bank
Washington, DC

Carole Elise Vinitsky
University of Miami
School of Law
Coral Gables, FL

Lowell A. Wakefield
University of Alaska
Port Wakefield, Alaska

James P. Walsh
U.S. Senate Commerce Committee
Washington, DC

J.S. Warioba
Government of Tanzania
Ministry of Foreign Affairs

James A. Wexler
NOAA
Redmond, WA

Allan E. White
Office of Naval Research
Arlington, VA

Ira M. Witlin
University of Miami
School of Law
Coral Gables, FL

Atwood C. Wolf, Jr.
New York, NY

Warren S. Wooster
University of Miami
Rosenstiel School of Marine Sciences
Miami, FL

Ralph Yalkovsky
Buffalo State University College
Buffalo, NY

Richard Young
Van Hornesville, NY

Joseph A. Zinna
Continental Oil Co.
Stamford, CN